SISKIYOU TRAIL

The
Hudson's Bay Company
Route to California

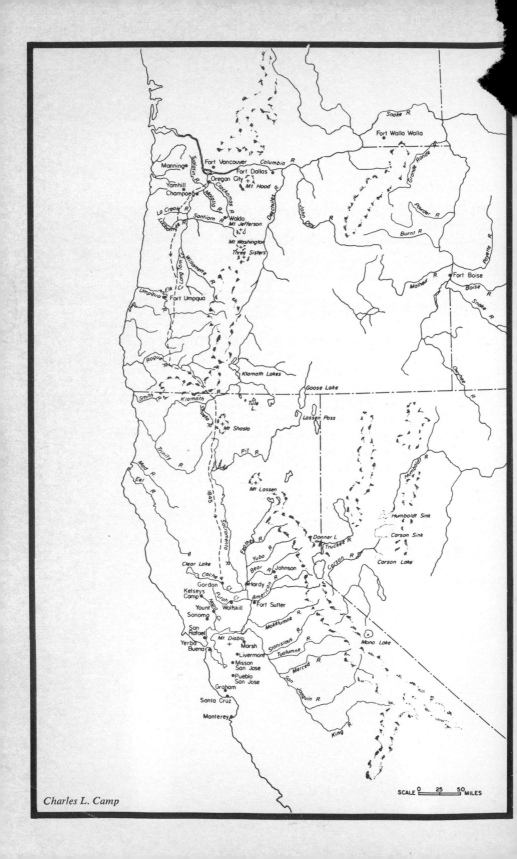

Charles L. Camp

By 1845, the various strands of the Siskiyou Trail were reduced to one well-worn route up the Willamette River from Fort Vancouver, over into the Umpqua and Rogue River valleys, across the Siskiyou Mountains to the Klamath and down the Sacramento Valley to San Francisco Bay.

Books by Richard Dillon

Exploring the Mother Lode Country
Burnt-Out Fires
Humbugs and Heroes
Wells, Fargo Detective
Fool's Gold
Legend of Grizzly Adams
Meriwether Lewis
The Hatchet Men
California Trail Herd
Shanghaiing Days
J. Ross Browne
The Gila Trail
Embarcadero

SISKIYOU TRAIL

The
Hudson's Bay Company
Route to California

by

RICHARD DILLON

McGraw-Hill Book Company

New York   St. Louis   San Francisco   Düsseldorf

London   Mexico   Sydney   Toronto

23456789KPKP798765

Library of Congress Cataloging in Publication Data

Dillon, Richard H
   Siskiyou Trail.

   (The American trail series; v. 12)
   Bibliography: p.
   Includes index.
   1. Northwest, Pacific—Discovery and exploration. 2.
Fur trade—Northwest, Pacific. 3. Hudson's Bay Com-
pany. I. Title. II. Series: American trail series (New
York); v. 12.
F880.D57   917.95′03′3   74-23553
ISBN 0-07-016980-2

for David Dillon

To the spirit of enterprise diffused
among the fur traders, from the earliest days
of the French down to the present time,
we owe almost all that we know
in these savage places.

—Alexander Ross, *The Fur Hunters*
of the Far West (1855)

Acknowledgments

I am particularly indebted to the kindness of Beaver House, London, archivists Mrs. J. Craig and Miss A. M. Johnson, and Retired Secretary of the Hudson's Bay Company R. A. Reynolds, who placed the original manuscripts of the Honourable Company at my disposal during visits to England in 1966 and 1971.

Others who aided and abetted the researching of the Siskiyou Trail story include: Richard Abel, Robert Becker, Eleanor Brown, Charles L. Camp, George Chalfant, Robert E. S. Clark, John Cleaves, John D. Cowan, Marty and Ferol Egan, Richard H. Engeman, Herb Garcia, the Reverend Maynard Geiger, Charles J. Gleeson, Carl R. Greenstein, A. B. Guthrie, Jr., Merrilee Gwerder, Arch Hanna, Mary Hill, Ray Hillman, John Hussey, Priscilla Knuth, Therese Lawrence, Millard McClung, John McDermott, the Reverend John B. McGloin, S.J., Michael Mathes, Dale Morgan, Irene Simpson Neasham, Andrew J. Osborne, Allan R. Ottley, P. W. Philby, Mrs. Miriam Pike, Douglas W. Polivka, Mrs. Hazel N. Pollock, Peter Tamony, John Barr Tompkins, and Thomas Vaughn.

Richard Dillon
1974

Contents

Introduction

JOHN C. FRÉMONT was not all that he has been cracked up to be in American history. Though an excellent explorer and naturalist, he was no more "the Pathfinder" than was Dolley Madison. Like almost every other United States government explorer, he was a path follower. The real pathfinders in the lands west of the Rockies, Cascades, Sierra Nevada, Siskiyou Mountains, and California Coast Range were the wide-wandering mountain men whom Washington Irving called "Sinbads of the wilderness."

The fur men who came up the Missouri and Platte rivers to the Rocky Mountains and Pacific Northwest were plainsmen as well as trappers. Those who drifted south and west from Quebec and Montreal brought the forest skills of *voyageurs* and *coureurs de bois,* the boatmen and woodsmen of French Canada.

Besides the Englishmen, Highland Scots, Irish, French-Canadians, and Anglo-Saxon Americans who scouted the Siskiyou Trail, there marched Spaniards, Mexicans, Orkneymen, Shetlanders, Norwegians, Swiss, Germans, Black Americans, Iroquois, Abenaki and other partly "civilized" Indians, Walla Wallas, halfbreeds, and Hawaiians.

They came not only from St. Louis and Montreal, but from Fort William and Grand Portage on Lake Superior, from Hudson Bay, from Fort Garry or Red River (Winnipeg), from Taos and Santa Fe. Their first destinations were the streams and "holes" (highland valleys) of the Rockies, but they soon pushed on to the *terra incognita* of the Columbia. Once established in Oregon, their curiosity was

INTRODUCTION

piqued by the legend of California. So they reversed the traditional westward course of empire by exploring not only eastward into by-passed Idaho but by also penetrating southward into California, to San Francisco and beyond.

The California fur trade is a story as colorful and adventurous as that of the Gold Rush, the classic drama of the Far West. Yet it has been badly neglected by writers and is almost unknown today. It was eclipsed by the romance of El Dorado, which saw the whole world turned topsy-turvy in the rush for gold. Although Americans and Canadians had opened trails to Mexican California long before the pioneering Bidwell-Bartleson party of 1841 laid out the California-Oregon Trail from the United States, only a handful of rugged individuals made the annual marches of the fur brigades, whereas tens of thousands of adventurers flocked to the placers. There was, alas, no host of chroniclers for the fur rush, unlike the Gold Rush, and no Francis Parkman appeared to make literature of history.

Documentation of California's first boom—the trade in furs—has been fragmentary, at best. The record was more often oral than written, and it was easily, and early, lost. Men at the top like Dr. John McLoughlin of Fort Vancouver were intelligent and educated gentlemen, but the bourgeois leaders out on the trails were laconic reporters, and their *engagés* (or engaged servants—Hudson's Bay Company employees) and free trappers were lucky if they could scrawl their own names. Hence the rent in the fabric of California's early story which this narrative is meant to patch.

Twenty years before the Gold Rush, Hudson's Bay Company trappers opened a route to California from the Columbia River by way of the Siskiyou Mountains, which separate the modern states of California and Oregon. In time, it became a road followed by gringo fur men, government explorers, cattle drovers, horse thieves, settlers, and El Dorado-bound argonauts. With the rapid development of California in the 1850s, the same line of communication became a horse trail for pack trains, then a wagon road, and finally a rugged turnpike for Concord stagecoaches. Finally, with the driving of the last spike in 1887, the old Hudson's Bay Company Road between Fort Vancouver and San Francisco—the Siskiyou Trail—became the roadbed for the railway which still ties the states of Oregon and California together, and which is now tightly paralleled by one of the major thoroughfares of the continent, Interstate Highway 5.

California was but a minor source of beaver pelts. It was the child of the richer Oregon and Idaho fur trade. But the discovery of gold in 1848 (by a one-time Siskiyou Trail wayfarer), with the fur trade only a few years in its grave, revived the trans-Siskiyou Mountains route of the fur traders. It became not only an avenue of access to the placers of California's "diggins" for Oregonians, but the line of travel by which an economically brawny California shortly made Oregon into a satellite.

The "semi" rigs on Highway 5 and the piggybacks of the SP which hurtle northward and southward today, linking Washington and Oregon with California, are following the general trend of the moccasin-pounded Siskiyou Trail, albeit one consolidated and straightened out considerably by explosives and bulldozers from the wriggling map line of the 1830s and 1840s.

SISKIYOU TRAIL

The
Hudson's Bay Company
Route to California

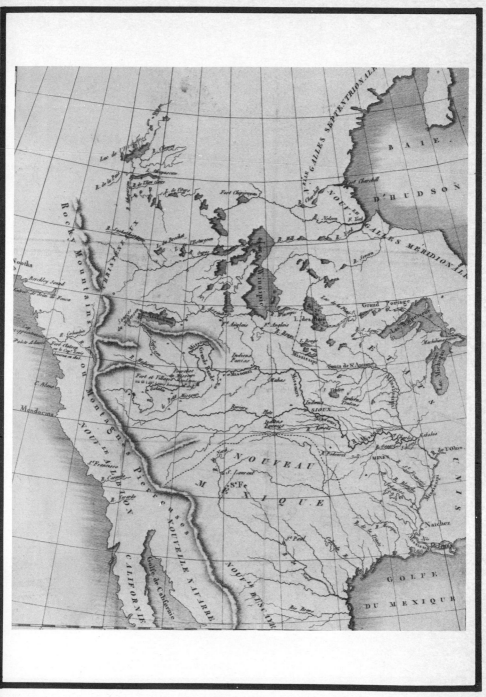

Even after the exploration of Lewis and Clark in 1804-1805, French and other European map-makers had a truncated view of the Far West, combining Rocky Mountains with the Cascades and California's Sierra Nevada. Until the late 1820s and the opening of the Siskiyou Trail, the land between San Francisco and the Columbia River (still termed Drake's New Albion on this French map) was *terra incognita,* a blank on the map.   *Sutro Library*

Joe Meek was a typical Oregon mountain man, like many (including his brother Steve) who made the march southward into California over the Siskiyou Trail. *Sutro Library*

The one man more responsible for the blazing of the Siskiyou Trail than even Peter Skene
Ogden or Jedediah Smith was Dr. John McLoughlin, chief factor at Fort Vancouver and—to
the Indians—the White-Headed Eagle.   *Oregon Historical Society*

Although Jed Smith and Ewing Young had a hand in the laying out of the Siskiyou Trail, most of the work was done by Britons—or, rather, Canadians. However, two Yankees put the trail "on the map"—Lt. George Emmons and Passed Midshipman Henry Eld of the U.S. Exploring Expedition, in 1841.

A California mountain man, pictured by the state's first real artist, Charles Christian Nahl.

This lowly rodent, *Castor canadensis,* was as important to the frontier economy of Oregon and northern California as the bison or American buffalo was to the High Plains. *Sutro Library*

The Spaniards in California were quite aware of the beaver in the territory, but looked upon the animal as a zoological curiosity (as in this illustration from the history by Venegas) rather than as the foundation of a commerce which would create new trade routes, including the 850-mile-long Siskiyou Trail.

Sutro Library

Photographs of mountain men are rare, because the beaver trade was dying as the daguerreotype worked its way West. But this one anonymous fur trader can stand as the epitome of all the "reckless breed of men" who traveled the Siskiyou Trail between Oregon and California.

A domesticated "Captain of the California Trail"—Michel Laframboise in 1856 with his wife (Emelie Picard Laframboise) and child, long after his retirement from trapping the Siskiyou Trail.
Courtesy of Mrs. Harriet Munnick

Where the Siskiyou Trail began . . . The interior of the Fort Vancouver compound, photographed circa 1860 by Capt. Charles J. Darrah, R. E., a member of the British Boundary Commission.
Victoria and Albert Museum Library

In the mid-1840s, John C. Frémont, the so-called Pathfinder, cut the Siskiyou Trail in several places, including the Sutter Buttes (above), which he climbed for a view of the Sacramento Valley and the Sierra Nevada to the east. *Bancroft Library*

The Siskiyou Trail, where the Sacramento Valley pinches out at its northernmost end. *Sutro Library*

Travelers on the Siskiyou Trail described the Siskiyou Mountains-Shasta area as one of "Alps upon Alps." Here a party makes camp in the lee of Mount Shasta.   *Sutro Library*

Fort Vancouver, Hudson's Bay Company post and beginning point of the Siskiyou Trail to California.   *Sutro Library*

Peter Skene Ogden.

On July 29, 1845, Siskiyou Trail mountain man Jim Clyman described Castle Crags: "Northwest of our camp is an awful steep craggy cliff of grey granite rock, the pineceles of which look as sharp as Icyceles."

Mary Hill—California Geology

Castle Crags as they appear today, a California State Park.

California Department of Parks and Recreation

Astorians,
Nor'westers,
and the Honourable Company

By RIGHTS, Francis Drake should have founded the California fur trade in 1579, when he sojourned on the coast just north of the Golden Gate after beaching and careening his leaky *Golden Hind*.

The Miwok Indians who crowned him King of Nova Albion wore animal skins to fend off what Drake's chaplain denounced as "the nipping cold . . . thicke mistes, and stynking fogge" of California's backward summer climate. But the garments were not of beaver fur, for *Castor* did not find the thick, fluted, and fibrous-barked *Sequoia sempervirens* to its taste. Commoners shivered in deerskins or elkskins, while the chief wore "a coate of the skins of conies" in lieu of royal ermine. The rodents were not true Barbary conies, of course, but either pocket gophers or ground squirrels.

Forty-five years before Drake, Jacques Cartier opened the St. Lawrence River and made possible the American fur trade in which California eventually played a modest role. When the Dutch, operating out of Albany, New York, with Iroquois agents, threatened to cut this French trade route, Médard Chouart, alias Sieur des Groseillers, and Pierre Esprit Radisson came up with a plan to get peltry to Europe quickly, economically, and without Dutch interference, by way of Hudson Bay.

Not only did the French governor turn down the proposal, he taxed Radisson and Groseillers for their pelts and then fined them for illicit trading. Undaunted, the rebuffed traders approached Great Britain, which had everything to gain and nothing to lose in hearing them out. The English were receptive. Sir George Carteret presented the two men to the King. But, still recovering from the plague and fire of 1666, London was not quick to adopt the ambitious plan until the King's cousin, Prince Rupert, took up the American fur trade as a commerce which not only promised sweet profits but which would open up a larger trade with Russia. Moscow wanted furs; England needed Baltic naval stores if she was to compete with Holland for control of the high seas.

Prince Rupert interested courtiers and merchants, who sent an awkward little ketch, the *Nonsuch,* to the southernmost reach of Hudson Bay in September 1668. The traders wintered in a cabin grandiosely called Charles' Fort, the ancestor of all fur trading posts in the West. They lived on ship's stores of bully beef and salt junk (pork), augmented by whatever fish and game they could take locally.

Three hundred Indians accompanied rising temperatures to Charles' Fort in April. They were eager to barter beaver pelts for trade goods and the *wampum* of white Long Island seashells which Groseillers brought. He had no trouble negotiating a treaty with *les peaux rouges* for a vast tract of land. When the Rupert River ice broke up, the *Nonsuch* sailed for the Thames with prime beaver skins worth £10–12 each. The £60,000 cargo was not enough to pay all costs of the experiment, but quite enough to convince the project's backers that one could sail directly from London Bridge to Hudson Bay and that future voyages would bring handsome profits.

On May 2, 1670, the interested gentlemen-merchants incorporated as the Company of Adventurers in England Trading into Hudson's Bay, with Prince Rupert as Governor. The firm, soon dubbed the Honourable Company, was modeled along the lines of the Muscovy and East India companies. The Royal Charter made the investors into the true and absolute lords and proprietors of a million and a half square miles of Hudson Bay watershed, the greatest beaver preserve on earth and almost forty percent of modern Canada.

The rim of the grant extended all the way to southern Alberta, tantalizingly near the coveted Pacific. Such a domain was too much for Rupert's fellow adventurers to administer, much less exploit or control. The problem was the "spirit-breaking distances." York Factory and other posts remained for years as ignorant of the whereabouts of the undefined western boundaries as was London itself. It was all the English could do to fight off their French rivals on Hudson Bay proper.

So tenuous was the Company's hold that it could not send out a genuine exploring expedition for almost twenty years, in spite of exhortations from the directors—the Governor and Committee resident in London. In the 1690s, Henry Kelsey wintered in the valley of the Saskatchewan River, but the Company was so enfeebled that not until 1754 was Anthony Henday, an outlawed smuggler-turned-explorer, able to winter on Alberta's Red River within sight of the Rocky Mountains.

The Rockies—the Montaignes Rocheuses—had been sighted earlier by Pierre Gaultier de Varennes, Sieur de la Verendrye. Henday found it impossible to persuade western Indians to trade at far-off Company posts, instead of swapping their plews or pelts for brandy and trade goods at the nearby French posts founded in Verendrye's wake. The first "western" outpost of the Honourable Company, Cumberland House on the Saskatchewan, was not planted until 1774.

The Company was heartened, naturally, by the cession of French Canada in 1763 at the close of the Seven Years War. But, to its chagrin, the expulsion of France only seemed to revitalize competition. The French traders of Montreal now wrapped themselves in the Union Jack and threw in with canny Scots businessmen attracted by the lure of sure profits. Boldly, they outflanked the ponderously moving frontier of the Company's fur empire. By 1784, nine Montreal fur interests were amalgamated as the North-West Company. Its men moved westward at a smart clip from Fort William along the old *voyageurs'* route of Rainy Lake, Lake of the Woods, and Lake Winnipeg. The newcomers appeared bound for mysterious Oregon and bent on transforming the charter of Charles II into a mere scrap of parchment.

Court proceedings and other legal maneuvers in England were paralleled by rivalry and even violence in America. The forts of "the English" were sometimes built almost chockablock with those of "the Canadians" or "the Pedlars," as the rivals fought to control strategic trade routes. A North-West Company explorer staggered to a seaside boulder in what was later to be British Columbia to smear on it, with vermilion and bear grease, "Alexander Mackenzie, from Canada by land, the twenty-second day of July, one thousand seven hundred and ninety three." By 1804, Nor'westers Mackenzie, Simon Fraser, and David Thompson had completely seized the initiative from the London company.

Mackenzie tried to get Thomas Dugdale, Fifth Earl of Selkirk, to buy a controlling interest in the older firm, so that it could be absorbed. But Selkirk held onto his shares, instead, and set out to reorganize the decrepit and almost moribund Honourable Company. At the same time, he launched an agricultural settlement on Red River near Lake

Winnipeg, to help Scotland's destitute crofters—and to block the Nor'westers' road to New Caledonia, as British Columbia was then called.

The exasperated Nor'westers resorted to war. A party of *métis* or half-bloods attacked the settlement in 1816 and killed twenty men, including the governor, at Seven Oaks. This massacre by the so-called *bois brûlés* caused the surviving settlers to flee for their lives. But Selkirk not only reestablished the colony, he captured the North-West Company headquarters at Fort William in reprisal, before the Colonial Office could intervene to prevent more violence.

Selkirk died in 1820, as did Mackenzie. Several North-West Company wintering partners, including Dr. John McLoughlin, decided that more than a truce was needed. They ended the disastrous competition by arranging for a merger of the two firms into one bearing the name of the old company.

An act of Parliament confirmed the antique charter of the Honourable Company, but now granted it sole rights to the fur trade in the Hudson Bay basin *and* in the drainage of all rivers falling toward either the Arctic or Pacific oceans. The monopolistic license was subject only to the Convention of 1818 with the United States. This accord provided for joint occupancy of Oregon Territory and, thus, gave Americans equal rights to the fur trade there.

Long before the merger of the companies—as early as 1810, in fact—the richest fur magnate in the United States made his move. John Jacob Astor organized a Western subsidiary to his American Fur Company. He called it the Pacific Fur Company, and he meant it to hunt the blank space on maps which stretched from Russian Alaska to Spanish San Francisco Bay.

Oregon was to be the heart of Astor's fur empire, but he hoped to hunt down the coast into unoccupied northern California. Washington Irving said of Astor: "He considered his projected establishment at the mouth of the Columbia as the emporium to an immense commerce; as a colony that would form the germ of a wide civilization; that would, in fact, carry the American population across the Rocky Mountains and spread it along the shores of the Pacific."

Three of Astor's partners were experienced fur men, ex-Nor'-westers he lured away. But he wondered at the depth of their personal loyalty to him. Since he had been able to buy their services, he knew that they could be bought back by the Britons; so he gambled in choosing his principal partner. He named Wilson Price Hunt, a gentleman with no fur trade experience. But Hunt was utterly dependable and loyal, just the man to be Astor's agent. Alas, Astor passed over a future giant of the fur trade, Donald McKenzie, and chose a weak man (Duncan McDougall) to back up Hunt.

Astor planned well, sending both a land and a sea expedition to found his post, Astoria. But, when the *Tonquin* reached the Columbia bar, two boats were swamped in the savage surf and eight men were drowned. The superstitious *canadiens* crossed themselves and pronounced the deaths of their comrades to be an ill omen for Astor's venture.

McDougall hurried the building of the fort on a jut of land called Point George on the south bank of the Columbia near its mouth. Captain Jonathan Thorn took the *Tonquin* to Nootka on a trading cruise. McDougall also sent out men to spy on the North-West Company. He found, to his relicf, that its nearest post was Spokane House, far to the east. One of the scouts, Gabriel Franchère, at this time noted for the record the mouth of the Willamette River where it entered the Columbia from the south. This was Lewis and Clark's Multnomah River, and the future gateway to the Siskiyou Trail. Franchère recalled later: "Our guide informed us that up this river about a day's journey there was a large waterfall and, beyond it, the country abounded in beaver . . . ."

Still, when a party was sent from Astoria to found an outpost, the Willamette was not chosen for its site. The post was set up far to the northeast, to counter Spokane House expansion and to keep that fort under surveillance.

The Astorians became interested in the Willamette Valley, but hardly as a highroad to California. Washington Irving echoed their feelings when he described the sixty-mile-wide trough between the mountains as ideal for settlements: "Through the center of this valley flowed a large and beautiful stream, called the Wallamot, which came wandering for several hundred miles through a yet unexplored wilderness. The sheltered situation of this immense valley had an obvious effect upon the climate. It was a region of great beauty and luxuriance, with lakes and pools, and green meadows shaded by noble groves . . . finely diversified with prairies and hills and forests of oak, ash, maple and cedar . . . with elk and deer . . . [and] streams well stocked with beaver."

On December 5, 1811, the partners finally heeded the claims of the Indians that the Willamette was rich in beaver. Robert Stuart made a reconnaissance of its banks and, shortly, William Wallace and J. C. Halsey set up an outpost in the valley. It was more of a meat-hunting camp than a trapping headquarters; but, when they returned to Astoria from their cozy winter quarters, Wallace and Halsey brought out seventeen packs of beaver skins. (To trap beaver, men waded into the water, placed their traps in the streambed about four inches below the surface, depressing the springs with their feet or a "squeezer" of two strong sticks. They then extended the trap chains for their full length in deeper water and drove the hard stakes, or float sticks, solidly into the bottom. The last chore was the baiting of a switch of willow or other wood, which they jammed into the bank. Smears of castoreum [beaver musk] from their bait bottles did the trick.)

In addition to skins, the two men brought thirty-two bales of dried meat. The venison jerky was more welcome than the beaver plews, because fresh meat spoiled quickly in the moist and mild coastal climate, and all attempts to dry or smoke meat there had failed.

Trapper-chronicler Ross Cox never ascended the Willamette more than a few miles above its mouth, but he, too, became a convert. He boasted of its relatively mild and dry clime, its rich and abundant soil, its fruits, roots, and native tobacco, and its elk, beaver, and deer. He differed from another literate Astorian, Alexander Ross, only in his describing the natives of the valley as tranquil folk. Cox did not envision the river as a road to California, but he predicted that, when "improvements of scientific cultivation" were extended to the Willamette country, it would become one of the most delightful districts west of the Rockies.

McDougall made Astoria into a wilderness Gibraltar. A stockade ninety feet square was formed of palings or timber pickets, loopholed for muskets. The compound was guarded by two bastions mounting four four-pounder cannon to further protect the dwellings, powder magazine, and storehouse. But the garrison, snug in its fortress, received a terrible blow to its morale when it learned that the *Tonquin* had been cut off and seized by Indians at Nootka and the crew murdered. The last survivor, the wounded ship's clerk, Mr. Lewis, had put a match to the vessel's powder supply and blown himself, the *Tonquin*, and sundry red-skinned pirates to hell.

Word of the disaster spread rapidly among the tribes. McDougall had to resort to a desperate and despicable stratagem to awe the local Chinooks. He showed a stoppered bottle to an assembly of Indians and declared, "The white men among you are few in number, it is true, but they are mighty in medicine. See here. In this bottle I hold the smallpox, safely corked up. I have but to draw the cork and let loose the pestilence to sweep man, woman and child from the face of the earth." The Indians were horrified and filled with dread of the Scot, whom they now began to call the Great Smallpox Chief.

Astoria's first reinforcements were the pinch-gutted members of the overland party led by Wilson Price Hunt and Donald McKenzie. They staggered into the compound in batches during January and February of 1812 after incredible hardships and privations in the boiling whitewater "caldrons" of the Snake River canyons. They gave the hated river a new name—La Maudite Rivière Enragée, the Damned, Mad River. They had eaten or traded away for food all of their horses but one, which they had killed and skinned to make a horsehide coracle. On its maiden voyage, the bullboat overset and drowned its one-man crew and was given up as a bad idea.

Ross Cox described the new arrivals, who had set out from Mackinac as cocky recruits with ostrich feathers and rooster tails in their hats: "Their concave cheeks, protuberant bones, and tattered garments strongly indicated the dreadful extent of their privations." One man, John Day, lost his mind because of his suffering.

In May 1812 Astor's relief ship *Beaver* brought more reinforcements, rations, and trade goods. As a result, two more outposts were established but, again, the Willamette Valley was spurned. However, Robert Stuart had reconnoitred it again in April with Regis Brugier, and Donald McKenzie shortly explored its course for a hundred miles with Louis La Bonté. He discovered its largest affluent, which was later named for him. Unfortunately, the enmity of the Calapooya Indians was aroused when Joseph Gervais struck a warrior. Their hostility, combined with illness in the party, persuaded McKenzie to return to Astoria around February 1813.

The Calapooyas bided their time, nursing their desire for revenge. The following year, they laid a trap for McKenzie at the mouth of the Willamette. He had no inkling of an ambush till an Indian messenger delivered a warning note from McDougall. It was almost too late. McKenzie had beached his boat and the river's tidal waters had left it stranded, high and dry. He feigned confidence in the Indians, told them that he intended to set up a trading post there, and loudly ordered his men to gather firewood and to clear a space for a camp. McKenzie then told the plotters that he would make a survey of the site next morning. While they gloated over their prey later that night, he stole away with his men the moment the returning tide freed his craft.

The Irish bourgeois John Reed took some men to the Willamette,

7

also, but to feed them rather than to hunt beaver. Food was growing short in Astoria. When they returned to the bastion on March 30, 1813, they described the valley as charming and abounding in beaver and deer. Company returns verified the fact: with no real effort, the Nor'westers took 775 beaver and seven otter skins in 1812–1813.

Donald McKenzie was on the Willamette again in 1813 and, indeed, was headed back there when he ran into Nor'westers coming to take over Astoria because Britain and the United States were now enemies engaged in the War of 1812. His expedition aborted and he returned to the fort. He found McDougall with a fleet of boats ready, ostensibly to transfer stores for a last-ditch defense on the Willamette, should a British sail appear off the Columbia bar. But it was a bluff, like McDougall's later shutting of the gates and training the cannon on the Nor'westers. It was all face-saving. Scot McDougall was not going to fight the War of 1812 for the Yanks.

Back in the States, Astor asked the government to send soldiers to garrison Astoria. He received no reply. He then hurried another supply ship out in March 1813. But Astor's luck had definitely changed with the *Tonquin* disaster. The *Lark* did not even reach Oregon; she was wrecked off Hawaii.

While Hunt was away with the *Beaver,* McDougall began to lose his confident air. He grew uncertain, then despondent, and began to predict failure of the establishment. When John McTavish of the North-West Company told him that a British naval vessel was coming to seize the fort, McDougall was completely dismayed. He decided that the best way out of his dilemma was to sell out before Astoria could be seized by force.

Washington Irving, in his floribunda prose, wrote that the return of the Willamette men with their numerous packs of beaver skins heartened the Astorian partners. "These were the first fruits of the enterprise gathered by men as yet strangers in the land, but they were such as to give substantial grounds for sanguine anticipation of profit when the country should be more completely explored and the trade established."

But all sanguine hopes of profit were dashed by McDougall's craven decision to abandon Astoria to the North-West Company. Hunt returned too late to stop the transfer of the post for a third of its value. According to Irving, beaver plews worth $5 each went for $2, and sea otter skins valued at from $45 to $60 sold for $12 a skin. Astor received $40,000 instead of the $100,000 his property was worth when Astoria changed hands on October 16, 1813.

McDougall always insisted that he had done the right thing by Astor, had swung the best possible deal in the circumstances. Perhaps —but he did not convince Astor, or even his own partners. And when the Scot reentered North-West Company service, Astor was sure that he had been sold out, betrayed by McDougall's capitulation. He wrote to Hunt: "Had our place and property been fairly captured, I should have preferred it. I should not feel as if I were disgraced."

Still, there was no doubt that Astoria was doomed by the outbreak of war. On the last day of November 1813, *H.M.S. Raccoon,* a twenty-six-gun Royal Navy sloop-of-war, anchored in Baker's Bay just inside the Columbia. Captain Black was annoyed to find that his proposed attack on Fort Astoria was no longer necessary, thanks to the commercial arrangement. Nevertheless, being a stickler for ceremony, he insisted on the formal raising of the Union Jack over the settlement on December 12 to assert possession of the surrounding country by His Majesty. Then, with the ensign tied snugly in place, he smashed a bottle of wine and rechristened Astoria, calling it Fort George. The North-West Company had complete control of Oregon.

The Nor'westers kept up the relief post of the American huntsmen in the lower Willamette Valley, because food shortages at Fort George did not cease with the dipping of one flag and the hoisting of new colors. Franchère (who stayed on in North-West Company employ, like many Astorians), in fact, took a hungry party to the valley on February 7, 1814, in order that they might subsist better. He found William Henry already there, in charge of a party of meat hunters.

Franchère was enthusiastic: "I found it a superb river as I traveled up it. It is, in fact, one of the most beautiful of all the rivers that flow into the Columbia. From the confluence to a falls of considerable size the country is, in truth, low and marshy; but at the falls the banks begin to rise on either side and, above it, they offer the happiest and most picturesque of views, laid bare of trees in several places and rising gradually in the form of an amphitheater. Deer and elk are to be found here in great numbers. The post has been established for the purpose of keeping a number of hunters engaged to provide the fort with venison."

Like Franchère, Alex Ross switched to North-West employ. Soon, he was second only to Hudson's Bay Company Governor George Simpson as a critic of its operations. The latter found the wild extravagance of Fort George appalling at a time when the post was giving away a quarter of its profits, in freighting and marketing charges, to the American bottoms it had to use because the East India Company

9

had a monopoly on British trade with the Far East. Instead of living off the land, the Fort George gentlemen imported great quantities of clothing and even food from Europe. Simpson tartly described their profligacy—"All this time, they may be said to have been eating gold." Worse, the bungling management of the Columbia Department negated the heroic efforts of field commanders like McKenzie. With such absurd imports as ostrich feathers and coats of mail lying in the Fort George warehouse, Simpson was entitled to describe the Columbia scornfully as the "scene of the most wasteful extravagance and the most unfortunate dissension."

As for Ross, he could not convince his new superiors that the sawed or split cedar boats of the Astorians were better on the broad Columbia than the traditional birch rind canoes which the Nor'westers brought from Athabaska. And, because fixed trading posts worked well in Ontario and Manitoba, the conservative partners frowned on the idea of wide-ranging brigades and far-flung interior outposts in Oregon, which he and McKenzie advocated. The real problem was that McKenzie was of a lower caste than the snobbish partners. His ideas were dismissed as those of a man "that was only fit to eat horse flesh and shoot at a mark."

Alex Ross saw that the managers of Fort George were imitating their masters in Fort William and Montreal. The latter were self-indulgent and squandering princes of commerce, men who threw away their money on fine clothing and silver horseshoes. Ross was particularly scornful of the table etiquette and other punctilios which the clerks insisted upon in rude Fort George. Seating at table was by a kind of business-rank protocol. There were three grades of tea poured, for the three castes of diners, and even three grades of sugar served— refined loaf, common crushed, and (for the local serfs) the inferior brown.

Shortly, Ross had something more important than table manners to be caustic about. The district's "booshway" (bourgeois), John McTavish, tried to awe Indians who had wounded some of his men. But his nerve failed him; he panicked and pulled out with his small army of Fort Georgians. Some of his men were so ashamed that they turned off and went up the Willamette—"to hide their disgrace," in Ross's words. Bitterly, he summed up this major operation of the Nor'westers: "They, therefore, without recovering the property, firing a gun or securing a single prisoner, sounded a retreat and returned home on the ninth day—having made matters ten times worse than it was before. Thus ended this inglorious expedition."

When asked about the humiliation of McTavish, Ross said that Nor'westers knew how to travel in Athabaska, but not in Oregon. In the latter area, the Americans knew best how to move about. In fact, said Ross, the Astorians had penetrated all the way to "the frontiers of California."

The wintering partners could not keep down as good a man as McKenzie. Montreal ignored his rough manners and hired him to head up all interior operations. Ross welcomed the new orders, since he was McKenzie's staunchest ally. But he groaned at the other news: Montreal was sending Iroquois trappers to reinforce the Oregon contingent. Ross had no use for the (half-)civilized Christian Indians of the East. After several exasperating experiences with them, such as when they deserted and gave away furs, traps, everything for the favors of some local "squaws," he referred to them as "Iroquois and other refuse."

Donald McKenzie made changes immediately. He expanded trapping of the rich Snake River country and replaced comfortable, but misplaced, Spokane House with Fort Nez Percés. Also dubbed Fort Walla Walla, it became his entrepot and depot for most trapping parties. In 1816 orders came to trap southward through the area Ross (forgetting his earlier boast about the Astorians) described as a new and unexplored tract.

But the first move toward California came from a ludicrous quarter—the guardhouse at Fort George. An American schooner handed over to the Nor'westers a Russian known only as Jacob. He was in irons, and the fetters suited him. The Slav had plotted mutiny, piracy and murder at sea. Once in custody ashore, however, his demeanor became as saintly as that of an archbishop. His conduct was so good that he was soon released from his chains and made a blacksmith. He was even admitted to the guard. One evening when he was on night watch, Jacob sneaked away. He took eighteen Owyhees— or "Sandwich Islanders," as the Hawaiians were called—with him. They headed for California where Jacob assured the *kanakas* their fortunes would be made.

After only a few days, the Russian's recruits had second thoughts. They redeserted and came back. But Jacob remained at large. He joined a band of disaffected Indians, turned renegade, and became a sort of white chief like Daniel Boone's enemy, Simon Girty. At least twice, Jacob scaled Fort George's walls. Once he broke into a storeroom to carry off some booty. On another occasion, he brazenly entered the fortress in broad daylight, as a spy planning a raid with his red-skinned desperadoes. However, he was dressed as an Indian woman!

Jacob became such a nuisance that Ross applied for permission to capture him. He took out a force, rounded up the rascal, and locked him in the fort until a vessel could take him to Hawaii. The last time the Nor'westers saw him, he was being rowed out to a ship. He took off his cape and waved it in the air like a flag, shouting, "Huzzah! Huzzah for my friends! Confusion to my enemies!"

Shortly, the first beaver trapping party started south, up the Willamette. The ten trappers were warned by Calapooyas not to continue hunting without paying tribute. The mountain men brushed the warnings aside, sure that the Indians were only bluffing. But, as they advanced, the Nor'westers found both river banks lined with warriors "in menacing postures," to use Ross's words. They called the Indians' bluff but had enough sense to paddle in midstream. They were shortly the targets for a shower of arrows. They returned the fire, with effect, but decided to turn back after one trapper was wounded. The first Willamette expedition was abandoned.

A short time after the return of the rebuffed party, a clerk took twenty-five men to again attempt a breakthrough to the beaver grounds. Since the earlier company had killed a chief, the Calapooyas would not dicker without compensation for his death. The matter was compromised with the presentation of gifts. But the Nor'westers were again stopped, a little further upriver. They were forced to fire at a menacing knot of Indians, killing three, before retreating downriver. That night, a raiding party got into camp and severely wounded one of the hunters. In Ross's opinion, only darkness saved the others from death. The second attempt to open up communications to the south via the Willamette was another fiasco.

The whites had considered the Calapooyas to be dull, inoffensive folk. Now they learned that, when aroused, the tribesmen could be dangerous. "By the disaster of this trip," wrote Ross, "every avenue was for the present shut up against our hunters in the Wallamite direction." He chided his colleagues for their latest blunder, which he would have avoided by paying the tribute demanded—a few twists of tobacco. "The result of this disaster," he reiterated, "shut us out entirely from the southern quarter."

Ross was put in charge of a third expedition strong enough to buffalo any Indians. He chose Peter Skene Ogden as his second-in-command. When the three boats reached the falls of the Willamette, Indians gathered to prevent further ascent of the river. Ross prudently camped on the opposite bank, under the muzzles of his two fieldpieces. Early on the fourth day, he attempted negotiations, but his invitations to a parley were refused. He crossed the river, boldly held out his hand in friendship, and offered to smoke with the Indians. But they still refused all communication with the whites, and continued their war songs and dances.

Ross did not panic and run like his predecessors. Nor did he attack. Determined to win peace, he just sat tight where he was. He would outwait the Indians. Years after, he wrote of the stand-off: "Patience and forbearance do much on these occasions. It is the best policy to be observed with Indians." His waiting paid off. Some chiefs who crossed to meet him, finally, were hostile and silent, at first. From their camp came loud wails of advance mourning. When Ross offered them the pipe of peace, they would not take it. Suddenly, the head chief asked bluntly in his own tongue: "What do the whites want?" Ross was angered by the Calapooya's spurning of the traditional pipe, but he held his temper and answered politely: "Peace. Peace is what we want." Presenting a flag to the headman, he added, "Here, the Great Chief of the whites sends you this as a token of his love."

Several moments of silence were broken by whispers. The chief accepted the flag and also Ross's offer of peace. He was gratified with the present, he said. Now he wanted to smoke. He laid a painted and feathered calumet before the white man. In return, Ross gave him the pipe which he had earlier turned down. The visitors began puffing in the ceremony preparatory to a palaver. When they were done with their showy inhaling and exhaling, the several Calapooyas got up, one at a time, to make speeches for fully two hours. Ross patiently heard them out. Mostly they spoke of grievances and their redress, and threats of resistance should the whites attempt to go upriver.

Ross then stated the white man's case against closure of the river. He began by trying to prove that the Indians had fired first at the trappers. Soon, he realized that he was getting nowhere. So he cut the affair short by agreeing to pay for the dead man. It took him a whole day of negotiation and three trips to the Indian encampment, but Ross finally won his demand of free access to the Willamette Valley. The supreme chief scraped up a little dust, threw it in the air and said, *"Hilow*—it is done." He then gave Ross a slave to show him that he might treat all of his people as slaves if they were unfaithful to their word. The bourgeois released the symbolic slave to the chief, paid for the dead, and took his leave.

Aleck Ross knew that his Willamette treaty could be upset in a day. He admitted: "Their acknowledged authority is but very limited, their power as chiefs but small; so that any rascal in the camp might at any time break through the most solemn treaty with impunity." But he was lucky. The Indians faithfully observed their part of the agreement for years, until the lower Willamette Valley was pacified and half-civilized by the fur men.

The conditions of the accord were few. The river was to be open to unmolested travel by whites; in the event of misunderstandings, the natives were not to resort to violence but to seek redress, via their chiefs, from the White Chief at Fort George. The trappers were not to take the law into their hands, if aggrieved. The chiefs were held accountable for the conduct of their people.

Back at the fort, Ross's superior, the taciturn James Keith, not only gave him one of his rare smiles but actually praised him aloud: "Your success removes my anxiety and is calculated not only to restore peace in the Willamette but throughout the whole neighbouring tribes."

But peace was not complete in the Willamette Valley, and Ross was the first to know it. When he led a forty-five-man party to the river's mouth a short time later, he was met by Indians who began to stretch arrows in their bows. Two Iroquois cocked their guns in response to the menace, but Ross stopped them from firing. The Indians finally withdrew, but remained "shy"—aloof. This was a bad sign, but Ross managed to extricate his followers without an altercation.

This incident at Multnomah Island was the exception to the rule. But the Nor'westers did little with the Willamette; there were just too few men spread too thinly over an immense area. Fur men like Ross and Ogden were not afraid of dangers of the long march to California. As the former wrote: "An experienced person in the Indian countries, with only one or two men, their guns and a few loads of ammunition, would think no more of crossing the desert from the Atlantic to the Pacific in the most wild and unfrequented parts, than any other man in ordinary life would do to cross a country parish from one side to the other." The time simply was not ripe for expansion southward of the fur trade.

Not until the Cowlitz River on the north shore was closed by Indian trouble did the North-West Company finally direct its attention again to the upper Willamette. Tom McKay led a party of sixty men to its very source (briefly called McKay's River), then crossed the divide to drop into the Umpqua River Valley in 1819–1820. McKay found the Umpqua to be rich in furs and the Indians peaceful and unused to contact with whites. But his men mistook the Indians' timidity for hostility. They bullied them, threatened them, and, finally, seized their horses to insure the return of some visiting redmen. The Umpquas, naturally, could neither understand or accept such outrageous behavior. They resisted. The trappers fired into them and fourteen inoffensive Indians soon lay dead. They had not drawn a single bow, so there were no casualties among the "civilized" combatants, even when they pursued the "savages" into the woods.

Shortly, the Canadians came to their senses. They were isolated in Indian country more than two hundred miles from Fort George. They hurriedly retreated. Their fear infected the fur hunters on the Willamette, who joined the rush downstream. Five men were sent ahead as expresses to Fort George to give an account (much colored in the trappers' favor, complained Ross) of the "battle." But, while they were camped at Oak Point, the four whites were killed as they slept. Only the Indian messenger escaped to spread the word. The murders, committed within twenty miles of the fort's cannon, were the work of the local Cathlanahquiah Indians. The Umpquas made no real pursuit.

Such atrocious murders, almost at the fort's very gates, called for exemplary revenge if the North-West Company were to survive. Three parties of whites, half-bloods, and Indians were hurried out. They arrested five men for the murders. Four were convicted after a long trial and executed. But nothing could be done about the Umpquas except to give them a wide berth. This was done by free trappers La Bonté, Gervais, and Etienne Lucier, who tamed the lower Willamette in the 1820s, giving the valley such place names as Lac La Biche (Elk Lake) and Rivière du Boudin (Pudding River—for a feast of venison, topped by blood pudding, enjoyed after a period of virtual starvation). Ross estimated that the trapper's massacre of the Umpquas cost the North-West Company four thousand beaver pelts a year—£6000. He added: "The dire effects produced on the natives by the heedless conduct of our people took years to efface."

Although the late fur trade historian Dale Morgan insisted that Nor'westers never worked as far south as 42 degrees, there were always tales—like Ross's—of loners venturing to California for furs. In 1820–1821, Indians told their Franciscan mission padres of buckskin-clad, rifle-bearing strangers in the hinterland. These may have been freelance trappers like Louis Pichette, alias Dupé or Dupré, and his sidekick, Louis Kanota, either a Hawaiian or a Nipissing Indian. In July 1822, a "Simeon Frazer" told Edwin James that he had "often" been in northern California. But, by and large, California—and most of Oregon—remained untrapped during North-West Company days.

The deed poll of March 26, 1821, which merged the North-West Company into the Hudson's Bay Company (which took Ross, McKenzie, and other Nor'westers into its employ), did not open up the Siskiyou frontier.

McKenzie, even more than Ross or Ogden, was perfectly capable of opening the trail to California. Ross's thumbnail biography suggests the kind of man he was. His confederates teased him as "Fat McKenzie," since he was a corpulent 312 pounds in his prime. But he was an intrepid explorer, who thought little of mushing 600 miles on snowshoes. He was, as well, an impressive figure in his elkskin surtout, a sort of arrowproof armor along the lines of the leather cuirasses worn earlier by California's *soldados de cuero*.

McKenzie's friend, the "scribbling clerk" Ross, wrote of him: "Capable of enduring fatigue and privations, no labour appeared too great, no hardship too severe. Bold and decided in the presence of danger, he was peculiarly adapted to strike awe into the heart of the savage, who has instinctive reverence for manly daring. . . . To travel a day's journey was his delight. But he detested spending five minutes scribbling in a journal. His traveling notes were often kept on a beaver skin, written hieroglyphically with a pencil or a piece of coal, and he would often complain of the drudgery of keeping accounts. . . . Every man he met was his companion; and when not asleep he was always on foot, strolling backward and forward, full of plans and projects, and so peculiar was this pedestrian habit that he went by the name of 'Perpetual Motion.' "

But McKenzie could not be spared from the rich Snake River country, whose returns were almost enough, alone, to counter the general mismanagement of the Columbia Department by the gentlemen of Fort George. And so it was that the Siskiyou Trail was not pioneered until later—and not by stout McKenzie but by Ogden, Jedediah Smith, and lesser mountain men like Alexander R. McLeod, Michel Laframboise, and Francis Ermatinger. After the 1821 merger, Chief Factor McKenzie went east to Fort Garry, where he closed out his career in brilliant fashion as Governor of Assiniboia for eight years, before retiring with the well-earned title of "King of the North-west."

Snake River Outfit

GEORGE SIMPSON was a bastard. The dynamic illegitimate son of George Simpson of Ross-shire, Scotland, earned the epithet not so much because of his sinister genealogy as for his example as a stern, demanding—even carping—taskmaster, a disciplinarian of Company clerks and servants. Simpson suffered from that common birth defect of natural sons—he was born with a chip on his shoulder.

Born in 1792, the driving Simpson was short of stature but long on executive ability, and tough as a coal miner's Shetland mule. He entered Hudson's Bay service in 1820, just in time for the merger. It proved to be the perfect combination of man and moment. He arrived in time to rescue a fagged-out firm which was swallowing an equally exhausted North-West Company. By 1824, the influence of the frenetic little inspector general in speeding canoes and dogsleds was having its effect. In that year, a trader wrote that the Northwest was finally beginning to be ruled with a rod of iron.

Colin Stewart, sizing up Simpson at Fort William in 1821, misjudged him. He damned him with faint praise by describing him merely as a pleasant little man who was so full of spirit that he personified ambition. Simpson soon changed, if Stewart was right. Long before he was made Governor-in-Chief of Rupert's Land (all Hudson's Bay Company territory in Canada), Simpson was becoming dictatorial, a Napoleon of the fur trade. During forty years of service to the Company in Canada, the domineering Simpson was the most relentless critic and foe of any and all Yankee interlopers in John Bull's beaver preserve. He was marshal of a small army of trappers fending off the Americans who would eventually philosophize their aggression by the term "manifest destiny."

As governor-in-chief, Simpson hid his toughness under a surface ease and affability. Thus, he had little friction with his subordinates, whom he awed in any case. But he confided his true opinion of them to his journals and especially to a secret notebook. Like Wellington, he considered the men serving under him to be a rabble. He rated individuals and races alike with Solomonic aplomb. Canadians were to be preferred to Orkneymen, he insisted, for, although the latter were less expensive fellows, they were slow, less strong in physique and spirit, and obstinate if brought into the service as young men. As for the Scots and Irish, he pontificated that they were not only too independent but quarrelsome and mutinous. His American rivals, of course, were roughnecks and scoundrels.

No element of Hudson's Bay Company affairs escaped Simpson's personal attention and scrutiny. To save money—like many a self-made Scot, Simpson worshiped thrift and order—he introduced York boats for freighting when they proved practical to replace the traditional but inefficient birch peel canoes. He stopped the bestowing of gifts on the Indians and instituted more liberal payments for their skins and a policy of advances for clothing available at the company stores. Critics said that this was debt slavery. They also quipped that the H.B.C.-lettered Union Jack which was the Company's flag stood for "Here Before Christ" and that the motto *Pro Pelle Cutem* of the firm's coat of arms meant not "Skin for Skin" as claimed, but really described the Indians as being "Skinned, for Skins."

Simpson took in hand a self-styled "company of adventurers" which, though charged by its charter with the duty of exploration as well as trade, was more timid and indolent in 1821 than adventurous. Its men in the field, mostly plodding Orkney Islanders, could not even hold their own with the North-West Company's *mangeurs de lard,* or pork eaters—the canoe men of the Montreal–Fort William run. The real adventurers of the fur trade were not "Bay" men at all, but the North-West Company *voyageurs* and *coureurs de bois,* the boatmen and woodsmen of the fur frontier, the true *pays d'en haut* (upper country, or outback) which stretched westward to the Rockies.

Luckily, with the conciliation of the two merchant companies there came an infusion of Highland Scots and French-Canadian blood which reinvigorated the ancient company. Thirty-two of the first fifty-three commissioned officers (chief factors and chief traders) of the new company were Nor'westers.

The Governor and Committee in London asked Simpson to survey the Columbia Department. The international situation in the much controverted Oregon country was fluid, even mercurial. Russia, Great Britain, and the United States all claimed sovereignty over the land between Spanish territory and Alaska, a land whose borders were all de jure, not de facto. The Columbia Department had been a losing proposition under the North-West Company, but Simpson's London superiors advised him that, if he could reduce its annual loss to a small sum, he was to retain the area for the Company and Britain, for strategic or political more than economic reasons.

Governor Simpson was way ahead of London. He had already evaluated the Columbia region and was optimistic that it would not only serve as a barrier to keep Americans away from the Company's inner sanctum of the fur trade, New Caledonia or British Columbia, but that he could shift its operations from the red to the black columns of the ledger. The ordinary clerks and servants thought little, if at all, about their roles as agents of British expansion, but Simpson was not unaware of what later would be called geopolitics. He realized that by maintaining a British presence in jointly occupied Oregon Territory, he was serving the Crown.

Simpson knew just the man to make a success of the Columbia operation, so bungled by the Nor'westers. He was Dr. John McLoughlin. At first blush, Simpson's confidence in the nonpracticing medic seemed inexplicable. The entry for McLoughlin in the Governor's little black book (titled *Book of Servant's Characters*) was highly critical. However, it was also ambivalent—and no one ever secured a "passing grade" from the impossibly demanding Simpson. Few, it turned out, fared any better at his pen than the doctor.

Simpson found Chief Trader McLoughlin to be an active—indeed a bustling—man. He was capable of getting much business done, but he lacked system and regularity in his habits. In Simpson's ken, he did not even have the talent to properly manage the clerks under his authority. The governor admitted, however, that he was zealous in discharging his duties and was a man of strict honor and integrity.

To Simpson's mind, McLoughlin was too great a stickler for right and privileges, a man who liked too much to set himself up as a righter of wrongs. Had he had the influence and tact to attract a following, Simpson thought that he might become a troublesome man to the Company and eternally embroiled in so-called affairs of honor. The governor put him down as a man who would be a radical in any country, under any form of government, and chastized the future

"Father of Oregon" for his ambition and his violent and ungovernable temper, which reduced his influence among his colleagues. After calling attention to McLoughlin's good points, chiefly his influence over the Indians and his tolerable fluency in their tongues, Simpson exhibited the ambivalence which almost subverted his criticism into praise: "Altogether a disagreeable man to do business with, as it is impossible to go to him in all things, and a difference of opinion almost amounts to a declaration of hostilities, yet a good-hearted man and a pleasant companion."

By September 1822, London had discarded any thought of withdrawing from Oregon. At the same time, the United States pressed its claims and the Czar issued an ukase claiming the Pacific Northwest coast for Russia, all the way down to the Fifty-First Parallel.

London's decision was to make a permanent stand on the north bank of the Columbia, to enter the coastal trade (until now an American monopoly), and to strengthen the Columbia Department and fight a commercial holding action in the area south of the Columbia.

Simpson accordingly reorganized the whole trading system. He abandoned the supplying of Fort George by sea and substituted a land communication with York House on Hudson Bay via Norway House, north of Lake Winnipeg. He gave notice to the Boston skippers and began a Company fleet by chartering the brig *Lively*. And he began to plan a new headquarters for the Department, safe on the right bank of the Columbia. It would replace Fort George, which was obviously going to fall, eventually, into American hands.

At the same time that he upgraded operations, Simpson cut costs. He reduced the number of employees from 151 to just 83, saving £2000 a year. He reappointed factors and traders to posts instead of transferring them out just as they grew experienced. Most important, he contributed new life to the Department by sending some of his best men there, including two rising young clerks named Peter Skene Ogden and John Work. Simpson planned farms on the Columbia, Cowlitz, and Willamette rivers to make Oregon self-sufficient without the import of foodstuffs. The Governor and Committee in London not only went along with him but suggested a broadening of the base of the trade by marketing products other than furs.

Far more important than the diversification of trade, however, was the boom in peltries from the Snake River country. In 1822 Spokane House received over 4000 beaver pelts. The next year, Alex Ross's brigade brought in 4900 skins.

Although international tension relaxed in 1824 and 1825, with the Czar's territorial claim retreating to 54° 40′ and the United States and Great Britain agreeing to continue the status quo of joint tenancy, the Company went right ahead with its plans. On July 22, 1824, Simpson was ordered to abandon Fort George as soon as he could establish a new post. The fort at Astoria had been, technically, returned to the Americans after the War of 1812, but it was still in North-West Company possession in 1821 and therefore passed into Hudson's Bay Company control. U.S. Commissioner J. B. Prevost had ceremoniously hoisted a Stars and Stripes over the stockade in 1818 in a gesture meant to show its recovery by the United States. But no Yankees came to reoccupy it. The hardly convincing fiction was that the British were only holding it and protecting it for the United States until the President should ask for it!

The Council which convened at York Factory on July 10, 1824, appointed Dr. McLoughlin chief factor of the Columbia Department. He was Simpson's pick and no better choice could have been made. The six-foot-four-inch muscular giant was sometimes rash and impulsive, but he was as well-meaning and good-hearted as he was energetic and forceful. He gave away something to McKenzie and Ogden as a field man but was their superior in the desk work of the administrator —which was just as important to Company success. Though only thirty-nine, McLoughlin was a veteran of twenty-one years in the fur trade. And he was tough enough for the job. Simpson described him well: "He was such a figure as I should not like to meet in a dark night in one of the bylanes in the neighbourhood of London, dressed in clothes that had once been fashionable but were now covered with a thousand patches of different colours; his beard would do honor to the chin of a grizzly bear; his face and hands evidently shewing that he had not lost much time at his toilette; loaded with arms, and his own Herculian dimensions forming a *tout ensemble* that would convey a good idea of the highwayman of former days."

Born in Rivière du Loup on the St. Lawrence below Quebec in 1784, McLoughlin was of Irish, French-Canadian, and Scots descent. He was baptized a Catholic but raised a Protestant before being apprenticed to a doctor in Quebec when he was fourteen. In five years he became Dr. McLoughlin, licensed to practice surgery, medicine, and pharmacy. In 1803 he joined the North-West Company as an apprentice surgeon on the promise of a quick rise to a high post. Instead, his advancement was glacially slow. But when he traded his scalpel for a skinning knife, his talents were more readily recognized by his employers. By 1814, he was a wintering partner. Eventually, he became a leader in the "revolt" which led to the North-West Company's absorption into the Honourable Company. McLoughlin was rewarded by being promoted to chief factor when the firms amalgamated.

McLoughlin's dominating blue-gray eyes, under thick, bushy brows, commanded respect. They were complemented by a powerful voice and an imposing manner. He was stubborn, as easily angered as Simpson claimed, and was used to having his own way. Yet, withal, he was kindly and as renowned a host (to Americans as well as Britons) as Captain John Sutter of California, who became a legend as a philanthropic boniface of the overland trail to California. Sympathetic and compassionate, McLoughlin was also a good thinker and conversationalist. His was an inquiring mind, and while stationed at Rainy Lake he wrote a thoughtful essay on the Ojibways of the area. Most important to Simpson, his competence and integrity were unchallenged. Approval of the choice of McLoughlin was almost unanimous. His many friends saw him as the right man for a demanding and critical task. His few enemies mistakenly thought of the transfer as a banishment for an embarrassingly obstinate and impetuous troublemaker.

Typical of McLoughlin was the dispatch with which he moved to take over the fur barony. Just seventeen days after the vote of the Council, he was leading fourteen men westward in two canoes. But even McLoughlin was no match for the frenetic Simpson. He had decided to personally supervise operations from Fort George. Although the governor dawdled until August 15 before setting out, he overtook McLoughlin near the Athabaska River on September 26, to the astonishment of the doctor. When the two parties, traveling together, reached Fort George on November 8, 1824, Simpson had been just eighty-four days on the road. The prodigious traveler had beaten the record passage by a full twenty days.

Simpson and McLoughlin found the Columbia Department to be virtually a limitless territory. There were no firm boundaries save the rolling surf to the west and the crest of the Rockies to the east. The border of New Caledonia to the north was a blurred line. Somewhere to the south lay Spanish California, now a part of newly independent Mexico.

The governor was annoyed upon his arrival to find the officers in charge of Fort George at play. They were amusing themselves with a sailboat instead of working. He thought it typical of their lackadaisical management. Or *mis*management. Not only did Simpson dislike Fort George's bastions and its two eighteen-pounder cannon standing post in front—he thought the Astorian fortress possessed an air of grandeur and consequence which simply did not become a fur trade factory. Everything on the Columbia, in fact, was on too grand a scale—everything except the beaver harvest! He had cause to criticize; four forts in almost virgin territory had yielded only twenty thousand skins over a period of fourteen years.

Simpson found the natives to be amiable, verminous, and venereal. Drunkenness was ruining the local economy since rum-sodden Indians did not make good beaver hunters. He discontinued the old policy of awarding them a bonus of a bottle of rum for every ten skins delivered, a variation of the traditional *regale* of the Canadians. This was a drunken binge indulged in by the *québecois* at the end of any journey of conesquence. He proudly reported to London in 1825 that he had put a stop to the liquor traffic on the Columbia.

McLoughlin went along with his superior's teetotaling policy, as did the doctor's strong right arm, Peter Skene Ogden. But the latter sometimes envied the lack of scruple of his American rivals toward mixing Indians and spirits. After he was worsted in a collision with Yankee trappers in 1825, he groused: "Had I the same opportunity or the same advantages they have, long since I would have had a good stock of liquor here—and every beaver in the camp would be mine."

The four months which Simpson spent at Fort George turned him into a confident booster for the Oregon country. He all but forbade the import of food, since there was fish aplenty in the Columbia and potatoes in Fort George's fields. He expected McLoughlin to develop his own supply of beef, pork, corn, and butter. It had commonly been felt in London that farming and fur trading were incompatible. Simpson reversed this policy, with McLoughlin's help, and got London to like it. He felt that any endeavor which lightened Company expenses was a legitimate branch of the trade.

Finally, since the Company and the Crown now bowed to the inevitable and abandoned all hope of holding the lands south of the Columbia for many years more in the face of American expansionism, Simpson decided on a radical policy, one of ruthless expediency. He would combine short-term profits with long-range political strategy by having his men literally hunt out the contested regions. They were to strip the streams bare of beaver, down to the last cub. He planned to leave the Snake, Willamette, and other expendable fur areas so barren of peltries that the Americans would find them no attraction

23

and would turn away without threatening the Columbia's north shore.

Nor'wester David Thompson had once said: "A worn field may be manured and again made fertile but the beaver, once destroyed, cannot be replaced." The American fur trader, William H. Ashley, felt differently about the recuperative powers of beaver colonies: "Leaving the streams undisturbed for five or six years, they will, at the expiration of that time, be found as numerous as when first trapped." Simpson chose to believe Thompson—but not to accept his maxim as a warning; rather, to take it as a challenge. He would make Oregon (and California) south of the Columbia into a barrier—in terms of the fur trade—resembling the Great American Desert just reported by Major Stephen H. Long in the High Plains in the lee of the Rocky Mountains. Simpson wrote London: "The country is a rich preserve of beaver . . . which, for political reasons, we should endeavour to destroy as fast as possible."

It was as part of Simpson's deliberate policy of destruction of the beaver in Oregon (and northern California) that a road was driven up the Willamette Valley to the Umpqua and Rogue rivers and over the Siskiyou Mountains. The Siskiyou Trail came into being strictly as an incident to Simpson's scorched earth policy and was an accidental road to California. It was meant only to penetrate into the heart of a no-man's-land which the Scot planned to turn into a beaver desert.

The Governor ordered McLoughlin to find a site on the Columbia's north shore for a headquarters which would be strong and self-sustaining. The chief factor explored Cape Disappointment and Baker's Bay near the river's mouth but regarded them as unsuitable. He worked his way slowly upstream, finding the right bank either too high, rocky, and steep or too low and swampy in almost every instance. Not until he was one hundred miles from the sea and six miles past the mouth of the Willamette (on the opposite bank) did he find what he sought. It was a gently sloping point backed by a higher prairie, with a second bench rising above the little river plain to some sixty feet of elevation. The site was so superior to any other he had examined that it won his complete approval. It was sufficiently elevated to satisfy London's instructions. The mile-wide and three-miles-long plain, although backed by a parklike landscape of firs, was treeless enough to be called a prairie by early rivermen. It already had three names—Jolie Prairie, Belle Vue Point, and a Klickitat name which translated as "Place of the Mud Turtles."

Only the strip of shore adjacent to the river was subject to flooding, but McLoughlin chose a site for the stockade set far back from the shore. High and dry, it also offered a commanding position, one easily defended against hostiles approaching from the river. The field of fire was made to order for defensive action. Jolie Prairie was also almost directly across the Columbia from the mouth of the Willamette, the avenue to southern Oregon which, when developed, would make Fort Vancouver the northern terminus of the Siskiyou Trail.

According to McLoughlin's friend, lieutenant, and successor, James Douglas, the doctor had still another reason for his choice of site—the beauty of the location. Visiting botanist David Douglas of London wrote (on April 13, 1825): "The scenery from this place is sublime—high, well wooded hills, mountains covered with perpetual snow, extensive natural meadows and plains of deep, fertile, alluvial deposit covered with a rich sward of grass and a profusion of flowering plants." From the benchland, a viewer had the whole sweep of the Columbia River Valley and the unending forests surmounted on the horizon by lofty, snow-capped Mount Hood. Such latecomers as Lieutenant Charles Wilkes, U.S.N. (1841), were as impressed with the beauty of the happily named Jolie Prairie as were McLoughlin and Douglas.

There were a few drawbacks to McLoughlin's choice of site. It was far from the Columbia's mouth, which it was supposed to command. But he stressed in his report that nowhere downstream had he found an eligible situation, as required by London's instructions. The fort was a stiff walk from the river bank; there was no spring or other source of drinking water on the stockade site; and McLoughlin was not sure that ships of deep draft could reach the mooring below the fort. But a well was successfully dug, and the landing was found to be on water deep enough for the ocean-going vessels of the day.

McLoughlin's party of laborers reached the site either late in November or early in December, 1824. The men fell to work, guided by the doctor's occasional supervisorial visits. As early as March 1825, Simpson reported that a three-fourths-acre plot was picketed, with structures within. He was a little premature. The two storehouses, the Indian hall, and the "dwelling house" were almost certainly not completed. The temporary quarters of the workers were tents, skin lodges, and bark huts. But most of the buildings were begun, and progress was satisfactory if not hurried.

The prairie sod was broken for potatoes and other crops. Canoes began to transfer goods from Fort George to the new depot. By mid-

March most of the property of any value had been cleared out of the old Astorian headquarters. McLoughlin reached his new base of operations on March 18, 1825. Fort George was completely abandoned. (But, since the Americans did nothing with it, McLoughlin revived it as a small trading outpost in 1829.)

Simpson was absolutely delighted with Fort Vancouver. The always pragmatic governor liked the great extent of pasture nearby and was sure that both Indian corn and European grains would thrive on the tableland above the river. And, while not as interested in esthetics as the doctor, he was no philistine. He crowed: "It will in two years hence be the finest place in Western America. Indeed, I have rarely seen a gentleman's seat in England possessing so many natural advantages, and where ornament and use are so agreeably combined."

The "Napoleon of the Fur Trade" was always fond of pomp. When he traveled long distances, he sometimes had a bagpiper droning and squealing away, as well as a bugler trumpeting in his fast express canoe. And his paddlemen were led in traditional *chansons* like *Très Beaux Canards, À La Claire Fontaine*, and *En Roulant Ma Boule* by a chorister. Small wonder, then, that, before his departure for York Factory on March 19, Simpson felt it to be only fitting and proper to muster the entire company, as sunrise gilded the stockade, for ceremonies in connection with the founding of the new trading post.

Simpson had the flagstaff stepped. He formally baptized the post by smashing a bottle of rum on the butt of the flagpole and shouting to the assemblage: "In behalf of the Honourable Hudson's Bay Company, I hereby name this establishment Fort Vancouver. God save King George the Fourth!" Simpson's words were echoed by a chorus of three cheers from the crowd before he gave orders for the issuance of a few drams of liquor to all persons present.

Still as concerned with British strategy as with Company profits, he wrote in his journal that evening: "The object of naming it after that distinguished navigator is to identify our claim to the soil and trade with his discovery of the river and coast in behalf of Great Britain."

Before Simpson took his leave, he gave McLoughlin supreme authority over the Columbia Department. The doctor's predecessors had been hesitant in criticizing or overruling other commissioned gentlemen in charge of the satellite posts.

After Simpson departed, McLoughlin continued the stripping of Fort George. But he also got cracking with the fur trade itself.

Soon, he had sent out so many men in fur hunting parties that he had only a corporal's guard to defend his new headquarters should Indians attack. He could muster a garrison of only two servants, a clerk, seven common laborers, and a visitor or two, like botanist Douglas or one of the itinerant free trappers of the lower Willamette.

Simpson did not want departmental headquarters moved permanently to Fort Vancouver. He feared that even the north bank would fall to the Americans. He preferred a site quite distant, one which he fancied to be on a natural road to the interior, the Fraser River. Unlike McLoughlin, he did not realize that the Fraser was no possible rival to the Columbia, since it was unnavigable.

McLoughlin laid out grain fields and put in appletrees and grapevines. The latter were the result of a handful of seeds placed and forgotten in an Oregon-bound gentleman's coat after a London meal. The post's first harvest was a bountiful one for an isolated agricultural outpost in a wilderness of firs and furs. McLoughlin secured nine and a half bushels of peas and nine hundred barrels of potatoes. In 1826 he planted the first two bushels of wheat in the Pacific Northwest, and also some oats, barley, corn, and timothy. He predicted that, by 1828, his wheat fields would supply not only all the flour needed by his resident servants and laborers, and quiet the ravenous appetites of his Snake River and Southern trapping brigades when at home, but provide enough for all the Company posts west of the Rockies. (In 1838, when pioneer John Sutter saw Fort Vancouver, he was so impressed that he took it as his model for New Helvetia, or Sutter's Fort, far down the Siskiyou Trail.)

McLoughlin hoped to increase the herd of stock transferred from Fort George. He forbade the killing of cattle. The taboo was observed as religiously as if Jolie Prairie were Delhi itself. It was not until 1836 that the doctor allowed a cow to be butchered. In March 1829, he found that he had 153 head of neat cattle, not counting calves. Also fifty goats, some chickens, and two hundred hogs rooting contentedly on the prairie. Barrels of cured salmon soon were loaded on ships bound for the London docks. In 1827 McLoughlin suggested the opening up of a timber trade to California and Hawaii. Two years later, Simpson's examination of Willamette Falls led him to enthuse that enough saws could be employed there to load the whole British Navy.

As early as 1825, Simpson began to have doubts about his projected Fraser River headquarters. By 1826, he was speaking of the Columbia as the only navigable stream into the interior. The

London directors grew leery of the Fraser scheme, too, and allowed it to die an unlamented death. At the same time, they gave Simpson's combative stance before the Americans their blessing. In fact, they repeatedly urged him to acquire and erase the fur trade south of the Columbia and to oppose vigorously any American penetration of the Oregon-Idaho-California buffer zone protecting New Caledonia. Typical of their communiqués to Simpson was one of March 12, 1827: "It is extremely desirable to hunt as bare as possible all the country south of the Columbia and west of the mountains."

In lieu of violence, McLoughlin was to use his skills as a trader, discouraging Yankee competition not with Tower muskets but by hunting clean the countryside and consistently paying the Indians and free trappers more for their skins than his American competitors. Also, he was to sell supplies and equipment cheaper than they could. This was a reversal of long-standing mercantilist policy. The monopolistic directors of the Company had long been used to buying furs at the lowest prices possible and charging all that the traffic would bear for traps, gunpowder, and other supplies.

The old company changed its spots quickly. When Ogden's men deserted him in 1825, for better fur prices (plus whiskey) from the Americans, the new tariffs went immediately into effect. Ogden quickly recaptured control of the fur trade in the most critical area, the Snake River country, then set about securing Oregon and northern California.

Peter Skene Ogden was a man of great endurance, courage, and modesty. David Douglas met the brigade leader in 1826. He found him to be a man of much information and a very friendly gentleman. Lieutenant Charles Wilkes met him fifteen years later and was much taken with Ogden's wit, describing him as a general favorite, and adding: "There is so much hilarity and such a fund of amusement about him that one is fortunate to fall into his company."

Unfortunately, Governor Simpson's greatest weakness was his professional jealousy. It was probably the product of a heavily masked inferiority complex. This paranoia led him to constantly underrate and downgrade any subordinates who might (even remotely) become threats, one day, to him. Thus he badly misgauged Ogden as a man of boundless ambition who was superior to his colleagues, to be sure, but who was a cool, calculating fellow uninfluenced by any good or honorable principles! He thought that Ogden was capable of doing anything to gain his ends. He wrote privately: "In fact, I consider him one of the most unprincipled men in the Indian country." Yet he appreciated Ogden's gifts of leadership and his rare appetite for exploration. He possessed a genuine geographical curiosity akin to that of Jedediah Smith. Ogden was also a far better journal keeper than most of his colleagues, since he was blessed with intellectual curiosity and was a keen observer and an interesting chronicler. In his later years, he wrote an anonymous treatise entitled *Traits of American Indian Life.*

Combining—or, rather, confusing—the intellectually inclined Ogden with the rough-hewn giant Donald McKenzie, historian T. C. Elliott absurdly described the former as scrawling his journals on indifferently cured sheets of beaver skin tied with leather thongs. All very romantic and colorful—but Ogden did not tolerate badly tanned skins and would never have wasted a thirteen shilling plew for singeing and scraping into parchment, since his packhorses always bore pens, ink, and journals of watermarked English paper, bound in stiff marbled boards.

Ogden, however, did start out in the fur trade very much on the wrong foot. Born in Quebec in 1794 of American Loyalist parents, the Tory's son spurned family urgings toward the ministry and legal profession. He became a clerk in Astor's Montreal warehouse when only a lad, then shifted in 1810 to a clerkship in the North-West Company. He betrayed a youthful, reckless bravado by buying a sharp dagger, a real Highland *skeene* or dirk (and his middle name was sometimes spelled Skeen) for his trip to the West. Sadly, Ogden soon put the knife to work. Carried away by the emotional rivalry between his own firm and the Hudson's Bay Company, he attacked Peter Fidler of the latter's Lac La Crosse post. Luckily for all concerned, he only cut the trader's coat and pricked the skin a bit.

When Ross Cox visited him in 1817, the Irish "scribbler" described Ogden as "humorous, honest, eccentric, law-defying Peter Ogden, the terror of the Indians." Cox was probably referring to an 1816 incident at Green Lake in which Ogden was accused of "the most barbarous murder of an Indian," or possibly a similar "tragic event" reported earlier in 1817 at Ile à la Crosse. Whatever the case, Ogden fled westward across the Rockies almost a year ahead of a bill of indictment for murder.

Once in Oregon, Ogden was given command of a punitive expedition against the Cowlitz Indians, who had murdered an Iroquois trapper. They had to be administered a lesson or no trapper would be safe. The expedition went badly; Ogden's later gifts of leadership were nowhere in evidence. His drunken, irresponsible Iroquois massacred a Cowlitz village, including the women and children, and he had to pull the party out. The Cowlitz Indians were so alienated that they put a stop to all trapping north of the Columbia for a considerable time.

Ogden won no honors on the Cowlitz expedition. But it was, indeed, an ill wind on the Columbia which blew no good. With the north bank closed to trapping, Nor'wester (and, shortly, Hudson's Bay Company) interest was re-aroused in the Willamette. Also, the Cowlitz expedition proved to be a turning point for Ogden, personally. He seemed to mature overnight as a field commander. Now, he made few—very few—mistakes in Indian country. He became a tough but fair frontier diplomat, as Meriwether Lewis had been in 1804. In six long, dangerous, and exhausting expeditions between 1825 and 1830, "M'sieu Pete" lost only a handful of men to illness and Indian arrows.

Ogden was no Indian-lover, but he was no longer Cox's "terror of the Indians." He was ethnocentric, like most of the English and Scots of his day, but a pragmatist who judged each tribe by its actions and merits. Thus, he liked the Nez Percé, Flathead, and Cayuse Indians. He married a Nez Percé girl, who accompanied him on some of his expeditions. He hated, but respected, the murderous Blackfeet, but he despised the *gens du serpent*, the Snakes of Oregon and Idaho and their Nevada kin, the Bannocks and Paiutes. Sometimes, he expressed sympathy or compassion for these "insolent scamps" because of their sheer wretchedness, as when he found the so-called Diggers ("Shuckers," he called them) existing on roots, grass, prickly pears, and ants. But, because they stole horses and ambushed straggling trappers, he detested them. He once burst out in exasperation: "How long will the Snakes be allowed to steal and murder I cannot say." And, again: "As an individual, acting for myself, I will not hesitate to say that I would most willingly sacrifice a year and even two to exterminate the whole Snake tribe, women and children excepted, and in so doing I am of opinion [I] could fully justify myself before God and man. But I full well know [that] those who live at a distance are of a different opinion." Ogden ran a tight brigade in Oregon and California and had little trouble with the Indians of the Siskiyou Trail, though he was hardly less jaundiced of eye toward them than toward the Snakes.

Because he knew that every beaver hunter needed four stout horses to work his traps, transport supplies, and pack out pelts, and because good animals were in short supply, Ogden placed a high value on his *remuda* or horse herd and a very low value on Indians who raided it: "Were they dead, few would regret them." Pacific Northwest historian Keith Murray's point is well taken: In a society where a horse meant not only the difference between profit and loss on a fur hunt, but perhaps even survival, theft of horses was more of a crime than murder. Not only was a horse necessary for the march and the hunt, it was a walking commissary—a last-ditch supply of food when a famished man reached the end of his rope.

Outfitting a brigade with horses was always disheartening work. Most of the mounts which survived one expedition were gathered up for the next, though mere bags of skin and bones. Each year, Samuel Black at Fort Nez Percés bought 250 horses, but the Indians always gave him culls—either racks of bones or untamed mustangs. Again and again, Ogden urged the Company to pay more and get better animals. The investment would be returned many times over in greater beaver catches as his men gained more mobility. He wanted a hundred good horses for each trip out, not the "trash" always given him. But the pence-pinching was continued, and Ogden had to make do with nags and cobs, animals ready for the boneyard.

Peter Ogden had been given a partner's share in the North-West Company, but when the firms combined he found himself one of three Nor'westers blacklisted for reputations of violence. His name was not carried over to the Honourable Company roster. The infuriated outcast went all the way to London to plead his case. He won. Ogden was belatedly appointed a first-class clerk with the salary of a chief trader. He was given the command of the Spokane District, replacing Ross, who was disliked and denigrated by Governor Simpson. The latter claimed that Ross was "full of bombast and marvelous nonsense." Probably he was thinking of Ross, too, when he mused that some gentlemen in savage regions imbibed the exalted notions of Indian chiefs.

One of Ogden's most difficult charges was locating the Buenaventura River. The Buenaventura was a product of wild cartographic imagination. It was supposed to flow from Lake Salado (the Great Salt Lake) all the way to the Pacific—some, identifying it with the Sacramento, said it proceeded via San Francisco Bay. Simpson thought that it might be the Umpqua of southern Oregon. (He placed *its* headwaters seven hundred miles too far east.) It was of a piece with the fabled Northwest Passage and Straits of Anián of myth-making map engravers. Even the Lewis and Clark map showed the Multnomah (Willamette) rising in a lake south of the Snake and flowing north and west, unimpeded by the Cascades, to join the Columbia. As varied explorers as Lieutenant Zebulon Pike and the so-called "Lost Trappers" believed in a single great fountainhead in the Rockies. There, perhaps in the Wind River Range, a whole group of rivers was held to have its source—the Arkansas, the Columbia, the Rio Grande, the Colorado and the mythical Buenaventura and Los Mongos.

Simpson had a field man of McLoughlin's mettle in Ogden, a worthy successor to Ross and McKenzie—and then some. The Snake River country was too rich to spare him for the detailed exploration of the Willamette and Umpqua rivers and Siskiyou Mountains. But Ogden proved to be such a prodigious explorer ("a man of great leg") that, eventually, the doctor (with amazing geographical assurance— and ignorance) asked the impossible of him: to tie the Snake to the Willamette. (Like Lewis and Clark, he was ignorant of the Cascade Range.) Amazingly, Ogden did just that. And, as a sideline, he investigated the Klamath Lakes basin, the Siskiyou and Shasta barrier, California's Central Valley, and even "the Spanish River," the Colorado! Easily the Company's ablest field commander, he trapped more and explored farther than any other individual in the trade, with the possible exception of his American rival, Jedediah Smith.

Almost immediately upon taking command of the Snake River Brigade from Ross at Flathead Post, Montana, in November 1824, Pete Ogden ran into Jed Smith. The latter had rescued some Company Iroquois led by Old Pierre Tevanitagon, who had been robbed by Bannocks.

Smith wished to winter at Flathead Post, then accompany the Britishers out in the spring until he could separate for a return to his associates at Green River in the Rockies. To Ogden, it seemed that Simpson's worst fears were correct: The Americans were trying to open a road to the Columbia via the Snake. Although he resented the Iroquois "vagabonds" having sold Smith all their 105 beaver pelts for horses and equipment (he doubted that they were *that* "pillaged and destitute"), Ogden preferred to have the Yankees nearby, where he could keep an eye on them; so he made no objection to their staying.

But Ogden did not wait for spring. Instead of wintering at the post, he led out a new expedition on December 20, 1824. It was his largest brigade, a small army. Simpson's economies had not yet taken effect. He had ten engaged servants, forty-five freemen and boys, thirty women, and thirty-five children. Smith and his *bostonnais* ("Bostonians," that is, Yankees) followed Ogden as he headed for the Bitterroot Valley. They camped near him, but not with him. On March 19, 1825, they pulled away at the Big Bend of Bear River, in Utah. But Ogden had a hunch he had not seen the last of Smith. His second-in-command, William Kittson, wrote: "About noon they left us, well satisfied, I hope, with the care and attention we paid them. For, since we have had them, no one in our party took advantage of, or ill treated them. One Jedediah Smith is the head of them, a sly, cunning, Yankee."

Ogden tried to keep gambling and drinking out of his brigades. They both spelled trouble. But his men smuggled decks of cards from Fort Vancouver. He never really understood his mercurial Frenchmen. "However fair Canadians promise," he wrote, "still, they always deviate from their instructions." Much later, he added, "Canadians are certainly strange beings—in the morning more curses were bestowed on me than a parson could bestow blessings in a month, and now [that] they find themselves rich with food, with a fair prospect of soon reaching the end of their journey, I am, in the opinion of all, a clever fellow for coming this way."

The chief trader had more confidence in his French-Canadians, however, than in the so-called civilized Indians of his brigades. But he had to be philosophical about them, like his shabby horses. "Indians do not answer with trapping parties. But to make up our number, we are obliged to take them and they are miserable substitutes. No dependence can be placed on them for day or night watch, and in an attack they are the first to conceal themselves."

Ogden was aware of Simpson's attitude toward the Americans, of course. The Governor labeled them a motley crowd, without rules or regulations, who were never on their guard and always having their camps plundered. They were, he said, "people of the worst character, outcasts of society and jail runaways, acknowledging no master, no discipline." Ogden had more respect for the Yankees, though he noticed, too, that Indian raiding parties preferred Americans (as easy marks) and ofted skirted Company camps to get at the *bostonnais*. Later, Ogden noted in his journal: "The last party of Americans we lately joined never keep watch. Not long since, they had them [their horses] stolen. Still no guard, and [they] appear quite indifferent about them. Happy men!"

Ogden, when in enemy country, ran his own brigades like paramilitary units. He advised John Work, his successor on the Siskiyou Trail: "No man exempted from going on discovery [i.e., scouting], or to any place required for the general interest; no man exempted from the night watch except the day guard; no man is allowed to start before the leader is ready & gives the call, the same in regard to camping. When two-thirds of the trappers have their traps in the water it is understood you remain in camp."

In dangerous country, Ogden warned his men against absenting themselves too far from camp, and forbade anyone visiting his traps without at least one companion. The American fur trader, William H. Ashley, incorrectly accused the British of supplying the Indians with arms (which took American lives) in exchange for furs. But almost never did Ogden swap even a rusty old Northwest musket, though he might trade a bit of lead or powder for pelts. It would have been idiotic for him to arm Indians; it might mean his own scalp.

Ogden was not unwilling to praise his men, but he often tempered such praise with criticism. Thus, when he wrote Work to advise him to trust "leading men" Louis Kanota and François Payette for their knowledge of the country, he added a warning: Work was never to accept any other kind of information from them. They could not be relied upon. "To suit their own interest or view, [they] will assert anything."

Although he treated his men well by the standards of the time and place, even doctoring the sick with purges and vomits, doses of gunpowder and vinegar, and even practicing phlebotomy or venesection ("bleeding"), he often had to quell incipient mutinies and to win over wrong-headed freemen who bore him no personal loyalty and had no sense of duty to the Company. Often, he had to use his wits and quietly, unobtrusively, consign his men to the devil after patiently hearing out their complaints, plans—and even plots and threats.

The worst crisis in Ogden's career came on May 25, 1825, at Deserter Point on Utah's Weber River. An uncouth, illiterate free trapper, Johnson Gardner, backed by twenty-five to thirty armed followers, buffaloed Ogden and persuaded twenty-three of his Iroquois and French freemen to desert, taking their horses, traps, and 750 furs. The rowdy Gardner, ostentatiously flying the American colors, then rudely ordered Ogden out of U.S. territory, adding: "You will see us shortly, not only on the Columbia but at the Flatheads and Kootenais, as we are determined you shall no longer return in our territory."

Ogden refused to be goaded into a fight, nor would he pull out of what he considered to be Oregon Territory, open to free trapping by citizens of both countries. He said that he would leave when his government told him to do so, and not before. Gardner warned him that he remained at his peril. But he was bluffing; he made no move toward a real fight.

Simpson would have liked to send a strong force to call the boisterous American's bluff, once he heard of the setback. But he knew that the brigades faced hostilities enough from Indians, without letting Yankees pick a fight with them. Still, he took some action. He tried to cut back on the number of freemen with Ogden. They were paid only for the furs they raised in their traps and, to his mind, were congenitally disloyal. He hoped to increase the number of *engagés* or servants, hired hands paid £17 a year by the Company, whatever their luck with their traps, to replace the independent, undisciplined (and often mutinous) free trappers.

Ogden also urged competitive pricing of furs and supplies and an end to the company store mentality which kept free trappers and servants in peonage or involuntary servitude (and resentment) by means of debt slavery. Once Simpson saw how counterproductive was the victimization of the *engagés* by the "big medicine" of weights and steelyards at Fort Vancouver, which always seemed to dip in the Company's favor, he lined up with Ogden. Goods were soon made available to the engaged servants at "European" prices without markup. Hunting implements, including traps, made by the smith at Vancouver were sold at inventory prices, without gouging the buyers.

When the Governor wrote London on September 1, 1826, to justify the reforms, he pointed to hunters who had taken 150 beaver each and still had not cleared enough to pay for their traps, especially if they had lost traps or horses to the Indians. McLoughlin, like Ogden, wholeheartedly urged such long overdue changes. He wrote Simpson (on March 20, 1827) about their happy effect on his trappers: "It secures their fidelity, equips them completely, and stimulates them to exert themselves."

With Wyoming's Teton Mountains in view, Ogden received a message from Simpson by a Flathead runner. The Governor pointedly reminded him that he was to trap his way home via the Umpqua and Willamette rivers. Although Ogden confused the Great Salt Lake with Klamath Lake (five hundred miles west) and believed that the Umpqua lay but ten days away, he declined to blaze the northern section of the Siskiyou Trail at this time. After the desertions, he fancied himself surrounded on all sides by enemies, with his own force shrunk to sixteen men.

This weakness was not Ogden's only reason—or excuse—for paying no mind to Simpson's instructions. He was afraid that he would lead the Americans right to the Columbia by way of the Willamette— the one thing, above all else, that Simpson did not want. He thus excused himself for failing to follow orders: "[Even] allowing my numbers to have been greater, I am not of opinion it would have been good policy in me to have open'd a short cut for the Americans to

Fort George." Moreover, Ogden was in a funk. For the first time in his career, and perhaps the last, he was demoralized, defeatist in spirit. He morosely predicted to Simpson: "You need not anticipate another expedition [in the] ensuing year to this country, for not a freeman will return and, should they, it would be to join the Americans."

So, Ogden came out not by the Willamette but via the Walla Walla River and Fort Nez Percés, on November 2, 1825. He had only four hundred skins, far from what he had a right to expect. He needed three thousand for a profitable expedition. Ogden warned Simpson that the entry of the Americans might, in time, reduce the Company's catch to nil. But he blamed his cowardly freemen for the failure of his hunt, and he promised Simpson: "You can rely on my exertions to find beaver."

The Governor was distressed by the Americans' presence, by the failure of the hunt, and by Ogden's decision not to connect Snake and Willamette via the Siskiyou Mountains (as yet unnamed) and the Umpqua River. But he took Ogden up on his promise and quickly sent him back out.

Already, to make sure that the Willamette-Umpqua area should not be neglected, Simpson had planned an expedition composed of Fort George freemen and supernumeraries under Finnan McDonald and McLoughlin's stepson, Tom McKay. Their route was to be up the "Oulamat" and across the mountains ("Which we know little about," admitted Simpson) to the Umpqua River and thence back to the Columbia. The exploration, planned for May 1825, had to be postponed because of Indian trouble near Fort Vancouver. But Simpson did not lose interest in it. Nor did McLoughlin. The doctor reported from Indian conversations that a beaver-rich stream lay just three days south of the Umpqua. There, the natives wore robes of beaver fur! The doctor also reported word of a great lake (Klamath Lake), supposedly rich in beaver, lying southwest of Fort Walla Walla. McDonald and McKay finally got under way on August 19, 1825.

On his new march, Ogden was to trap the Snake, investigate Klamath Lake's reputed beaver colonies, and then link up with McDonald and take command of the united parties. Simpson, still trying to curb "extravagances," limited the total strength of both companies to fifty men and forbade any women or children to go along. Since McDonald already had thirty men, Ogden could take only twenty trappers, mostly tired veterans of his just-returned expedition. Worse, he had to use the skeletal horses which had staggered into Fort Nez Percés with him, only two weeks earlier. He considered himself optimistic when he guessed that two-thirds of them would die on him during the winter.

The chief trader's route took him in November 1825 from the Dalles to the John Day, Deschutes, and Sylvies rivers and Harney Lake. His orders were to trap close. Ogden rarely questioned Company policy and was, in any case, no conservationist or ecologist. (Neither term, of course, had been invented.) He was a ruthless hunter, ready to ruin the region between Snake and Willamette. Thus, he wrote: "If the Cayuse will not ruin the beaver in their own lands, we must for them at least diminish the number, and if we do not, others probably will for us at no distant period."

But Ogden sensed that something was wrong with Simpson's scorched earth policy and his comments began to change as time went on. In October 1827 he would write: "The once-famed Snake country for beaver is a ruined one now and, granting it were allowed repose, which few on either side concerned are willing to do, it would require four years to recruit." Finally, he began to feel guilty over his role in Simpson's questionable strategy, writing: "It is scarcely credible what a destruction of beaver by trapping this season. Within the last two days, upwards of fifty females have been taken and, on an average, each with four young, ready to litter. Did we not hold this country by so light a tenure it would be most to our interest to trap it only in the fall, and by this mode it would take many years to ruin it."

Sadly, Ogden commented on *Castor canadensis,* hunted by Britons, Americans, Indians, otters, and wolves—"Well may it be said beaver have many enemies, while they alone wage war with none." The only thing which delayed extermination of the beaver in the West was the animal's sagacity. As Siskiyou Trail trapper George Yount later put it: "No animal is more sly, cunning and sagacious than the beaver. His instinct almost amounts to reason and intelligence."

The chief trader closed with Finnan McDonald's company, trapping along the way and writing in his journal (without irony), "All well, and starving." He joined the Willamette party in December 1825 at the mouth of Crooked River on the Falls (Deschutes) River. McKay explained why they were so far north: Klamath Lake was destitute of beaver. Their expedition, in fact, was a failure; in four months they had taken only 460 skins. Ogden later reported to McLoughlin that he attributed the party's meager success to the poverty of the country in furs, not to any want of exertion by McDonald and McKay.

Finnan McDonald was an experienced mountain man. A wild-bearded, red-haired giant of six feet, four inches, he was a Nor'wester of 1804 who had hunted the Columbia way back in 1807–1812. A real Highlander from Inverness, McDonald's first language was Gaelic, and his English was mediocre. He had commanded Spokane House and twice whipped Piegan Blackfeet war parties—no mean feat. In '23 he had replaced Donald McKenzie over the Snake River Brigade. In spite of a battle in which he killed sixty-eight Blackfeet while losing only six of his own men, he had managed to bring out 4459 peltries. But never again, he swore. He wrote a friend: "I got home safe from the Snake Cuntre, thank God, and when that Cuntre will see me agane, the beaver will have gould skin."

McDonald and McKay had set out from Fort Vancouver with the visiting botanist, David Douglas, on August 19. They took an old Indian trail up the Willamette. Douglas had admired the forty-three-foot drop of Willamette Falls and poked about a village of Calapooyas —as peaceful as Quakers now for all their orneriness of Nor'wester days. The botanist had then explored the Willamette and Yamhill rivers and camped four miles up the Santiam. There he hunted and botanized so zealously that he was given a new name, besides "King George's Chief," by the Indians. It was "Grass Man." Douglas had been intrigued by the large pine nuts carried by Indians in their pouches as food, especially when they indicated that they came from cones the size of breadloves. He named the new tree, the sugar pine, *Pinus lambertiana* without seeing it, but he vowed that he would find specimens. However, as McDonald and McKay headed for Klamath Lake, Douglas had to retrace his steps to Fort Vancouver.

The only welcome news which McDonald brought for Ogden was confirmation of McLoughlin's rumor of a great river south of the Umpqua in the land of the "Clamut" people. Immediately assumed to be the elusive ("missing") Buenaventura, it was really the Klamath River.

Ogden refused to waste any more valuable time looking for the hidden river in what McDonald described as a beaver desert. He left his friends to make their way down the Deschutes to the Columbia while he headed back to the more promising tributaries of the Snake east of the Cascades. He found the bleakness of the central Oregon desert to be incredible, and the Indians were the most wretched-looking beings he had ever seen. Glumly, he wrote: "The further we advance, the less we find. . . . Had we not our traps, we must have starved to death. . . . Our hunts are damn'd. . . ."

Even Ogden's place-names document the hostility of the desert country east of the Willamette Valley and Cascades—the Malheur ("Unfortunate") River, the Brûlé ("Burnt") River, the Malade (or "Sickly") River. On the latter, beaver ate water hemlock (poison parsnip) without ill effects—in fact, they grew fat on the plants. But the trappers who feasted on *Castor's* oily and slightly musky meat and succulent tail became deathly ill. Ogden described a case of "the beaver illness" or wild parsnip poisoning. "One of the Canadians, seriously ill, attributed to the beaver meat. He was suddenly seized with a violent pain in his loins and from thence his head, and shortly after, lost all motion of his limbs. He is now nearly recovered by drinking pepper and gunpowder mixed in water. For nearly four hours he suffered great pain."

Ogden still talked of winding up his expedition with a look at Klamath Lake, not far from the future Siskiyou Trail. But, beginning to appreciate the vast distance from the Snake to Fort Vancouver via the Umpqua and Willamette, and very conscious of the starved country en route, he made no real effort to reach his base by such a Robin Hood's barn route. He could not blame his freemen this time. Though they were forever urging a return to proven hunting grounds when exploration failed to reveal rich new areas, he found his men could be depended upon, when the chips were down: "Many of the trappers came in almost froze and without setting their traps. Naked as the greater part are and destitute of shoes, it is a surprise to me how they can exist; and to their credit, be it said not a murmur of complaint do I hear."

Since Ogden's geographical ideas were almost as twisted about as Simpson's, he thought (while he was on Oregon's Bruneau River) that he was near the Colorado River drainage, the Klamath Lakes, California, and the Snake watershed—all at the same time. He had David Thompson's map of 1818, with its details from Lewis and Clark, and possibly a copy of Clark's 1814 map showing a mythical Upper Multnomah. Almost certainly he had the popular Arrowsmith map, printed in London with many errors. He may have been familiar with a John Melish map showing the Willamette rising near a fountain feeding the Rio del Norte, or Rio Grande, and the Buenaventura connecting a Rocky Mountain lake with San Francisco Bay. (Later this stream was renamed the Timpanogos and the Buenaventura was moved south to briefly attach itself to the shallow, almost underground,

Salinas River.) If Ogden thought that the Umpqua was the rumored Los Mongos River, cutting through the mountains to reach the sea near modern Port Orford, he did not mention it. Soon he would realize that the Umpqua was much too short to fit the description of Los Mongos, Buenaventura, or any other fabled watercourse.

Naturally, Ogden mixed up his Pacific and Gulf of California drainage. He reported some fine streams draining into the Gulf of California; but to reach them he would have to traverse *mauvaises terres*—the badlands—destitute of any provisions. According to the Indians, starvation had driven the Americans back. But he was sure that they would try to find the three large rivers rumored to flow through the "Clamnitt" (Klamath) country.

For all of his geographical confusion, Ogden had a remarkable sense of direction on the ground by dead reckoning. He crossed the Cascades to tie together for Simpson the Snake and Willamette drainages. He set a course for McKay's Nole (Knoll) on July 7, 1826, well to the north of the Siskiyous, and reached the headwaters of the Willamette by way of Burnt Encampment. He reached the valley floor on July 16 by dropping down through hills of good soil and natural gardens of hazel nuts and berries. There, an Indian whom Ogden hoped to hire fled from him. He penned his puzzlement: "It is rather strange, considering the trappers have been residing amongst them for the last fifteen years, and have had an establishment on their lands nearly as many, that they still should be wild as the Snakes."

Ogden accomplished the Cascades crossing with little labor, yet he doubted that the Company could use his route as a practical road between Fort Vancouver and the Snake, via the Willamette. "The distance is far too great and the resources of the country not to be depended upon." On the other hand, he anticipated the later Siskiyou Trail by recommending a route up the Willamette and over the mountains to the Klamath area as feasible and highly advantageous.

The explorer was much impressed with the lower Willamette near its junction with the Columbia, where Portland would spring up. He doubted that a finer stream could be found in Indian country. He totted up its blessings for settlers—wood, water, good soil, edible roots, red deer and small deer, salmon and sturgeon. He guessed that a colony would soon flourish on the river.

On August 20 Ogden reminded Simpson that Fort Vancouver was still trying to implement his recommended southward push: "The 2d trapping expedition which I beg leave to call to your attention is in a direction due south from this establishment. An attempt was made last year to reach it by Mr. Finnan McDonald but, owing to various circumstances, particularly being too weak in numbers, they were obliged to abandon it, having proceeded some distance on the journey. So far as they went, beaver were not overabundant."

Ogden had not had a chance to explore the Willamette to its head or to investigate the Umpqua Valley as a route from one side of the Cascades to the other. Thus, he was as interested as McLoughlin when chief trader Alexander McLeod returned from his expedition with word that Indians had reported a large river, abounding in beaver, only two days' march south of the Umpqua. Almost certainly, they meant the Rogue River, rather than Ogden's elusive Klamath. But none of the fur men knew this, so it immediately became a prime candidate for the role of the mythical Buenaventura.

Ogden offered to lead the next expedition over the mountains to the Klamath basin, urging Simpson not to lose any time if he proposed to beat the fast-moving Americans. But McLoughlin could not spare Ogden from the Snake's lucrative beaver grounds in order to blaze a route through the Siskiyou Mountains via the Rogue River. The Willamette, Umpqua, Rogue, and Siskiyous would be only a secondary zone of hunting and exploration for the doughty chief trader. The doctor intended to send his Southern Brigades out under Alex McLeod.

CHAPTER THREE ══════════════════

"Blanks and Prizes"

ALTHOUGH PETER OGDEN returned to the field with a third Snake Country Expedition on September 11, 1826, he was determined to find a better connecting link between Snake and Willamette. So, while he joined Tom McKay and the horses at the Dalles, he sent Jean Baptiste Gervais—called "Batice Jervey" by his Anglo-Saxon associates—up the Willamette with some mules and horses to rendezvous with him around the end of September.

Astonishingly, McKay was about the only first-rate hunter of game that Ogden had. He wrote Simpson that his freemen and engaged servants, alike, were in no sense hunters. When they could not find beaver, they had to eat their horses. Out of a party of thirty-five mountain men, only Gervais, an Iroquois, Louis Shanagoronte, and a sixty-two-year-old freeman, William Cannon (Oregon's only Revolutionary War veteran), were huntsmen.

The horse herd was not big enough, and not good enough by half. Those which were not worn out from the prior expedition were nearly wild mustangs. Packed for the first time in their unruly lives, the untamed animals promptly bucked off their loads, scattering supplies in so many directions that Ogden never did find one sixteen-pound keg of refined tallow. But, aside from the horses, Ogden was well fitted out. His beasts were laden with ammunition, leather lodges (skin teepees), lodgepoles, and *apishamons* (or deerskin saddle blankets which doubled as tarpaulins). As for rations, there was grain, tallow, tea, chocolate, salt, sugar, corn, flour, molasses, dried peas, rice, and even butter and a modest "cellar" of brandy and Demerara rum. In trade goods he had variety enough to tempt the most *caveat emptor'*d redskin—awls, scalpers and common English butcher knives, blue and green glass necklace beads, blankets, blue and red baize, brass rings and wire, fishing lines, Fort Vancouver-made axes, hawk's bells, bastard files, Highland garters, combs, East Indian print cotton, corduroy, flannel, scissors, looking glasses, buttons and European cloth jackets—the latter slightly damaged goods. Ogden even had some gunpowder, lead and two old second-hand muskets for the most demanding barterers. He was a strong believer in trading for furs as well as trapping them: "Were men constantly employed going from [Indian] nation to nation, the Columbia returns would increase one-fourth." Like McLoughlin, he was chary about giving guns to Indians, even the cranky old trade muskets, Brown Bess, or Tower pieces from London or the Northwest guns sometimes called "Hudson Bay fukes" or "Mackinaw guns." He knew that the hostile tribes had too many arms already, taken from murdered whites and Iroquois, looted from caches, and purchased from unscrupulous traders.

As he left the Columbia, Ogden took a long, hard look at the river. He recalled his privations and sufferings of the last march and prayed silently to God that he would reach the river again in safety and with bales of furs. Since half-starved Indians were everywhere, he kept a strict watch by night and day, particularly over his horse herd. His men were happy because the redmen traded them fresh salmon and plump dogs to eat.

Gervais rejoined Ogden on Crooked River near its confluence with the Deschutes. He brought a tale of woe. Horses had strayed, one had been stolen, one was sick, and another had died. And his remaining stock had not exactly fattened on the Willamette march. But Ogden was in as good a mood as his men. When they got the first traps of the season wet they began to take beaver. But not many; the animals were few and wary, since the streams had been hunted in the past. Ogden admitted that the streams needed a rest of several years to recover. When the men raised their traps on October 3 he noticed that they averaged but one beaver to every ten traps set.

Meanwhile, the Snakes fired at his men, stole his horses, set the grass around his camps ablaze and, finally, robbed and wounded two trappers. The latter caused him to say, "We have sustain'd a most shameful defeat." He tightened security, showered curses on the Snakes, and wrote in his log: "If ever Indians deserved to be punished, they certainly do. They were well treated and fed by us and, in return, they attempted to destroy us. This is Indian gratitude, and this is not the first instance I have experienced of their villainy for kindness shown them."

Tom McKay was a major source of support to Ogden. He was the son of a North-West Company partner, Alexander McKay, and his half-Cree wife. His father had brought Tom to Oregon on the *Tonquin*. The eleven-year-old escaped the shipboard massacre because he was detached to help build Fort Astoria. When his widowed mother remarried, it was to Dr. John McLoughlin. By the fall of 1813, McKay was in the Willamette near Champoeg, twenty miles above the falls. Alex Ross described him as being "brave as a lion." A fall from his horse during an Indian campaign dislocated one knee and hip and left him lame for life. But it did not slow him down enough. Not only did McKay participate in the massacre of Selkirk's colonists at Seven Oaks, he apparently went berserk with bloodlust. Witnesses reported that he shot to death an unarmed man while the pitiful fellow was on his knees before him, begging for mercy. McKay fled with Samuel Black and joined Ogden, then very much the bullyboy. And all three were temporarily blacklisted by the Honourable Company when it took over the Nor'westers.

McKay, tall, dark and vigorous, accompanied Ogden to Fort George and seemed destined for success. When he was attacked on the upper Willamette during the 1819–1820 season, he left the Indians so badly beaten that they made no further trouble for years. He later crossed to the Umpqua River and built the first Fort Umpqua, about thirty miles from its mouth and west of what was later the Siskiyou Trail. He managed the post at Champoeg, married the daughter of Concomly, chief of the Chinooks, and was chosen to meet Simpson when the Governor was en route to Fort George in 1824.

Simpson gave McKay several assignments, including the post of second-in-command on Finnan McDonald's exploration. But McKay disappointed the demanding governor. By 1826, Simpson had written him off as incompetent to command. He remained a clerk. To Simpson, "the Terror of the Indians" was a confirmed liar, a man of little judgment, and one who should be kept under close observation—if not restraint. Luckily for Tom, Chief Trader Ogden still had confidence in him. He remained Ogden's trusted lieutenant.

With only empty traps being fished out of the water and prospects gloomy, with his hunters unsuccessful ("Should we not soon find animals, horses will fall for the kettle"), Ogden confessed to his diary that he was at a loss how to act and what to decide. By November 5 he had decided to turn his back on the desert rivers of the Snake country and head for the untrapped "Clameitte" River. The route, almost due west, made Ogden almost as disheartened as his men, but he could not show it. He had to keep morale high or all would perish in the desert. So he promised them a river ahead, while he wrote in his journal: "This is really a wretched country, and certainly no other inducement but filthy lucre can induce an honest man to visit it."

Paulina Lake was reached on November 15, but Ogden did not realize that Oregon's High Desert was now behind him. He wrote disconsolately: "Our hunters returned late in the evening without success. Starve we must." There would be no starving; next day, he reached the Little Deschutes River about three miles from modern Lapine, Oregon. McKay had been there with McDonald, so now Ogden had a guide. Camped on the very spot where old Finnan had built canoes to descend the Deschutes, Ogden was pleased to hear his clumsy nimrods firing away. "No men could have exerted themselves more than they did, if in vain." But, for all of their blasting away at game, they got only seven white-tailed deer. Ogden lost his patience with them eventually and wrote (on December 21): "Our hunters are not even deserving of the name and, altho constantly in motion, can scarcely support themselves."

With hungry horses straying from camp and hungry freemen plotting their usual machinations, Ogden started over the high "Umpqua" Mountains, the Cascades and Siskiyous. He would go as far south as McDonald had gone, if not further, though no one could tell him if that country—toward Spanish California—was rich or poor in beaver. Since the waters of the Klamath basin did not drain into the Columbia, there had to be another large river in the area. His hunch was that it was Simpson's Buenaventura. On its way to the Pacific he would surely find deer and elk, even if it should prove to be empty of beaver.

The first day of December 1826 brought Ogden's two expressmen safely back to camp from Fort Vancouver. They brought a letter from McLoughlin in which he replied to Ogden's worries about venturing into California. The chief trader had recalled that the Spaniards (i.e., Mexicans) had remonstrated with the Company in 1825 over his trespass on their territory. The doctor quoted Governor John Pelly's communication to George Canning, Great Britain's Secretary of Foreign Affairs, advising him that Spain, by the convention of 1798 after the Nootka Sound Affair, had relinquished all claims beyond lands she did not actually hold by settlement. And, of course, Britain held Mexico—Spain's successor in California—to the bargain. McLoughlin cautioned Ogden against infringing on the rights of others, and he was to avoid armed collisions with Americans or "Spaniards" at all costs. But he must not acquiesce to the mere assertion of territorial rights by others.

Ogden was pleased to have his orders clarified, but his party was still in dire straits. One woman was ill, having been lost eleven days without food before being rescued. She was being given broth. Six inches of snow fell before turning to rain. There were *no* beaver on the shores of mighty Klamath Lake. He wrote: "All looks gloomy. What will become of us? Two horses already kill'd for food, and appearances bid fair that more will fall soon, and I cannot prevent it. . . ." Shortly, his half-starved men were suffering from bouts of indigestion. After their long involuntary fast, they glutted themselves on dog meat and paid for it in discomfort and pain. Wrote their chief: "Canadians cannot withstand temptation, and the consequence is, this day, they are suffering."

Slowly, conditions began to improve. The terrain and climate were better than the desert, although the dense fogs were as annoying as the muddy trails. There was no frost, even at night. There was grass in plenty for the horses, dogs, *camas* and other roots, and fish (suckers?), which Ogden called carp, to buy. While no land of milk and honey, Ogden felt it safe to leave the sick woman with a Klamath chief, at her request. He gave her a horse and orders to steer a course for the Willamette when she recovered.

Though Ogden was a natural skeptic (for all of his chasing of the Buenaventura), his men tended to believe everything they were told—even by Indians. Thus, they began to scheme to pack up and leave for the (nonexistent) *buffalo* country of Oregon! Ogden snorted his derision: "This with their horses in their present state! They never can. Independent of this, before they proceed one-fourth of the distance, they would quarrel and separate. . . . I have no idea they will dare make the attempt. No application has been made to me and when they do, I am prepared for them." As usual, it was all talk and bluff. The separatist plans and plots of the trappers—and would-be buffalo hunters—vanished into the mild Klamath air.

Peter Ogden explored Klamath Lake and Link River, noting that ahead, as far as his eye could reach, there stretched a continuous swamp of lakes all run together. On December 19 he found a fine looking "river"—actually Willow Creek, which fell into Lower Klamath Lake. In it were the abandoned stone barriers of old fish weirs. Although it was an attractive stream, his men could find only one beaver lodge and were able to take only two animals. Nor did their nets yield any fish. A puzzled Ogden wrote in his daily log: "All these waters must discharge in some large river, which I hope we shall ere long see, and if no beaver [are] in it, I shall certainly be at a loss what course to take to find beaver."

The chief trader tried to send word of his progress to Fort Vancouver, but all Indians refused his bribes, claiming that the route across the Siskiyous was impassable during the winter.

Because his dates were off by one day, Ogden celebrated Christmas on December 24, 1826. At the request of his followers, he did not raise camp, although it was his inclination to do so because of his short food supply. On Christmas Day itself, all were on the march. Ogden noted five more lakes in the distance and observed, sadly: "This certainly is a country of lakes, but not of rivers or beavers."

The Klamaths who visited the whites wore blankets or cloaks of duck and goose feathers as winter clothing. This did nothing to reassure Ogden as to the presence of beaver in the locality.

It was on Christmas Day that Ogden first saw the most prominent landmark of the entire Siskiyou Trail: Mount Shasta loomed up like an immense white beacon. He promised himself that he would visit the massive peak, come spring, and wrote: "On both sides of us the mountains are very high, one in particular high above all others, pointed, and well covered with snow, and from its height [it] must be at a considerable distance from us. Our guides inform'd us beyond these mountains reside the Sastise [Shastas], a nation they are at present at war with, and this is one of the principal causes they do not wish us to visit them at this season. At all events, from the depth of snow we cannot, but in the spring we shall, if we find no beaver in this quarter."

Since McKay was sick, Ogden replaced him with Francois Payette. He sent him on a reconnaissance, to determine if the mountains to the south could be crossed in spite of the Indians' warnings of lack of water and the presence of many "cut rocks" in the passes. The scout reported back that the company could skirt the "chain of rocks," so Ogden ordered his men forward. Two of his freemen balked. They had gone three days without eating and did not want to kill off their few gaunt horses for food. They were determined to return to Klamath Lake. Ogden replied tartly: "Your sufferings are in common with others'. As long as I had food to give you, you received your share. Provided we can find water, I am determined to advance but I do not intend to do so without first examining the road, and I shall send an advance to examine it." The two trappers did not desert him.

With discontent increasing in reverse ratio to the success of the unlucky hunters, Ogden sent a recuperated McKay on scout. Briefly feeling sorry for himself, he wrote: "We have yet three months of winter. God grant they were well over and our horses escaped the kettle. But I fear not. I truly believe, without exception, I have been the most unfortunate man that ever visited this barren country. The Lord's will be done to me, situated as I am without remedy."

Thinking that it was New Year's Day, Ogden tried to pull his men out of their funk on December 31. He issued them a dram of liquor each, some tobacco, and his best wishes for success in 1827. He was probably near Gillem's Bluff in the Modoc Lava Beds near Tule Lake. There, his hunters killed a "goat"—probably a mountain sheep rather than a mountain goat, but possibly an antelope since the Canadians called them *cabris,* "kids" or "goats." When McKay returned from reconnoitering, he brought bad news. As far as he could see to the southward with a glass there was nothing but a continuous chain of mountains without the least appearance of a river—or of any water at all. Worse, from his departure until his return, he had not seen the track of a single animal! Faced with mountains flanked by a lava *malpais* or badland, Ogden gave up the idea of going further south until spring: "Return we must, and seek food where we can find it."

The brigade began its retrograde march, demolishing abandoned Indian huts for firewood during its retreat northward. Ogden left payments behind, so that the natives would not see such actions as confiscation, vandalism, or robbery. "I should certainly regret that our side should cause a quarrel with these Indians for, so far, their conduct towards us has been certainly most correct and orderly, and worthy of imitation by all." Marching, hunting, and chasing strayed horses when not trapping (with minimal success), the men returned to baffling Willow Creek. There, Ogden observed: "I cannot but again remark what a fine river for beaver, nor can I account for it there is none."

When a scout reported that he thought that the Klamath River could be reached without rounding the huge lake, Ogden sent Payette to check on it. He returned convinced that the lakes and marshes made it impossible. Ogden was now reconciled to the need to traverse a long and circuitous route to the river, which he was eager to examine. The natives, of course, reported it a-crawl with beaver. But they had said the same thing about Klamath Lake and Willow Creek, and Ogden had found the contrary to be true; so he no longer put any stock in their claims.

By January 12, 1827, Ogden reached the Klamath River—and California. By his calendar, it was Friday the thirteenth. Certainly it proved to be the proverbially unlucky day. There were no amphibious rodents, which now would have been welcomed more for their flesh than their fur. At Hot Springs, near modern Beswick just south of the Oregon line, the sight of a small black insect swimming on the surface led a trapper to test the hot water. He put a finger into the boiling spring for perhaps a second. It was a painful, if enlightening, experience. The skin peeled off his finger shortly after immersion. Ogden found the deep and wide Klamath apparently turning into a lake. Again, he expressed his befuddlement: "This is certainly a strange country. In no direction can we possibly travel without seeing lakes, and nearly all connected together."

Few deer could be killed and young, fat dogs for eating were now becoming expensive. Four rings or buttons bought just one; a scalper was worth only two canines. To the astonishment (and delight) of Ogden, the Klamaths remained honest. They even delivered up a strayed horse, voluntarily. But his attempts to recruit them for guides proved unsuccessful. So fearful were the Klamaths of their warlike neighbors, the Shastas, that even in midwinter they kept a strict watch out for raiding parties. Again they warned him not to visit the Shasta country. But Ogden reminded his men: "Our object is beaver. [We] have nothing to do with their disputes or war affairs."

The ever-disgruntled freemen represented to Ogden that they would advance no further in exploration but would cross the height of land to the east in the spring, to hunt the Snake where they knew that beaver existed. Tired of their endless, mutinous bickering, Ogden glumly wrote: "A porter in London is a king in comparison with me at the head of freemen. He carries his burden, has a meal to eat, and sleeps soundly. Far different is the case with me. But all this would be a trifle could I but find beaver, and not be obliged to return empty-handed, as from our present prospects we certainly shall."

Plots occupied much of that night, but, come morning, not one voice countered the chief trader's orders to cross the stream to the north bank with the help of two canoes. Ogden knew why a mutiny was averted. "At this season, even if so inclin'd, we cannot return to the River of the Falls [Deschutes], and this the freemen are well aware of." He swore: "Cursed country! I not only feel but *am* wretched and unhappy. God grant we were all safe out of it and in a country of beaver."

Finally, Ogden's bad luck broke a little. He was finally able to persuade a Klamath to guide him over "The Mountain" (i.e., the Siskiyou Mountains), by promising to protect him closely. The Indian had originally balked because he feared that his enemies would kill him on the trail. Ogden swore by the heavens that he would safeguard him. He was delighted to provide a close guard, for it would also prevent his guide's desertion. "I have now taken every precaution for our safety and success, and if we do not find beaver the fault is not mine. More I cannot do."

Along the river bank moved the company, the wet road proving to be very fatiguing to the horses, who sank into the mire. The hapless hunters saw only two hares and the old tracks of red deer. The hoofprints heartened them, even though last season's tracks added nothing to the larder. They knew that, eventually, they would have success. The very next day, the Iroquois hunters killed seven red deer. This was a great stroke of fortune. The Klamath guide was as surprised as the huntsmen. He had told Ogden that no game was left in the area. The news of fresh meat spread, causing an unusual joy. The sight and smell of cooking venison soon created "a general smile" in camp. Ogden was particularly pleased, since he had just decided to sacrifice five horses to the cooking pots.

A beaver lodge was found before the men camped at the rapids marking the limit of ascent of salmon in the Klamath. Trappers then examined a small fork which, not many years before, had obviously been stocked with beaver. The guide explained that the Klamaths had destroyed them all. Worried Ogden: "I fear all the streams we shall find, if ever there were beaver in any of them, the natives have destroyed all."

On or near Camp Creek, Ogden left the river and turned southwest to Cottonwood Creek just north of today's Hornbrook. The constant rainy weather suggested to some of his men that they were nearing the seacoast. But Ogden (correctly) disagreed. He said that he had enough room, if there were beaver, to employ his traps for years on the Klamath. He saw that the soil was good and he guessed that the river was navigable for large craft up to the rapids, from the ocean itself. He had not seen the whitewater rapids downstream.

A heavy, all-night rain flooded the camp, sending newborn

rivulets through Ogden's lodge. Rising water carried off the traps set in the evening, too, except for four which were quickly raised. But, after the storm, more beaver were taken and deer became numerous. Things were looking up. The guide turned up some Indians who explained the local shortage of beaver. They hunted the animals and singed the fur off their skins! The chief trader had seen beaver meat in lodges, but never any pelts. This explained one puzzle. He wrote: "I am in hopes my trappers will leave them few, even if they should be inclined to singe."

The ambivalent Ogden, ready to carry out Simpson's war without quarter against the beaver, himself, chided the natives for burning the stream banks in dry weather, to kill off the animals: "From appearances," he added, "they have destroyed no small number." Ironically, at the same time that he was scolding the Klamaths for their destructiveness, London was reiterating to Governor Simpson: "It is extremely desirable to hunt as bare as possible all the country south of the Columbia."

Ogden lamented the lack of a well-marked trail over the Siskiyous to link Fort Vancouver with the Klamath area by way of the Willamette: "It is to be regretted this country has been allowed to remain so long unexplored, altho certainly our establishments are not far distant from it, now that the mountains of the Willamette have been explored. But why go far in quest of beaver when the Willamette afforded a sufficiency to supply the freemen and the indolent natives? But now it is the reverse. . . . Although it may be considered as a new country, it is almost an exhausted one. . . . The rivers in proportion to its size are certainly few in number and have been not only by us but by the Americans repeatedly trapped, and the Spanish trappers have also met with the same fate." Here, Ogden badly overstated the case: There were few American and no Mexican trappers about.

Though local trails were in a horrid state, Ogden liked the oaks, maples, the six-inch-long green grass, and the snowless climate of the Klamath. Hunting was not going well, however, and he groused about the rifles introduced by the Americans to replace the old smoothbores. The Yankees bragged of their rifles' accuracy and, therefore, of their savings in ammunition. But Ogden believed the reverse to be true. The rifles were "easily deranged," as he put it. And they had to be sighted in again after repairs by the wasteful firing of twenty shots at a target. Finally, he knew that his hunters were as vain of their marksmanship as they were poor shots. They thought that a ball from one of their rifles would hit the mark at any distance. He guessed that, of ten shots fired by them, only three ever hit anything. But a hunter with a short-range musket would take the precaution of slipping up close to his quarry till he could hardly miss. Of every ten shots, at least six would bring down the prey. Sniffed Ogden: "We are indebted to the late American Fur Company for introducing rifles into the Columbia and I, for one, do not feel obliged to them for it."

The chief trader was also annoyed by those hunters who sold deer meat at the rate of a beaver skin per deer. He tried to prevent it by feeding the needy himself, but he had to admit: "Of the two evils, we must choose the least, for if they were prevented from purchasing meat they would, from hunger, be under the necessity of killing their horses." Luckily, Ogden's best hunter was so heavily in hock to the Company that he had to collect a lot of venison to pay off his debts.

With trappers out and hunters scattered to the four winds in search of deer, Ogden suddenly realized that he had only four men to defend the camp, should it become necessary. He quipped: "What a noble prize, with our horses, we would be, were we in Blackfoot country!"

"M'sieu Pete" was shocked by the wretchedness of the Indians when he visited a hut with his guide. He found three women and a boy, living only on acorns. They were not alarmed at him but suddenly began to cry as his guide appeared. He learned the cause of their distress: The guide told him, freely, that he had killed the women's husbands in a raid, the summer before. The chief trader was now not so happy with his choice of pilot: "The wretch, from his conduct, appeared to be fully convinced of his power over them and, probably, were we not here, would be base enough to kill all."

The country was backward, puzzling. Besides the mild winter climate, there were beaver in fast and rough currents, at times, with none in the deep and still water they always preferred. Ogden wondered if the hot springs caused such a strange situation. They should have mattered little, for the dams were frozen and most animals snug in their lodges.

Because so few beaver were up and about, Ogden sent traders out to buy pelts from the Indians. Some of the trappers, desperate for profits, took some raccoons. They found the skins hardly worth preserving, but the flesh proved to be an excellent change in their diet. Now, they could share their food with the local Indians, leading their chief trader to comment: "Only a few days since, we had not a sufficiency for our wants, and now we have an abundance and can assist the needy. Such is the hunter's life, today starving and the following, an overabundance."

Early in February, two of the men became lost. They fired their weapons and the men in camp returned the salute, then built a large fire to attract their attention. When only one man made his way in, Ogden climbed a high hill and fired more signal shots. But he received no reply. At dawn, he ordered the signal fires continued, and at 10 A.M. the man staggered into camp. During his all-night wandering he had lost one shoe. Ogden was surprised that he did not lose his feet, too, from frostbite. But only one foot was slightly frozen, for, despite the snow, the weather was mild. Ogden warmed him up, gave him hot broth—and then sent him cracking, right back out to find his horse, blanket, and beaver furs, if not, perhaps, his missing shoe. The chief trader was, frankly, tiring of the carelessness of his men. That anxious night led him to recall that a Company official had urged that young gentlemen of sixteen to eighteen years be sent to Canada, without trial or training, since they were "most fit"—presumably by breeding—for the fur trade. Ogden wanted steady men about whom no one had to worry when they absented themselves from camp.

Of his current crew, he observed: "My green hands acquit themselves so far as regards trapping, but in every other respect they are most careless. An instance of this, not more than three days since, occurred. One of them left his traps and gun on the road and ascended a hill to examine the river. He was absent upwards of one hour and, during his absence, three others, happening to pass that way, secreted them. On his return, finding all gone, he return'd to camp and informed his companions that the Indians had stolen his gun and traps. Payette . . . made preparations for starting for the Indian camp, when the men who had taken the property arrived. . . . [This] would have caus'd probably a serious quarrel with the natives, and blood to have been shed, and [all] allowing to the carelessness of this man."

With the old hands, Ogden sometimes had trouble in camp where they were idle. And, heaven knew, they ate twice as much when lazing about a juniper or artemisia campfire than when attending their traplines. Only his prior knowledge of their probable intentions frustrated them when they exercised their natural penchant for plotting. But when they were in the field they were fairly vigilant and seldom met with accidents of any kind, because they knew that it was to their advantage to be careful.

On February 6, the guide told Ogden that he would have to leave him in the morning, but that he would be replaced by two Indians who knew "The Mountain." Ogden had a long conversation with the strangers. He learned that they had never heard of the ocean, but they reported beaver on the far side of the Siskiyous. While he prepared to cross the range for a look-see, he sent Payette down the Klamath with nine men. Before he was even under way, an Indian arrived to report that Payette's party had been attacked, a horse killed in the skirmish, and the Canadian's cache looted of meat. The furs in it had been left. "I cannot blame them," said Ogden of the redmen; "they are in a starving state, subsisting entirely on acorns."

During his own march, Ogden found many huts, but all were recently abandoned. He did not allow his men to take any of the Indians' paltry possessions. He feared that mere contact with the whites would make villains of the natives, as was the case (he said) with all Indians in touch with civilization. "Their petty thefts do us but little injury. Still, it is a convincing proof they are not honestly inclined and [that] fear alone is the cause of their not being more daring than they are."

All along the Klamath, the marchers found almost one continuous rapid. They ascended a fork trending into the Siskiyou Mountains and did well by trapping. Ogden then broke up the brigade even further, sending thirty men in advance of himself, to trap in three separate divisions. "By this plan, no stream will escape observations. . . ." The road was villainous—hilly and muddy. When the horses were unloaded they lay down in the muck and remained there until evening. Ogden had never seen them so tired. By February 7, the company was in the higher, more rugged portion of the Siskiyou Mountains, which he described: "The country around us presents a gloomy and barren aspect. Mountains covered with snow of an extraordinary height . . ."

Sticking to a west-northwest course, Ogden succeeded in traversing the range to the Little Applegate River without much difficulty, for the greatest depth of snow he encountered was no more than a foot. The ascent was gradual, but the descent was steep, and all hands had to work hard to prevent the horses from falling down the slopes with their loads. He was pleased with his relatively easy negotiation of the barrier: "The first Mountain since my sojourn amongst freemen that I have succeeded in crossing without sacrificing horses, either in summer or winter." He liked the looks of the Little Applegate, too, with its grass already green and four inches high, and oaks double the size of any he had ever seen. It was as if he had blundered into a forgotten patch of summer.

Shortly after the men set up camp, an Indian boldly entered Ogden's tent. He presented the trader with a fresh salmon and a beaver skin, then informed him that few beaver in the lower part of the Little Applegate had escaped the hunting of his kinfolk. However, the Applegate River itself (he said) was full of beaver. Ogden was tempted to believe him, though he was becoming a doubting Thomas where Indians were concerned, if only because he knew that most Indians were able to take beaver only in narrow streams, not large rivers. He was also cheered by the fact that his informant was completely ignorant of the Pacific Ocean. This meant that it was far enough away so that his men could do a heap of trapping before reaching tidewater. (Not until the trappers reached California's Delta and Suisun Bay did they abandon the gospel that salt water or brackish water and beaver did not mix.)

Ogden was absolutely delighted with the intramontane Siskiyou area: "This is certainly a fine country and probably no climate in any country equal to it." The Indians told him that winter was over. It was February 9! The singing birds, croaking frogs, and flowering plants seemed to verify their extravagant claim. Though the loftier mountains ahead bore snow, all of the hills surrounding the camps were bare of it. The area was rich in oak and pine, and the soil seemed well adapted for cultivation. Ogden believed the Indians when they told him the hills were thick with deer, for the simple reason that his informants were all well clad in buckskins. The new Indians, whom he took to be Shastas, were bold, stout-looking fellows who made their caps and arrow quivers of beaver skins.

Although, like McKay, Ogden had long held the sobriquet "Terror of the Indians," and though he wrote of the Shastas, "I am of opinion if, on first discovering a strange tribe, a dozen of them were shot, it would be the means of preserving many lives," he was peaceful toward his red visitors. He refused to take sides in the Klamath-Shasta controversy: "So far as regards their quarrels, we shall give ourselves no trouble and they may destroy each other, the more the better if they are fond of war. Let them enjoy it, and we in the intervene will endeavour to wage war with their beaver."

There was no lack of beaver in the Little Applegate, but the Indians had made them shy by breaking up their dams. And the animals were not so well outfitted with fur as others taken earlier.

Ogden blamed it on the mildness of the climate. He figured that the animals would be wretched, not worth trapping at all, in summer. The only way to take them was to let the traps remain undisturbed in the same place for two or three nights. During the first night, only three drowned beaver were found in the traps, plus some raccoons. But, after the second night, when the sixty traps were raised they brought twenty beaver with them.

Now Ogden realized why the local animals were so "wild." Many of the carcasses bore arrow or spear wounds. The Shastas used snares to take them, too, and earlier he had seen Indians netting beaver. He was almost ready to adopt snares himself, for sixteen of his steel traps were broken because of the inferior quality of the metal. They had to be repaired in the field. The Fort Vancouver blacksmith had told Ogden that the fault was not his. He did the best he could, but the steel was bad, not the kind which should be used for traps. Beaver were strong, their resistance incredible. The Americans had superior traps of Juniata steel, and Ogden treasured the six which he had in camp. They were more slender than the Canadian model but far stronger. The six had been in constant use for seven months and were as good as when purchased.

Ogden was so stubborn about his sense of direction that he was reluctant to believe the Indians when they told him that the streams which he was hunting—Yale Creek and the Little Applegate—did not connect with the Klamath but another stream. The latter headed westward, while the Klamath pitched south for a time during its dash for the sea.

Nor did the Indians think Payette would be successful in crossing the Siskiyous from the lower Klamath. He would have to come back upstream and follow Ogden. The latter was uneasy about the party, of which he had had no word since the rumors of the skirmish. But, since it was composed of his steadiest men, it did not preoccupy his mind. Ogden was intent on following the Klamath-Buenaventura to the sea. Unconvinced that he was not on one of its tributaries, he announced: "We shall for the present follow down trapping this stream and in six days hence, should we see nothing of the Clammitte River, we must seek for it."

Not that Ogden wished to leave the Siskiyou range, for "all the Indians agree in saying the farther you advance, the more beaver you will find." His expectations were now more sanguine than when he had first spied the Siskiyous, but he warned himself against over-confidence and reminded himself that fur trapping was a chancey thing: "It is all a lottery, and we are more subject—at least, *I* am—to draw blanks than prizes."

The local Indians were an impressive lot. For one thing, they ate beaver meat raw. And a one-armed warrior coolly explained about his missing limb: He had been wounded; the arm did not heal, so he had cut it off, himself, about three inches below the socket with his flint knife and axe. He had suffered great pain during the amputation, but the operation was a success and he had healed the stump with an application of roots.

Monday, February 12, brought an unpleasant night. McKay aroused Ogden at midnight. An Indian messenger had just brought word that a war party was on the point of attacking the camp. All the men leaped to the alert, but it was a nervous time for Ogden. Because he had scattered his men so, he had few camp guards: "Our numbers amounting to only eight men, and one-half never [having] fired three shots, our resistance would not have been long and of little avail. The night was certainly favourable for them, very dark and blowing a gale." Ogden was never sure if it was a false alarm or not, but no Indians attacked.

Next day, the chief trader wrote: "All was quiet during the night and, this morning, our scalps and—to us, almost as valuable in this country—our horses all safe." Nevertheless, he was annoyed with the natives. "I have, since my first entrance into their country, made it a point of informing them that the object we are in search of is beaver and not war, and to trade with them." He was inclined to believe that the redskinned courier had brought him a false report in hopes of currying favor or, rather, being rewarded. He knew that this was frequently the case on the Columbia. The Indians there were so frequently rewarded for falsehoods that they enjoyed hearty laughs when seeing whites out in the rain all night, on guard against invisible (and nonexistent) enemies.

But Ogden could not take any chances with potential hostiles, so far from home: "We all know Indians are a treacherous, blood-thirsty set of beings, and I shall watch their motions." Angrily, he added: "The sooner the extermination system be introduced amongst them the better." He sent word to the trappers trailing him not to raise camp until he should meet them. They were careless fellows, but the Canadians, at least, knew how to defend themselves when the chips were down: "The last American war [the War of 1812] is convincing proof," he reminded himself.

One day, Ogden did not raise camp because of stormy weather

and the need to skin and dress forty beaver. Fortunately, the women were as skilled in crafts as their husbands were not. "It is a pleasure to observe the ladies of the camp vying with each other, [as] to who will produce on their return to Fort Vancouver the cleanest and best dress'd beaver. . . ."

Next morning, St. Valentine's Day, was an exciting one for the horse herders. They found a Company animal killed and another, along with a freeman's mount, wounded by arrows. Ogden had been warned (even by the chief, who slept in camp), but he could not believe the warnings. "I have been mistaken," he admitted, "and to our cost. One cause assigned to it is that the Indians are displeased at seeing us daily destroy their beaver, and say they will, in consequence, starve."

The brigade leader not only resumed posting a night guard but also reestablished the day watch: "Otherwise, we stand a chance of losing our horses." The danger would be great while he was short-handed, until the split-off parties should rejoin him. He led his men down the Little Applegate to the Applegate itself, which he misjudged in size. It was a fine-looking stream, to be sure, and skirted with such beaver vittles as aspen, willows, and poplars, but hardly the size of the Willamette, as he wrote. He took the opportunity to do a bit of place-naming: "This river I have nam'd Sastise River, also a mount equal in height to Mount Hood or Vancouver I have named Mount Sastise. . . . I have given these names from the tribe of Indians who are well known by all the neighbouring tribes. . . ." Mount Shasta the peak remains to this day, outlasting Jedediah Smith's name of Rogers' Peak (for his clerk); but the name Shasta River has shifted to the south and attached itself to the stream at the base of Mount Shasta, rather than Ogden's stream, now called the Applegate.

With a good catch of beaver, otter, and deer, Ogden was pleased with the Siskiyous, though the Indians gave him some uneasy moments. Most were peacefully collecting dead salmon in the streams, especially the most putrid specimens, but a few were acting boldly, even insolently. Wrote Ogden: "One of the trappers reported that, within a short distance of the camp he met with three Indians who, on seeing him, strung their bows and made preparations for sending him a few arrows, at the same time making signs for him to leave their lands. He instantly drew the cover from his gun and was in the act of giving them a salute when they took flight. An example must be made of them, and soon, if we wish to remain in the country without being molested."

Beginning to worry about long-absent Payette because of this show of hostility, Ogden left him a note and had his men mark their trail very plainly. Of Payette's party, he wrote: "From their non-appearance, I conclude they have found beaver—or are destroyed by the natives." It would be impossible for him to find them, since he had no idea where they had left the Klamath to cross the Siskiyous.

The trappers reported indifferent success now—and numerous insolent natives lurking about their horses. "They appear determined to oblige us to leave the country," wrote the journal keeper, "and we are equally so not to leave it until we examine it farther." He set three men to work making a canoe so the trappers could work the far side of the Applegate. When the river subsided after the rains, he sent men across in it and crude rafts. The next day's return was only thirteen beaver, and not of good quality. Ogden was bewildered again: "It is really surprising that in a river where beaver have an abundance of food and at this season, they should be so miserably poor, scarcely an oz. of fat to be found in one of them, and their fur can almost be compared to summer beaver, their skin remarkable for its thickness."

Ten Indians paid the camp a call. They professed peace and advised him that he need not guard his horse herd so closely while in their country. Ogden had to let the animals graze at night, in any case, for if he kept them tightly guarded they would not feed well enough to regain their strength and soon they would be of no use to him. The presence of the Indians led him to worry about Payette. "Day after day passes, and still no accounts, no accounts of our absent men, and many and various are the conjectures concerning them. . . ."

But on the twentieth, the nine-man Payette party arrived. The men had taken only seventy-three beaver and nine otter, though they had descended the Klamath to a point only four days from its mouth. They had seen many wonders—villages built of "cedar" (redwood), lodges holding twenty to thirty families each, and fine planked canoes resembling those of the Chinooks at the Columbia's mouth. The natives had trade goods like knives, axes, and even tea kettles, and they were helpful. They had pointed out where beaver were likely to be found and had rendered other services without demanding the least reward. The only drawback was that their track downriver had been a stony one. This Ogden could believe. The exhausted horses were still lying on the ground. He doubted that he could recover the use of them, because of their battered hooves, before June.

The trappers who had crossed the Applegate returned with but few beaver, but at least with deer meat. They had barely been able to hang onto the venison, for no sooner had they shot a buck than six Indians appeared out of nowhere, like wolves. As the hunters cleaned the animal, the Indians drank the deer's blood and devoured the entrails without even cleaning them. They wanted more meat than just the guts and did not take off until the whites began to heft their guns in a menacing manner. "They were miserable looking wretches," wrote Ogden, "and certainly in their present state would be fit subjects for the Missionary Society, and the sooner they come the better."

That evening, fifty savages assembled near camp and asked to parley and make peace. Ogden *wa-waw*'d with them and awarded them two dozen buttons as an amity offering. They appeared ready to return the favor but were so impoverished that they had nothing to offer but a dance, which they performed before they left. "With the exception of their bare coverings," noted the trader, "their bows and arrows is all they possess in this world, or will probably in the next."

That night, Ogden checked his statistics. "We have this day 15 beaver, which completes our first thousand and leaves us eight to commence our second with. We have certainly travell'd far to complete this number."

The weather grew stranger still. Fourteen inches of snow fell from Ogden's supposedly coastal skies. Then the temperature rose and made mountain traveling impossible. This led him to predict: "Should we not find beaver in the lower part of the river, starvation will soon make its appearance." One squaw was so weak that she had to be tied onto her horse, and the chief trader was sure that part of his horse herd was bound to be sacrificed for the cooking pots.

Now the Indians grew bolder. They brazenly stole a trap. But they quickly returned it when Ogden sent an ultimatum: If they did not bring it back he would send a force to kill all of them. They did not doubt for a moment that he meant what he said. Wrote the trader: "It is to be regretted that the chief had not been caught in it. . . . If they do not comport themselves with more propriety, ere long, some of the trappers will, without doubt, make an example of some of them, and this alone will be security for the remainder."

On February 25, 1827, Ogden decided to bid adieu to the mountainous Applegate country, retracing his steps downstream and commenting, "There is nothing for us here excepting black tail deer." He sent men ahead to examine the lower Applegate, then again divided

61

his main party. McKay took thirteen men to look over some forks of the Klamath noticed by Payette. Ogden then followed his scouts down the Applegate with twenty-four men.

Ogden passed a large village which was abandoned by its citizens, hiding in the hills. "As they can render us little or no assistance, they may remain in their present wild state the remainder of their lives," he opined. In a second village, he saw a sickle and two china bowls. He figured that they had come from either the coast or California in the hands of Spanish traders. Unable to find a canoe on his side of the rain-swollen river, he had a man swim the Applegate. He could not stay where he was. "Fair or foul, tomorrow we must start; otherwise, we must commence killing our horses for food." Luckily, the swimmer found a canoe on the far side and took it, leaving its value in trade goods. Trappers crossed and were astonished to find on a large fork (Jump-off Joe Creek) the tracks of horses. In puzzlement, Ogden wrote: "We are at a loss to know who this can be, who travels with horses in this quarter." Probably it was the track of Michel Laframboise, out on scout for Alex McLeod. Apparently he had trapped the creek; Ogden found numerous signs of beaver, mostly old, but took precious few animals when his traps were raised.

Probably few of the natives had seen Laframboise, for it was obvious that horses were new to them. They stared at the animals in disbelief. Ogden mused: "A finer country for horses I have not yet seen and it is real surprising they have none. A few years with a band of mares [and] this country would soon be overstock'd. The Snakes or Blackfeet could never reach here."

As usual when beaver was in short supply, Ogden's freemen became grumblers. They regretted not having gone with Tom McKay. Ogden just shrugged and wrote in his book: "It is with him, as well as with us, a lottery."

On March 7 Ogden's men found the Applegate discharging into a river (the Rogue) which the trader still thought must be either the Klamath or its Sasty (Shasta) branch. He crowed: "Altho the Indians in the upper part reported it had no communication with it, I was of contrary opinion; indeed, it was almost impossible two such large rivers should flow nearly in the same course and not connect together sooner or later. It now forms a large river . . . and more appearance of beaver."

The men took twenty-eight beaver and two otter the first evening and agreed with Ogden that the area (around Grant's Pass) was a fine country. He appreciated its timber and pasture too but again wondered if he were getting too close to tidewater. He remembered how the effects of the Columbia's tidal bore were felt at Fort Vancouver, a hundred miles from the bar. As he planned a descent of the river, he again reminded himself, "When once we see the tide we may lose no time in returning. Beaver and salt water do not agree."

On the Rogue River Ogden met a chief who spoke Umpqua. He learned that the Umpqua River was far away but that the local natives traded beaver and *hyaquois* (dentalium shells, for wampum) for axes and knives. This explained the manufactured articles he had seen in the villages. The chief told Ogden that the lower river was stony and without beaver but that another large river, not distant (presumably the Coquille), was so well stocked with the animals that the Indians there made robes of the fur. The chief offered to pilot the whites there.

Other Indians who came in gave differing distances to the beaver-rich river, from three to eight days. Ogden did not know what to think. He did not believe this time that he was being deliberately misled. "This is certainly a wide difference as regards time; but, probably, they have never seen it and their information may be derived from report." Probably the chief referred to the Elk River as three days distant and the commoners meant the Coquille, eight days away.

Cursing the rain, which was rotting the "leather tents" or teepees and which made necessary the quick dressing of green skins, before they spoiled, the trappers crossed the Rogue River. Ogden swore that his own blankets had not been dry for twenty days. When fair weather finally turned up, men and women hurriedly dressed beaver pelts and the women also dried meat in case Ogden should seek out the new river. Since Indians were becoming both numerous and troublesome again, he decided not to let the camp fall too far to the rear of his advance parties.

Briefly, Ogden allowed himself the luxury of deploring the waste of the Company's "hunt clean" policy: "It is almost a sin to see the number of small beaver we destroy and to no purpose. Some of the females taken have no less than five young . . . [and] rivers subject to overflow their banks require double and treble the time to recruit after being trapped." He remarked, too, how thinly scattered was beaver in southern Oregon—one small stream in the Snake Country would equal the whole Siskiyou shebang!

Ogden was at a loss now whether or not to proceed to the supposedly beaver-crowded river. The Indians stole two traps and then scattered like quail. He could not hire a guide from among them. Finally he sent some men out and they dragged in an unwilling pilot.

He was alarmed and wild. "We must endeavour to tame him," said Ogden. Only a constant guard kept him from deserting. Reluctantly, he led them to some redskins drying *camas* roots. Ogden gave the miserable looking people some rings. But the guide was no horseman. He fell off his mount so many times that Ogden was persuaded to lead his horse as he rode. Finally, he had to tie the Indian on with a rope, like the sick woman. "It caused no small diversion to the men to see me driving him along," he noted.

Since March 14, 1827, began with snow and ended with rain, with no respite between the storms, Ogden and his followers holed up in camp for a much-needed rest. He seized the opportunity to indulge in a rare philosophical soliloquy: "It is certainly most harassing for the poor trappers to trap in such weather, obliged to sleep out, and two-thirds without a blanket to cover them. Still, not one complains, but [all] exert themselves to procure beaver with all their might and main. Poor fellows; at times, at least, when I see them arrive, which is too often the case in this rainy climate, drenched in rain and shivering with cold, [I feel] most keenly for them. The life of a trapper, altho at times he has some idle hours—which, however, does not often happen—is certainly a most laborious one, and one [which] in four years makes a young man look almost as if he had reached the advanced age of sixty. Of this, many convincing proofs are now amongst my party. The cold water which, more or less, they are wading in two-thirds of the day, added to the cold and sleeping often without fire and wet to the skin, conduces to ruin their constitutions. Well do they earn their ten shillings per beaver. A convict in Botany Bay is a Gent living at his ease compared to them. Still, they are happy and, amidst all their sufferings and privations, if they take beaver—all is well. Thoughtless beings, how much more comfortable and with less labor could they earn an honest livelihood in their own country than they do in this. And many are aware of this, but a roving life pleases them and, with nearly all, it would be viewed more as a punishment than a favour to send them to Canada. God grant some kind friend would succeed *me,* and I would most willingly steer my course from whence I came altho I am not [French-] Canadian."

On the march again, more useless traps (one with a snapped chain and four with broken jaws) led Ogden's freemen to curse him and the Fort Vancouver smith alike. At Allen Creek, Indians buoyed Ogden's hopes up by informing him that there were plenty of beaver in the big river ahead. He tried not to be overanxious: "However, well do I know what an Indian calls a river of beaver, and probably we may be disappointed." There were tracks of elk, deer, and grizzlies all around Allen Creek, leading him to hope that beaver were abundant, too.

A couple of freemen asked if they could go back to trap the forks of the Applegate and Rogue in the party's rear, then descend the stream to rejoin Ogden. He refused. He told them that he was aware that there were still beaver behind him, but he reminded them that he would need them for food as well as for furs if he was to successfully extricate the party from the wilderness. He reminded them further that two-thirds of the return march would have to be performed in country which was destitute of beaver, whether he decided to bring them out via Flathead Post, "Fort Nee Percy," the Dalles, or the Willamette.

Although he was closing with the Umpqua and, therefore, a straight run home to Fort Vancouver by way of the Willamette, Ogden apparently did not seriously consider using that route to get back. He planned to return by the roundabout route by which he had come, the Snake Country trail, even though he noted in his journal that, by making use of the Willamette, he could make it to the fort without starving—"With good hunters, a party not over-numerous may succeed in procuring a meal every two days."

The catch was fair, and the fur was superior to that which they had taken earlier, too. Ogden put his thoughts into writing: "Those taken in small streams are far superior to those taken in large; in the latter the water is not so cold as in the former . . . nor do the beaver remain so quiet as in small streams."

An old Indian was brought trembling into camp by trappers. Fed and given beads, he calmed down and conversed with Ogden, who now learned the reason for the Indians secreting themselves, as well as their reluctance to serve as guides. Tidings of the coming of the white men had spread throughout the Siskiyou Mountains, but the story was told that the pale strangers came not for beaver but to enslave Indians.

Ogden blamed the Klamaths for spreading the malicious rumors, in hopes of keeping the trappers in their own country. The local Indians were scarecrows. They looked as if they had not tasted food, other than roots, for ten years. He knew that some of them took beaver with spears, wooden traps, and fire, though many warriors lacked even bows and arrows. He thought: "What a noble prize they would be for the Chinooks, who commerce in slaves." The chief trader stuffed his visitors with meat and when one finally volunteered to lead him to the big river of the beaver, he immediately took him up on the idea. Afraid that he would desert in the night, Ogden deceived him by telling him that he would not set out on the morrow, although he fully intended to do so.

The guide took the whites from Allen Creek over a rugged mountain covered with trees, through which a passage had to be chopped with axes. Although the guide said that it was impossible to cross the range with horses, Ogden was determined to prove him wrong. Of the many mountains which he had crossed, none had more impediments to negotiate than the particular Siskiyou ridge blocking his way. It was a mass of dense timber, steep hills, and "cut rocks." But only one horse was seriously injured by a fall, and none of his men was hurt. A pleased Ogden wrote of the horses: "It is to me almost surprising that they were not all killed."

After a strenuous day, camp was set up and the tired men relaxed by cussing out Ogden and his pilot—when safely out of the former's hearing. But the Indian who promised arrival at the river next morning delivered them there, on time. Ogden did not know it, of course, but he was not on Elk River or the Coquille but simply on another stretch of the Rogue River, writhing its way through the folded Siskiyous to reach the sea. He was welcomed to the Grant's Pass area by a wind- and rainstorm so violent that, for almost the first time on the expedition, his men were unable to stake out the traps.

By now, his trappers were predisposed to disappointment, but Ogden insisted that the new stream be given a fair trial before being condemned. He sent six men upriver just before he received bad news from his guide. Local natives had told him that an Umpqua chief and six trappers had recently cleaned out the stream. This must have been Little Chief, with McLeod and Laframboise. He had been on the South Fork of the Coquille on December 9, 1826, and must have made it over to the Rogue, too. The natives also persuaded Ogden that he was not on the Umpqua and that it lay across a range of mountains necessitating a march of several days.

The men sent upstream reported a few beaver but so many "cut rocks" on the shore that they had had to cross and recross the water on rafts. It had been impossible to trap it to its source. Nevertheless, Ogden sent a party with Gervais to explore it and see if a transit could be made over the mountains to the Umpqua, thereby opening up a segment of road back to Fort Vancouver. He thought that such a road should have been made years before, since it could have been done with facility. He ordered Gervais on to Fort Vancouver when he was done, with a letter for McLoughlin. Before the Frenchman left, confident of a good march and hunt, the chief trader gave him orders not to leave an area until he had examined and trapped every stream he should find. With beaver scattered so thinly over the Siskiyous, this was the only way to carry out Simpson's "wasteland" strategy.

That same March 26, 1827, was a busy day for Ogden. After wishing Gervais bon voyage, he sent men after a stolen trap. The Indians had taken out the beaver, to eat, then thrown the trap into the river. Ogden wasted no compassion now on the nearly starving natives. With deer in abundance, he blamed their plight on their inept hunting methods and just plain laziness. Later, the guide led Ogden over a point of land to reach the rushing, dangerous Applegate again at their old campsite, then followed it down to the large river which, unknown to him, was the ubiquitous Rogue *again,* which he had just left across the mountain. He managed to find a canoe to ferry everyone safely across, but this was not the end of the day's adventures.

Some of the men wounded a grizzly. One of the local Indians, eager to prove Ogden wrong in his low opinion of them as hunters, borrowed an axe. He then stripped himself naked, took the axe and his bow and arrows and rushed on the bear, though the aghast whites tried to restrain him. Ogden recorded the scene: "He paid dearly for his rashness, and from the wounds he received it is not supposed he will recover. He has received considerable injury in the head and shoulder, also the loss of one eye, which was actually torn out; a more frightful looking being they never beheld."

When the chief trader found the banks of the Applegate covered with white clover, he once more waxed enthusiastic about the Siskiyou meadows: "In all my travels, I have not yet seen a finer country for pasture than we have travelled over for some time past. Probably one cannot be found to equal it, and, consequently, our horses are certainly in prime order." He compared his "new" stream favorably with the Sasty (Applegate), still not realizing that he was on but another reach of the same twisting stream, finding its way out of the tangled, tortured ridges and canyons of the Siskiyou Mountains.

The Applegate, here, gave the appearance of harboring beaver. But when traps were set by night and raised in the morning only two beaver and one otter were in them. The explanation was not long in coming. Crossing a point of land to avoid innumerable boulders in the riverbed, Ogden came upon a large track made by travelers on twenty to thirty horses. Apparently, he again had stumbled on the trail of his colleagues, Alex McLeod and Michel Laframboise. When one of his Iroquois, probably mistakenly, told him that he thought he recognized a mountain as one said to be in the Umpqua country, Ogden made up his mind. He would remain no longer in the Siskiyous; they were getting too crowded. Thus he did not close a gap in the nascent Siskiyou Trail, but pulled out. On March 27, 1827, he wrote that he saw no reason to follow the track of the other party, since it would not increase his returns. He sought out a guide to get him back to the Klamath without loss of time, but via a different route from the one he had used to penetrate the Siskiyous.

Before he left them, Ogden described the local Indians as being the closest to Christians in terms of funeral customs of any he had seen. They sunk five- or six-foot-deep graves, wrapped the dead in deerskin winding sheets, and always placed the corpses with their heads to the east. They even erected foot-square plank "headstones" and "footstones" over the graves. He talked to some squaws and elderly men but could get information only on funerary customs, nothing on transmontane routes—nor could he obtain a guide.

The great number of graves spelled starvation to Ogden. This was curious in a fine country of grass and clover. Again, he felt sorry for the natives: "It is distressing to see human beings suffer in this way while others are enjoying life subject but to few of its inconveniences. . . . I have observed the natives from the dawn of day until late in the evening employed in digging roots, and the greater part of the night is spent in pounding and preparing their food; nor do they appear to collect more than sufficiency in one day's labour than one meal. Wretched and forlorn beings, and amidst all their sufferings they also live in dread of enemies. But with the exception of their scalps, I see nothing they have that can attempt an Indian to travel a mile in quest of them."

Back over the Siskiyous marched "M'sieu Pete" Ogden at an early hour of April 2, 1827, toward California. By midafternoon on April 3, he was pleased to see the mountains dropping away behind him. He was amused, too, to see Indians fleeing him and he remarked: "Poor creatures, we mean them no harm." Traps were set at all halts, even old campsites where they took two beaver when, earlier, eighty had fallen. Ogden's intent was now survival, however, rather than profits or laying waste the countryside as per Simpson's instructions: "Our horses were certainly low when we encamped, but we are now in a starving state and until we find beaver, push on we must or kill our horses for food, and I fear they will inevitably fall."

Still trying to untangle the geography of the Siskiyou barrier, Ogden came to believe that the Klamath formed a junction with the Applegate and the Rogue. If the mysterious trappers, whose tracks he had found, had not yet examined the lower river, it could easily be done from the Umpqua. Therefore, he was eager to explore south of the Klamath and hopeful of finding Simpson's Buenaventura.

After two days without food, an elk, a deer, and a grizzly fell to the company's rifles, to add to beaver in the traps. But rain, snow showers, strayed horses, and the need to "dust" (shake) and dry the skins, to keep damp and vermin away, slowed the brigade's wandering way. Ogden could not hurry the march, in any case, since McKay was to join him on Klamath Lake. He was anxious to hear of the halfbreed's success, thinking it could not possibly be worse than his own.

On April 19, on the bank of the Klamath, Ogden found a letter from McKay, concealed under a tree. The latter was crossing a mountain with a guide to "five rivers of beaver," presumably the Pit and its forks. He suggested that Ogden join him there. However, the chief trader felt that it would be more prudent to await him at Klamath Lake, as arranged, and to send a messenger to McKay.

Ogden was presented with the first salmon of the season by a visiting Indian, but his mind was more on his tenderfooted, limping horses.

McKay surprised Ogden by arriving in camp on April 22, ahead of his party. He had had double his chief's success, taking 735 beaver and otter, mostly in two small streams tributary to the Klamath. He had been turned back by deep snow from the river reported (by the Indians) to be rich in beaver. His men had had to kill three of the horses when their feet gave out. Considering the severity of the season and the time lost by lack of familiarity with the country, Ogden was quite satisfied with the entire brigade's returns, which now stood at 2230 beaver and otter.

Great flocks of gray and white geese honked overhead as the combined parties made an abortive beginning of a march to the rumored five rivers of beaver. Some Indians visiting the Klamaths stole three traps and killed a Klamath woman who informed on them. Ogden put it to his men: Should he pursue the murderous thieves or not? When only McKay and three others volunteered to go after them, he gave up the idea and raised camp to ascend the Klamath.

He hoped to set traps as he moved and, still, make two winter days' travel into one. But the horses' hooves were so bad that such a pace was completely out of the question.

Ogden traded for four hundred "carp" to use as iron rations while McKay rounded up some guides. On the borders of a lake, perhaps Tule Lake, Indians warned him of stony country ahead. On the fourth, Ogden reached his old December 31 campsite. It marked his most southerly penetration of the season. For the first time, mosquitoes became a nuisance at night after sultry days. The terrain, over which he set a southeasterly course, was barren except for "Norway pines"—piñon trees? It was a land without Indians, game, or the tracks of a living creature. Probably they were skirting the Modoc Lava Beds, scene of California's only major Indian war just forty-five years later. But at noon of May 6 they reached a fine stream, well wooded with willows on its muddy banks: "Ten minutes after," recalled Ogden, "not a trap remained in camp." Though wood was still scarce, Ogden now had open country ahead and a much better road, one free of the lava stones which cruelly punished the horses' hooves, already soft and tender from the long rainy season.

Ogden was not yet on the much-touted Pit River, but on one of its affluents, Turner Creek. Shortly, he found the river proper and finally reached the Buenaventura, in a sense. For the latter came to be the Sacramento and the Pit is really the main fork of the upper Sacramento River. The higher portion of Turner Creek was soon crowded with traps, since the Indians reported no beaver in its lower stretches. The Indians were right. And, as they had predicted, no animals at all were in the Pit itself.

The locals, whom Ogden found to be "daring" warriors, warned him to be careful on their riverside paths, which were pocked with pitfalls for deer and wolves. Nevertheless, three mounted men fell into the traps. Miraculously, only one of the riders was hurt and only one horse killed. Some of the pits, if Ogden did not exaggerate, were thirty feet deep, and armed with sharpened stakes. Remarked the chief trader: "It is almost incredible the number of pits the Indians have made along the river on both sides of the track as well as in it. They are certainly deserving of praise for their industry, but from our not seeing the track of an animal I am not of opinion their labour is rewarded from the number of pits. So as to warn others who may chance to travel in this quarter, I have nam'd this river Pit River. It is true we have lost a horse and a most valuable one, and it is now almost surprising to me we have not lost more."

Ogden's eyes kept returning to the snow-covered heights of the Warner Range, where he correctly supposed that the Pit took its rise. Perhaps it would offer him a passageway through the high country barrier to the east. But first he had to clean the Pit River area of its fur. Two miles east of the modern town of Canby, California, Ogden examined another stinking, sulfurous, boiling spring. Once again, he had a minor "casualty" in the ranks as another inquisitive trapper had to dip his finger, gingerly, into the bubbling water. Of course, he paid painfully for his folly. This accident was soon followed by a genuine tragedy. A trapper's child fell into the Pit, and, though he was fished out and Ogden tried desperately to save him, he could not be revived. The little drowned boy was buried beside the river.

The chief trader learned that the empty huts along the Pit were only momentarily abandoned. Their owners were in the mountains, in search of food: "Well do they require to go somewhere, for here they would soon starve for, without exception, it is the most barren country I have ever travell'd over."

Trappers higher up reported that the Pit split into two wooded forks without rapids—"in a word, beaver streams," exulted Ogden. He ruminated on how vexing it was to find so many likely streams empty of beaver, but he thought that he had the explanation: "The rivers of this country would certainly be better stock'd in beaver than it is but, in my opinion, from the poverty of the country in [game] animals. [This] obliges the natives to destroy beaver for support, for almost in every part of the rivers they have been working and the few that escape are, consequently, very wild."

With the Pit as disappointing as the Klamath and Rogue, Ogden was momentarily puzzled as to where to turn, next. He mused: "We travel, as it were, in the dark, as from our Indian guides little reliance or dependence can be placed on them, and we must act for ourselves and trust to chance, and it may probably prove to us a broken reed."

Ogden now had to make some hard decisions. Having been scolded by Simpson for not following through on orders, he was careful to remind himself: "I must make the attempt and follow my instructions in taking a southern course, and if I should find nothing I shall then take an eastern course with the hopes of falling on the waters of the Snake Country." He asked McKay to return on the brigade's track to look over a river reportedly seen, three years earlier, by one of the men. If he found nothing, he was to explore the true sources of the Willamette, which, Ogden noted, had not yet been examined. Surprisingly, McKay declined and Ogden dropped the idea.

So, Ogden sent out scouts "on discovery." They returned to report the mountains ahead to the south (the Shastas) to be impossible to cross because of deep snow. They estimated that it would take four days to cross even in summer. When another scout came in, he reported a narrow escape from thirty Indians, whom he took to be Snakes. They had surrounded him and were preparing to discharge arrows into him, until mollified. They told him the country to the south had no beaver. Ogden was impressed that these Indians agreed with the Klamaths. Nevertheless, he was mindful of Simpson's instructions to explore and trap widely, and to seek the great River of the West, and not simply retrace his steps; so it was with reluctance that Ogden gave up: "Were there a possibility of crossing, I would still steer my course southward." But, with his way blocked by deep snowdrifts of the Shasta-Cascade mountains, Ogden gave up his quest for the Buenaventura River on May 5, 1827.

Ogden led his men up the Pit until it divided into three forks. (Had he gone downstream, he would have reached the Buenaventura—the Sacramento—proper.) Ironically he was just two hundred miles north of the man who would find the river and blaze a major portion of the Siskiyou Trail alongside it. Jedediah Smith was camped on another major fork of the Sacramento, the American River, near the site of the present Folsom.

Pete Ogden now abandoned the future route of the Siskiyou Trail entirely and headed for Goose Lake, which he called Pit Lake, on the modern California-Oregon border near the Nevada line. He found old dams and beaver huts aplenty; but traps set in the streams drowned nary a beaver. He learned the reason: Four years earlier, the natives had burned the stream banks, dams, and lodges during low water. An angry Ogden scribbled in his journal: "It is a lottery with expeditions. . . . This is certainly strange and almost vexing, to see so many fine streams and find nothing. Nor can I account for its being so, for if one-third of the rivers we have discovered this year had been stock'd in beaver, we should now have more than we could transport."

Shortly, Ogden fell ill—like many of his men. A rack of skin and bones, he steadied his pen and wrote: "Of all situations a man can be placed in, I am fully of opinion none can be more wretched and forlorn than being sick on the plains, exposed to a burning sun and deprived of every assistance and comfort that can tend to alleviate his sufferings."

Somewhat recovered from his illness and malaise, Ogden resumed his homeward march, cursing the Indians who had killed, by his estimate, sixty thousand beaver by burning over the narrow streams. In his opinion, it was the most destructive way of hunting beaver—and he was an expert on beaver destruction. Because of the shortage of game in the area, Ogden did not believe that the beaver would ever recover. The Indians would kill every surviving rodent which poked its nose above water.

Chief trader Ogden reached Fort Vancouver, via the Snake, on August 5, 1827, and shipped his furs. His pelts ran about a pound apiece in weight and his catch amounted to 2188 beaver and 79 other skins (chiefly otter), totaling 2817 pounds. Since "made beaver"—that is, prime adult skins and their equivalents in the pelts of young cubs, otter, and sea otter skins—cost 13 to 14 pence each, the Company would clear almost 100 percent profit if it could get 20 shillings a skin.

Ogden's task had been hunting beaver (to extinction) and searching for the hidden Buenaventura, not laying out the Siskiyou Trail. Hence his wandering, backtracking route. In his log he had written: "Now we know the country between this and the Clammitt, it is scarcely credible the circuitous road we made last fall." Nevertheless, he had blazed a portion of the ultimate road over the Siskiyous, and his Pit River route became an alternate road to the more directly north-south passage lying to the westward of Mount Shasta.

In July 1827 Simpson reiterated to London that the best protection the Company could secure against competitors was by exhausting the country south of the Columbia, since its beaver offered the greatest temptation to the Yankees. Accordingly, in September 1827, the tireless Ogden was back in the field. He was not confident of success, even though he hunted the Snake rather than the Umpqua-Siskiyou-Klamath area: "My expectations as far as regards success is far from being sanguine; still the attempt is worthy of a trial." He was back in the fort on the last day of July 1828 with a pretty fair catch.

Ogden's fifth expedition left Fort Nez Percés on September 22, 1828, and struck across the Nevada desert to a stream he called the Unknown River, then Mary's River—for his wife, Mary Rivet Ogden. (Frémont renamed it the Humboldt.) Ogden was worried about bumping into Alexander McLeod's Willamette party, far to the westward of him, until he learned that no salmon ascended his Unknown River. He shortly found that it squandered its alkaline waters in a desert sump, and felt better. "With this [discovery], I am well pleased, as it might interfere with Mr. McLeod's trapping party and prove injurious to both parties should they come into contact with each other. . . . As I have no guides, I travel along, as it were, blindfolded. . . . It is to be regretted that there is no water communication from this country to the Willamette."

At the end of May, on the bleak Humboldt Sink, Ogden met hostile Paiutes who were well armed. He guessed how they had possession of modern arms: "I am of opinion [they] must be some of the plunder of [Jedediah] Smith's party of ten men who were murdered in the fall and, from native to native, had reached this. They would not inform me from whom they had received these articles; this looks suspicious. . . . More daring and bold Indians seldom, if ever, have I seen." More likely, the weapons were not trophies from Jed Smith's disaster on the Umpqua (see next chapter) but, rather, booty from the massacre of Ephraim Logan's trapping party of early 1828, near Twin Falls.

On the last day of May 1829, Ogden again betrayed his geographical uncertainty, truncating the area between Great Basin and Willamette-Sacramento valleys. He turned back, fearful of trespassing on McLeod's preserve if he continued westward. "Granting the season was not so far advanced, it is contrary to my wish to infringe on Mr. McLeod's territory, as the waters that discharge in the ocean I have nothing to do with, and if Mr. McLeod has succeeded in reaching the Bona Ventura, he must have crossed the stream the Indians inform me of." Not so: The stream was probably the nearby Carson River, flowing eastward out of the Sierra Nevada to die in Carson Sink, just across the Forty Mile Desert from the Humboldt. But Ogden turned back and made his way to Fort Vancouver via Oregon's Blue Mountains and Fort Nez Percés, on July 24, 1829.

On his sixth and last Snake Country Expedition, Ogden explored and trapped a very large segment of the Siskiyou Trail, which was beginning to take shape. All of his journals were lost. In their absence, details of the journey are scant; but bits and pieces can be put together from a few of his letters, from other Beaver House documents, and from the pages of his anonymous essay of 1853, *Traits of American Indian Life & Character*. He explained his task of September 1829: "In 1829 I was appointed to explore the tract lying south of the Columbia, between that river and California. For five years previously I had been similarly employed [largely] to the eastward of that tract, where I had had many rencontres with the warlike tribes."

Ogden's thirty men were well equipped, except (as usual) for horses, though he joked later that his men, in pursuit of "vile lucre," could not boast the India rubber pillows and boots, the preserved meats and dried soups of more famous travelers, who explored for science or amusement, rather than profit.

Winter came early that year and dashed his hopes of a fall hunt on Mary's River in Nevada. He pushed on south to the desert oasis of Walker River and Walker Lake and was disappointed to find both destitute of beaver. Continuing across what he called the "Great Sandy Desert of Great Salt Lake," he now paralleled the San Joaquin Valley portion of the later Siskiyou Trail but was blocked from it by the mighty High Sierra.

Ogden's men suffered greatly from hunger and thirst in January 1830. Some of his worn-out horses had to be butchered and eaten and their blood drunk. He lost many horses, but all of his men survived. Apparently, Ogden crossed the rugged White Mountains, possibly discovering Westgaard Pass, and dropped into Owens Valley. He found the Owens River devoid of beaver—but not of Indians. They were wild as deer, but he captured two warriors. He treated them with as lavish a hospitality as his straightened circumstances permitted. After pumping them dry of geographical information, he dismissed them with enough baubles to prove his good intentions.

Later, Ogden had serious second thoughts about the policy of kindness which was more generally followed than not (if only for self-preservation) by trading and trapping parties out West: "I will venture the opinion that had it, on the first discovery of new countries, been resolved to treat the savages with the greatest severity, the eventual sacrifice of many lives on their part would have been avoided."

The reason for Ogden's mistrust of kindness as a weapon was the fact that the Indians, perhaps Monos, loosed a shower of arrows into camp. The men were unscathed, but they wounded three precious horses. Still unwilling to start a general war, Ogden, nevertheless, had his patience sorely tried by this raid: "I considered it high time to convince them that we could resent the unprovoked attack." He ordered just one man to fire on the Indians. The trapper discharged his rifle and a warrior fell. It was lesson enough; the Indians fled, leaving the body of their companion on the ground. Ogden hoped that the lesson would teach the Indians not only of his superiority in arms but of his desire to be lenient with them, so long as they behaved themselves. But from past experience he did not hoist his hopes up very high.

Traveling across a country "as barren as ever Christian traversed," Ogden reached another tribe, probably the Mojaves. He strongly suspected them to be the perpetrators of Jed Smith's first massacre in 1828. He later recalled: "My men were eager to revenge the massacre upon them, but as I had no proof that these were the guilty persons, I withheld my consent to their entreaties." On the Mojave River (which Smith had dubbed Inconstant River because its scant flow was seldom boosted to the surface sands by underground rock dikes) the Indians began to ask for trouble. They swarmed over the camp in great numbers, each man carrying not only his aboriginal weapons but a long stick over his shoulder in derision of the musket and rifle-packing mountain men.

Ogden quietly doubled his horse guard, warned his men to hold themselves in readiness for a fight, and imitated Jed Smith's earlier action when in the same bind. He had his men tie butcher knives to poles with thongs, to fashion rude spears or lances. He then gave them orders to fire once and not try to reload after the first volley but to charge the hostiles with cold steel. "I was apprehensive lest, during the interval of loading, the Indians might make a rush and overpower us. And that a speedy attack was meditated I could no longer doubt."

With all preparations completed, Ogden remarked: "Danger is an excellent disciplinarian." He admitted a few Mojaves to camp, hopeful that his obvious defensive posture would deter an attack. But the Indians' lust for horses and other booty was too powerful. They struck, wounded a guard, and tried to steal the horses. Ogden long remembered those critical moments. It was no time for a warning shot, a token resistance, if these were, indeed, the victors over Jedediah Smith. "This was sufficient for me. They had shed the first blood and I was resolved that theirs should repay it; and as it was now for life or death with us, I ordered a general discharge, to be followed up by a charge with the spear. The first, however, sufficed; for, on seeing the numbers of their fellows who, in a single moment, were made to lick the dust, the rest ingloriously fled and we saw no more of them. Twenty-six dead remained on the field."

Ogden had no qualms about this slaughter of the Mojaves. They had attacked him in spite of his peaceful manifestations, and they, very likely, had murdered Smith's men earlier. Besides, he blamed them in part for the deaths of an estimated 350 beaver men, Britons and Americans who had fallen victims of the Indians during twenty years of the trade all over the West.

Finding few beaver in the Mojave, which he called the southwest branch of the Colorado, Ogden pulled out and headed north so as to give the "Spanish" settlements of California a wide berth. It is not clear whether he reached the Colorado River itself and the Gulf of California at its mouth. He told John McLeod, Sr., that he had, in a letter of March 10, 1831; but he may have been content with the beaverless Mojave River, which he took to be a fork of the Colorado.

Crossing the Tehachapi Mountains, Ogden reached the San Joaquin Valley. In his letter to John McLeod he described his luck after he struck the tail end of the Siskiyou Trail proper, the San Joaquin Valley from the Kings River on north: "I was not so successful in my last year's expeditions as the year preceding, although I extended my travels by far greater distance, to the Gulph of California, but found beaver very scarce. . . . [But] by following the mountains, I could examine the different [Sierra] streams and, at the same time, avoid meeting with the Spaniards, and on the South Branch of the Boreantura [i.e., the San Joaquin], which I trapped from its sources to its discharge in the Gulf of San Francisco, I was fortunate in securing 1000 beaver. I say fortunate for, when on the eve of leaving it, I was joined by an American party with a Mr. [Ewing] Young from St. Fee, well loaded with traps, who were in quest of the Boreantura and Willamette. We kept company for ten days when we reached Pitt River, now found to be the north branch of the Boreantura, when, finding Mr. [Alexander] McLeod's trapping party's tracks, they retraced their steps, empty-handed."

Ogden was back at Fort Nez Percés on June 30, 1830, after an eleven-month absence. He left his surviving horses there and started down the Columbia in a rickety boat. At the rapids of the Dalles, he continued on foot after the portage. This was not because of any premonition of danger, for the boat bobbed in apparent safety below the stony channels, but because the heat of July 3 was already intense in the gorge, which stunk of putrefying salmon. Though it was long past breakfast time, Ogden decided to walk on a bit and have a bite to eat, further down. He set forth, idly watching the boat skirt a string of small whirlpools in the defile, then shoot majestically forward across the water.

Ogden recalled: "I half repented my resolution of walking, envying the swan-like ease with which she appeared to descend, so contrasted with my own fatiguing progress." But suddenly the way of the boat was checked, as if the craft were gripped in a giant, invisible hand. The rowers were nearly thrown from their seats. They regained their balance and dug the blades of their oars deep, to pull free of the whirlpool which tugged at the boat. But their straining muscles could not break its grip. The vortex began to form, sucking the boat round and round, down and down, as a horrified Ogden watched, utterly incapable of helping his companions in any way. He heard his bowsman shout, *"Ramez! Ramez! Ou nous sommes pais!"* ("Row! Row! Or we are lost!")

The stern dragged lower and lower, the bow rose, and Ogden saw the boat disappear from view. The whirlpool soon filled itself again and the surface of the treacherous river stretched out smooth. In a few moments, paddles, setting poles, and other buoyant gear began to appear on the water. Then Ogden saw a few struggling men—but, one by one, the figures disappeared in the depths, pulled down by lesser vortices.

Twelve years later, Ogden still vividly recalled the horrible scene: "After a brief interval, nought was to be distinguished but the mournful rustling of the waters, and I sat down with the consciousness of being left, in the fullest sense, alone."

Ogden had no hope of any of his comrades surviving. But one did: Baptiste, the steersman, who seized four kegs which were lashed together. He rode out the disaster and was picked up by Indians, miles downriver. The bodies of his friends were not found until long after, when they were cast ashore on widely separated beaches.

Thus, Ogden's last Snake Country Expedition ended in disaster. He had explored the California portion of the Siskiyou Trail, but he lost in the wreck not only twelve of his associates, including such stalwarts as François Rivet, Jr., Antoine Sylvaille, and Joseph Portneuf, and three hundred beaver pelts, but every last word of his journal of exploration.

Back in Fort Vancouver on July 6, 1830, Ogden was worn out from his unrelenting efforts to carry out Simpson's charge, even without the emotionally shattering experience of the Dalles disaster. The Governor, once so critical of him, now praised him highly in reports to London: "I cannot quit the subject of our trapping expeditions without expressing my utmost satisfaction with the zeal, activity and perseverance manifested by Chief Trader Ogden in the very arduous service on which he had been employed for some years past; while I am sorry to intimate that the injury his constitution has sustained by the privations and discomfort to which he has been so long exposed will render it necessary to relieve him as soon as we can find a gentleman qualified to fill his place to advantage."

It would not be easy to find a replacement for Ogden. He had taken better care of men, horses and equipment than any brigade leader or American trader. He kept his gear dry, his leather lodges solid, his horse tackling in good order. He so encouraged his trappers and their wives to carefully clean, stretch, dry and shake their beaver skins that he got them bonus payments for such splendid pelts. When his men fell ill, he treated them like doctor and nurse combined. Seldom did he lose a patient—or even his temper over a patient. (An exception was an 1828 case in which the sick man was so ornery that "Dr." Ogden exclaimed: "It is his *duty* to recover, for he can expect, no longer, any assistance from me!") He ran his brigades like paramilitary units, never allowing himself to be surprised and ambushed like his chief American rival, Jed Smith.

Simpson gave Ogden responsible positions, after he recovered his health, on the Russian-Alaska frontier and as Chief Factor of New Caledonia or British Columbia, an area four times the size of Great Britain. He won praise when in 1847 he ransomed the survivors of the Whitman massacre.

Ogden had done his job well. He had pretty well exploded the myth of the Buenaventura and/or Los Mongos River, though Frémont would administer the coup de grâce. He had hunted out a great swath of beaver country for Simpson and the Crown. Proof of his success was in the decline of the beaver catch in the Snake Country (and portions of the Siskiyou Trail area), which sank from 2099 skins in 1826 to 788 in 1832 and only 220 in 1835.

There still remained much to be done in the Snake Country satellites of Siskiyous, upper Willamette, and Sacramento-San Joaquin rivers as Ogden retired from the scene. Simpson indicated his continuing interest in a communiqué of July 10, 1831, to his London superiors: "The Snake Expedition penetrated from the interior as far south as some of the headwaters of a river running into the Bay of St. Francis, which we understood to be the Buona Ventura, but is now ascertained to be the Sacramento. From Chief Trader Ogden's report I am concerned to find that the country is much less exhausted, and still overrun by American trappers."

Simpson replaced Ogden with John Work, who most nearly measured up to him. He used Work, Alex McLeod, Michel Laframboise, and Francis Ermatinger to clean out the last of the buffer zones to be cleared of beaver. This was the wilderness barrier cut only by the thin trace of the Siskiyou Trail.

A Sly, Cunning Yankee

NO SINGLE INDIVIDUAL blazed the entire Siskiyou Trail—not even the redoubtable Peter Skene Ogden. The route was put together in bits and pieces at different times by Americans and Britons, the trappers who were Robert Glass Cleland's "reckless breed of men," John G. Neihardt's "splendid wayfarers," and members of Herbert E. Bolton's "rollicking brigades."

But the man who pioneered a large portion of the trail in California, whose exploits persuaded the Hudson's Bay Company to make it a permanent route, was the greatest American explorer after Meriwether Lewis. He was Jedediah Strong Smith, proponent of Manifest Destiny and possessed of what Ogden called "the spirit of enterprise which seems to be inherent in the Anglo-American race, and which rejoices to meet and overcome every kind of difficulty."

Jed Smith was in the Far West a scant eight years before Comanche lances stabbed the life out of him on the Cimarron River in 1831. But "Old Smith" (thirty-two at his death) was the first Anglo to reach California from the east, the first to cross the Sierra Nevada and Siskiyou Mountains, and the first to explore the Great Basin. He made the first effective discovery of South Pass. He helped Ogden and Frémont lay to rest the mythical Buenaventura, Timpanogos, and Los Mongos rivers.

Smith was an authentic hero, a leader of genuine character, and, like Ogden, a prodigious pedestrian. He was an Argus-eyed observer and possessed the curiosity of a Meriwether Lewis about terrain, Indians, flora, and fauna. Perhaps it was his keenness of observation

81

which led Alexander Ross to size him up as another secret U.S. Government snooper, like Captain Benjamin Bonneville and Lieutenant William A. Slacum. Writing of his lost Iroquois, Ross said: "With these vagabonds arrived seven American trappers from the Big Horn River, but whom I rather take to be spies than trappers."

An unidentified eulogizer paid tribute to the great explorer, geographer, and cartographer in the June 1832 issue of the *Illinois Monthly Magazine*. The anonymous obituarist recalled words of Jed's which would have served him well as an epitaph, had his bones ever been found: "I started into the mountains with the determination of becoming a first-rate hunter, of making myself thoroughly acquainted with the character and habits of the Indians, of tracing out the sources of the Columbia River and following it to its mouth, and of making the whole profitable to me, and I have perfectly succeeded."

The New York-born Smith was one of the young men who answered William H. Ashley's 1822 St. Louis ad for trappers. Ashley and his partner, Andrew Henry, could not compete with the Hudson's Bay Company, head-on. But they hit upon innovations which made competition possible. They chose free trappers rather than employees for their far-ranging forays, and they supplied them neither in St. Louis or at expensive forts maintained in the Far West. Instead, they invented the rendezvous.

The Rocky Mountain rendezvous, 1825–1839, has often been sung in American history and legend, but its chroniclers have not yet done it justice. In terms of color and drama, it is to America what gladiatorial combats were to Rome or joustings to medieval England. It deserves a Dante, a Chaucer, at least a Daumier. The rendezvous was a barbaric trade fair, as exotic as a Stamboul bazaar, where painted savages and atavistic trappers of almost equal barbarity mingled to barter pelts for new outfits. There was usually enough company credit for a couple of weeks of drunkenness and debauch before the hunts were resumed.

The rendezvous was like a gathering of the clans crossed with a French-Canadian *regale* and just a touch of a Roman orgy. Mountain men who had been abstemious (involuntarily) for months now steeped themselves in popskull rum or whiskey between amorous bouts with lissome young Shoshone girls encamped at the great meeting-place. The gathering had elements of the circus and California rodeo with races, feats of horsemanship and enough showoff marksmanship (including the blasting of whiskey cups off each other's heads with Hawken rifles) to please a *Schutzverein*.

The Siskiyou Trail was controlled by Forts Vancouver and Umpqua (and later Sutter's Fort), so the rendezvous was never introduced to it. But the American interlopers in the Company's beaver pasture were *all* trained by it and the Britons found its products, Jed Smith, Ewing Young, et al., very professional mountain men.

Smith demonstrated his courage early, in the Rockies, and his ability, as well. Alex Ross described him in 1824 as a shrewd and very intelligent fellow and the leading man among the trespassing American trappers near Flathead Post. Ogden's clerk, William Kittson, was not so flattering. He branded Jed as a "sly, cunning, Yankee."

By the time he was twenty-seven, Smith had "arrived" in the fur business. He was a partner in the firm of Smith, Jackson, and Sublette which succeeded Ashley and Henry's company in July 1826. " 'Diah" hoped to open up new beaver grounds to the south and west of Great Salt Lake. The Bible-toting (and quoting) mountain man later insisted that he had not meant to go all the way to California but had found himself in the middle of the Colorado Desert when it was too late to turn back and had pushed on to the Pacific to survive. But Smith, phrenologically speaking, had a "bump of curiosity the size of a goose egg." And he later confessed: "I started . . . for the purpose of exploring the country southwestward, which was entirely unknown to me and of which I could collect no satisfactory information from the Indians who inhabit this country on its northeast borders." Like Ogden, he was also intrigued by the Buenaventura of the imaginative map makers. These creative cartographers, descendants of medieval chart makers long on sea monsters and unnamed islands, gave their minds the loosest rein in order to fill in ugly blank spaces on their maps.

On August 15, 1826, Smith treated his seventeen men to rum in the traditional *regale* or farewell party—then, next morning, casually led them out on his great South West Expedition. As Bernard De Voto observed, Smith would set forth across an unmapped wilderness with the aplomb of a farmer strolling down to his barn. He was the antithesis of the "typical" mountain man, who was likely to be as brutal, debauched, and profane as he was hardy and courageous. The ex-Ohioan was a devout, Bible-perusing Methodist teetotaler. He neither smoke nor drank unless spirits or "bacca" were necessary in the transactions of Indian diplomacy. He was apparently as celibate as St. Simon Stylites himself, inviting no squaw of record, however comely and willing, to warm his "buffler" robes. He was quite literate and, like Ogden, blessed with an inquiring mind.

Smith rode to Utah Lake from Cache Valley, thence to the Virgin River—supposedly named by the Spaniards for the Virgen María but, just possibly, for one of Jed's trappers, Tom Virgin (who must have suffered an awful lot of ribbing from his bawdy pards). The Mojaves who met Smith were more curious than belligerent, and he led his men safely across the Colorado, the first Americans ever to reach California overland. From the Needles area he pushed across the Mojave Desert to reach the capricious Mojave River, which he named Inconstant River, then clambered over the San Bernardino Mountains to reach Mission San Gabriel on November 27, 1826.

Jovial, fat Father José Bernardino Sánchez made the gringos welcome with wine and fresh beef. Smith's clerk, Harrison Rogers, described the padre as a fine man, very much of a gentleman, and Smith named the whole northern Sierra Nevada Mount Joseph for him. Jedediah went to San Diego to call on Governor José María Echeandía, who had chosen this place of residence because its climate was warmer than the capital, Monterey, and because (it was whispered) of the warmth of his passion for a San Diegueña named Josefa Carrillo.

Like most governors of Mexican California, Echeandía, who towered over six-footer Smith, was skilled at temporizing. When Smith begged permission to continue his march northward to the Columbia through Alta California, Echeandía hemmed and hawed and hemmed again. He did not like the idea, though the trespasser carried a license from General William Clark, Superintendent of Indian Affairs in St. Louis, to establish a trading post, Fort Defiance or Fort Defence, on the Buenaventura (presumably, on a portion of it in Oregon, not Mexican California). Also, the passports which *"Smit"* carried were American, not Mexican, and for fifty-seven men, whereas he had only sixteen with him.

Smith put Echeandía down as "much of a gentleman, but very suspicious." Only when Jed won new friends among Yankee shipmasters in California waters, who signed a document attesting to his good character, did the governor give up waiting for a word of guidance from Mexico City. Although he still thought Smith to be more *espía* (spy) than *pescador* (fisher) of furs Echeandía issued him a permit to leave the province via Russian Bodega and then via the desert route by which he had arrived.

The Bostonian sea captains were pleased to help Smith. They were very proud of their fellow American's exploit in crossing the impossible, "impassable," mountains and deserts to reach California.

Captain William H. Cunningham of the *Courier* wrote a letter home which was reprinted in the *Missouri Republican*. In it he asked rhetorically: "Does it not seem incredible that a party of fourteen [*sic*] men, depending entirely upon their rifles and traps for subsistence, will explore this vast continent and call themselves happy when they can obtain the tail of a beaver to dine upon?" Britons as well as Yankees in port were impressed by Smith's exploit, though James Wolfe, aboard *H.M.S. Blossom* in San Francisco Bay in November 1827, remarked on Jed's sangfroid: "Mr. Smith seems to think very lightly of his trip across the continent."

Jedediah Smith led his expeditionaries out of San Gabriel on January 18, 1827. He was curious about the unexplored coast north of the Russian settlements and thought that there ought to be plenty of beaver there as well as along the Oregon coast. Unaware that the Siskiyou Mountains pushed into the sea, he believed that there was an easy shoreline route to the Columbia, too. Echeandía insisted that he and his beaver "fishers" bypass all settlements as he exited from the province; so, equipped with sixty-eight fresh horses (some too-fresh, wild *broncos*, in fact) he rode to the Victorville area of the Mojave River in a feint, then took a dogleg course to avoid the desert. He wished first to trap Lake Chintache (Tulare Lake) in the San Joaquin Valley, where few Mexicans and no *yanquís* had ever ventured.

Smith had heard rumors of great numbers of beaver congregating at the huge lake or slough in the *tulares* or bulrush swamps. Californians did not bother to trap beaver, largely because there was no market for their furs. He hoped for a good spring hunt before the shedding season of summer should ruin the animals' pelts. Dropping down from the Tehachapi Mountains to a *laguna* (which he took to be Chintache, but was really the combined sumps of Lakes Kern and Buenaventura in a very wet year), he crossed the Kern River near modern Bakersfield. Making his way to the true Tulare Lake, he found trapping difficult because the surrounding terrain was so drowned by floodwaters. He bade the impossible area *adiós*.

Smith then moved to the Kings River, El Río de los Santos Reyes, usually considered in later years to mark the very end of the Siskiyou Trail. He named the stream Wim-mul-che for a band of Indians of the Yokuts nation. They seemed to thrive on a diet of fish, skunks, worms, seeds, acorns, grass (probably clover), grasshoppers, caterpillars, the seeds of flags or cattails, and the larvae of yellowjackets. They had domesticated the dog, but raised him for grub, not companionship. Their artifacts were modest in quality, except for their six-foot long *balsas,* or reed canoes, and their fine bows. These could send an arrow in a quarter-mile arc through the air.

North of the Kings, which flowed into Fresno Slough and then into the San Joaquin River, Smith found the country growing more fertile and attractive. The streams were increasingly dressed with fringes of oaks and sycamores. He continued on to the San Joaquin at its great bend near present-day Modesto. Beaver were scarce, but deer, elk, and "goats" or *cabris*—antelope—were abundant. Across the San Joaquin, Merced, and Tuolumne rivers Smith moved his party. They explored and trapped the Appelaminy, as Smith called the Stanislaus, and the Calaveras, which he called the "Mackalumbry." Then, confusingly, he called the true Mokelumne the Rock River; the Cosumnes he dubbed Indian River. Finally, Smith reached the stream to be named for him and his men, El Río de los Americanos—the American River. He called it Wild River.

Surprised that California beaver did not care for height, unlike their Rockies kin, and seldom lived above a thousand feet of elevation, Smith learned fast. He trapped only the valley floor and the lower reaches of the Sacramento's tributaries. Miwoks, perhaps of the Mokelumne band, broke some traps and attacked the party. This little brush jolted Smith out of his dangerous complacency. Peace was quickly restored when, five times, his long rifles spoke and five warriors fell. Only a few months earlier, the Cosumnes Indians had killed a score of Mission Indians and repulsed a Mexican punitive force. Now, reported Lieutenant Ignacio Martínez to Governor Echeandía, May 21, 1827, the Mokelumnes were quickly "appeased" by the American *rifleros,* or riflemen, and became their friends.

Before striking out for the Columbia, Smith decided to attend the annual rendezvous near Bear Lake, Utah. This side trip was a march of seven hundred miles across snowy American alps and blistering New World sahara. Late in April, he left most of his men camped between modern Folsom and Sacramento and tried to cross the Sierra by way of the American River canyon. Deep snow in the High Sierra turned him back after he lost five horses. He then retreated down to the Stanislaus near its junction with the San Joaquin and established a base camp and supply cache there. This was the equivalent of the Fort Defiance which General Clark had authorized him to build, and the cache a place of safekeeping for his 1500 pounds of furs.

When Smith set out again for Utah, he took only Robert Evans and Silas Gobel, and he left the company under Rogers's command. He started up the North Fork of the Stanislaus on May 20, 1827, reached Hermit Valley at the head of the Mokelumne, and crossed the summit by 8700-foot Ebbetts Pass, losing only two horses and a mule. After twenty days of hellish travel across the Nevada desert, the three men made it to Skull Valley. Though Evans gave out, Jed got him and Gobel safely to rendezvous at Bear Lake. Smith laconically recalled: "My arrival caused considerable bustle in camp, for myself and party had been given up for lost." A small cannon, dragged all the way from St. Louis, was loaded and fired in a salute to the strong-legged mountain man.

After penning a note to General Clark to complain of Echeandía's treatment, Smith attended to business with Jackson and Sublette, mentioning the $9000 worth of pelts he had in his Stanislaus River cache.

Smith was no man to waste time. Having arrived the day after the Glorious Fourth, he was on his way back to his California camp on the morning after Bastille Day. Evans balked at recrossing Hell, but sixteen adventurous fellows (intrigued by Smith's description of winterless coastal California) followed him out. They were the usual mixed bag—Americans like Gobel and Henry (Boatswain) Brown, French-Canadians, a "Spaniard" or Mexican, Gregorio Ortega, a Black or mulatto, Polite (Paulet?) Labross, and two Indian women. One of the Yanks was John Turner, destined to play a considerable role in the history of the Siskiyou Trail.

Jed Smith had promised Harrison Rogers that he would return to the Stanislaus camp, of course, but he had other reasons for hurrying west. "Of course, I expected to find beaver, which with us hunters, is our primary object, but I was also led on by the love of novelty common to all, which is much increased by the pursuit of its gratification." In other words, he wanted to see some new country—northernmost California and Oregon.

Smith's route ran from the Bear, Weber, and Provo rivers to Utah Lake and his old trail near the Virgin River to reach the Colorado. En route he heard rumors of another trapping party and even saw signs of its passing; this was Ewing Young's company.

On the Colorado on August 18, 1827, Smith made the first of three disastrous mistakes of his lifetime. (Trapper George Yount blamed all three of Smith's debacles on sheer carelessness.) His laudable unwillingness to accept the frontiersmen's dictum—that the only good Indian was a dead Indian—betrayed him. He was lulled into a false sense of security by the peacefulness of the Mojaves during his earlier visit. He did not know that, after that visit, the Mojaves had been battered in an affray with Ewing Young's trapping party. A chief and sixteen braves were killed by the mysterious "Spaniards and Americans" of whom Smith had heard on the trail.

As Smith and his compatriots began to cross the wide Colorado on rafts which his men had constructed with the help of the Mojaves, the latter struck. Pretending to help with the ferrying of men and goods, they treacherously fell upon the whites still on the east bank. According to Jonathan (José Joaquín) Warner, they also swam up to the last raft, clambered aboard and butchered its complement. All ten men on the east shore were killed as Smith watched, helplessly, from the far bank. Among the bloody corpses on the river bank lay Gobel's. The Indians spared only the two women, whom they took prisoner.

Smith did not know the real cause of the attack, vengeance for the Mojave defeat by Ewing Young, so he blamed the *californios*. Writing General Clark, later, he said: "The Governor had instructed the Muchaba [Mojave] not to let any more Americans pass through the country on any conditions, whatever." Of course, the Mojaves did not take orders from the weak California government, and, being a warrior nation, they needed no excuses to make war, in any case. Revenge and booty were sufficient for the Mojaves.

Half a thousand Mojaves rushed across the river to finish off Smith and the eight other survivors of the ambuscade. Quickly, he spread out his goods on a sandbar in hopes the Indians' greed for spoils of war would delay an attack. The ruse did not really work, but he had time to fall back and fort up in a clump of cottonwoods. He had his men clear a space behind a natural breastwork of fallen limbs, then had them make rude lances by lashing their butcher knives to cottonwood poles. Smith had only five rifles. He gave orders that not more than three were to be fired in a volley, then waited the charge of the horde of warriors.

When the attack came, two of his men fired and brought down two Mojaves. Curiously, this was enough to drive the others off like frightened sheep. Smith wrote: "We were released from the apprehension of immediate death." He later described to Ogden his next actions: "Any attempt at pursuit [by us] under such circumstances had been in vain. Such was the situation in which I found myself, with property to the value of ten thousand dollars, and rather than the villains who had so deeply injured me should reap any benefit from it, I had the whole thrown in the river. We then made a raft and crossed over, when we found the bodies of my unfortunate men so mutilated as to be scarcely recognizable. We consigned them also to the keeping of the deep, for as you well know, not even the dead are respected by the wild tribes of these parts."

When it was nearly dark, Smith led his men out on the desert without guide, horses, or rations beyond fifteen pounds of dried meat. He placed his trust in his memory and instinct and neither deserted him in his hour of need. He crossed the desert in less than ten days, whereas it had taken him sixteen days on the prior march. This time, he found the "Gap of the Mountains" (Cajon Pass) and threw himself on the unfailing kindness of Mission San Gabriel. Tom Virgin was so battered by a Mojave war club that Smith left him at Rancho San Bernardino. He let Isaac Galbraith go, too, since the free trapper was also wounded; the Herculean Maine-man had been struck in the head by a musket ball. But the combination of a powder-pinching warrior (and, thus, a spent ball) and the resistance of a paper packet of vermilion inside his hat band caused the lead slug to bounce off his skull without dashing his brains out.

Once he was rested, Smith hurried north to his base camp on September 18, 1827. He rejoined his eleven comrades there and ended his long and disastrous detour within two days of the time limit he had set for his return. It was a briefly joyous reunion swiftly damped by sadness as he informed his men of the Mojave ambush. He recalled: "I was there by the time appointed but instead of bringing them the expected supplies, I brought them intelligence of misfortune."

Smith was pleased to find the camp safe. He learned from his clerk, Rogers, that both Indians and Mexican soldiery had visited it, without any trouble arising.

The fact that the Mexican military had not bothered Rogers led Smith to blithely pay a call on Mission San José to explain his continuing presence. He was ill prepared for the hostile reception there. Father Narciso Durán was as inhospitable as Sánchez had been kind. Smith was placed under house arrest—not close confinement, but restricted to "a dirty hovel which they called a guard house," in his own words.

While the American was moved under a military escort from San José to Monterey and its "calliboose" (*calabozo,* or jail), the governor soaked up all rumors about Smith. The latter was said to have claimed land along the San Joaquin and to have encouraged Christian Indians to desert the missions for the back country. Echeandía, understandably nonplussed by the return of Smith and his *norteamericanos,* complained: "It is not possible to trust them further." For his part, Smith growled: "It seemed as if this man was placed in power to perplex me and those over whom he was called to govern."

Eventually, the Mexicans' chief informer was flogged for his lies. Smith was not sent to Mexico (at his own expense!), as the governor had planned. Once again, the Yankee shipmasters came to Jedediah's aid. They signed a bond for him and Echeandía granted him permission to leave California for "the Salt Lake deposit" via Mission San José, Carquinez Straits, and Bodega. He was not to delay on the way, or move toward the coast, make any hostile excursions or wander anywhere south of 42° without a U.S. or Mexican passport.

On November 15, 1827, Smith sold 1568 pounds of beaver to the captain of the *Franklin,* which was lying in San Francisco Bay, for $3920, plus another $20 or so for otter skins. That day, Echeandía gave him his passport for seventeen men, one hundred mules, and 150 horses, mainly in order to get rid of him as a problem. Smith wrote: "I think he did not wish to have my party try their rifles on his soldiers, for there were some terrible stories in circulation about the shooting of my men. It was said that they were sure of their mark at any distance." Isaac Galbraith, now recovered from his concussion, had, indeed, amused himself by shooting the heads off of little *chenates,* or blackbirds, at twenty paces, and James Wolfe of *H.M.S. Blossom* wrote of Smith's *yanquís*: "Each individual is necessarily a good shot with his rifle, performing—as we are told—the feat of William Tell frequently, for pastime."

Smith moved to Monterey from the Presidio (Fort) of San Francisco to join Rogers and his men. He went to San José and told Father Durán that he needed more grass for his herd, moved his company to the Mission's San Lorenzo sheep ranch (near modern Oakland), and then slipped away to the San Joaquin Valley. He rode to the Old River branch of the San Joaquin, calling it the Pescador River, then swam his stock across the Peticutsy (San Joaquin) on January 3, 1828, and floated his property over on a crazy raft of poles and reeds tied together. Though many of his horses were wild mustangs and easily spooked, he did not lose a single head. This was because he built a corral on the river bank and drove a small band at a time into the pen, then into the river. He had paid $10 a head, expected to get $50 each at rendezvous, and hoped to begin a horse trade between California and the Rockies as a by-product of the fur trade.

With the wide San Joaquin now an effective moat between himself and Echeandía, Smith loosed a sigh of relief. He wrote in his journal: "Having been so long absent from the business of trapping and so much perplexed and harassed by the folly of men in power, I returned to the woods, the river, the prairies, the camp and the game with a feeling somewhat like that of a prisoner escaped from his dungeon and his chains."

Smith next trapped the French Camp area of the San Joaquin. While some of his men searched for beaver sign, he had others build elkskin canoes or bullboats to insure that his forty-seven traps would do the most damage. His little fleet worked. In just two days, his nine trappers caught forty-five beaver though the lowlands were inundated. The low, flaggy ground was so covered with water that it was impossible to go to the river on foot for several miles above and below his French Camp bivouac. But the reedy and rushy banks of pools continued to yield some beaver and when Smith made his count he found that he had sixty-one skins. Good weather and friendly Appelaminy Indians further cheered him and his first two canoes returned with thirty-three pelts. Then Rogers brought in four elk and trappers James Reed and Louis Pombert paddled up with twenty-two pelts in their canoe.

Very pleased with French Camp, Smith sent Reed and Pombert back out with orders to meet him in eight days at the Mokelumne. Since his horses had eaten off all the grass around camp, he pulled stakes and lit out from Lone Tree Creek or French Camp Creek for the boggy Calaveras. He crossed it with his men on felled trees while the animals were made to swim for it from a riverside corral. It took all day to make the crossing and the far bank was so swampy from a week of sheeting, sluicing rains that Smith had to set his men to making a corduroy road in order to extricate his laden animals.

Twice, Smith and his men shot huge grizzlies but could not bring them down. Many Indians were in the area, but they were as meek as the so-called "white bears" were bellicose. A few redmen ran off, but none showed hostility, only fear. Even though the countryside was rolling, the ground was so spongy that Smith's horses sank almost to their knees at every step during downpours. By January 22, Smith was out of provisions but managed to kill some deer and buy salmon, fifteen to twenty pounders, from the Indians with tobacco. He finally abandoned his plan to visit Bodega and Fort Ross when two local chiefs, who had offered to serve as guides, backed out.

By and large, Smith found that he got along well with the Indians, who were half civilized—that is, they wore Spanish blankets (*serapes*) and shirts and, to his surprise, showed little disposition to theft. The one naked fellow who failed to return a loaned blanket proved the exception to the rule. The Indians lived in permanent lodges of grass and mats, eating acorn mush and a bread resembling the persimmon bread which Smith associated with the Indians of the lower Mississippi.

Slogging on through the drowned countryside to the Mokelumne, Smith waited for Reed and Pombert, drying and stretching skins as he waited. Curiously, although the rain continued the Mokelumne began to fall. Many Indians visited him, including the hostiles of the previous summer. To keep the peace Smith gave them presents of sugar and tobacco.

Smith began to fear the worst as Reed and Pombert's canoe failed to appear. He left notes for them and personally searched all the way to the Sacramento River with Abraham La Plant and an Indian who spoke a little Spanish. He sent a party of local Indians to hunt for the missing men. Only on February 9 did the true situation dawn on Smith. He made a search of the camp and found that the two men had taken all of their possessions with them. Belatedly, Smith realized that he had been deserted. His belief was confirmed when Indians reported the trappers far up the Sacramento. The men constituted a small loss; Reed was a troublemaker whom Smith had twice had to flog, and Pombert was a drifter who had joined him as casually as he had left. Good riddance. But they had taken eleven of the traps, leaving him with only a dwindling supply of traps. And, doubtless, they were taking *beaucoup* beaver with them, too.

On February 12, Smith camped on the east bank of the Sacramento. He found the "Buenaventura" here to be three hundred yards wide but turbid and seemingly slow-moving. Floundering alternately in liquid mud and water standing two or three feet deep, his men herded the "cavallard" (*caballada,* "horse herd") north along the shore, timbered with cottonwoods, ash, sycamores, elm, and a few oaks. An old chief, acting as a guide, left him and Smith gathered that he was entering an area claimed by a tribe of more warlike mood. Trapper A. Lazarus not only had a trap stolen but found himself surrounded by threatening Indians. In the nick of time, he was rescued by some of his friends. They drove the redmen away and would have punished them but for the miry ground which restricted their movements.

The day after the near-fight, Smith soliloquized: "The river was quite rapid and the rushing of the water brought fresh to my remembrance the cascades of Mt. Joseph and the unpleasant times I had passed there when surrounded by the snow, which continued falling. My horses freezing, my men discouraged, and our utmost exertion necessary to keep from freezing to death, I then thought of the vanity of riches and of all those objects that lead men in the perilous paths of adventure. It seems that in times like those, men return to reason and make the true estimate of things. They throw off the gaudy baubles of ambition and embrace the solid comforts of domestic life. But a few days of rest makes the sailor forget the storm and embark again on the perilous ocean and I supposed that, like him, I would soon be weary of rest."

Washington's Birthday saw the trappers crossing the American River, probably near modern Folsom. They swam the horses and ferried their goods in a skin canoe. It was difficult to tell where river stopped and flood plain began, so swamped was the area. The Sacramento Valley was becoming one vast slough, leading Smith to write: "So muddy that the horses could not travel. . . . I hardly know what course to pursue, for it is impossible to travel north and useless to travel up Wild River, on which I am camped, for there was no beaver in that direction." Already, Smith knew that all the bait in the world would not bring beaver to High Sierra traps.

When the weather cleared for a spell, Jedediah hurried his men out in the general direction of Oregon. At one point, he found hewn logs where whites should never have been before. He used them for a raft, speculating that that was the purpose for which they were originally cut. Free trapper John Turner ran into trouble with the Indians on the American River. To Smith's distress, he and Toussaint Maréchal had to kill a native and wound another. As ever, the trader was trying to keep peace with the Indians. He scolded the men and punished them by prohibiting them from trapping for a time and assigning them the most menial tasks around camp. He commented: "I was extremely sorry for the occurrence and reprimanded them severely for their impolitic conduct."

The run of bad luck continued. Near the junction of the American and Sacramento rivers, the inhabitants fled a village as the whites approached. All but one fled; a young girl actually dropped dead, apparently from shock. The devout Smith was horrified by the bizarre happening. He pondered: "Can it be possible that we who call ourselves Christians are such frightful objects as to scare poor savages to death?" Tenderly, he covered the girl's form with a blanket and left gifts on the ground beside her, to convince her people that he had meant them no harm and particularly regretted her death.

Smith led his men toward the Feather, which he called the Yaloo (i.e., Yolo) River, traversing an aquatic countryside of so many ponds, mires, lakes, and sloughs that progress was almost impossible at times. But he could not really complain; he negotiated Bear River, which he called Brush Creek, safely; his men were bringing in three or four beaver every day, as regularly as clockwork; and he and his hunters were killing the company's fill of deer and elk.

Nor were his men fussy about what they ate. When they killed a brown bear and feasted on it, he wrote: "Yes, I repeat it, *feasting,* for the hunter of the Buenaventura Valley at the distance of 2,000 miles from his home may enjoy and be thought thankful for such blessings as heaven may throw in his way." Shortly, heaven overdid it. In an area of lodges which reminded Smith of Pawnee homes, a curious form of manna was delivered from on high. A grizzly bear was the prize this time—but one with a strong aversion to cooking pots. The beast cruelly mauled and bit Rogers, even though the clerk put a rifle ball through its body. Rogers's companion, John Hanna, then put another ball into its breast. The gunshot only seemed to annoy the bear, which returned to claw Rogers some more. Hanna ran to camp for help and Smith carried his friend to safety. He washed Rogers's painful wounds with cold water and plastered them with the only "medicinals" he had, soap and sugar.

So painfully wounded was Rogers that he could not be moved. Smith laid over a week while the "petit booshway" mended somewhat in a camp below the junction of the Feather and Yuba rivers. He sent out men to plant the remaining twenty-eight traps, while he strolled about, making friends among the Indians. The largest *ranchería* which he visited contained about fifty lodges. He found the natives to be without civilized goods and generally naked, though the women wore a fringe of bark or of flags around their hips for modesty's sake. A few wore dresses of net work and some of the men had feather robes. The menfolk smoked wooden pipes and manned log rafts, on one of which Smith crossed the river. He traded meat, beads, and pieces of flannel for feather headdresses, fishing nets, and dishes. Since the latter were obviously of great value to the redmen, he returned them after examining them with exaggerated interest and appreciation. Smith's *pescadores* made a fine catch in the meantime, taking twenty beaver in one day, as compared to earlier good catches of from eight to fourteen pelts. When the Americans left, the Indians were so sorry to see them go that they broke into what passed for weeping among that stoical people.

Smith explored up the Feather River and took the east fork, the Yuba River, which he called the Hen Neet. Crossing it, he advanced ten to twelve miles up its north bank to Honcut Creek (his Red Bank Creek), above its forks. He found little beaver sign. The Feather was, by now, so unproductive he moved the traps to the Yuba.

The advancing season began to dry out the Sacramento Valley and Smith realized that it was, betwixt floods, a firm and dry country quite fit for cultivation. He again made friends with the Indians. They were wary but less miserable-looking than those from Deer Creek south. They were also skilled in trapping geese and brant in nets. When Smith's hunters fired on some sitting honkers without effect, they learned how skillful the Indians were as decoy makers, too. Nevertheless, Smith could not give Sacramento folk a very high rating. He found them inferior to the beaver in building homes for themselves and called them, in fact, "the lowest intermediate link between man and brute creation." The locals had a particularly absurd and disconcerting idiosyncracy: They thought that they could talk to the whites' horses and chatted as much, orally and in sign language, with the dumb beasts as with the men of the South West Expedition.

Smith was genuinely puzzled as to why such a bounteous land did nothing to expand the Indians' creative energies. He investigated some baskets and found them loaded with acorns, pea vines, and a few fish and fowl. He mused: "They live in a country where the soil is good and the climate pleasant with the exception of two or three months in the winter, when there is too much rain. There is seldom any frost and I have seen snow but once in the Valley of the Buenaventura." At least, he found the Indians to be as honest and peaceable in their dispositions as they were numerous: "If missionaries could be useful in civilizing and christianizing any Indians in the world, their efforts should be turned towards this valley."

It was well for Smith that the redmen were friendly. Their skill with bow and arrows was considerable. When hunters cut up a grizzly they had killed, they found an arrowhead driven so deeply into its chest that there was a three-inch stub of the arrow still attached to the point, and all of it healed over. Smith gave all of the entrails and some of the meat to the Indians. They were soon "puffed up like bladders." He was pleased that the Sacramento's mosquitoes were more troublesome than its Indians.

Jed Smith guessed that the presence of so many "grisly" bears indicated a superfluity of game animals as the valley drained off its floodwater. There were elk, deer, antelope, wolves (more likely coyotes), beaver, otter, raccoons, swans, geese, ducks, brant, loons, cranes, and herons, plus the ubiquitous scavengers—the crows, ravens, magpies, and turkey vultures or buzzards.

With Harrison Rogers somewhat recovered from his mauling by March 26, Smith left the Feather via a double-sandbar ford which made swimming easy for the horses. He ferried the goods in a hide canoe, at a point about five miles northeast of modern Biggs, then reached the Sacramento via Butte Creek. He found the river two hundred yards wide, quite deep and rushing along. Here, near today's Jacinto, the Sacramento was lined with sycamores, cottonwoods, oaks —and beaver lodges! His men took twenty beaver in just twenty-eight traps set. Small wonder Smith exclaimed: "I consider it great trapping!"

Smith forded and examined Deer Creek, calling it Black Sand Creek, and found Mill Creek so deep and fast that he had to go up it for three miles to find a safe ford. On April 7, nearby, Jed had another encounter with *Ursus horribilis*. With several men, he followed a wounded grizzly into a thicket—on foot because it was too dense to admit a man on horseback. Recalled Jedediah: "As we advanced, I saw one and shot him in the head, when he immediately fell—apparently dead. I went in to bring him out without loading my gun and when I arrived within four yards of the place where the bear lay, the man that was following me close behind spoke and said, 'He is alive!' I told him in answer that he was certainly dead, and [I] was observing the one I had shot so intently that I did not see one that lay close by his side, which was the one the man behind me had reference to. At that moment, the bear sprang towards us with open mouth, making no pleasant noise. Fortunately, the thicket was close on the bank of the creek [which Jed, shortly—and naturally—dubbed Grizzly Bear Creek] and, the second spring, I plunged head foremost into the water. The bear ran over the man next to me and made a furious rush at the third man, Joseph Lapoint. But Lapoint had, by good fortune, a bayonet fixed on his gun and, as the bear came in, he gave him a severe wound in the neck which induced him to change his course and run into another thicket close at hand. We followed him there and found another in company with him. One of them we killed and the other went off, badly wounded.

"I then went on horseback with two men to look for another that was wounded. I rode up close to the thicket in which I supposed him to be and rode round it several times, halloeing but without making any discovery. I rode up for a last look when the bear sprang for the horse. He was so close that the horse could not be got under way before he caught him by the tail. The horse being strong and much frightened, exerted himself so powerfully that he gave the bear no opportunity to close upon him and actually drew him 40 or 50 yards before he relinquished his hold. The bear did not continue his pursuit but went off, and [I] was quite glad to get rid of his company on any terms, and returned to camp to feast on the spoils and talk of the incidents of our eventful hunt."

Smith went up his Grizzly Bear Creek to the foot of the first small range of Sierra foothills. From this viewpoint, he noticed that the Sierra, or Mount Joseph, looked lower than further south, and with less snow on its summit.

Continuing up the Sacramento River, Smith decided (even before reaching Iron Canyon) to give it up as a route to Oregon: "The mountain beyond appeared too high to cross at that season of the year, or perhaps at any season. Believing it impossible to travel up the river, I turned back into the valley and encamped on the river with the intention of crossing." To the west, the Coast Range was dusty with snow but less rugged and high than the Shasta mountains due north. Smith misjudged the difficulty of the Sacramento canyon (though it would not prove an easy stretch of the Siskiyou Trail) and, at the same time, underestimated the difficulty of crossing to the coast. He wrote: "Far off to the north, very high peaks of the mountain were seen covered with snow."

On April 11, Smith crossed to the Sacramento's west bank just above Red Bluff. He lost only a colt as he swam his herd. Abandoning the future Siskiyou Trail, he aimed for a gap in the coastal mountains, counting (like Ogden and McLeod) on finding a surfside trail northward to the Columbia River. Hardly had he left the route of today's Interstate 5 and Highway 99 for Highway 36 when he spied little Indian children darting into holes, disappearing like young wolves or prairie dogs after the briefest of views of the strangers. It was not a reassuring sign. Sure enough, on April 15 he found a fresh arrow projecting from the neck of one of his horses. Smith barely had time to shout an alarm before the air was full of flying shafts. The crack of the Hawken rifles brought down three of the dozen leading attackers. They managed to crawl off, but the other rabbitskin-robed root diggers gave up the battle. Still, Smith had to abandon a horse and mule out of a total of eleven animals wounded.

From increasingly rugged ridges timbered with oaks and "bastard cedars" (redwoods?), Indians harassed the company despite Smith's peace signs. When two Indians were shot in a skirmish, he thought it best to pen up his animals at night under a guard. But he dismissed the watch at midnight, figuring (correctly) that the cold air draining down the mountain slopes so chilled and benumbed the Indians that it was all they could do to huddle together for warmth. They would be in no mood to go raiding during the wee hours.

Advances were only six to twelve miles a day as Smith crossed the divide and reached the Trinity River. There, in Hay Fork Valley, he and Arthur Black were attacked by a dozen Indians on April 19, 1828. Smith ordered four horses caught and led a spirited, if impromptu, cavalry charge that scattered all of the attackers save two, who fell kicking in the dust. "After this," wrote Jed, "they troubled us no more." His assumption was premature. They continued their harassment and now the weather also turned against the whites. Smith lamented: "My horses freezing, my men discouraged, and our utmost exertion necessary to keep from freezing to death."

Horses grew lame and the terrain slanted so precipitously that a good day's march was a couple of miles. It seemed to make little difference if he chose canyon or ridge, the going was very rough everywhere: "I had flattered myself that I was nearly over the bad traveling. But I find this day of the old kind. . . . I made an attempt to go down and travel along its [the Klamath River's] banks, but I did not succeed and was obliged to wind about among the hills and mountains."

One day, though the men labored until nightfall, they advanced just two miles and two horses were dashed to pieces in falls from cliffs. Other animals were mangled in lesser falls and Smith had to leave packs in a ravine all night, under guard, when the animals simply could not proceed with them. Luckily, the Indians were—temporarily—friendly until May 19, the day that Smith spied the ocean from a little prairie near modern Orick. Rogers and Virgin, ahead on scout, had to flee an Indian attack. And then they reported that traveling on the beach would be impossible except at low tides. There was no coastal shelf. The mountains pitched abruptly into the sea.

Smith turned inland again, slowly hazing his three hundred animals over densely timbered, brushy mountains lost in fog and rain. He recalled: "My men were almost as weak as the horses, for the poor venison of the country contained little nourishment." About the only thing which Jed found admirable about the north coast of California was its stands of *Sequoia sempervirens,* or redwoods: "Some of the cedars were the noblest trees I had ever seen, being 12 or 15 feet in diameter, tall, straight, and handsome."

June opened badly for Smith; he was kicked by a mule and hurt pretty badly. But on the third he noticed both beaver and tide in the lower Klamath, incongruous but encouraging signs. And *Castor* was supposed to avoid salt water! Before he could puzzle this out, Peter Ranne, his Black trapper, got into a shooting scrape with Indians. Recorded Smith: "As he was not a good marksman, I presume he did them no hurt."

On June 19 Jed swam Smith River, named for him, on horseback. He was pleased to see beaver sign on the stream and camped, next day, almost on the present Oregon line, in a little prairie of good grass, many deer, and—alas!—mosquitoes, horseflies, and gnats. But the worst of the traveling seemed to be behind them. Smith's last day in California, forever, was on June 23, 1828. His last camp was near Castle Rock; his final fording of a California stream was his wading of Castle Rock Creek.

On the Chetco River, Jedediah found that the natives dug animal traps like those on Pit River. Some horsemen fell into these elk pits, ten to twelve feet deep and much wider at the bottom than at the narrow, camouflaged mouths. They got themselves and their mounts out with considerable difficulty but no serious injuries. If Smith or Rogers ever looked out to sea for a sail, neither chronicler mentioned it. From the Chetco's abandoned villages they marched their men north past Whaleshead Creek over country cut by dark ravines from which Indian bowmen wounded two horses and, presumably, killed another which did not show up. When the men went out to look for lost horses now, they were greeted with howling imprecations and launched arrows by Indians in hiding.

An old Indian trail led the expeditionaries to a camp on Pistol River. Taking to the beach, Smith led them next to the Rogue, where the men had to tear down lodges to construct rafts. June 28 was a bad day, an exhausting one. It started well, for Smith spotted some beaver sign; but in crossing the river he lost between twelve and fifteen animals, bringing the total loss for only a three-day period to twenty-three mules and horses. But he managed to scramble onward, over Humbug Mountain and across Brush Creek again and again. (Lieutenant Rodney Glisan counted the creek crossings of the Indian trail in 1856; there were seventeen fords in four miles by actual count.)

But Smith was lucky again: He lost but one pack mule in a fall over a cliff.

On the Sixes River Smith again saw beaver spoor. Game was scarce, but no one suffered because he had laid in a good supply of jerky. He passed the rocks or "stacks" lying offshore called Los Monges (the Monks) by early navigators and corrupted into Los Mongos by Anglo-Saxon mapmakers, who gave the name to a second-rate Buenaventura.

In camp on the night of July 3, 1828, Jed Smith made his last journal entry at Whiskey Run. (Rogers kept his journal going until July 13.) It was an entry which must have made him apprehensive of trouble. On the Coquille River he "discovered some Indians moving as fast as possible up the river in a canoe. I ran my horse to get above them in order to stop them. When I got opposite to them & they discovered they could not make their escape, they put ashore and, drawing their canoe up the bank, they fell to work with all their might to split it in pieces." The fleeing Indians left behind a ten-year-old slave boy, from the Willamette. The American adopted him and named him Marion.

Independence Day was no day of rest. The mountain men made a difficult nine-mile march to Cape Arago, crossing the bad ravines now called the Seven Devils. Indians came to tell Smith that he was only ten days from "Cata-pos" (Calapooya) on the "Well-hamet" River. This was good news, indeed. The Americans were nearing the home stretch to Fort Vancouver. Their troubles would soon be over.

For several days, camps were made around Coos Bay. Smith traded with one Indian who wore a Hudson's Bay blanket capote— possibly taken from the corpse of the Iroquois, Ignace, killed there on March 27. The very next day, the Coos Indians shot eight of Smith's animals with arrows. Three mules and a horse died of their wounds. Rogers explained: "They tell us that one Indian got mad on account of a trade he made and killed the mules and horses."

Smith bought beaver pelts and the skins of land and sea otter and cubs. He chided the natives for killing his animals, but they said they had not been a party to it. Rogers noted: "Finding them so numerous and the traveling being bad, we thought it advisable to let it pass at present, without notice." Smith got all his animals safely across the wide North Slough, even a badly wounded mule. Rogers watched him. "Capt. Smith swim the mule alongside one of the canoes. He was somewhat of the opinion the Indians had a mind to attack him from there behavior and he crossed over where the swells were running pretty high."

Friendly-appearing Indians welcomed the travelers to a campsite on the south shore of Winchester Bay at the mouth of the Umpqua River. They sold the whites fish and berries before they crossed the river and camped near modern Gardiner. There, one of several Kelawatsets tagging along with the party stole an ax. Reported Rogers: "We were obliged to seize him before we could scare him to make him give it up. Capt. Smith and one of them caught him and put a cord around his neck, and the rest of us stood with our guns ready in case they made resistance. There was about 50 Inds present but did not pretend to resist tying the other."

The camp had been the site of a heap of trouble. Smith hoped that it had all blown over, but he moved camp anyway. On Sunday, July 13, 1828, he was still in the vicinity, but now camped opposite modern Reedsport at the mouth of a north-bank tributary to the Umpqua. Dr. McLoughlin called it Bridge River, and today it is Smith River, but for years it was known as Defeat River. Everyone was heartened by the news from the Chinook-speaking natives, familiar with Fort Vancouver, that from a point only twenty miles upriver there was a good trail to the Willamette. Thus the words of Harrison Rogers—the last he would ever write—"We will have good traveling to the Wilhamet or Multnomah, where the Calipoo Inds. live."

Bastille Day—July 14—1828 was as peaceful as a church social, until Arthur Black had to order a Kelawatset chief to dismount when he brazenly seized one of the horses and began to show off by riding around camp. Black made no threatening moves, but his request that the chief get down was backed up by the rifle he carried loosely in his hand. The Indian, now sullen, dismounted. Unfortunately, the rider had been the very peacemaker who had persuaded the Kelawatset band, the night before, *not* to go to war on the whites for putting a halter around the neck of the ax thief. He was no friend to lose.

Although Smith noticed that the Kelawatsets were gathering in large numbers, he was not alarmed. He had plenty of confidence in his clerk. So he set out to find the road up the Umpqua, taking no precautions other than to remind Rogers not to allow Indians in camp while he was away. He then got in a canoe with John Turner, Richard Leland, and an Indian guide, and pushed off to pass between Goose Island (now Perkins Island) and the north shore, to enter Bridge River.

The usually reliable Rogers was not alert. He let the Kelawatsets enter camp as some men were asleep, others lazing about. A few were eating, still others mending canoes and cleaning rifles. Without warning, the Indians—perhaps one hundred of them—fell on the camp. The surprise was more complete than even the Mojave trap. The Americans did not have a chance. Arthur Black was cleaning his gun when two Indians grappled with him for the weapon, cutting him on both hands with knives. A third rushed at him, to brain him with an ax. He managed to avoid the blow, partially, but the weapon slammed painfully into his back. He let go of the rifle and sprinted for the woods.

Black's last view of the Umpqua campsite was a horrible one. Two Indians were atop Thomas Virgin, on the ground, killing him. Thomas Dawes was floundering in the blood-tinged shallows, but Indians were drawing up on him in a canoe to finish him off. A third gory figure, whom he could not even identify, was lying on the ground, literally being hacked to pieces by Kelawatsets.

Some time later, Smith returned to camp from his reconnaissance. He was unaware of the tragedy, but something made his hackles rise as he neared the beach. Probably it was the uncanny silence of the area. Before he could back-paddle to halt the canoe, or take any other action, an Indian popped up on the river bank and signaled to Smith's guide. The latter turned around in the craft, grabbed Jed's rifle, and dove into the stream. At the same moment, Indians hidden on the bank began a hellish yelling and opened fire on the canoe. But Smith was no Rogers. Unflustered, he grabbed up the weapon of one of his companions. It was an old fusee with a bent barrel. The ball went wide of its mark so that Smith, in disgust, threw it into the bottom of the canoe and took up his paddle to dig in for dear life. His companions followed suit.

Getting to the far bank, Smith left Turner and Leland to guard the craft. He climbed a hill until he could spy out the camp. He saw no signs of life. From such a distance, he could not make out the mutilated corpses of his men. Concluding that his party had been wiped out, to a man, Smith struck out for the safety of Fort Vancouver with his two followers. It was 150 miles in a straight line, much further via the Willamette, toward which he shaped his course.

Meanwhile, Arthur Black may have lost consciousness for a time, from the shock of the dreadful war ax wound. But the urge for survival ran strong in him, and he moved like a deer for the cover of the forest, hid there, and eluded his pursuers. For four days he wandered until he fell in with the ocean again only two miles north of the Umpqua. He had a general idea of the whereabouts of Fort Vancouver, so he started following the coastline northward. The first Indian he met tried to pillage him of his knife, his only remaining weapon. Black was determined to sell his life dearly. He resisted, kept the knife, but ran into seven more Indians. They forced him to give them his clothes, except for his pants. And, presumably, he hung onto his blade. He watched for his chance, and when another party joined his captors and a quarrel erupted over him, he slipped back into the woods and hiding.

Finally, Black found his way to the "Killimaux" villages. He got some friendly Tillamooks to escort him overland to the Willamette. There a freeman forwarded him to Fort Vancouver. He arrived, to the astonishment of Dr. McLoughlin, at ten at night, August 8, 1828.

Smith and Turner and Leland were moving slower than the fleet Black. They found the mouth of the Alique River, now the Alsea, then Jed led the way to the Tillamooks. Villagers guided them, too, to the Willamette and Smith, and his comrades reached Fort Vancouver at noon on August 10.

CHAPTER FIVE ════════════════════════

Terra Incognita

WHILE THE PROTEAN Peter Skene Ogden was trading, exploring, mapping, and trapping (and ruining) the beaver country, and trying to determine the whereabouts of the Buenaventura River, Dr. McLoughlin was sending less roundabout reconnaissances southward from Fort Vancouver. These were meant to open the upper Willamette, the Umpqua, the Rogue, and the sierra linking Cascades and Coast Range but blocking access to California. This barrier was sometimes called the Klamath Range, California Mountains, or Boundary Range, instead of the Siskiyous, and McLoughlin hoped that it could be outflanked on its seaward side. These brigades, not Ogden's Snake River outfits, eventually laid down the Siskiyou Trail.

Simpson believed that southern Oregon would pay off: "We have every reason to suppose that the country is rich in furs." And he could not stand the idea of Snake River men loafing about Fort Vancouver during the slack seasons. He decided to keep the would-be idlers busy by sending them up the Willamette to open either an interior route (the ultimate line of the Siskiyou Trail) or a coastside bypass. The hunters were to push on even if catches were small and of "unseasoned" (i.e., out of season) animals, with poor coats. And always in the back of the Governor's mind was the need to create a buffer zone, a vacuum, by pillaging the beaver frontier in order to turn the Americans away.

McLoughlin was tempted to give the command of the parties called variously the Southern, California, Umpqua, and Buenaventura Brigades to Chief Trader Alexander Roderick McLeod, who had

105

joined the North-West Company in 1802 as a young blade of twenty years. He had risen to the command of Forts Perseverance and Good Hope in Canada but had been relieved of duty for "preposterous and galling use of authority." In a way, McLeod was being banished when he was transferred to the Columbia in 1825.

Simpson, as early as March of 1825, sounded out some Willamette freemen about a trapping venture to the Umpqua. Normally, the free trappers were eager to court (to seduce, if need be) Lady Luck. But the Governor found them "shy" this time. At first, he thought that their change of heart was due to their growing families, busily setting roots in the Willamette prairie. Then he realized that the bad reputation of the Umpquas was a factor. However, the timidity of the freemen did not stop his plans. Simpson commented: "We are, however, perfectly independent of them and, on the whole, I would be better pleased that they did not go."

The Governor planned the first expedition personally. He would use supernumeraries not assigned to regular brigades, plus the more willing freemen squatting near Fort Vancouver. He chose John Work and Tom McKay to lead the fifty to sixty men—then had misgivings about their leadership and put Finnan McDonald over them and added Alexander McLeod to the command as a kind of insurance. McDonald had told him that he wanted to retire, but the Governor persuaded him to lead one last hunt.

Anxious to beat his American rivals to the last untrapped beaver kingdom on the continent, the *terra incognita* between the Willamette and San Francisco Bay, Simpson hoped that his men would push on all the way to the Colorado River! To his immense disgust, the top-heavy party, loaded with leaders, did not even reach California. McDonald crossed the Cascades from the Willamette, probably by Santiam Pass, wandered up the Deschutes River to the unexplored Klamath region, and then (as we have seen) called it quits and united with Ogden's party from the Snake. When they rendezvoused, Ogden decided that it was too late (it was December) for a California reconnaissance, especially since he had no guide and the local Indians represented the tribes to the south to be hostile.

Since McLeod was now familiar with the Willamette, Deschutes, and Klamath areas, he became McLoughlin's choice, on Finnan McDonald's retirement, to head the Umpqua Brigade. The doctor posted Donald Manson to it as second-in-command. Briefly, McLeod used him as his amanuensis, although the clerk had no experience as an expedition journalist. The Company demanded a daily log of its "booshways," and McLeod excused himself from the chore with claims that he had more than enough other business to attend to in conducting the expedition.

All arrangements for the march were completed by May 5, 1826, except the arrival of McLeod himself with the horses from Fort Vancouver's so-called Upper Establishment, Fort Nez Percés. So Manson led off, taking a boat to the falls of the Willamette with a large supply of traps made by the fort's smith and provisions supplied by Vancouver's *dépense* or storekeeper. Manson was accompanied by engaged servants, tame Indians, and "Michel the Interpreter." This was Michel Laframboise, thirty-three-year-old veteran of the *Tonquin* voyage of 1810, who, one day, would succeed to the command of the Siskiyou Trail expeditions. With him was an Umpqua Indian he had brought to the fort at the end of McDonald's march. He was now escorting him home.

Water was high in the Willamette, but the current was not strong, so progress was satisfactory—even pleasant when the boat was accompanied by frolicking seals. The animals were too shy to be approached closely, but their very presence told Manson that salmon would be numerous at the falls. Flying showers of rain obliged the clerk to give orders to set up camp, but, next day, Willamette Falls was reached. All hands had to fall to, to move property across the portage around the "chutes" and away from greedy-eyed Indians. Once Manson had his goods safely stacked under guard above the falls, he had Laframboise spread the word that he was interested in buying horses. To break the commercial ice, Laframboise traded a few beads and some ammunition for two small salmon and some reed and grass mats. The Indians apologized for the lack of fish, explaining that the high water had temporarily drowned the fishery.

Since there was no food from that quarter, Manson ordered Pierre Charles and William Cannon to take twenty musket balls and some powder and to bring in some deer. He had the rest of his men collect the *agrés* or outfit (pack saddles and other horse gear) and get it in order, while the women sewed saddle bags. Both hunters had fair reputations as marksmen, the old Revolutionary War veteran being the best of the whole party. Manson was not sure that his nimrods would be successful, so he took the precaution of bartering two dozen brass rings for four small salmon trout. It was well that he did; his hunters returned empty-handed, though they had seen a good many deer.

Manson was pleased to hear from Laframboise that horse-owning

Indians would be in to talk trading. But he was annoyed to learn that the handful of freemen in the valley had already spoiled the horse trade. For the record, he observed that French-Canadians never hesitated a moment in giving away all they possessed for a fine horse.

The clerk soon found that the Indians were not really inclined to sell their horses, or even to bring them around. He sent Laframboise to the village with orders to try to buy as many as possible. The *canadien* returned to report that the Indians had agreed to sell only one and were asking a second-hand gun and a fathom of strouds, or Indian blanket material, for the beast. But, when he grudgingly offered them their outlandish price, the Indians found imaginary faults in the blanketing and claimed that the measure was a short fathom. It was obvious to Laframboise that the redmen were not really interested in trading.

Manson took advantage of clearing weather after an all-night rainstorm to send Laframboise to McKay's (i.e., Depaty's) Old Fort, to trade for horses. The clerk still had hopes for venison in camp, so he sent Cannon and an Indian along with Laframboise, with orders to hunt for meat. The interpreter tried one last time to buy horses at the falls, but his very good offer was refused.

Meanwhile, Manson had his men move the boat across the portage and into the river above the chutes, with the help of Indians hired for five loads of powder each. As a consort, Manson chartered an Indian canoe for ten musket balls and some powder. Next morning, he set out for McKay's Old Fort, near modern Newberg, Oregon. While ashore, having breakfast, the clerk was surprised to receive a visitor. It was freeman Etienne Lucier. He changed his mind about going down to Fort Vancouver and decided to tag along with Manson. Perhaps they were already friends; in any case, the clerk married Lucier's fourteen-year-old daughter, Félicité, in 1828. Lucier was a welcome addition, since he owned horses and promised to try to get more for the brigade.

Numerous tracks of deer and the reports of guns as he neared McKay's Old Fort that evening caused Manson's stomach to rumble more than usual. But when he reached the old post in the morning, he found that Cannon had killed only two deer. Laframboise had killed none. Worse, the hunters themselves had eaten most of the meat from one animal and had left the other carcass cached in the forest. Manson hurried the Hawaiian laborer, America, out of camp with Cannon, to retrieve it. Cannon was under orders to hunt his way out and back, too.

The *kanaka,* America, was an ex-Nor'wester of nine years in the fur trade, typical of the score of Sandwich Islanders or Owyhees (Hawaiians) in Oregon Territory. Though Alexander McLeod had little use for them, and Alex Ross was of mixed emotions about the Islanders, some had proved themselves to be good hunters and trappers. Travelers to "Wahoo" (Oahu) always described the Hawaiians as graceful and muscular men, active both on land and sea. But Ross found them dull and awkward in the Pacific Northwest, though willing and honest workers. No one denied their great skill as boatmen, divers, and swimmers, even in the cold waters of Oregon. Few goods were lost overside from capsized canoes for long, and rarely were there drownings, when canoe crews included *kanakas.*

Probably, Manson was as aware as Ross of the paradox of the Polynesians, the contrast between their capacity for work in Hawaii and their incapacity in Oregon. Ross had thought them (in the Islands) the most active people he had ever seen. He was probably right in blaming their diminished showing in the fur trade upon Oregon's climate. Constant rains, cold, whistling winds and snow all led to pneumonia and consumption among the displaced South Sea Islanders. Simpson admitted that Ogden's "Islaween" were not very good for laborious duties, but he admired the Islanders' courage and insisted that "they can be depended on in cases of danger from the natives."

Since his gunpowder was affected by damp, Manson took advantage of the sun which beamed on the camp on May 12. He spread the powder to dry as he waited for America to bring in the deer. The day grew even brighter when Lucier turned over to him two horses which Laframboise had left in his care after Finnan McDonald's expedition. One had a sore back but the other was fit for immediate duty. But Lucier's good news was word that freeman Ignace (Little Ignace) had a cache nearby containing not only eight to ten red deerskins but also some dried deer meat—venison jerky. Manson sent Laframboise with an Indian guide to loot the Iroquois's cache of everything which might be of service. Before he was back with the skins and 120 pounds of meat, Cannon brought in two small deer and was followed by Lucier with four more.

Because Pierre Charles still could not hunt—could barely hobble with a festering foot—Manson put him to work helping the Iroquois bowsman, Michel Oumantanie, a man of thirty years' fur trade experience. Old Michel was covering the saddles with Ignace's deerskins. Since the only treatment available for the limping Charles was the application of poultices of flour, there was no reason why he should not keep himself busy covering saddles and making saddlebags.

On May 14, 1826, Chief Trader Alex McLeod left Fort Vancouver to join Manson. His men were worn out because heavy rains had caused them to drive the horses along the unflooded foothills, so he let them rest at the falls and hurried up the Willamette with only an Indian guide. But the next day the horse party came up, and the Umpqua Brigade was complete as McLeod bought ten mares and horses and two colts from Lucier, at £1.14 a head.

That same day, a messenger arrived from McLoughlin with letters for McLeod. He was instructed to send Manson back and to substitute Laframboise as his second-in-command. The doctor also put his earlier, verbal, orders in writing. The chief trader was to collect as many furs as possible, but since McLoughlin's knowledge of southern Oregon was so limited, he would offer him no advice as to what measures to adopt. McLeod should be guided by his best judgment. He should keep one thing in mind, however: he was due back at Fort Vancouver by August 25.

McLeod sent Manson back to the fort in a boat which Depaty and McDonald had left at McKay's Old Fort. (This was the much "injured" craft which had caused Ogden so much annoyance by its absence.) Though the party was shrinking, it was still hungry. Rations per day were a bit of oatmeal and a piece of venison—when the chief trader could "afford" the latter. But, now, Cannon began to hit his stride as a hunter, bringing in from one to three deer each day. If only there were not so many mouths to feed! Besides Laframboise and Cannon, McLeod had three French-Canadian laborers, Jeaudoin, Joyalle, and Gobin, also three Hawaiians, whom he rated as inferior, America, Dick, and the tongue-twisting Tourawhyheene. He had two Iroquois, Big Michel Oumantanie and Little Michel Otoetanie (or Otoetanin), three Columbia River "partizan" Indians, and the unnamed Umpqua with Laframboise. The latter was, as yet, of no use as a guide. McLeod had only his own limited knowledge of the country, the not too dependable advice of freemen like Lucier, and Laframboise's memory of the earlier expedition. But since Michel Laframboise told him that he had seen vestiges of beaver in two small streams heading not far from the sea, McLeod directed his course to that quarter.

McLeod felt that he had far more trade goods than he would find a market for in lonely southwestern Oregon. He wished that he were half as well supplied with horseflesh. He was not optimistic about accomplishing very much with his worn-out nags in the three months allotted to him. Nor had he any hope of being able to buy new animals as replacements, since the Indians were setting exorbitant prices on their horses. With time as precious as prime beaver plews, McLeod had to sit in camp, writing of the horses: "A considerable time must elapse before they become in a condition for a regular journey; otherwise, we would not wait a day longer here. . . . We must, of necessity, stop here several days to allow our horses to recruit."

The men who had crewed Manson's boat returned, to report that they had had to leave it above the falls since the Indians would not work as packers for any terms. Even with his entire party reassembled, McLeod could not leave. He was dickering for horses with the local Indians, though in vain.

On May 21, McLeod shifted camp but advanced only a few miles because he was finally able to do some horse trading. But the mare and foal which he acquired still brought his herd to only thirty-nine animals, old and young—too few for comfort. Nevertheless, he decided to weed them out before heading into the wilderness. He turned the weakest ones over to an Indian caretaker who looked trustworthy. No sooner was the march renewed than one of McLeod's "good" horses up and died. It was not a cheery omen for the success of an already slow and halting Umpqua reconnaissance. Since the country was hilly, though open, McLeod forbade anyone's riding the already staggering horses except the far-ranging hunter, Cannon, and the lame Charles.

The rain finally subsided as the little brigade, guided by Laframboise, plodded along the mucky north bank of Chehalem Creek to reach a copse of trees. Ax men felled one of the tallest across the stream and used it for a bridge to carry men and baggage, while McLeod and Cannon pushed ahead to find a ford to swim the horses across. By dusk, the bourgeois rejoined his men in camp.

During the next few days, with Cannon always on scout for game, the party crossed a prairie drained by several streams, probably branches of the North Yamhill River. Because of their improving skill in felling trees for bridges, the men were not delayed. In the oak-clumped foothills of the divide between Panther Creek and the South Fork of the Yamhill, the Yamhill Indians finally decided to sell a few horses. The future now looked a little brighter, especially since the condition of all the horses began to improve. But McLeod feared the effect of the rougher country ahead, even on lightly laden animals. He was sure that his herd would remain poor all summer.

111

Each day was a monotonous routine of marching, hunting deer, trying to trade for fresh horses, and curing what little venison Cannon brought in—all of this in a steady downpour of rain. As yet, there was no beaver trapping. In the lee of Trask Mountain, McLeod left the interior valleys route of the future Siskiyou Trail and headed into the Coast Range, though the Indians warned him that the path across was a bad one. It was hardly surprising news to McLeod, but he tried to prepare better for the difficult climb by adding Jeaudoin and Joseph Louis to Cannon's one-man hunting party. Alas, they all met with bad luck.

Ten times the men crossed a stream trending westward through the coastal range. This was the Indians' Kellymoux, but it was actually the Big Nestucca rather than the Tillamook (Kellymoux) of today. They followed its lower channel to the ocean on June 1, 1826. Laframboise reckoned that they were south of the stream where he had seen beaver spoor, so McLeod sent him upcoast towards prominent Cape Kiwanda. He was to trap for ten days, then send a message as to his success. If unsuccessful, he was to march south and join McLeod.

To spare his skin-and-bone horses, McLeod left all of his heavy gear and the seven most broken-down animals in the custody of an Indian recommended by Laframboise. A fine beach then led him southward in an easy march toward difficult Cascade Head of the steep, muddy, and brushy slopes. His failure to find beaver there was made all the more painful when McLeod learned that the Indian guide-interpreter whom he had hired to meet him there had waited for a couple of months for the delayed expedition, then had despaired of McLeod's ever coming and had decamped.

Laframboise was not so well skilled in local tongues that he could be an adequate substitute. McLeod checked his entire party and noted in his log that no one was up to the task of translating the local idiom. He moved slowly down the coast, making only a few miles before encountering the Little Nestucca. It was difficult to communicate with the Indians on it, and he could get no information on beaver. But he managed to hire a damaged old canoe with which to ferry men and equipment.

In the next stream, probably Neskowin Creek, McLeod found signs of beaver at last. He had his men set their traps for the first time. In order to hunt upstream, the chief trader was obliged to pay the ridiculously high price of four inches of tobacco for the hire of a canoe. He was amazed how few canoes the coastal Indians possessed, what with rivers, creeks, lakes, and ponds galore, not to mention the entire ocean. He thought that it was due to the curiously scanty and dwarfed timber on this particular portion of the generally well-wooded Oregon coast. There simply was no wood locally available which was suitable for boat construction.

McLeod's day was brightened considerably when an Indian agreed to guide Cannon and a Hawaiian to a beaver stream which the native had seen a long time before. But when the three men got there they found the colony's lodges abandoned, the dams broken, and the creek hunted out. The guide was clearly disappointed too— and not dissimulating. He offered to show his new companions beaver lodges still farther upstream. McLeod encouraged him with the present of a *parfleche,* or skin bag, and two inches of tobacco. This was against the protests of the guide. He was the very personification of the legendary "Honest Injun" and he observed, either vocally or by signs, that he had not yet found any beaver for his white friends and, therefore, deserved no reward.

McLeod tried the Neskowin. When the traps were raised, dripping, above the surface they were all found to be empty. This was only the beginning of the bad news. Cannon and his men returned to report no beaver on the upper waters, either. Shortly, McLeod learned the reason for the complete absence of the rodents from such a likely creek. A villager told him that Depaty had come down to the Umpqua via this stretch of coast. He had retraced his steps to the Willamette, disappointed in the meager beaver resources of the coast, but not before he had skimmed off what beaver there were.

There was no point in examining the watershed any further. So, although Cannon now joined Charles on the sick list, McLeod decided to push on to the Umpqua. He hoped that he might find streams which Depaty had overlooked. He wrote: "We cannot glean anything in this quarter."

Shortly, McLeod ran into an Indian with two otter skins. He refused to sell them, but told the Scot that he had obtained them in trade beyond the Umpqua. This encouraged the chief trader to keep pushing southward. But, with his horses fagged out and the underbrush and downed timber so thick that a trail had to be literally hacked out with axes, McLeod made slow progress. At least, two elk were killed for the larder and the skins used as *apishamons,* saddle blankets and all-purpose covers. After treating some visiting Indians to elk meat, McLeod left a note for Laframboise, urging him to hasten but to take good care of his horses.

At last, on June 8, 1826, a beaver was finally caught. The animal was the sole return of ten traps left in the water for ten days. Two days later, McLeod seized a rare cloudy-bright day and devoted it to drying meat and preparing deer and elk skins as saddle blankets and fur bale coverings. He found the tasks awkwardly done. Strangely, none of his frontiersmen were familiar with such routine wilderness chores.

McLeod moved out again in mist and rains over a very bad, spongy road into which the horses sank to their fetlocks. By a path much obstructed with underbrush, McLeod finally brought his party over rugged Cascade Head to a camp on Salmon River. On the steep hillsides his horses fell and rolled but none was killed or even badly injured. Indian messengers brought word that Laframboise was on his way. With Cannon and Charles still sick and rough trails and foul weather dead ahead, McLeod decided to wait for his interpreter to try to parley with the Indians. He gathered that they had never seen white men before. Certainly, there was a communication problem with them, as he discovered when he tried to borrow a canoe: "Indeed, our defective means of communicating our ideas is much against us and occasions much delay and disappointment."

Sure that Laframboise would come up soon, McLeod moved camp to a grassy point near the Siletz River after a series of rainstorms abated. In a nearby lake, Indians had tried to kill beaver—or so he interpreted their sign language. Although Cannon was still so ill that he had to have an Indian carry his hardware for him, he managed to set three traps, which took two beaver and cheered him up somewhat.

A local chief was trying to understand McLeod's *wa-wa* when Laframboise arrived. McLeod broke off his dickering for a seagoing canoe in which he hoped to speed up his reconnoitering. The interpreter had nothing to show for his hunt but six beaver, and he had had a horse killed in a fall. McLeod was most unhappy with Laframboise: "He has led us to anticipate an abundant hunt, which evidently proves his erroneous judgment." He blamed the loss of the horse on the Canadian's inattention, sourly noting that it was not one of the worn-out stock, either, but one of the expensive animals bought from Lucier.

Resuming the parley, McLeod also sent Laframboise to examine the canoes. They were awkward craft. McLeod was reluctant to trust his party to them in the surf of such an exposed coast, especially when he learned that the Indians never dared take them beyond the

Econne (Yaquina) River, which lay far short of the Umpqua. The natives described the land route as being much safer than the sea, with its rocks and surf, even though the beach was blocked completely by an enormous point of land eighteen to twenty miles south. There was no beach around it; it would have to be surmounted. But, the Indians added, beyond the great headland lay a fine, rock-free beach.

Conscious that he was running out of time, McLeod toyed with the idea of a genuine sea voyage along the coast in order to examine the more southerly rivers, which the Indians reported to be rich in beaver. Land travel was very, very slow. He was perplexed, confessing in his journal: "We are undecided what method to adopt. Prudence would dictate to continue by land for, otherwise, we run a risk, the loss of property if not of lives." On the other hand, he knew that dilatory travel on the shore at the mercy of mercenary Indians would not even halfway achieve his mission. He decided to compromise and do a bit of both.

McLeod swam the horses across the wide but shallow Yaquina River without difficulty. The Indians provided canoes in which he sent six men to hunt upstream while he had the others scatter their traps along the river to avoid crowding. Even Cannon got up early and staked his traps before joining McLeod as "garrison" of the camp. Though the Indians had little to trade other than raspberries and shellfish, McLeod managed to secure three pelts by barter.

When Laframboise brought in two beaver from his four traps, and Cannon one animal, McLeod's spirits rose. He wrote: "Great hopes exist of taking some beaver in this vicinity." Charles and Louis came in with four, and Cannon found an otter and another beaver when he lifted his traps to move them. On June 22, one beaver was caught and, next day, Jeaudoin and Laframboise each brought in one. Laframboise had an otter, too. This was enough to buoy McLeod's hopes; but most of his men had little luck. They blamed their failure on the weak traps made at Fort Vancouver, like Ogden, but McLeod disbelieved them and charged their lack of success to their clumsiness and inattention.

The Yaquina was easily the most productive, as well as the most pleasant, camp of the expedition. Besides the modest beaver catch, it offered grass for the horses and game for the hunters. And, with meat in camp, everyone was reasonably content, though all were eager to try the reputedly richer streams to the south.

McLeod was giving the orders to hobble the horses preparatory to a move just as Dick and his two fellow Hawaiians got back to camp.

They had been gone eight days and had only two beaver and an otter to show for their efforts. But they admitted that they had missed many: "This is a very prevelent complaint and echoes from every mouth," reported McLeod. Cannon found the local beaver to be "shy," too, and he and his party got only six more. But he reported good prospects on the upper Yaquina and blamed his small catch on the fact that he had been constantly in motion, hardly wetting his traps before he was lifting them to move on again. He felt that the upstream area was worth a couple of weeks of intensive trapping. Since McLeod had built up some confidence in the old soldier, he thought that he was a good judge of the situation. Accordingly, he gave him permission to take six men to trap for five or six days, higher up. He ordered him to get word back of his luck.

McLeod raised camp and followed the beach to Beaver Creek, which he called the Nackito River. He traded for a few skins and fed his men, some of whom had fasted (unwillingly) for a few days. Then he hired a canoe and searched the stream, already trapped by his advance men. He found more feet than bodies in the traps and noted some traps missing. Jeaudoin accused an old Indian of having stolen them, but McLeod thought the charge unfounded. He was anxious to keep the peace, so he scolded the Canadian: "I availed myself of the opportunity and acquainted the accuser, Jeaudoin, to be more cautious in future and not to attach blame without sure grounds of complaint and, in any debate with the natives, not to allow their passion [to] predominate over their judgment, so as to avoid unnecessary difficulties [which] thus might arise, and not to proceed to violence without my being previously acquainted with the circumstances, and concluded by observing that they should appeal to me and say nothing to the Indians." McLeod was right. A few days later, the missing traps were found.

At this point, the *kanaka* Dick went with one of the Columbia River partisans and a local guide to one of the reportedly rich beaver streams. The chief trader promised his guide remuneration in the form of a calico shirt if he should turn up *Castor*. Charles was up and around again, walking on his game leg. But now America was ill with chest pains, leading McLeod to write: "Since leaving Fort Vancouver, we have not been free from invalids tho our party is small. It is remarkable that seldom less than two or three are ailing." Charles took two men to trap the next river to the south, the Alsea, accessible via a smooth sand beach. Near the base camp, beaver were seen swimming in Beaver Creek in broad daylight, but the returns were minimal.

America was now so sick that McLeod felt it best to disperse his traps among the other men so that they would not be wasted. He also sent an Indian to check on Cannon's party from whom he had not heard a word.

McLeod was now glad that he had decided against a coasting voyage in canoes to investigate the mouths of large streams by putting into them from the sea. This mode of travel would have allowed him to cover more ground, but such amphibious exploration would neglect the smaller streams inland, the tributaries. And he found *no* beaver in the mouths or lower reaches of large rivers—only some distance up from tidewater. Thus, he was really vindicating his position when he wrote in his official journal for his superiors' eyes: "The knowledge we now possess of the country justifies the plan of continuing our further progress by means of horses, otherwise many tributary streams that contain beaver would be passed by unnoticed were we to proceed by water. . . . In every little stream, vestiges of beaver is to be seen and, as they are but a short distance from each other, much delay will consequently occur and our progress proportionately [be] protracted for the sole purpose of trapping, which leads me to conclude that our journey will terminate at no great distance from hence."

The men who had ascended the Alsea to the head of canoe navigation reported little beaver sign. Their twenty-two traps took but seven animals. Furs continued to reach camp but in small numbers. It was a rare day when McLeod, by nightfall, could count more than a few pelts peeled from carcasses, scraped of fat and flesh, and secured with sinew to hoops made of willow withes.

As McLeod slowly poked down a beaver-poor coast in that July 1826, Simpson was urging McLoughlin to make extra efforts in the untrapped fur land toward the Siskiyous: "It is intended that a strong trapping expedition be kept up to hunt in the country to the southward of the Columbia, as while we have access thereto it is our interest to leave it in as bad a state as possible for our successors. This party may be called the Snake, Umpqua or any other Expedition you please, but our wish is that it should scour the country wherever beaver can be found but, on no consideration cross the [Rocky] Mountains, take its return to Fort Vancouver annually in a sufficient time to be sent home by the ship of the season, and return to its hunting grounds immediately."

When his upper Yaquina party rejoined him with only twenty-four beaver after twelve days, McLeod raised camp. He sadly noted:

117

"Poor prospects for a new country that was seldom if ever hunted."
He lost time ferrying the Alsea in hired canoes but led the way down
the beach until it was blocked by huge Heceta Head, of which the
Indians had warned him. To McLeod, who scouted the mountain
personally, it looked impossible to move horses across it. So, blocked
by the headland, he reversed his recent decision and took to sea, noting: "Our progress with horses must terminate here."

McLeod left all animals and unnecessary baggage with an apparently reliable old Indian, sent Laframboise to the Yaquina to add
two more craft to his one-canoe fleet, and waited for calm weather to
make his seagoing expedition. When Cannon and an Iroquois asked
permission to hunt high up the Yaquina again, he granted it. He saw
no alternative to splitting his party into small units, so scattered were
the beaver. And time was running out.

The chief trader observed of his trappers: "The space of country
they have to hunt is not so destitute of beaver but what they might
do something, altho their endeavours hitherto is no proof of it." In
fact, he felt that they might do as well taking the beaver missed by
the brigade in its rear as they would do up ahead in new country.
He echoed Ogden's feelings about the fur trade, exactly: "It is all a
lottery."

The weather cleared but the velocity of the wind intimidated
McLeod from venturing out to sea on St. Swithin's Day, so he scouted
the shore ahead on foot, managing to make ten miles. He took only
Gobin and an Indian, leaving Laframboise in command of his camp
with orders to proceed by sea in the canoes should the wind drop
enough for safety. On his march, McLeod ran into a very intelligent
Indian, who reported beaver abundant in the rivers and small lakes
ahead. He ended his hike over dunes and beach at the mouth of the
Siuslaw, three hundred yards wide at ebb tide, very deep, and with
a strong current.

The Umpqua Indian was now McLeod's best linguist, but it was
increasingly difficult to converse with the natives as he made southing.
None of them knew a word of the Chinook which the Umpqua spoke
and which the trader had been sure would be the *lingua franca* of the
coast. He was now less trusting of the information he received but
hoped that it was true that the Umpqua lay only twenty miles south
of him.

Retracing his steps toward Heceta Head, McLeod had not made
three miles before he saw the canoes approaching with sails set. They
put their prows into the Siuslaw just in time. A blustery, bullying

wind was beginning to whip whitecaps on the waves, and two of the fragile craft shipped a lot of water in passing over the bar.

The reunited brigade set up camp at the mouth, from which McLeod ascended the Siuslaw to its first fork. There he set up a new camp, between two Indian villages. The redmen bartered berries and *camas* roots, and a leader, whom the Canadians dubbed Little Chief, traded fifteen beaver skins for *hyaquois* shells, prized by the Indians as both jewelry and wealth. McLeod scattered his men as hunters and trappers, keeping camp only with Laframboise and the Iroquois, whom he found more useful than the Sandwich Islanders. He grumbled in his journal that the latter were always disabled by illness. At the moment of writing, two of the Owyhees could hardly walk. But it was a lucky day, otherwise. The men were finding drowned beaver in their traps; Little Chief had a source of pelts to trade. The Indian sold McLeod eighteen more beaver and an otter, for which he was paid a calico shirt, a tin dish, and some of the precious dentalium shells.

Jeaudoin tried to survey the North Fork of the Siuslaw but found canoe navigation impeded by fallen trees. Since he saw no sign of beaver anyway, he gave up. By now, McLeod had abandoned the practice of hiring Indian guides. They wanted too much for their information, and they deceived him.

Little Chief, having traded forty skins, told McLeod that he was going to the next big river beyond the Umpqua, for more. This was the Coacuss (Coos) River. Knowing that McLeod would soon have to leave the area, he promised to collect skins for a return visit by the white men. His braves had none at present. Until the coming of the "white skins," only youngsters had hunted beaver—and then for amusement. (Adults occasionally took the animals to make winter robes.) Little Chief reported the land between the Umpqua and Coos rivers to be particularly rich in beaver, especially a lake drained by a tributary of the Umpqua, which had never been seen by whites.

McLeod's men were having mediocre luck with the streams draining into the Siuslaw. As usual, McLeod blamed it all on his men's incompetence, especially that of the *kanakas*. He reserved his choicest spleen for Tourawhyheene, saying that the Islander possessed "very bad perfection. I believe he is both indolent and slothful to a degree beyond bearing."

Nor was trading brisk after Little Chief left, though the Umpqua swapped his two and a half-point Hudson's Bay blanket for a robe of eight beaver skins. So small were the returns that McLeod seriously considered collecting deer hides, for buckskins, so that he should have something to show at Fort Vancouver for his exertions. He gave up the idea when he saw how clumsy were his men at tanning skins and dressing leather. The local lakes were trapped but yielded no beaver at all. All the while, the natives kept assuring McLeod that there was a country well-stocked with beaver, always just ahead.

When Little Chief returned with only nine pelts, apologizing for having gone no further than the Umpqua, McLeod decided to pull up stakes. Little Chief suggested that he go home via the Umpqua, and inland, rather than up coast. The going would be easier on loaded horses, and the men could trap the sources of a number of streams. He even offered his services as guide. But McLeod had to turn him down. It was getting close to his deadline. He could not even consider exploring a new route to the fort. "In a few days hence we must trace back our steps, agreeable to appointment, and defer to another season to acquire further knowledge of the country and its resources to the southward of this stage, as our progress in that direction terminates here."

On the last day of July, McLeod moved his party to the seashore for a feast of beaver, venison, seal meat, and whale. The whale meat and blubber were particularly welcomed by men tired of a restricted diet of lean venison and beaver.

August 1, 1826, saw the brigade sailing northward up the coast minus McLeod. Perhaps a landlubber, he took a small party overland. They found the horses safe behind Heceta Head, so McLeod sent the canoes back to their owners and awaited Cannon and the Iroquois. He took the opportunity to air his furs, which were becoming damp. When Cannon came in, it was to report terrible fortune. He had taken only seven beaver between July 15 and August 4.

Having crossed the Yaquina, the men were blocked by a flood tide which stole their beach, so they whiled away their time by receiving five Tillamook visitors. They bore a puzzling report: Fort George had been reestablished by strangers who claimed to be the sole proprietors of the soil of Oregon Territory!

Jeaudoin now joined America on the sick list, and everyone was hungry again. Although they shot seals in the water, they could not retrieve the animals since they had no canoes. They lost all but one, collected by an Indian who swam out for it. (McLeod does not seem to have tried his Hawaiians—excellent swimmers—in the surf.) At the Little Nestucca, Indians were spearing salmon but would sell only a few. Without further explanation, he noted in his journal that "their

superstitious ideas prevented us from obtaining as many as we wish'd."
He put his men on iron rations, issuing them each only a pint of corn.
Most of the Tillamooks, except the salmon fishers, could not be help-
ful, since they were starving.

Back in their May 29 campsite on August 11, having made good
time to the Yamhill country, McLeod released his Umpqua interpreter. He had served him well, and McLeod compensated him hand-
somely as he turned back for his far-off village. Aside from the annoyance of wetting furs in the Little Nestucca and Tillamook rivers and
having to halt to dry them, the return passage was uneventful. Mc-
Leod met Little Ignace, the Iroquois freeman whose cache he had
robbed. He had the decency to offer the plundered man a piece of
deer meat.

Fine weather, at last, after one of the soggiest seasons on record
in Oregon, accelerated the party's return. Willamette Mountain was
passed and a "channel" of the Willamette River reached in Multnomah Slough, in the Burlington area of what was later Portland. On
August 19, McLeod trudged into Fort Vancouver with a disappointing catch of only 285 beaver, thirty-six land otter, and three sea
otter. This was only 395 pounds of furs by McLoughlin's figuring.
And he had secured fully half of it by trading, not trapping.

Naturally, Alex McLeod tried to explain away his mediocre
showing. He claimed that he had been too busy examining the shore
for a good hunt. Moreover, beaver were scarce on the coast, as were
beaver cuttings and other signs. All of this was very true, and he
really did not have to fib as he did and suggest to McLoughlin that
he had reached the Umpqua when he had made it only to the Siuslaw.

The portly, florid McLoughlin was vexed by McLeod's failure
to "scour" Oregon of beaver and to carry out Simpson's orders to
acquire "as ample an occupation of the country and trade as possible." His blue eyes snapped his disapproval. He passed on word of
the scarcity of beaver, but he could not believe that there was not a
natural low-level trail to California along the coast. And he was intrigued by the mysterious river reportedly only two days beyond the
Umpqua. Perhaps it was the elusive Buenaventura! So, McLoughlin
decided to hurry McLeod out again, and back to the littoral, rather
than up and over the interior Siskiyous.

CHAPTER SIX ══════════════════

Umpqua Brigade

ON SEPTEMBER 15, 1826, less than a month after his return from the Siuslaw River, McLeod had to set out again for the Umpqua and points south. Again Laframboise and Manson were ordered to assist him, along with eleven French-Canadians, five Hawaiians, and two Indians. Fine weather alternated with light rain as he collected horses, ferried men and supplies, and pushed up the Willamette toward a rendezvous with the rest of the brigade at McKay's Old Fort.

This time, McLeod planned to use the natural highway of the Willamette more, before cutting over to the coast. To his distress, he found that the Indians were burning off the grass in the valley. The Willamette country was so overrun with grass fires that he had difficulty getting the horses through, "owing to their alarm, caused by the devouring element."

The Indians put great tracts to the torch in order to make easy the collecting of winter rations of grasshoppers and honey, also to force deer to congregate in cramped islands of grass where they could be more easily taken. But not only were the trader's horses spooked; they were made to go hungry for lack of pasture. McLeod found the west bank so destitute of grass that he had to swim his horses across the Willamette. Even then, he had to post guards to keep them from straying in search of feed.

McLeod hoped to recruit freemen to bolster the brigade's strength. Little Ignace and Lucier paid him a call, and the latter was inclined to join him, to work off a heavy debt to the Company. Then Jean Baptiste Dubreuil—a *milieu* or middleman, in the old *voyageur* terminology (which still rated servants as bowsmen, middlemen, and steersmen)—came in with an Indian and three horses.

But Dubreuil was not McLeod's last reinforcement. Manson arrived on September 22 with the balance of the brigade's supplies. McLeod welcomed them but damned the lack of tobacco, so essential to trading or even parleying with Indians. He was also bothered by the fact that the fort made no allowances for his Indian partisans. He had to make up packages of supplies for them himself. He testily explained in his journal: "Consequently, we shall be deficient in some necessary articles."

With Manson was McLeod's most curious reinforcement. It was the discoverer of the Douglas fir, the namer of the Cascades, the twenty-one-year-old Scots botanist David Douglas, on a scientific mission for the Royal Horticultural Society in London. Like his hosts, he was traveling light. Besides his rifle he had only a brace of pistols, six precious quires of paper for mounting dried botanical specimens, a small copper kettle, some tobacco, and a few trifles to give to the Indians as presents. Aside from the clothing he wore, he took only two extra shirts, one of flannel and one of linen—but indulged himself, as he put it, because of Oregon's famous cold rains and brought along two blankets and a tent.

Since he had arrived at Fort Vancouver in April 1825, Douglas was familiar with Oregon's sopping climate. Between August 19 and August 30, 1825, he had explored the Willamette with a party of hunters to a point twenty-five miles above the falls.

This time, Douglas had accompanied Manson to the falls, where a damaged boat had to be repaired by "gumming its seams." The naturalist seized the opportunity to examine the twenty-five-foot sheer drop of an entire river over a basaltic ledge which cut it into a cascade of channels between rocks and islands. He found the surrounding valley an impressive and highly diversified country of hills and dales in addition to a well-watered (often, *too* well-watered) plain in the sixty-mile wide trough between Coast Range and Cascade Mountains. The varied soils, ranging from bottomland black alluvium of muck to sandy loam, and on to the red clay of the higher timbered zone along the two-hundred-mile valley, boasted a surprising array and variety of beautifully flowering plants for so late in the season.

McLeod sent men back to the fort with replies to McLoughlin's dispatches. The doctor had stressed the importance of his having a "personal communication" with the natives of the unnamed large river beyond the Umpqua. The doctor wanted to open up a trade with them. Also, McLeod was to keep his men busy all winter, trapping. If he could spare Laframboise, he was to send him back, however. Again pleading ignorance of the country, McLoughlin gave his subordinate virtual carte blanche; he was to be guided by the circumstances of his expedition.

McLeod's one great worry was transport. He hurried men out to look for strayed horses and kept them out until every animal was recovered. He did some hard trading, giving a gun, a three-point blanket, and a pound of transparent trade beads, but he was gratified to be able to add two Indian horses to his herd.

On the twenty-seventh, the chief trader set out, but only on a shakedown march of five miles. He then sent out meat hunters and bade adieu to Manson, who would take his messages to Fort Vancouver. Already, McLeod found some of his equipment superfluous so he sent it back with the clerk. He meant to perform better, this time, and that required that he travel farther and faster. And this, in turn, meant going light.

On the Yamhill, which cut through an area of rich, reddish soil, foot-high red clover and other grasses, and abundant oaks, McLeod found Yamhill Indians with a few pelts to trade. But their inflated prices precluded any bargaining. He complained: "The intercourse these people have had, and indeed all the Indians of the Willamette, with freemen has rendered them very unfit subjects to have any dealings with."

Alex Aubichon, a freeman and ex-Nor'wester, served as guide, but his track was so meandering and circuitous that the chief trader began to consider him only indifferently qualified for the task. Worse, deer were both scarce and shy. Even the Indian hunters "fared scantily," to borrow David Douglas's phrase. The Indian-set fires frightened all game animals away.

Marches averaged from a dozen to eighteen miles per day, though to the botanist's aching feet they must all have seemed twenty-milers. The fires had burned away the ubiquitous blackberry patches and the thickets of "brakes," or bracken; but the blackened stubble of the ferns made for slow going. Burned stumps of brush tripped boots and moccasins alike, and even the stubs of strong grasses cut toes and made walking torture. But Douglas was game, determined to keep up with the mountain men, although the grass fires also made botanizing slow and very difficult.

The weather, at least, was good—unusually so. Although it was broken from time to time with rain and lightning, Douglas found plenty of clear weather in which to collect interesting specimens, such as the stinking camphor weed of the banks of the Santiam River. Douglas learned that the Indians used the plant to stupefy fish. He was amused when "McKay" (Depaty) did some botanizing himself one day. The *canadien* served shoulder of doe for breakfast, basting it with Canada mint and sugar and serving it on salal leaves in lieu of plates.

On this trip, McLeod was no longer bewitched by the idea of a coastal road, as were McLoughlin and Simpson. He knew that no shoreline shelf existed. Mountains plunged directly into the deep without terrace or even beach, like Oregon's Heceta Head and (unknown as yet to him) California's King Range, far to the south. So he followed the advice of Depaty and Little Chief and made as much southing inland, via the Willamette, as possible. Only then did he turn west to follow orders and seek the coast.

October 1, 1826, found McLeod leaving the Willamette and taking the uphill pull of the high road to the Umpqua, still called the Arguilar by some. This was a corruption of the Aguilar, from Sebastián Vizcaino's pilot, Martín Aguilar, who sighted the Rogue or Umpqua as well as Cape Blanco in 1603. As Little Chief had predicted, McLeod found it a well-beaten path. Indians dogged his heels on it, trying to sell him horses, but at outlandish prices. He refused to buy, fearing that such payments would establish a bad precedent for future travelers.

David Douglas noted that the only distinguishing marks of a Sunday on the trail were a changing of linen by some of the more fastidious mountain men and a perusing of Catholic religious tracts in the evening. The naturalist did not keep the Sabbath overly well himself. He spent a part of the Lord's Day hunting a giant grizzly bear with John Kennedy, a twenty-six-year-old ex-Nor'wester from Sligo, Ireland. The monster was hiding in a hummock of brushwood. Because it was dusk and the light was failing fast, the hunters decided to give up the search. It was a judicious decision. Douglas made another search for *Ursus ferox* at daylight, but he was gone, perhaps luckily for the botanist. He liked to hunt with the men but he must have known that he was no "grisly" bear hunter. He was well aware of the animal's ferocity, since he had read Meriwether Lewis's comments in journals of the Lewis and Clark expedition.

October's unseasonal heat, combined with the lack of pasturage, was hard on the horses. McLeod had to camp anywhere his animals could find pickings on the cutbanks of streams or on the margins of woods, where the Indians' fires had turned back or died out before destroying all grass. Because of their hunger, there were always strays to be pursued. A more unusual delay occurred on the second. McLeod laconically entered in his diary: "Obichon's woman was delivered of a female child. In consequence of her indisposition, we had to stop in the rear." Aubichon *et famille* rejoined McLeod before he broke camp on the fourth.

The next day was so hot and sultry that, after eighteen miles, the horses were exhausted. With Mount Jefferson in view to the east, the party was rejoined by Depaty, who had gone ahead to hunt toward the Umpqua with Little Ignace. He told Douglas that he had asked one of his hunters to bring back some of the huge cones of the sugar pine which so excited the botanist's interest. Douglas had only seen seeds and a few scales, so far, in the possession of an Indian. From Depaty, Douglas got a grizzly bear skin in trade for an old blanket and some *tabac*. The Scot wanted it for an underrobe in his bedroll as much as for a natural history specimen. Depaty also promised to kill him a male and female grizzly so that he might be able to measure them, if not skin them out.

Although the Indians were as poor as Job, Douglas noticed that McLeod did not falter in his policy of flattering and mollifying them It was simply good diplomacy. He journalized: "Some of them came to our camp in hopes of finding a morsel treat, with which they were gratified."

On October 8, McLeod saw the first faint sign of *Castor*. He camped on the edge of an old beaver dam. This was also the day when John Kennedy was attacked by a grizzly. The beast was but a few yards distant when the hunter saw him. It was impossible to outrun the animal, so the Irishman threw his gun up and fired, point-blank. The ball had almost no effect. The grizzly shook off the shock of impact like a bee sting and charged. Kennedy had time to climb up a small oak, but the bear caught him with one paw under the right arm and the left on his back, as if the brute were picking up a parcel. Fortunately, Kennedy's clothes were old, worn and weak, or he might have been tugged to earth to be mauled to death. His blanket, coat and trousers were shredded from his body and torn to pieces by the angry monster. But the Irisher was rescued by some of his mates, all of whom were amazed to find him without serious injury.

The country grew more wooded as the trappers left the plains and climbed into the foothills, where the first elk were seen, crossing three ranges via Pass Creek and Elk Creek. The *biches* or elk (wapiti) were really tough customers—tough to kill and tough to eat. It was not surprising that their meat was lean and chewy. Douglas saw hunters put eleven musket balls into one five-hundred-pound buck before they could bring the animal down. McLeod named Elk Creek, calling it Elk River, when he camped near modern Elkton.

The eleventh was a red-letter day. Two beaver were caught; the first of the season. Unfavorable weather stopped progress for two days, then McLeod's unfavorite trapper, Tourawhyheene, lost his horse with all of his traps and other property. But a party found the animal and gear, so all was well again.

McLeod and Douglas customarily led the line of men, but now the chief trader had Depaty and two Indians in the van, breaking trail. It was not easy work. They had to hack off the lower limbs of trees to permit the horses to pass through the dense conifers. Though the rains were light, they greased the roads so effectively (with the help of fogs) that the safety of the horses was endangered. Some of the pack animals were injured in falls as the brigade dropped down from ridges of about 2700 feet above their bases in order to reach the Umpqua via Red Deer River. Actually, this was but another stretch of twisting Elk Creek. Fortunately, trees, brush and rotting stumps, and deadwood stopped the falling horses before they were lost for good. In spite of the tumbles, of all goods hauled over the mountains only a canvas bag of rifle balls was lost from a saddlebag. But because of the frequent falls, Douglas adamantly refused to allow his specimens to be packed on the horses. He carried his collection on his back, including deer horns. And since footing was so bad that he, too, fell from time to time, Douglas wrapped his specimens in a cushiony grizzly bear skin for protection.

There were threats to secure footing other than muddy trails. Numerous fallen pine trunks had to be clambered over. Douglas estimated that some were 250 feet long! But he was much more interested in the aromatic Oregon myrtle (the California bay or laurel). The trappers boiled the bark to prepare a tealike beverage, and the Indians roasted the olivelike nuts in embers for food. So powerful was the spicy fragrance of the bay tree that the scent emitted merely as the result of its leaves rustling in the wind was enough to induce fits of sneezing among the more allergic of the company (hence another alias for the myrtle on California's Redwood Coast—pepperwood). Douglas hoped that the tree was his discovery, but George Vancouver's naturalist, Archibald Menzies, had found it when he landed at Trinidad in April 1793. Years before that, of course, the

Spaniards knew it as *laurel silvestre*. But Douglas's bay nuts and seeds would prove to be the first to reach England for planting in botanical gardens. And his discovery of the Western chinquapin, or golden-leafed chestnut, was a genuine botanical "first."

With food supplies exhausted and his horses breaking down from hunger, McLeod divided his party. He scattered small units to forage for themselves, then took Depaty on a deer hunt, while Douglas made himself useful by setting up camp, chopping wood, and kindling a fire. At twilight, the botanist and camp tender refreshed himself with a bath in the cold Umpqua River. From the vegetation about him—*Menziesia ferruginea* and *Pinus canadensis*—he guessed that he was lolling only thirty to thirty-five miles from the sea.

McLeod wounded a doe, but it got away. So it was a supperless night for Douglas. It was almost sleepless, too. Oregon he found cold by night, even this close to the coast, and the packhorse carrying his blanket was one of the laggards. Douglas did not plan to lie down at all that night. He sat up until 2 A.M., when McLeod took pity on him. The chief trader loaned the scientist his own blanket and buffalo robe and took a turn, himself, at sitting up, wrapped in his greatcoat or capote of Hudson's Bay Company blanket material. Though the mercury did not sink below 41°, Douglas found that night brought a damp, penetrating cold settling about the camp. Even with McLeod's blanket and buffalo skin "horse rug" (saddle blanket), he could not keep the chill from congealing the very marrow of his bones. Three times during the night he got up to rekindle the guttering campfire.

McLeod apprized visiting Umpqua Indians, next day, of the peacefulness of his intentions. As he did so, his men placed the first traps in the river and the women skinned out a doe and a buck for the meal. Douglas waited impatiently for his tardy horse. The exhausted beast did not reach camp until 4 P.M. Repeated falls by the animals had bruised the botanist's tin specimen box all out of shape. But the contents, including his prized notebook, were safe. In fact, only a small case of preserving powder was actually spoiled, although his spare shirt was reduced by chafing until it looked like "surgeon's lint," or bandages. Once again, Douglas congratulated himself on not having trusted his fragile specimens to the wobbly pack animal.

Douglas set off by himself to botanize on October 18, 1826. He took a route parallel to the modern road from Elkton to Oakland, Oregon. Accompanying him was one of Depaty's hunters, an eighteen-year-old lad of some unknown tribe. He had been captured as a slave until released by Depaty. Like his master, he was fond of the life of a free trapper and had not the slightest desire to return to his own people, could he have found them. He spoke Umpqua, as well as the Chinook trade patois or *lingua franca*. Douglas found little difficulty in conversing with him, though he was reticent, like most Indians.

Douglas sought the home of the great-coned sugar pines, which he already had named *Pinus lambertiana* from the scales and nuts in his collection. So he headed for the mountainous source of the Umpqua. Not toughened up like the trappers as yet, by half, the Scot soon got himself into trouble. He built a raft to cross the river only nine miles from the set traps and blistered his hands so painfully that he had to send his companion to camp with a note to McLeod about his difficulty. Before his friend could respond, the naturalist got himself into a real fix. He chased a buck and fell into a deep gully full of deadwood. He passed out from severe chest injuries. Though he later claimed to have been only stunned, it was obvious, from the time at which his watch stopped, that he lay unconscious for five hours. Calapooya Indians found him, extricated him from the natural trap into which he had tumbled, and helped him saddle and mount his horse. The fierce pain in his chest prohibited him from walking. But he fell off his horse and was creeping along with the help of a walking stick and his gun, used as a makeshift cane, when he was re-rescued by Kennedy.

Because of Douglas's accident, Kennedy did not find Chief Centernose of the Umpquas, whom he was seeking. But one of the chief's sons came into camp with a message that his father would visit McLeod in a few days' time. Douglas enjoyed the rest, and gallons of tea, as his hurt ribs repaired themselves. Since bleeding was very much in vogue among doctors in 1826, Douglas prescribed a little bloodletting to himself. And, since he was the nearest thing to a physician or surgeon south of McLoughlin, Douglas operated on himself. He opened a cut in his left foot, let it drain a bit, and convinced himself that he felt better.

The accident was not serious, and Douglas was soon himself again. However, it proved to be a bad omen. In July 1834, the scientist lost his life on Mauna Kea, on the Island of Hawaii in a similar accident. He fell into a pit, an animal trap. Unfortunately, it was already occupied by a wild bullock, which trampled him to death.

While he waited for the chief's arrival, McLeod explored westward down the Umpqua. He set up a base camp on a plain near an Indian village near today's Scottsburg. In the village, the women wore beauty marks like those which Jed Smith had seen on the lower jaws of Mojave lassies—tattooed lines running from mouth to chin. Douglas appreciated such cosmetology, writing: "It is considered a great mark of beauty. I have little doubt that such a lady in London would make a fine figure, particularly when a little red and green earth is added to the upper part of the face."

When two of the Iroquois returned from a canoe-renting visit to the village, they brought not only the craft and some salmon of excellent flavor, but also Little Chief. McLeod was pleased to see the beaver-trading chieftain of his prior expedition. On the twenty-second, the principal chief of the Umpquas, Centernose, paid his courtesy call. His Highness was much gratified by the present of some trifling articles which McLeod forced on him. Shortly, he reciprocated with gifts of salmon weighing fifteen to twenty-five pounds each.

McLeod spent most of the Sabbath planning his journey to the coast and thence south along the littoral from the Umpqua to the unknown river beyond. Centernose kindly agreed to serve as his pathfinder and appointed one of his sons to be Douglas's guide on a second attempt to find the sugar pines. That day, Douglas examined a very large black-tailed deer shot by McLeod. It was a stray, since it was far north of its range and well into whitetail country. Incredibly, he found that the Indians could take such powerfully built animals in snares made of wild iris fiber. Though thin it was strong enough to hold an elk. Douglas suggested that it would probably tame a buffalo too, should bison ever venture as far westward as the Umpqua.

A recuperated Douglas set out on October 23 with his guide and two horses. One carried his blanket and specimen paper. The other he could ride, if need be. He was determined to snare the elusive sugar pine, this time—the most princely of its genus, perhaps the grandest specimen of vegetation! (Only later would he visit California, see the giant redwoods, and revise his opinions.)

McLeod led a small flotilla of canoes down the Umpqua, detaching craft to explore the tributaries and trap them, if beaver sign could be found. He gave the men in these waterborne detachments orders to return to the main camp, where Laframboise remained, within ten to twelve days. By that time, he hoped to be back from his coastal sortie.

McLeod's fleet shrunk until he had but one canoe besides his own when he reached tidewater. It was that of the Old Chief, or Centernose. In his own boat he had five trappers and two Indians. At dark, McLeod led everyone ashore. He was within sight of the sea after twenty-seven miles of travel though not quite at the river's wide mouth. The Umpqua was only a hundred yards wide where Laframboise tended camp; here it broadened to a mile and a half before it met the sea.

McLeod encountered two canoes cargoed with berries, to be traded for salmon. The craft were crewed by timid natives. After they hove in view, they would not come near him until he sent Centernose's canoe out to intercept them. He wanted no berries, but he did barter trinkets for salmon, for supper. Along the way, he saw plenty of wild fowl which would have brightened the cook pots. But he could lose no time in hunting.

At the river's mouth, the travelers were well received in a two-house village. After a breakfast of sturgeon and salmon, which he paid for with a few trifles, McLeod had the canoes secured on shore. He then set briskly out with all baggage snug in his men's knapsacks. After three hours of trudging, he led his men to a stream only thirty yards wide but teeming with salmon trout. He calmed the fears of Indians at the fishery with his elaborate pantomime of friendship. It was obvious that the jittery locals had never seen a white in their lives. When he camped at a lagoon behind the beach, he sent a messenger ahead so that his party would not frighten any more Indians.

Wednesday, October 25, dawned in a cold drizzle which discomfited the explorers, since they had no covering but their coats and a blanket apiece in their rucksacks. But they pushed on to Coos Bay, where McLeod stared long and hard at the "mainland." It was one of lofty mountains topped with impenetrable forest. Much time was lost in finding a guide, then in slogging through dunes of sugar-fine sand heaped up by savage onshore gales.

When the winds absented themselves for the moment, McLeod hurriedly put to sea in a hired canoe. Centernose and his court declined the honor of braving the sea with him, but four Indians attached to the chief trader's party were willing to have a go at becoming sailors. The guide urged them to negotiate Coos Head only at ebb-tide. Since the ebb came after dark, "Captain" McLeod turned the conning of the craft over to the eagle-eyed Indians. They navigated well, sailing a westerly course for three miles, then making a dogleg to the south which carried them beyond dangerous Coos Head. They headed directly for shore and paddled up an inlet to await daybreak. McLeod then led them on to a safe place to secure the canoe and reverted to shank's mare again. Leaving some woods, he marched south over a fine, flat, hardpacked beach to reach the Coquille River on October 26. The Indians called it the Shequits. So broad was its mouth that it appeared to flow through a lake before it mingled its fresh water with the salt surf of the Pacific.

Local Indians told McLeod that beaver were in great number upstream. He doubted this usual greener-grassing: "That, like every other Indian report of the kind, deserves little credit." He quieted the anxiety of the local folk with little presents and assurances that his only interest was beaver. Then he asked them to ask their friends to bring him pelts. Before his fire was kindled, messengers were on their way to spread the news of hairy strangers who offered the sacred *hyaquois* for mere beaver skins! Indeed, the pale-visaged strangers seemed to use the fur of the rodent as their own *wampum*.

McLeod kept a close watch that night. His prudence was justified, as twenty-seven natives came to visit. They were not hostile, but he could not fail to note the hush which fell over his own redmen. They were much in awe of these newcomers and he wondered if they were of the Umpqua band which had chased the Nor'westers from this country. He bought a fresh fish from them, patiently and politely explained that the men needed to rest, and, with relief, saw his guests depart. But they did not go far. They stopped at a nearby lodge where they put on a dance whose noise kept the whites in fretful sleep, if not awake, all night long.

In a borrowed canoe, McLeod paddled twelve miles up the Coquille. He visited hamlets where he saw beaver skins, but the Indians were reluctant to part with them. He also saw signs of beaver in the river. When he revisited the little villages, he managed to secure twenty-three large and small beaver, three common (i.e., land) otter, and three skins of the very valuable sea otter. Next day, he tried again and got forty-five pelts. On a third buying trip, he secured thirteen more—but no answers to his request for information on the country to the south. All the natives professed ignorance of it. None had ever been beyond a small river thirty miles distant, where friends lived.

When McLeod persisted, the Indians referred him to an old man who lived at the source of the Umpqua. He was said to be in the habit of visiting a river of some note to the south; perhaps it was McLeod's Great River. However, he never walked along the beach to reach it. He took a three- or four-day overland journey to what must have been the Rogue River.

The chief trader had to get back to his people. He knew that his nonappearance would worry them. He planned to return to them and the Umpqua by retracing his steps up the seashore, then to hook inland to the Great River (Buenaventura?) by the old man's trail. Thereby, he would establish a road from Fort Vancouver to the Buenaventura, if horses could possibly make the trip.

On the last day of October, McLeod headed back for base camp. Though high water had moved his canoe, he found it to be safe and sound. Camping in the rain, with "no other canopy but the heavens," he next moved his men around Coos Head on the ebbing tide, dropped his pilot, and, trading for ten beaver en route, was back in the headquarters camp on the night of November 3, 1826. He found Douglas already there and was pleased to learn that his scientific friend's botanical gleanings had compensated him very well for his hardships, fatigue, and an Indian scare or two.

While McLeod had been trekking southward, Douglas was being assaulted by violent winds and storm-driven rains which drowned his campfire and blew down his tent. He had shivered in his drenched blanket, suffering from headache, stomachache, and giddiness. After he treated himself to a whiff of tobacco (he was afraid to use up, so early, his only medicine, calomel), Douglas suffered a violent perspiration fit, but his fever subsided. He recovered and moved across the Umpqua near modern Cleveland. On the south side he discovered, straightaway, that not all Umpquas were as friendly as Centernose. He wrote, October 26, 1826, about his adventure on Sugar Pine Mountain west of Roseburg:

"About an hour's walk from my camp, I was met by an Indian, who, on discovering me, strung his bow and placed on his left arm a sleeve [bow guard] of raccoon skin and stood ready on the defence. As I was well convinced this was prompted through fear, he never before having seen such a being, I laid my gun at my feet on the ground and waved my hand for him to come to me, which he did with great caution. I made him place his bow and quiver beside my gun and then struck a light and gave him [tobacco] to smoke, and a few beads."

The two parted as friends. But, shortly, Douglas had a less amiable encounter. He had reached a grove of his long-wished-for pines, with their immense cones hanging like sugar loaves. But the cones were high above him, the trees much too thick to chop down, and the trunks without lower limbs for climbing. He recalled: "Being unable to climb or hew any down, I took my gun and was busy clipping them from the branches with ball when eight Indians came at the report of my gun. They were all painted with red earth, armed with bows, arrows, spears of bone, and flint knives, and seemed to me anything but friendly. I endeavoured to explain to them what I wanted and they seemed satisfied and sat down to smoke, but had no sooner done so than I perceived one string his bow and another sharpen his flint knife with a pair of wooden pincers and hang it on the wrist of the right hand, which gave me ample testimony of their inclination. To save myself, I could not do by flight and, without hesitation, I went backwards six paces and cocked my gun and then pulled free from my belt one of my pistols, which I held in my left hand. I was determined to fight for life.

"I, as much as possible, endeavoured to preserve my coolness and perhaps did so. I stood eight or ten minutes looking at them and they at me without a word passing till one, at last, who seemed to be the leader, made a sign for tobacco, which I said they should get on condition of going and fetching some cones. They went and, as soon as out of sight, I picked up my three cones and a few twigs and made a quick retreat to my camp, which I gained at dusk."

But that night brought little repose for the naturalist. During his sleepless night, he wrote: "How irksome a night is to such a one as me, under the circumstances! Cannot speak a word to my guide, not a book to read, constantly in expectation of an attack, and the position I am now in is lying on the grass with my gun beside me, writing by the light of my Columbia candle—namely, a piece of wood containing resin."

Next day, Douglas's guide was attacked by a grizzly, which the botanist shot. After boiling the last of his rice, a hungry collector started back for base camp. En route, his horse, which was one of McLeod's favorites, slid down a slope and became wedged between two trees. Douglas had to laboriously tie its legs and head, to prevent it from struggling and hurting itself (or him), before he cut away the lower trunk and freed the animal. When he finally reached the headquarters camp, he found no one there but Laframboise and an Indian boy.

The French-Canadian told Douglas that the Umpquas were becoming troublesome, with the trappers so scattered. That night, the campers raised a large fire but lay in the shadowy grass nearby, rather than in its warmth. Sure enough, around ten o'clock, some fifteen armed Indians crashed through the grass and bracken toward the flickering light. Laframboise and Douglas fired some blank rounds at them, sending them skittering back into the woods whence they had come.

The following day, Depaty returned to the base camp from the coast. He, too, reported Indian trouble as well as bad weather. He had never experienced such a stormy march, and the tribes were hostile, to boot. They had killed one of his men and carried off a hunter's Indian wife. This affair perhaps explained the curious incident of the thirty-first when Douglas had seen an Indian walking along in a hunter's coat and carrying traps. At the time, he had written: "All this looks very suspicious, but as we know nothing of his language and are too few to risk coming to a quarrel . . . we take, at present, no notice, hoping, too, that he may have only robbed and not murdered our poor countryman."

Douglas was delighted to see Depaty because he was a fine hunter. He would have fresh meat in camp in jig time. Soon the Canadian proved himself: He brought in a long-tailed doe. The botanist needed no urging to turn cook. He was proud of his kettleful of venison and rice soup but prouder still when, after the camp's population was swollen by the arrival of thirteen hungry trappers (who ended his fear of an Indian raid), his companions indicated their acceptance of the plant hunter as one of themselves. Happily, Douglas journalized: "I find that I stand high among them as a workman, and passable as hunter."

The botanist made a hike of a dozen miles along the steep, wooded banks of the Umpqua in hopes of meeting McLeod, who was expected momentarily. He missed him, though the leader reached camp that night. But Douglas was able to survey the Umpqua. He estimated that it was seven to eight hundred yards wide at one point, with a fall of four feet from the tide, whose effects he could see thirty miles inland. That night, he was interested to learn from McLeod that the river's mouth was three-quarters of a mile across, but blocked by a sandbar which would never admit shipping.

McLeod reported to McLoughlin by letter of November 5. He explained his poor catch of forty to forty-five beaver by reminding the factor that: "No success could be anticipated from this neighbourhood after its being so repeatedly hunted for several years back." He described the area beyond the Umpqua as seemingly favorable for beaver and its natives as "Children of Nature" who were well disposed toward strangers. He advised his superior that he was turning his horse herd over to Depaty to fatten up at "the Old Establishment," Old Fort Umpqua, where lines of traps could also be run. In the meanwhile, he would call on his new Indian acquaintances and, circumstances permitting, would visit the Great River. He would "sound the way and secure a welcome reception." He asked that his letter-bearers be sent back to Fort Umpqua. Before he signed off, he complained of the poor quality of the trade scalpers (scalping knives) supplied him by Fort Vancouver. The Indians preferred knives of their own crude manufacture. He also reminded Dr. McLoughlin that Indians preferred *hyaquois,* which they treasured as both jewelry and money, above all other trade goods.

Shortly, McLeod's Hawaiians got into his better graces. They used their swimming and diving ability to recover traps and other property on the river bottom after a gale upset a canoe. The *kanakas* were able to recover all the capsized goods, except two beaver skins.

In a dawn-to-dusk rain, McLeod ordered a return to the south coast. He hoped to revisit the Coquille and push on to the Buenaventura. Indians now told him that the mysterious river was as large as the Columbia. He guessed that it should lie at 41° latitude. He sent Kennedy and François Payette (*dit* Faneant) as his couriers to Fort Vancouver and detached Depaty to trap the upper Umpqua giving him three men as trappers-wranglers. At the same time, he took care of the horses. His own crew packed 215 large plews and sixty-four cub pelts, nineteen large and nine small land otter, and three sea otter skins in buffalo hide wrappers, for Kennedy to pack home.

When the rain subsided on November 7, Kennedy set off, followed by Douglas, Piette, and nine horses loaded with furs. At the same time, Depaty left. Provisions for Kennedy, Piette, and Douglas for a week's expected journey consisted of a few dried salmon and some of the mixed rice and corn (iron rations) brought from the fort. Douglas expected to be able to shoot deer or wildfowl on his way to the Columbia.

McLeod was genuinely sorry to see the botanist leave. He was fond of the indefatigable plant hunter, so devoted to his researches. He described him as being always the best of company during a journey. For his part, Douglas wrote in his journal that he would ever retain a grateful recollection of McLeod's uniform kindness. He promised himself to buy the chief trader a fine rifle as soon as he should reach London.

The journey to Fort Vancouver proved to be far more tedious than anyone could have guessed. It was a hard and hungry march of twelve days in cold, rainy weather. There was but one meager meal per day. Deer were scarce. Soup of powdered *camas* roots made Douglas sick. He was a crack shot (popping off pine cones had been child's play), but only a few geese and ducks came before his sights. And *how* he longed for the ultimate luxury—hot tea. He sighed:

"A little tea, the greatest and best of comforts after hard labour." The weather was so wet and cold that Douglas swore that it not only chilled him and his companions but bleached them, too.

For all of its fatigues and exposure, the march went without a hitch until it crossed the Santiam. Douglas had all of his nature specimens soaked and damaged. He was much distressed but tried not to show it so his companions would not take him for a complaining pork eater or greenhorn.

By November 19, 1826, the botanist was resting at Fort Vancouver, his ankles swollen and inflamed from the cold, wet, and strenuous march. He had to remain indoors and off his feet for nine days. But he put his enforced confinement to good use, drying out and organizing his plant specimens. From the fort, he had penetrated the wilderness of southern Oregon almost to the Siskiyou Mountains. In the Looking-Glass Valley (near Roseburg of today) he had been only one hundred miles from California.

McLeod did not break camp on November 9. He took six canoes and had his men trap the Cahourz (Coos) River. But two weeks yielded only fifty pelts. When his men reported nearby creeks to be devoid of beaver, he pushed all the way to the Coquille, using hired canoes. These he abandoned to proceed on foot in a difficult march over marshy ground, knee-deep in mire and water, which transformed a four-hour hike into an advance of just three miles. Again, there were only a few beaver and—an ominous new note—the Indians grumbled about strangers taking their beaver without paying tribute.

The chief trader sent Laframboise to look into this matter of rumored hostility as well as to look for a stolen trap. Laframboise found that two Umpqua youths who had attached themselves to the Iroquois, Ignace and Jacques, were "giving too much scope to their tongues." McLeod promised to give them a little wholesome advice. If that should have no effect, he vowed to take stronger measures to keep them in subjection. He was determined to maintain the peace at any cost. McLeod worried when he heard that reports unfavorable to the Umpqua Brigade were being circulated among the Indians. But he did not lose any sleep over it. By now, he accepted bad Indian rumors no more readily than good ones.

Laframboise took a message from McLeod to Depaty as constant December rains raised the Coquille and drowned all the traps. Since there was no hope of a beaver hunt until the river should fall, McLeod used the lull in the hunt to make his visit to the Great River. He ascended the South Fork of the Coquille on December 8, hoping to find a passage for horses and baggage from its source to the Umpqua. He found beaver vestiges all along the Coquille's banks but saw that the rise and fall of its waters would only thwart his men. He took only seven men, ordering the rest to sit tight in camp. They were not to trap but to remain on guard against any hostility from the natives. And he gave the Iroquois hunters enough ammunition to keep the camp in fresh meat.

Upstream, on foot, filed McLeod's group. When the canyon grew rocky and cataracted, the guide balked. It would be impossible to reach the large river because of the high water, he said. McLeod persuaded him to continue, since his goal was now only two summer days' travel away. But after having to ford the upper Coquille three times and rescuing one of his men from drowning, McLeod finally called it quits. He reported: "Seeing difficulties increasing without any advantage accruing from persevering further, I deemed it advisable to trace our steps back to examine the Indian route to the Umpqua." It was probably McLeod's presence on the upper Coquille which fostered the stories of nearby whites, passed on to Pete Ogden by Indians on the Rogue River.

Back on the lower river, McLeod was encouraged to stay by the villagers' assertion that the minor streams held beaver which the Indians had never molested. He had cause to believe his informants, this time, because of the beaver spoor he had seen himself below the forks. On December 12, he was back at the base camp. He tried again, choosing the same men, but opting for a different footpath to reach the source of the Coquille. This time, he followed the west bank of the middle fork. He found that the Indians' representation of the route was not far off the mark: It was a narrow mountain trail, unsuited for horses, but quite passable for humans in summer. Whether or not it could be used this late in the season was a moot question. Mountainous, broken country hemmed the river in on both sides as the rain metamorphosed into snow. But McLeod kept climbing doggedly toward the summit of the ridge and soon left the Coquille watershed to descend Looking-Glass Creek into the fine plain of the Umpqua, which was the appointed rendezvous with Depaty. He was nowhere to be seen.

From an Indian, McLeod learned that the Canadian was in camp downstream near Elk Creek, more toward the site of today's Roseburg. There, McLeod met the freeman. The latter's excuse for not meeting him was that he had received new orders from Dr. McLoughlin, orders to hunt. He handed McLeod letters from the

139

doctor dated November 15 and November 21. One missive informed him that eleven of his men would be needed to help build Fort Langley on the Fraser River. The doctor left it up to McLeod to decide whether to stay out with a weakened force or to return. He warned: "You will be too weak to stand your guard with the natives," but hoped he would visit the large river. The second letter suggested that he stay out until March or later, to spare the fort's scanty supply of rations. Trade goods were few, too. He informed McLeod that Fort Vancouver had only seventy-seven two-and-a-half-point blankets and no blue strouds (blanket material) at all.

McLeod holed up in a camp near Old Fort Umpqua for a few days because some of his men were ill. Two of the Hawaiians straggled in before he sent messages to Vancouver and dispatched Laframboise and three others on a sweep north along the coast. They were to go as far as the village of Cawais (Coos?), thence to the Umpqua's mouth, where he would leave instructions. Should they find no note there, they were to rendezvous with him on the Coquille.

The chief trader advised Dr. McLoughlin that he was nearing the mysterious large river and would reach it. But he warned that doublechecking of the natives revealed that it was more the size of the Umpqua than the Columbia, though its sources were far off in the Klamath country. They reported plenty of beaver on its banks. He apologized for turning back without seeing it, on the first attempt. But the advanced season had made it quite impossible to cross the mountains. He hoped to find a new route to it, come spring, one more to the east which had been recommended to him by Indians. He trusted that his efforts would add a few more beaver to the 150 he had on hand. But he felt obliged to reiterate how precarious was trapping along the entire coast. He closed his letter by asking the doctor to have a boat at the junction of the McKenzie and Willamette, McKenzie's Forks, in order to expedite his return to the fort. If not possible, perhaps a boat could be left for him at McKay's Old Fort.

In a heavy drizzle, McLeod led the main party up the Umpqua, dropped Depaty and the horses off at Looking-Glass Creek, then started back the way he had come over the mountains to his Coquille permanent camp. The march was without untoward interest, except that Little Michel got himself lost in the woods for a spell. At the Coquille, McLeod scattered men and traps but gave strict orders for all men to return to camp each evening unless granted a special leave of absence by him, in advance. Rifle shots at playful otter missed their targets but the traps began to claim beaver. Hunting downstream was luckless; McLeod blamed the lack of success on the ebb and flow of the tide, which played hob with the traps. He could get only scant information from the natives about the river to the south. What little he got was erroneous, and he concluded: "Fiction is a predominant failing with them."

On New Year's Day 1827, McLeod presented his men with a fathom of tobacco as a holiday treat. He moved his camp closer to the ocean when the catch failed to improve. There, he had a spot of trouble. An Umpqua, perhaps even Little Chief, seized an Indian boy with the intention of making him his servant, or virtual slave. McLeod quickly returned the boy and scolded the Umpqua for his aggressive act, which he feared would be blamed on the brigade.

Since the beaver catch was still almost nil, McLeod determined not to wait for spring but to head for the mysterious grand river immediately. Taking canoes to the Coquille's mouth, he marched his men down the ocean beach to the Sixes River, where the terrain forced them inland for four days. At a lake he met some Indians, probably the Kuatami, who (he thought) called themselves the "Got Tam You" tribe. (He must have guessed that the "God Damn You!" Indians had been in contact with whites.) But they fled their villages at his coming. For lack of timber, McLeod had to dismantle some of their huts to raft across the Squits En River (perhaps Mussel Creek), but to prove his good intentions he was careful to leave pay in trade goods.

Camped at Beaver Pond, his men shot at a beaver swimming in it, but missed. Later, they wounded a sea otter with a rifle shot but could not retrieve it in the surf without a canoe. The Scot followed a well-established Indian footpath over rocky but not wooded country. He noted that this portion of the coast offered nothing remotely resembling a harbor for sailing ships. He passed two small streams, only knee-deep at the ebb. He called them the Quatchen and Henne-Chenni, but they were probably branches of Elk River. Beaver muck was seen frequently in all the streams. It was apparent that the natives did not molest the animals.

It was with considerable difficulty that McLeod made friends with the wary natives. He did his best, by giving them food and other presents. On January 11, 1827, villagers on the Ukjeh River (probably Elk River) donned war garments instead of taking to flight at McLeod's approach. But his signs and gestures of amity won them over. They laid their weapons aside to receive "tribute" in the form of a few cheap gewgaws. He left them to hurry ahead to his Great

River, which they called the Tootonez, over a fine country of grass in full verdure.

McLeod was tremendously disappointed in the Tootonez, actually the Rogue River. It was no Columbia, no Buenaventura draining the Great Salt Lake and the Rockies. He made his impressions a careful matter of record: "It falls short of the description report has given in size and depth, for it does not exceed a quarter of a mile in breadth where we fell upon it about four miles from the sea."

There was plenty of beaver sign in the nearby creeks, at least. The Indians did not bother the furry creatures; they did not even know how to hunt them. Thus, they did not have a single pelt to trade. Of course, they repeated the familiar refrain—most of the beaver were far upstream. While McLeod sought more information and a strong enough canoe to breast the Rogue's current, his men pitched into a banquet of whale meat and blubber, a welcome change from an inadequate, sorely limited diet. They fired at seals and sea lions in the mouth of the Rogue, without success, but knocked down nine "bustards" to add to their rations.

McLeod hoped against hope that the Tootonez was not "the" large river of the south. But the natives were unanimous: There was no larger stream in the area; the Tootonez was the largest they had ever seen. He found it to be a mile wide at his camp, but its channel was blocked by gravelly shoals. Its mouth, between sandbanks, narrowed to three hundred yards at low tide.

Just as McLeod was about to backtrack up the coast, an Indian stole a small hatchet. When McLeod demanded either its return or payment for it, the chiefs gave him a hostage. They explained that the culprit had fled. The Scot made the best of a bad bargain by keeping the hostage for a time, to impress the damned "Rogues" or "Rascals" of his abhorrence of thievery. He explained: "It was not the value of the article as the act; to have passed it over in silence might not only leave a bad impression but actuate them to further violence."

And so the Tootonez got a name which it could not shake, Rogue River.

The seventeenth found McLeod back in his Coquille camp. He learned that Laframboise had not returned. Trappers who had gone to Coos River told him the Indians there were putting much too high a value on the few furs they possessed. No trading could take place. Someone had told them that he would pay above Fort Vancouver's

Indian tariff. McLeod would not do this, of course, since he was not authorized to exceed the going rate. And he knew that such action would be an inflationary precedent.

With few beaver still being taken, and barely enough time to get back to Fort Vancouver on schedule, McLeod issued orders on January 22 for all traps to be taken up. He settled his account with Little Chief and the other headmen. Because he knew that the Umpqua was too dangerous to navigate in the winter season, he decided to go up the northeast branch of the Coquille and to follow the Indian trail over the mountains to Depaty's camp on the Umpqua's inland plain. He let two Canadians, Little Ignace, and a Hawaiian (Tourawhyheene) go to the lower Umpqua to recover some of their property left there. But he ordered them to walk, not to use canoes. They were then to ascend the river and meet him at Old Fort Umpqua. He also gave Ignace a note for Laframboise, asking the latter to help the little party in any way that he could.

McLeod led the balance of his men up the Coquille. He hurried into camp in a heavy rainstorm, trying to protect his pelts from injury by damp. He had no proper skin wrappings, having sent them all to Fort Vancouver with the first load of furs. He had to make do with green elkskins, with the hair left on. They were makeshift coverings for turning aside the rain.

Because of the expiration of the contract of Cartreach, one of Depaty's servants, McLeod let him go to join his master on the Umpqua in order to give him tidings of the brigade, should Depaty be uneasy. No amount of compensation would tempt an Indian to go along as guide. All were ill-clad and unwilling to venture any distance in the snow. Cartreach set out alone. He returned shortly, completely intimidated by the awful aspect of the frozen mountains ahead of him.

Canoeing and portaging around rapids, McLeod's party continued its ascent. An Indian brought word that Depaty had had to kill the first of the horses to prevent starvation. He had also abandoned Looking-Glass Creek. The Scotsman, fearful of being caught without horses for the trip to Fort Vancouver, rushed ahead with only an Indian companion. He found Depaty gone from the rendezvous point, as the Indian had said.

McLeod followed Depaty's tracks along the Umpqua and discovered, to his joy, a tent looming up ahead of him. But, to his surprise, it was inhabited by Laframboise, not Depaty. Contrary to his instructions, the former had given up his coastal hunt and joined the freeman on January 10. He told McLeod that his associate was away on an upriver deer hunt.

The chief trader was perturbed by Laframboise's failure to obey instructions, but pleased to find that Depaty, with more judgment, had proposed a reconnaissance of the terrain between the Umpqua and Rogue rivers. Laframboise had agreed, and they had explored for twenty-five to thirty miles through a fine country. But neither had had enough gumption to try to cross the key barrier, Calapooya (or Canyon) Mountain. Thus, to McLeod's annoyance, they had left unexplored the essential link. It was almost certainly the tracks of Laframboise and Depaty north of Jump-off Joe Creek which had puzzled Peter Ogden's men and convinced them that the area had already been trapped.

Laframboise felt that he had a good reason for "disobeying" orders. McLeod's note had perplexed him. The Scot thought of it as an informal word of advice, thinking Laframboise would keep in mind his earlier oral instructions. But both Canadians had thought that his letter made for a conflict of orders. McLeod should have remembered how weak were Laframboise's memory and general intellectual powers.

The chief trader met Depaty at Old Fort Umpqua on February 6. He learned that his other men were making their way up the Umpqua, all but Ignace and an Indian, lying dead at Coos Bay. The story was so garbled that McLeod hoped that it was ill-founded. He sent Laframboise and an Indian to meet the men, then took some men and horses himself to meet the men coming via the mountain crossing from Coquille to Umpqua. He greeted the first of the men at dusk, then returned to the Scottsburg-area base camp.

Because he took a shortcut through a region of starving Indians, who were setting snares for game, McLeod missed Laframboise. The latter brought news of Ignace. But the trader found the Iroquois's companions at his camp. They corroborated the sad story. On Coos River, an Indian, hauling the trappers' canoe onto a beach, had caused a gun lying in the bow to discharge. The ball had killed the Indian instantly. The three men fled, leaving Ignace in the rear, ignorant of the mishap. He did not have a chance. The Iroquois walked into an ambush and was easy prey for the Indians, who misconstrued an accident as wilful murder.

Once more, McLeod damned the want of resolution in his Canadians and Hawaiians. He wished that he had time to disabuse the Coos Bay Indians of the idea that the Hudson's Bay Company men were aggressors. But it was too late. He could only tell the local natives to pass the facts of the misfortune on to their Coos River neighbors and to promise that he would return in good weather to settle with them. Deliberately, McLeod left to conjecture the manner of settlement. Since the locals were not friendly with the Coos Bay folk, he was sure that they would volunteer their services to cut off the whole Coos Bay tribe should he choose, later, to mount a punitive expedition.

McLeod devoted all day of February 15, 1827, to the difficult chore of rounding up his horses. All had been idle since November. They were wild, but in fine physical order for a change. By dusk, he reported most of them "hoppled." Next day, he received the property which he had left with the seemingly honest Indian. He was disappointed to find him unworthy of trust. The fellow was shame-facedly forced to make public restitution of the knives he had stolen. His mortification was keen in being humbled by the whites before his peers.

McLeod got the brigade in motion and proceeded to the northeast branch of the Umpqua, actually Bear River. There, he had his men form a human bridge across the stream to pass baggage to the far side before feasting on a dinner of venison and *camas*. The next camp was on the skirts of Mount Labish (La Biche—that is, Elk Mountain). On bad roads showered with rain and hail and drifted with snow the men followed La Biche, or Elk, Creek. After fording raging streams, they struck Grand Prairie. February was dying as McLeod made a hungry camp between the Lumtumbuff or Long Tom River and the Willamette. Heavy snow made hunting impossible on the march but, just north of today's Eugene, hunters killed four geese and traps yielded one beaver. The result was relative feasting. But at miry Long Tom River, Kennedy sold one of his horses for butchering by some of his comrades. And several of the trappers were now ill.

Since the brigade was in pretty bad shape, McLeod hurried two scouts ahead to McKay's Old Fort. They were to look for the boat he had asked for. They returned shortly to report no boat there. But spirits revived as hunters brought in geese, ducks, and even a wolf. The Long Tom was forded and, with borrowed canoes, the men crossed to the far side of the Willamette. When two men asked permission to forge ahead in a canoe they had bought from the Indians, McLeod readily gave his assent and added a letter to Dr.

McLoughlin. Then he led his slogging men down the inundated Willamette Valley, having to swim almost every little brook or swale, so overflowed was the plain.

The voyagers camped at the Teaute River and, with difficulty, managed to fell a tree to form a bridge across the main channel. Attempts which McLeod described as "furious" were made to kill deer grazing on the plain, but they failed. The long-continued filthy weather now threatened to damage the baled furs, since there was no sun to dry them out. Thus, McLeod redoubled his efforts to push on. He killed a horse for steaks to add to the venison of four deer finally killed on March 7.

Next day, McLeod reached the fir- and cedar-lined Santiam River, 150 yards wide where it met the raging Willamette. The horses were now so reduced that he did not dare try to swim them. He left most of them, with the traps, ammunition, and other gear, in a makeshift supply dump in charge of Depaty and Aubichon. He took some men and the fifteen best horses while the remainder proceeded in rickety Indian canoes they had patched up. It was on March 10 that McLeod ordered the peltries stowed in the crazy canoes commanded by Laframboise. The latter would meet him at McKay's Old Fort where, it was hoped, they would find canoes enough for all hands.

When McLeod reached Depaty's ("McKay's") old outpost, he found neither canoes nor Laframboise. Indians explained that he had left with his men that very morning, accompanying Lucier to the *chute* to secure canoes. The chief trader waited for Michel, reunited his party, and reached Fort Vancouver on March 14, 1827, after seven months in the field.

McLoughlin credited McLeod with 797 "made" beaver for his two expeditions. But even bearskins and deerskins had to be thrown in to reach that disappointing total. The doctor still could not believe that the coast was so beaver-poor. He sought other reasons for McLeod's failure, such as the time he had lost in returning to the post in August. Had he started properly and had he taken able and active men and good horses, he would have brought back 1200 made beaver. McLoughlin apparently pulled the figure out of the damp air of Fort Vancouver.

The beaver catch was a disappointment, but the truth about the Great River was a terrible letdown to McLoughlin. David Douglas, after chatting with McLeod, wrote: "The famous river, so much spoken of by the natives for its size, is by no means so large as represented. About 300 yards wide, bold, rocky banks, deep and very clean, navigable for small vessels thirty miles from the sea, [though] it has a sand-bar at its mouth."

McLeod's reconnaissances and Ogden's extended explorations, which just touched at Calapooya Mountain near Jump-off Joe Creek, should have ended tales of the Buenaventura and might have opened a high road over the Siskiyous to California in lieu of a nonexistent coastal route. But McLoughlin and Simpson were doggedly reluctant to abandon their preconceptions. Also, the border geography was still confused. Ogden stubbornly clung to the idea that the Applegate River was the Shasta and that McLeod's Tootonez was but a fork of the Klamath. For the moment, Ogden believed that the Buenaventura still did exist—and that it was the Klamath River!

McLeod's Great River quickly lost that appellation and a half-hearted search for "the" Buenaventura continued. Ogden, for example, hung the title on the Humboldt, first, and then the Sacramento, after giving up on the Klamath. McLeod's Tootonez River became simple McLeod's River or the Tootonez, not to be confused with California's McCloud River—also named for the chief trader, but misspelled. The great, but confused, London cartographer John Arrowsmith further complicated matters by putting the river on his widely used 1834 map under three names Tootonez, McLeod's, and Clamet! Worse, he appended a branch called the Shasty. As years rolled on, and the Tootonez portion of the Siskiyou Trail became notorious for Indian attacks, the stream came to be called the Rogue River, and so it is today.

Jedediah Smith was as bewildered by the rough terrain of the Oregon-California frontier as was Ogden, or McLeod. He believed that the Rogue and the Klamath were one river or that the latter was a branch of the former. For a land without telegraphs, news-papers, or mail service, news traveled fast in Oregon. Reverend Jonathan S. Green, in an 1829 report to friends in Hawaii, wrote optimistically about the possibility of settlement in southern Oregon: "Mr. Smith, an American hunter of whom you have probably heard, on his way from California to the Columbia last winter discovered a considerable river in the latitude of 42° 30'. This he judged to be navigable at the mouth. Should his opinion prove correct, the country about this river would probably be most favorable for such an object."

The ex-Honolulu divine was premature in dreaming of colonizing the Rogue-Klamath-Siskiyou country circa 1830. But the geographic knowledge, for all its fuzziness, was beginning to clarify the relationships among the coast, Willamette, Umpqua, and Rogue and the

Siskiyous. But if the discoveries of men like McLeod eventually reeducated McLoughlin and Governor Simpson to the need of an inland, river valley route to California, the fact was obscured by their monomaniacal insistence on turning the area into a beaver desert.

For the *n*th time, Simpson (on July 9, 1827) hammered at this theme: "The greatest and best protection we can have from opposition is keeping the country closely hunted, as the first step that the American Government will take towards colonization is through their Indian traders and if the country becomes exhausted in fur bearing animals, they can have no inducement to proceed thither. We therefore entreat that no exertions be spared to explore and trap every part of the country." Here a new note crept into the old refrain. Simpson, fearful of Yankee tampering with freemen and even H.B.C. *engagés,* added: "And, as the service is both dangerous and laborious, we wish our people to be treated with kindness and liberality."

Small wonder, then, that McLoughlin sent McLeod and his Umpqua Brigade back into the field on November 17, 1827. But a severe snowstorm negated all his efforts, and the luckless McLeod led his limping twenty-one-man party back to the post after wintering on the Umpqua. He had little to show for his efforts but fatigue and frostbite among his trappers.

In June 1828, McLoughlin had McLeod punish the Clallum Indians of Hood's Canal (in modern Washington) for killing five Company men. The punitive force killed twenty-two Indians, captured and burned two villages, and returned smartly to Fort Vancouver and praise. But, to McLoughlin's and McLeod's chagrin, London disavowed such harsh measures and punished McLeod by denying him a promotion.

McLoughlin strongly defended his lieutenant's actions. An opportunity came to show his continued confidence in McLeod. Less than a month after McLeod's return, Jed Smith and the other survivors of the Umpqua River massacre staggered into the post. Dr. McLoughlin was prepared to do more than make the distressed men comfortable. And McLeod figured largely in his plans.

South of the Siskiyous

JEDEDIAH SMITH led his edgy companions, Turner and Leland, into Fort Vancouver at noon, August 10, 1828. All three were fagged out from days of steady walking after the shock of the massacre. Smith had shaped his course to the seacoast and had followed the shore to the Alsea River and the Tillamook villages. From there, guides took him to the fort. He was astonished to find that Arthur Black had not only survived the slaughter but had reached the fort, dead with fatigue, shortly after nightfall of August 8. Smith learned from McLoughlin that the haggard Black had been so affected with emotion that he could not speak. When he recovered his voice, he asked the doctor to search for Smith and his companions, who might have escaped the treacherous Kelawatsets.

Black had described the surprise attack to McLoughlin and Ogden but repeated it for Smith. As Ogden recalled his words, "Soon after Mr. Smith's departure, while some of the men were cleaning their rifles, some cooking, and others trafficking with the natives, on a sudden, the latter—in number exceeding two hundred—with dreadful shouts rushed on us before anyone was prepared for defence. I escaped the general fate, being wounded and left for dead but, recovering, succeeded in effecting my retreat hither." (The formal, stilted tone suggests that Ogden rephrased the American's gasping account. Certainly, Black was not "left for dead" on the ground, or he would have been hacked to pieces with war axes.)

From Black, Smith put together a pretty good idea of the massacre. Two Kelawatsets had seized Black's gun, but he had clung to it for dear life. They were unable to wrest it from him until he was wounded in the back by a knife thrust delivered by a third warrior. Still another Kelawatset swung an ax at him. Black only had time to duck his head and take a glancing, but almost paralyzing, blow on his back. The pain forced him to release his hold on his rifle. But he had the presence of mind to sprint for the nearby woods. Desperation lent him added speed, and he outdistanced his pursuers.

McLoughlin welcomed Smith and his companions with the kindness and compassion which was becoming legendary. He took immediate action, though the chance of anyone else's having escaped was slim indeed. He sent runners to the Willamette Valley chiefs with presents of tobacco. The doctor asked them to search for survivors. He promised rewards for rescued Americans, punishment for anyone doing them injury. He began to muster a forty-man rescue party but had second thoughts about such a hasty, half-cocked measure, since the friendly Indians reported absolutely no survivors. He disbanded the relief party before it was really constituted, deciding to combine the search for Smith's property (and any possible survivors) with the regular business of his Umpqua Brigade—and then some, for the doctor planned to exploit Smith's reverse in order to penetrate deeper into Oregon and all the way into California, if possible.

During a fortnight of waiting, Smith mourned his dead and ruminated on his misfortune as, without a penny to his name, he ate off of Spode chinaware with the gentlemen in their Fort Vancouver mess. Although the Rockies were far more dangerous for trappers than Oregon (with 500 men murdered, according to Senator Thomas H. Benton's 1829 estimate), Smith's South West Expedition was wiped out. The Mojaves had killed ten men, two had deserted in California, and the Kelawatsets had murdered fifteen more. Smith must have agreed, with added emphasis, with the curiously understated views of Ogden and Simpson. The former said: "The life of an Indian trader is one of hazard and adventure." The Governor added: "So dangerous is the trade that, I lament to say, it has not been unattended with loss of life."

The Kelawatset attack was a shock to McLoughlin. The tribe sometimes sent men to trade at the post, and they had never made any trouble. Only a few hours after Jed's arrival, the doctor was writing London. He blamed the massacre on a quarrel. The Americans had demanded a stolen ax. But, more important, he reported that the Indians had realized that the "Bostons" were of a different tribe from the King George men of Fort Vancouver. Since the newcomers were rivals, perhaps even enemies, of the Britishers, the Kelawatsets had assumed that their attack would go unpunished.

They were wrong. The Honourable Company could not tolerate the murder of whites with impunity, even Americans, not if its own men were to sleep easily in Oregon. The Company never looked for a fight, but firmness toward the Indians was essential not only to success but to survival. McLoughlin, at the very least, knew that he must make a display of force. He would have to "show the flag" in the Umpqua area. He put it this way: "This unfortunate affair is extremely injurious to us, as the success and facility with which the natives have accomplished their object lowers Europeans in their estimation and consequently very much diminishes our security. As for us, every means in our power will be exerted to assist Mr. Smith in recovering his property."

The secret of the Hudson's Bay Company's success in dealing with Indians was its firm-but-fair policy, a "no-nonsense" policy. As early as 1683, its London officers had directed: "Draw downe the Indians by fayre and gentle means to trade with us." Even when the natives were shorted by the practice of the "Overplus," a kind of deduction from full measure of trade goods, the amount deleted was not used to feather a trader's nest but to pay for the gifts and liquor which the Indians expected on top of their payment in barter for furs.

But violence had to be met firmly, if not necessarily with more violence. Simpson attributed the change from hostility to peace by the Columbia River Indians to "the prompt and decisive conduct of the whites in never allowing an insult or outrage to pass without retaliation and punishment." Way back on May 20, 1822, Simpson had secretly told Andrew Colvile his philosophy of handling Indians: "I give my ideas thus freely for your private information. . . . If they were known by the very pious, I might be looked upon as a true North Wester. . . . I have made it my study to examine the nature and character of the Indians and, however, repugnant it may be to our feelings, I am convinced they must be ruled with a rod of iron to bring and keep them in a proper state of subordination. I have always remarked that an enlightened Indian is good for nothing. . . . They not only pick up the vices of the whites, upon which they improve, but retain those of the Indian in their utmost extent."

Smith reported to McLoughlin that he had lost 228 horses and mules, 780 beaver plews, 50 to 60 land otter skins, 2 or 3 sea otter,

200 pounds of beads, 100 pounds of tobacco, trade goods, and all of his traps and weapons.

Ogden was less interested in Smith's losses than in the reason for the Indian attack. He came to the same conclusion as McLoughlin. The Kelawatsets had realized that Smith's men were truly strangers, not related to the folk at Fort Vancouver. They had decided, therefore, to take advantage of the misplaced trust in them. Ogden paraphrased Smith's own words on this point: "Finding myself among Indians whom, from their possessing many articles of European merchandize and frequently naming you [Ogden] and several other gentlemen, I began to consider them no longer as enemies. I relaxed my usual vigilance. Having prolonged my stay for two days to recruit the worn-out animals I had purchased at St. Gabriel, on the third morning I directed Mr. Rogers, my assistant, to have everything in readiness, desiring the men also to clean their rifles preparatory to start on the morrow. I then, accompanied by two men, embarked in a canoe and proceeded in search of a suitable crossing place, the banks opposite our encampment being too steep for the horses to surmount. On my return after an absence of three hours, when within half a mile of the tents, I observed a number of Indians running towards us along the bank, yelling most fearfully. Immediately suspecting what had happened, we crossed over and secreted ourselves in the bushes, the Indians discharging their guns at us without effect. Anxious to ascertain the fate of my party, I ascended an eminence from whence I could plainly perceive that the camp was destroyed, and not a vestige of man, horse or mule to be seen. Though conscious that the wretches would not dare to pursue us in a country so thickly wooded, I yet considered it to be the most prudent to be concealed during the day and to travel only under cover of the night."

It is axiomatic that an ill wind always wafts some good fortune to someone. McLoughlin, though a compassionate man, saw Smith's disaster as a means of extending Company hegemony into the vacuum left by the ruin of the South West Expedition. London was still harping on ridding Oregon of Americans by trapping out all the beaver and by using sharper trading practices with the Indians. In February, the Honourable Committee had repeated itself: "We think it very important that you should have the means of gaining a firm footing in the coast trade and in all the country on the west of the mountains before the Americans arrive in greater force, as if they are met with a systematic and well-regulated opposition on the principle of underselling them, they will be less likely to persevere in their attempts than if they are allowed at first to make large profits."

Now, McLoughlin could convert the Umpqua Brigade into a Buenaventura or California Brigade. On August 7, 1828, he had reported to London that McLeod would trap south of the Willamette with freemen from that valley, and that he and Ogden would both return to the area in 1829. But now the doctor looked beyond the as-yet unnamed Siskiyou Mountains—all the way to California. Out of gratitude, Smith drew him a map of his track from San Francisco Bay to the fort. Small wonder that McLoughlin's new orders were to follow up the salvage of Smith's goods with a trapping *entrada* into California itself, to the very Buenaventura (Sacramento).

On August 26, the doctor dispatched Laframboise and six scouts. McLeod followed on August 28, having split his main party, which totaled only thirty-eight men, servants, and freemen, plus a few tame Indians. It was not a strong force with which to bully a tribe which had just cut the South West Expedition to pieces, but it was as big a company as McLoughlin could spare. Simpson had only 224 men in the entire Columbia District in 1828. But McLoughlin's belief in the importance of his "Buena Ventura Expedition" was revealed by the makeup of the force. Of the men, thirty-two were regular employees. This was as many servants as remained at Fort Vancouver and more than the strength of the Snake Expedition.

McLeod took Smith and five men up the Willamette in a leaking boat which required constant bailing since it was overladen with baggage. Tom McKay headed the overland party, which included Jed's comrades, Turner, Black, and Leland. McKay would rendezvous with McLeod at Sampou Yea (Champoeg) on the Willamette between modern Newberg and Butteville. The boat reached the falls on September 7, after a much too leisurely journey for Smith. With tobacco, McLeod hired Indians to portage his heavy baggage to a waiting boat above the chutes. He could learn nothing by questioning Indians at the falls about the ambush: "These people, like the generality in this quarter, are so subject to exaggeration that their assertions are entitled to little credibility. Therefore, their stories are treated with indifference."

The bourgeois found not only McKay's party in the Champoeg area, but Laframboise too, returned from a scout. The chief trader reported to the fort that Smith's case was even gloomier than anticipated. McLeod had been given carte blanche by the doctor to chastise the Indians, but he was undecided what to do. He reported: "With

153

the dull prospects before us relative to Mr. S's property, I am unable even to form an idea [of] what measures to adopt at this early period. However, I am not disposed to hostile measures. I must learn more than I know before proceeding to extremities." Perhaps McLeod was still smarting from the unexpectedly negative London reaction to his punitive expedition against the Clallums. Or he may simply have begun to believe that Jed Smith's braggarts had "asked" for the attack, with their arrogance and belligerence.

Laframboise had secured only a few of Smith's furs, all of which were branded by Jed for identification, and one horse. Even these he had traded from Willamette Indians, probably through freeman Pierre Charles, acting as an intermediary. He had had no dealings with Kelawatsets, or even Umpquas, so he could offer no information on their attitude. Smith must have thought Michel awfully timid for a mountain man. He wrote in his journal: "He had no personal communication with any of those Indians."

On the other hand, Laframboise told McLeod that the Umpquas still valued the support and friendship of the Company and were exasperated by the Kelawatset raid. They had picked up a few of Smith's horses, but his furs and property were dispersed all over the country.

McLoughlin's lieutenants, not as big men as the kind-hearted doctor, were not as sympathetic and compassionate toward Smith. Laframboise was careful to place the cost of his recovery of the little dab of stolen property to Smith's Fort Vancouver accounts. McLeod could not resist sneering at his temporarily down-and-out rival: "Mr. Smith's furs, that I have seen, are mere trash." Simpson's attitude suggested that he was more interested in driving a hard bargain with Smith than in extending succor to fellow "Europeans" in bad straits. He wrote Jed on the day after Christmas: "Your beaver is of a very bad quality, the worst, indeed, I ever saw, having in the first instance been very badly dressed and since then exposed to every storm of rain that has fallen."

McLeod did not hurry his mission. He sent Laframboise back to the fort with communications. He sent a Beaver Indian runner, Casino, to the Santiam and Columbia on errands. He just sat tight. With the country burnt-over and his horses in poor shape, as usual, and insufficient to the task assigned him, McLeod predicted (in self-fulfilling prophecy) that he would make slow progress toward California.

McLeod picked up the horses he had left near Champoeg in

March, 1828. He was shocked at their condition: "The ill usage of our horses got from the Indians will, I trust, be a lesson to us not to trust others again without guard." He continued to denigrate Smith, saying that he was undecided as to which route to follow back to the Rockies and that he was losing the loyalty of his comrades: "Turner seemingly declines exposing himself to further molestation from the hostile tribes of Indians over the mountains. Indeed, I am much in doubt that the trader (Smith) will leave us, as he seems so unsettled. I am the more confirmed in this opinion because his other men, I understand, are also resolved to object when the proposal is made to them for a move. . . . When the time comes, I shall do all that I can that the whole party go together."

The dilatory booshway gave his men a belated *regale* while an impatient (and temperate) Smith had to sit on his hands, virtually within hailing distance of Fort Vancouver. Most of McLeod's men drank themselves into a stupor over a period of three days, though some—"those who were not too much affected with liquor"—made saddles. Because of the burned-over prairie, his horses' hunger, his men's drunkenness, and "the molestation of the Indians," McLeod had a hard time rounding up his stock. Anything but a martinet, he let the spree run its sodden course. On September 11 he noted: "The men still enjoying themselves, but I am glad to observe that little liquor now remains in their possession." Teetotaler Smith was not enjoying himself, but was pleased to see the camp finally "drying out."

Even when his men were sobered up and all baggage and traps and other "rigging" was ready, McLeod did not move out of camp. His excuse was that Laframboise was not back from the fort. In any case, rain showers put a stop to what McLeod euphemistically called his progress. To kill time, Jed Smith went hunting. McLeod was pleased, since his drunken men's rheumy eyes had stared at few gunsights, of late. He noted: "Mr. Smith shot a small deer, which happened very opportunely as we had no venison."

Continuing to blame bad weather and strayed horses for his delays, McLeod did not move out until September 15. Even then, McKay and some others hung back, hunting for wandering horses, mostly half-wild *marrons* or mustangs. McLeod's "advance" was achingly, glacially, slow to Smith's mind, for the horse chasers had no better luck than McLeod's bagless hunters.

On the twenty-first, McLeod reached the "Chembukte," perhaps Mill Creek near Salem. Free trappers Depaty, Gervais, and the Iroquois, Louis Shanagoronte, drifted into camp. They brought disturbing rumors—word that the Kelawatsets had won the Umpquas as allies by giving them presents. A worried McLeod wrote of the Kelawatsets that eve: "Elated with their late success, they expect to make an easy capture of us as soon as we enter their country. It is said they are mustering to waylay us in the woody parts of the country. Pillage is their object, unmindful of the consequences."

Nervous or not, McLeod had his orders. He would follow the Willamette Valley to its head, cross the Calapooya Mountains (near modern Divide) to reach the Umpqua via the Calapooya River and a track passing nearby modern Oakland, Oregon. But not until September 22 did he even reach the Santiam, where the ford was buried deep beneath rushing water. He camped while Smith paced about, fretful over the unending delays. Three of McLeod's men were already ill, one with pains in his chest, another with sore eyes, and a third with a painful boil on one leg.

At the Rivière Coupé or Calapooya River, McLeod's rambunctious horses gave him so much trouble that he was of half a mind to abandon them because of the delays they caused. Fording the knee-deep Willamette, McLeod lost two packhorses which rushed into the water behind the headstrong *marrons,* missed the ford, and drowned in potholes. McLeod camped, hired some of the shy Indians with an ax and a blanket, and got them to dive for the valuable loads on the lost animals. They brought up nineteen of the missing twenty traps but could not find the other horse, which had been laden with lead. McLeod tried a grapple, without effect, then hired a slave belonging to Gervais because he had quite a reputation as a swimmer and diver.

While the underwater salvage operations were going on, Laframboise returned. He had been delayed by ill luck at buying horses from the Indians. He had secured only eight and had had to pay too much for them. McLeod grumbled: "Only our present situation could make us pay them so high. We require more to make us independent as, once out of this country, no means exist of procuring any."

Laframboise brought a letter from McLoughlin. It urged McLeod to use every means in his power to effect the restitution of Smith's property. But he left the decision of whether to take the Americans to the Umpqua entirely up to McLeod. The doctor added: "It seems to be in that state either that we must make war on the murders [sic] of his people, to make them restore his property, or drop the business entirely."

A still indecisive McLeod finally concluded to keep the Yankees with him, if only to bolster his small force: "I availed myself

thereof, as our number can't be too great in the eyes of the natives."
He was keeping in mind the doctor's admonition—"A failure in undertaking too much would make this unfortunate affair worse."

A second letter was addressed to Jed Smith. It expressed the doctor's sorrow at hearing from Laframboise just how badly scattered about were his stolen goods, and how unlikely their recovery. Earlier, Smith had suggested to McLoughlin: "Should you think it necessary for the benefit of our company to punish these Indians, you would confer a favor on your humble servant to allow him and his men to assist." But the doctor was not going to be pushed into anything. He made it clear that McLeod was in command of the expedition and would make such decisions. And he added: "As it would be worse than useless to attempt more than our force would enable us to accomplish, and as Mr. McLeod knows those Indians and knows best whether we can effect any good, he will decide on what is to be done."

The bourgeois gave up the search for the submerged lead finally, and on October 1 returned to his first order of business, the recovery of Smith's goods. He crossed the "Nontomba" (Long Tom) River, where Depaty and Gervais joined the brigade, along with family, friends and hangers-on totaling 20 men and almost as many wives and slaves or servants. The brigade was now big enough to make a "favorable" impression on the Indians and McLeod noticed that they were beginning to melt into the forests ahead of the company. But McLeod soon learned, to his disappointment, that his reinforcements were only temporary. Depaty and Gervais were loath to march all the way to California. The chief trader penned his annoyance: "Gervais, as usual, will soon get discouraged. . . . These people are not alive to enterprize and nothing but decisive measures will ever make them leave their favourite country, [the] Willamette."

McLeod passed La Biche (Elk) Mountain without having seen a single Indian. He had been warned against an ambush on Elk River but could not even find fresh traces of Indians there. When Laframboise brought in one of Smith's stolen horses, he also had news. The Umpquas, erstwhile allies of the Kelawatsets, were so shaken by the size of McLeod's force that they had fled into the mountains to hide.

Not until October 7 did McLeod even find the tracks of an Indian. It was probably the spoor of a spy, left behind to watch the movements of the invaders. Shortly, he picked up a rumor that the Umpqua chief was at "the Old Establishment" (Old Fort Umpqua), with some of Smith's booty. As he headed there, more information came in. The locals were losing their fear of the whites. Some finally visited the camp to report that many of Smith's animals had been killed by coastal Indians, while others had died while being driven to the hinterland.

By now, most of the men were enjoying ill health, complaining of various aches and pains. McLeod dutifully noted: "Not five sound in health." Nevertheless, he moved toward the Umpqua River, careful to send Indian messengers ahead to spread the word of his peaceable intentions. His efforts to appease both hostile and fearful bands were successful. On the tenth he invited the Umpqua chief to visit him and, the same day, received an intriguing rumor: "Indian intelligence purporting that four of Mr. Smith's men are in the custody of the Cahoose [Coos, not Cayuse] Indians. How these people escaped we are left to conjecture. Several Indians affirm that they are in existence. If the Old Chief confirms the report, [it] will remove my doubts on the subject."

When Chief Centernose appeared, he could neither confirm nor deny the rumor. To him it was just that, a "flying report." McLeod asked him to try to run it down. But Centernose (alias St. Arnoose, and Starnoose) had other information, when he led eight horses—to restore to Jed Smith—into camp. He had visited the Kelawatsets, who blamed the fight on the missing ax, the seizure and tying-up of the hostage, and the bullying and bragging of Smith's men. Centernose suggested that the ax had been lost in the sand, not stolen. And the hostage seized by Smith's men had been a warrior of rank, who had demanded retaliation. However, he had been overruled by another warrior of even more rank and prestige. Unfortunately, this peacemaker was the Indian rudely ordered off a horse and (perhaps) threatened with a gun! Nursing his wounded pride, the humiliated Kelawatset had reversed himself and joined the exprisoner of the whites in plotting a surprise attack upon them.

Centernose's explanation for the ambuscade jibed pretty well with those McLoughlin had picked up from Indian sources. The braggadocio and harassment by Smith's men had caused the bloody affair: "The Indians were much influenced," reported McLeod, "by the assertions of the other party [Smith's] telling them that they were a different people from us, and soon would monopolize the trade and turn us out of the country. These circumstances and harsh treatment, combined, caused their untimely fate at the moment they least expected it."

McLeod told Centernose that he would not remunerate the Indians for Smith's horses until all were in. When the chief asked him if he intended to make war on the Kelawatsets, McLeod said no. He only wished to reestablish peace and quietness and to restore Smith's property to him. The chief appeared satisfied. In fact, he was ready to join McLeod in any move against the Kelawatsets should the latter opt for war. The chief trader knew that this was so that the chief could "enhance his own merit" by hanging onto Company coattails. Still, Centernose could not understand why McLeod would aid "evil disposed" white men of another tribe, as it were, who boasted and threatened that they would take all the beaver away from him.

Smith did not deny the undeniable—that he had had braggarts in his ranks, loudmouths who swore that they would kick the Honourable Company out of Oregon. He guessed that the Willamette boy slave had passed their boasts on to the Kelawatsets. He admitted tying up the Indian after the ax incident, but reminded McLeod that he had set him free the moment the ax was restored (not "found in the sand") by the Indians. And he denied striking any Indian. Arthur Black acknowledged that he had ordered the Indian off the horse but denied threatening him with a gun, though he was carrying his rifle. Nor would he even admit to having worn "an irritated aspect," as the redman claimed.

By October 26, some twenty-six of Smith's animals were recovered. Centernose, unasked, proposed to accompany the brigade to the coast, supplying six canoes. McLeod welcomed the idea since the hire of a canoe usually cost him half an ax.

Smith doubted the rumor of his escaped men. He thought that the four Coos Bay prisoners might be the men who had failed to join him, as promised, at the rendezvous. They might have trailed him west from Bear Lake and right into a trap. (To this day, no trace of the foursome has been found.)

McLeod took nineteen men, including Smith and Laframboise, to the coast. He had men drive horses there, too, since a return in the canoes against the current would be tedious and dilatory. He would ride back to his base camp, left in McKay's charge. Though four of the freemen's Indians had deserted with their guns and some ammunition, he did not order McKay to mount a pursuit. He could spare neither men nor time. So far, he had only a few horses to show, had not even met the Kelawatsets, and had not trapped a beaver or neared the California country.

Centernose, speaking for McLeod, entered a Kelawatset village on October 21, ordering the villagers to return to the Americans all

159

stolen property. The lodges yielded a rifle, a musket, 2 pistols, Smith's books, papers and charts, and 2 vials of medicine. There were 139 large beaver pelts, 28 small skins, and 23 large and 20 small land otter skins—and 4 sea otter pelts turned up, too. Finally, 2 shirts and even a half-dozen lead pencils were surrendered. On the twenty-seventh, McLeod reached a lower village and recovered 10 pounds of trade beads, 1 trap, a fowling piece, a musket, and a cooking kettle. Next day, he reached the Pacific in fine weather and stopped at the "North Branch" of the Umpqua, where Smith's party had been destroyed.

On the stream, which he dubbed Defeat River (it is now Smith's River), McLeod reported: "A sad spectacle of Indian barbarity presented itself to our view, the skeletons of eleven of those miserable sufferers, lying bleaching in the sun." (The remains of the other four were probably in the river.) After giving the bones decent burial, McLeod and his party continued to the seashore but found no Indians in the area, which had recently boasted several villages. Moving northward, he took a rifle, pistol, 2 horses, and 15 beaver skins from a band of Indians on Tahkenitch Creek. He then camped on the Siltcoos River, where he recovered another of Smith's horses.

On the last day of October 1828, McLeod ascended the Siuslaw River and got a village to give up a blanket, a woolen shirt, 4 plews, some beads, a musket barrel, 3 horses—and information that friendly natives had turned 12 horses and 10 pelts over to the Tillamooks. As the men retraced their steps through wind and rainstorms toward the Umpqua's mouth, they recovered 2 kettles and 3 saddles near treacherous Ten Mile Creek, which McLeod named, equally descriptively, Quicksand River. The village of Chief "Nooze" (Centernose himself?) produced 3 more horses, 2 mules, 7 traps, a copper-covered kettle, a rifle and a rifle barrel, more beads, and the books, journals, and other papers of the murdered clerk, Harrison Rogers.

The twelfth of the month saw the brigade back at the entrance to Defeat River, camped either on Goose Island (now Perkins Island) or Black's Island. From there, Smith and his three companions fanned out and retrieved 7 horses and a mule. It was on the island that Smith decided to pull out of the Buenaventura Brigade. He would head for Fort Vancouver with his recovered goods. McLeod loaned him, as an escort, Amable Quesnel, William Johnston, and three Indians.

Jed Smith and his group took off on November 14 as McLeod headed for his Verveau camp, where he had left his horses and *agrés* (rigging) in the hands of friendly Indians. He found everything, for once, in high order. Laframboise had equally good luck on a special mission, too. He brought in the first pelts of the expedition (other than skins bearing Smith's brand), 72 large beaver and 16 large sea otter skins, traded from the Indians.

To his surpise, McLeod saw Smith returning to camp on the eighteenth. The latter had found his animals too poor to make it all the way to Fort Vancouver. And since he had found the Indians to be dependable, he had left the jaded stock with them, to recruit their strength before he tried again. In addition, Smith's run of bad luck was continuing. Johnston had wounded himself in the legbone while cutting a track through the brush, and Quesnel had been kicked by a horse and badly hurt in one knee.

When the chief trader tried to round up the horses he had left on Elk River, the Indians told him that his horse guard had abandoned them because Indian "stragglers" were circulating wild rumors of violence. With much effort, McLeod managed to assemble the herd, picking up two of Smith's strays in the process. Back at his base camp, he found that McKay, too, had recovered some stolen property. McLeod noted in his journal that he paid the Indians only for their services; he gave them nothing for the rustled stock they turned in.

McLeod had performed the first task assigned him. He had scoured the Umpqua country and found a surprising amount of loot, down to medicine bottles and pencils. He had done this without so much as a fight, much less the loss of men and animals. As a diplomat, he had performed as well as he had done as a scrounger. Also, he had explored and reexplored the critical connective area of the Umpqua, which tied Willamette to Rogue and opened the Siskiyous and California to trapping.

It is unlikely, however, that McLeod penetrated as far as Jump-off Joe Creek on this expedition. He mentioned neither stream nor man (Joe McLoughlin, the doctor's halfbreed son), so it is unlikely that Joe was with him and made a sortie to the stream. Probably, the naming of the creek occurred during McLeod's 1829 expedition, when Joe McLoughlin definitely was with him. Heading for camp one night, he walked off a bluff in the dark and received severe injuries in the fall.

November 23 saw Jed Smith's final decision. He would sell the horses and furs to the Honourable Company and head back for the Rockies. McLeod did not feel that he had authority enough for such a transaction, and referred him to McLoughlin. He let Smith have

161

Laframboise and two other men, to replace the banged-up Quesnel and Johnston, noting "The Indians seem intent on giving trouble." Smith left on November 28 and McLeod, exhibiting again the indecisiveness which kept him from fur trade greatness, started for Fort Vancouver in his wake, instead of opening up the Siskiyou Mountains.

McLeod, as an excuse for his unexpected return, took along two men who needed medical attention. He also brought the furs which Laframboise had bought, stating that he did so in order to save them from injury by wetting. He came upon an astonished Smith, camped in miserable weather on Elk River, and joined him. He quickly rushed ahead of the horse-herding Americans, however, and reached Yellow River on December 2. On this branch of the Willamette, he had his men build canoes. The flooded valley would have made travel on horseback difficult and perhaps injurious to the stock. From the Charlas Indians he received skins due the Company in payment of outstanding debts, but also twenty-three large beaver and one otter, all plainly marked with Smith's ownership brand.

On December 10, McLeod closed out his journal and started for the fort by canoe. He left Aubichon and two Indians as wranglers or horse guards over his herd. They were to move the beasts, once the rains should let up and the terrain should dry out, to winter pastures along the "L'Ommitomba"—the Long Tom River.

Without orders—virtually in defiance of orders—McLeod returned to Fort Vancouver on December 14, 1828—"for instructions," as he put it. McLoughlin's instructions had been plain enough: using Smith's map, trap into California after restoring the stolen items to the Yank. Eight days before Smith's arrival, McLeod aborted the first attempt by the Company to cross the still unnamed Siskiyou Mountains into California.

Smith was greeted by McLoughlin's customary hospitality but Simpson's lightly veiled hostility. The latter's letter, dated December 26, was devoid of Christmas spirit and reviewed Smith's actions and McLeod's findings with caustic "impartiality": "He [McLeod] learned that the melancholy catastrophe was occasioned by some harsh treatment on the part of your people towards the Indians who visited your camp, some of whom, they said, had been beaten . . . which treatment they further said corroborated in their minds a report that had preceded you from the Bona Ventura (for which it appears there were some grounds) and that, as a matter of self-preservation, they determined on the destruction of your party, which its injudicious conduct and unguarded situation enabled these savages to accomplish with little difficulty or danger to themselves."

When Simpson digressed, it was to blame McLeod's distraction to recover the loot for his loss of a whole season of trapping and his expenditure of £100 beyond the loss of normal fur profits. He carped: "Had you been in the condition of discussing terms with us, we should, as a matter of course, have insisted on your defraying the expenses . . . but you was not in that condition, consequently, nothing was said on the subject. . . ." He then offered Smith forty shillings for each of thirty-eight horses—take it or leave it. To drive a harder bargain, he claimed that McLeod had 150 head and did not need more horses. (Untrue!) "If you are not satisfied with that price, they are still quite at your disposal."

Small wonder that Jedediah Smith was ambivalent toward the Honourable Company, faced with the kindly McLoughlin and the ill-mannered Simpson. This ambivalence was reflected in Smith's later reports. Had it not been for Simpson's bullying, he probably would not have warned the U.S. Government against Company expansion in supposedly jointly held Oregon.

London's attitude was humanitarian and fair-minded, much closer to the doctor's than the Governor's. On October 28, 1829, the Governor and Committee expressed their approval of McLoughlin's efforts in Smith's behalf: "We are much gratified to learn that every hospitable attention and assistance were afforded Mr. Smith, the American, and his companions in distress after the horrible massacre of his party by the natives of the Umpqua, and from the humane feeling you have already manifested it is scarcely necessary to desire that you will in all occasions render any protection in your power to Americans, Russians, or any other strangers who may be in the country, against the treachery or violence of the natives, whatever may be the objects of the visits of such strangers, be they competitors in trade or otherwise, as all feeling of self-interest must be laid aside when we can relieve or assist our fellow-creatures."

A number of McLeod's associates were not surprised by his unauthorized return to the fort. Some said that he had come back simply because he was homesick; he missed his wife and family. Francis Ermatinger was convinced that McLoughlin had erred in choosing the erratic and delaying Scot to head up the new California outfit with the extra duty of rescuing Smith's goods. He much preferred the swarthy McKay, though he knew that the "breed" was "not gifted

163

with saint-like patience," to borrow the words of California pioneer Elijah Steele in the *Oregon Statesman* of 1865.

Tom McKay was a wiry, twinkling-eyed yarn spinner. With his white teeth clenched on the stem of a pipe as long as a churchwarden's, and stuffed with a mixture of *tabac* and kinnikinnick, he somehow managed to pour out "long sulphurous tales," accented with puffs of smoke. But more important than his role of campfire *jongleur* was his skill as a mountain man. He was as dependable as a Pennsylvania trap. Although he was gimpy, with a lame left leg from a poorly set broken bone, he was as fine a horseman as he was a marksman. At Fort Vancouver, a man named Anderson once showed his contempt of some men's shooting by pinning, with his sheath knife, a target of a piece of paper to a tree a long distance off. McKay warned him to remove the skinning knife or he would hit it. Anderson just shrugged, so the "breed" took aim, fired, and drove the blade into the trunk with his rifle ball. Simpson, chary of praise for McKay (or anyone) had to admit that McKay was well-known to every Indian in the Columbia Department, "having sent a few of their friends to the other world for their misdeeds."

Frank Ermatinger wrote his brother, Edward, about McKay on March 14, 1829, after a disgusted McLoughlin had hurried McLeod back to his stranded brigade: "I think he has accepted with indifferent good will. Mr. McKay is one of his party, I believe, and upon him I hold my hopes, for if Mr. McLeod was to go alone I am sure even the sight of so many horses, should he perchance fall in with them, would be alone sufficient for him to yield the field."

Dr. William Tod of the Company was a little kinder toward McLeod when he wrote Edward Ermatinger on July 15, 1829, for he blamed the elements more than the Scot for the fiasco of 1828: "He succeeding in recovering most of the furs but making considerable sacrifices and losing so much time that winter set in before he had the business settled, he was obliged to take up his quarters on his old hunting ground. He paid Vancouver a visit about Christmas time, much to the astonishment of the Doctor who, sanguine as usual, imagined him near San Francisco."

Simpson, visiting Fort Vancouver that winter, was as astonished at McLeod's appearance as was the doctor. But he was also busy denigrating Smith and the Americans. He boorishly reminded Jedediah how much he was in the Company's debt: "You are well aware that we have already experienced much inconvenience, incurred many sacrifices, and exposed the concern to heavy loss through our anxious desire to relieve, assist, and accomodate you. We are willing to do whatever else we can, without subjecting ourselves to further loss or expense in order to meet your wishes."

Simpson was pleased, at least, that Smith now gave up "the very hazardous journey" he had contemplated taking back to the Rockies and now accepted the Company's advice. This was to take the circuitous but safe route home to the United States via the Red River of the North. It was, in Simpson's words, "The safest course you can pursue and the most eligible plan you can adopt."

Smith, having accepted Fort Vancouver hospitality for so long, decided to sell his furs to the Company, in addition to his horses. He received £486.18.5, about $2369.60. The sum was based on a price of $3 per beaver, $2 for a land otter, and $10 for sea otter. The horses brought forty shillings each. The Company made a neat profit, kept the peace on the frontier, made something of a friend in Smith, and garnered useful geographical knowhow for its drive into California.

Smith was genuinely grateful for the Company's rescue of his pards and himself. He so stated in a letter to the Secretary of War, dated October 29, 1830. And he kept his trappers east of the mountains during the remainder of his short life, quite likely out of deference to McLoughlin's wishes.

Jed Smith did not actually follow Simpson's advice. When he heard of American fur parties near Flathead Post, he said a quick good-bye to the Britishers and headed that way on March 12, 1829. He took Arthur Black. Turner remained with the Hudson's Bay Company; Leland dropped out of sight.

Since Simpson had egged McLoughlin to get McLeod under way again, the doctor gave the Scot his orders on December 29—to hunt the "San Buenaventura." At the same time he ordered Ogden into California from the east (Snake) in a kind of pincer movement on the border beaver. Both men would follow trails blazed, and described, by Smith. McLeod actually set forth in January 1829, with Arthur Turner as his guide. He was to round up men for a hunt of twelve to sixteen months in California. There was a fresh reason for hurrying McLeod back out. Jed Smith had told McLoughlin that the "Spaniards" ignored their beaver, "an animal they hardly know by name, altho some of the rivers within a few miles of their settlements abounded therewith."

McLeod marched his brigade to what he took to be a fork of the Klamath River. It was actually the upper Rogue. He found the

"Rogues" rascally enough, for they took his traps and knocked them apart for pieces of metal to shape into arrowheads. He dropped down the stream to the mouth of the Applegate near modern Grant's Pass. His men caught a few beaver but lost some more traps to Indians. They gave him enough trouble for him to mention, without further detail, that his men had to resort to arms.

At last, McLeod marched over the Siskiyou Mountains. But he did not yet give them the name. In fact, he airily dismissed the barrier between Rogue and Klamath drainages as just "a height of land." When he reached the Klamath, he followed it to Upper Klamath Lake. Hunting continued to be poor, even in this well-watered area. He recalled: "A straggling beaver taken now and then was all the party could glean." Nor were game animals much more plentiful. His men began killing their horses to postpone starvation. For his own part, McLeod bought fish and eating dogs from the Klamath Indians. The latter then stole three horses—and with impunity because of McLeod's recurring vacillation. As usual, he had excuses: "We were too much pressed by starvation to take measures to recover them." Making no attempt to punish the horse rustlers, McLeod crossed his men over the "straits" between Upper and Lower Klamath lakes, then marched along the eastern shore of the latter to enter California, at last.

March 26, 1829, found McLeod halted on the Pit River, the main branch (or largest fork, however one looks at it) of the Buenaventura, the Sacramento. Here, too, the local residents stole horses and traps and, once more, McLeod feared that he lacked the strength to either recover the loss or punish the thieves. He was finally drawn into battle when the Pit River Indians grew so contemptuous of him that they attacked. Once the die was cast and he had to throw off his indecisiveness, McLeod recovered the doughtiness of his Scots heritage. He tore into the Indians and whipped them soundly. When the dismayed Pits left the field, seven or eight warriors lay dead.

McLeod, perhaps bucked up by this victory, set out in earnest to find the Buenaventura. "Conjecturing that we could not be very remote from the Valley we were directed to hunt, I sent a party down the [Pit] River to obtain information relative to the geography of the country. But no important information could be got, as the language of the natives is unintelligible to us. So we had to travel at random. Our conjectures, however, were not ill-founded." On April 6, 1829, two days after Indians robbed and killed one of his Indian trappers, McLeod found the Buenaventura (Sacramento) Valley. The very next day, two more trappers were attacked, but the Canadians killed two warriors and drove off the balance of the war party.

It was on April 9 that McLeod reached the Sacramento River bottom. He found it as thick with deer as Richmond Park. The hungry men, who had not seen a buck for a month, gorged on venison before wetting their traps in the Buenaventura for the first time. A week later, they were camped on the east bank tributary of the Sacramento now called Cow Creek, but dubbed Canoe River by the chief trader because he had his men build a little fleet of seven trapping canoes there, of cottonwood. He planned on giving his starved-thin and sore-footed horses a good rest in the vast natural pasture that was California's Central Valley.

The Canadians found it difficult to intimidate the local people, who loosed arrows at them without the slightest provocation other than their mere presence. The trappers killed a few attackers but more always replaced them and McLeod had to issue orders that all canoe men must return to camp each noon for reasons of security.

As the little fleet, with its escorting army, made its way southward along the eastern shore of the Sacramento River, it averaged a catch of fifteen to twenty beaver a day. When he left the area of the hostiles, McLeod was able to order the canoes out for longer hunts. They began to absent themselves from camp for periods up to a week in order to take full advantage of high water, as the sun began to bake the Sierra foothills, drying up *arroyos* and causing the river and its major affluents to drop. By now, McLeod had replaced the Buenaventura fables with a good idea of the real Sacramento: "It receives all the waters of the different rivers running through that valley, and, I believe, forms the Bay of San Francisco." It was a pleasant plain, except for one spot where salt-impregnated grass killed several horses before McLeod crossed over to the right bank.

McLeod was absolutely astounded when, on August 8, 1829, he received a note in English delivered by natives to his camp on the Quicksand (Mokelumne, today) River. It was signed by William Welsh, a fellow-Scot who had jumped ship, the *Lady Blackwood,* in Bodega Bay in 1821, to set roots quickly in Spanish California. His note inquired whether or not the party of strangers was American, and if it had come to settle the boundary line. McLeod recalled: "I replied in the negative and stated the object of our researches and sent back the messengers. We could not converse with those people as none of our party were acquainted with the Spanish language."

Back across the Sacramento from the Mokelumne went the

Buenaventura Brigade, to ascend one of the skimpy west bank tributaries. McLeod named (and misspelled) it D'Epatis River for Depaty, *dit* McKay. Some historians have guessed that it was terrace-banked Putah Creek near modern Davis, California. But if McLeod was correct in his estimate of the distance to Sonoma, "a Mission situated at the southern extremity of the mountain, about 70 miles from where we then were," then it should have been Stony Creek rather than Putah or Cache creeks, the only good-sized watercourses of the western side. Both of the other oak-belted streams, cutting through fine loam, are much closer to Sonoma. In order to find better grass and good water, the men followed the stream up into the hills of the Coast Range.

On September 19 the brigade was once again surprised by visitors. Five men appeared on a height and waved a white flag. They had been sent by the aptly named Fray Bonaventura (!) Fortuni of Mission San Francisco de Solano, at Sonoma, which McLeod called "St. Noma." The padre wished to ascertain the identity of the mysterious band whose presence had been reported to him by Indians. McLeod let McKay and two others accompany the neophytes, or Christian Indians, back to the mission. When they returned, next day, they brought Abel Stearns and four other foreigners resident in Alta California. They had been on the road to Russian Bodega when they had learned of strangers from the north.

Abel Stearns was looking for a fifty-mile-square landgrant on which to settle as a Mexican citizen. He passed on much geographical information to McLeod. In spite of recurring droughts and crop failures in 1828–1829, some of the missions still had herds of up to six thousand cattle and uncounted head of horses. As for beaver, the low water in the Sacramento (because of the drought) had driven most animals south and west, out of the river and its drying-up tributaries and into the marshy, tidal Delta, where the Sacramento and San Joaquin rivers joined forces for one last mighty rush to the Pacific through Suisun Bay, Carquinez Strait, and San Pablo and San Francisco bays.

The ex-New Englander warned McLeod that beaver skins were belatedly becoming an article of trade. Mission San José had collected 1500 skins from the natives for a pittance and sold them to ships at $3 apiece. Stearns, like so many other pioneers of Oregon and California, believed that beaver *must* be on the west coast. Thus he reported to McLeod, who repeated it to Dr. McLoughlin, that "the country to the northward of Bodega is said to be rich in beaver and no encouragement given to the Indians to hunt them." Wisely, McLeod (perhaps remembering the scanty returns on the Oregon littoral) spurned the coast and stuck with the Sacramento Valley.

Through the good offices of Stearns, McLeod secured twenty-three sound horses from Father Fortuni for thirteen blankets, some ha'penny knives, and a few files, axes, awls, looking-glasses, and rings for the Indian wards of the padre. Though three horses immediately strayed, it was an excellent bargain. McLeod's brigade was once more in good shape for traveling. Before he left, Stearns allowed one of his men, a Black American pioneer, George Washington, to join McLeod. The latter was pleased to have him, since he spoke Spanish well after six years in the province and knew the country, to boot.

The chief trader found the Sacramento Valley heavily populated with Indians. Great numbers crowded together at every watercourse, living on acorns, fish, deer, antelope, and bear. He estimated that some villages ran to 1500 inhabitants. On the D'Epatis River were sites covered with human bones. Stearns told him that they marked the scenes of battles or massacres of horse-thieving Indians by the Mexicans. McLeod did not doubt this, for he shortly cut the trail of a large party of horsemen towing a piece of ordnance. This was the track of Lieutenant José Antonio Sánchez and his forty-two-man punitive expedition of May, from the San Francisco Presidio. Sánchez had lost two soldiers killed and eight wounded, besides eleven of his Indian auxiliaries wounded, in a sharp fight with the Cosumnes Indians. The latter had not been awed by muskets or even the swivel cannon.

Someone, possibly Stearns, told McLeod that five whites had been killed by Indians, including Jed Smith's two deserters. Five men may have been killed, but not James Reed and Louis Pombert.

At one point, four hundred Indians rushed McLeod's camp. But, when they found the whites ready for them, they docilely unstrung their bows and let McLeod point out a place for them to sit for a spell. They later slunk off, meek as mudhens.

Trapping the streams flowing bayward from the Coast Range proved unrewarding. The ebb and flow of the tides alone played havoc with the traps, and thus the catch. "Missing" was the word of the day. The hunters' attempts to shoot beaver and otter as they swam on the surface only wasted ammunition. They envied the Indians' skill in netting occasional beaver as falling tides exposed the entrances to lodges. A man would break a hole into a den, and, when the frightened animals bolted, they became entangled in a net. The Indians bartered their catch at Sonoma Mission for clothing and the red and white beans which were so much to their taste.

Winter rations became a problem as McLeod saw his store of powder and ball dwindling away. He had his men collect and dry provisions, probably venison jerky, during August. Some of them imitated the Indians and swapped pelts at Sonoma for beans. The bourgeois was disturbed, too, by his men's reckless waste of ammunition: "My remonstrances on many occasions in the fore part of the season had not the desired effect of making them saving of what they had left in their possession. . . . To have wintered in this valley would have left us entirely destitute before spring, which would, most likely, involve us into difficulties."

For some reason, McLeod chose to winter neither in the Sonoma area nor in the Sacramento Valley, both having relatively mild winters, but to return to the highlands near Mount Shasta. Probably this was because he hoped to be able to run traps even in midwinter. He hoped to trap the uppermost Sacramento, the Pit, and the Klamath, and the streams of the "last height of land," the range he would shortly name the Siskiyou Mountains.

The Buenaventura Brigade left Putah Creek on October 8, 1829, and moved north to Cache Creek, the drainage of huge Clear Lake. A few beaver were taken, but the Indians welcomed their visitors with flights of arrows. A gunshot sent them scurrying for their huts. Crossing the Sacramento again to the better-watered east side, the fur men marched and trapped north along the main branch and its affluents, before retracing their steps of springtime to the Pit River.

More traps were stolen, more arrows dodged, more natives killed in self-defense. The luckless Jean Baptiste Jean, who had lost his horse by drowning in March (with all of his traps, ammunition, and extra clothes) now had his rifle stolen right out from under his Gallic nose while he was setting borrowed traps. McLeod recorded: "We lost many beaver taken out of traps by the natives but we never molested them in consequence, taking for granted that starvation compelled them to do it. But when traps were taken up, as was often done, we used every endeavour to get them back, but seldom succeeded. Their numbers precluded a possibility of detecting the guilty."

Two of the canoes sank and a third upset, sending twenty-nine traps to the bottom. Traps were becoming very scarce and some of the men were now unarmed—or "destitute of guns" as McLeod quaintly put it. Still, he was optimistic as he made his way up Clear

Water River, perhaps today's Fall River. He pronounced the thirty miles of terrain between himself and the Shasta Valley to be fine country for traveling, and unlikely to hurt the horses' feet.

McLeod had entered California east of Mount Shasta, like Ogden, but his return route was to be via the Shasta Valley, west and north of the great 14,162-foot mountain, smack on the main route of the Siskiyou Trail of later days. He felt that this central route was beyond the range of hostile Indians and only a third as long as Ogden's route back to Fort Vancouver.

While McLeod led an advance of foragers and scouts, trapping beaver more for food than fur, McKay commanded the main body. He led them to campsites pre-selected by his superior. November closed with a burst of fine weather, making traveling and camping easy and comfortable. McLeod sent Joe McLoughlin and Amable Quesnel to McKay to point out his trail.

Lulled by the mild weather into a leisurely pace, McLeod closed slowly with Mount Shasta and a stream which he called the Shasta River, but was not the river of that name today. There his men had to kill eleven Indians who shot some horses full of arrows and ran off others. McLeod still hated to have to fight the natives; he much preferred to feed Indians than fight them. But "they continued skulking about our camp in ambush, to do more mischief, and met their fate."

An early snowfall of November 28 might have served as a warning to McLeod, had it not melted off immediately. In any case, snow began to fall in earnest at noon of December 2, 1829. McLeod was completely unprepared. It was as if he had read and believed the tales of California being a land of subtropical milk and honey, from end to end. When the storm abated on the night of the third, the land was so deeply covered with snow that the horses could not paw their way down to grass. Frantically, McLeod ordered out all hands, to cut brush and to peel bark from trees as emergency feed for the stock. Notwithstanding the heroic efforts of the men, twenty-three horses died in just two days, December 3 and 4. On the fifth, the chief trader led a party out, personally, in hopes of finding exposed pasturage, somewhere. It was a forlorn hope; he was too high up, there simply were no sheltered spots. The farther he went, the deeper lay the drifted snow. Next day, another attempt was made by a hunter who had made himself a pair of *raquettes* or snowshoes. He mushed back to report the entire countryside to be covered with snow.

171

It was now impossible for the brigade to round Mount Shasta and drop into the true Shasta Valley.

The brigade leader was damned if he would let his horses die without a fight. He gave orders for his men to clear the banks of the nearby river of snow, so that brush and grass would be exposed. Despite their desperate work, he had to list nineteen more animals dead by January 10, 1830. Sadly, McLeod recorded the cold, hard facts of life for future sierra-winter travelers. The Donner Party of 1846 would have profited from his words. "Mr. McKay, who had attended with the men after the horses, informed me that no hopes existed of saving any of them. The feeding is supposed to produce a bad effect [that is, feeding them cottonwood bark, etc.] as they come unable to work, [and] of a sudden and almost immediately, fall dead, tho' not reduced." At least, the animals were not wasted; their frozen carcasses sustained the men during a long spell of boisterous weather which drove all game from near the snowbound camp.

The exact location of McLeod's cold and hungry camp is not known. But since the stream, whose banks he tried to clear, was "very rapidous" and took a southerly course to empty into the mainstream of the Pit, it must have been the McCloud, named for him but misspelled. In 1847 a wooden trough and some guns were uncovered on the North Fork of the McCloud, on Bartle's Ranch in Siskiyou County. Almost certainly, these relics were monuments to McLeod's tragic blunder. It was a terrible place in which to winter, even if his men did catch a few beaver. His men—and his herd— would have wintered easily in the Sacramento Valley. On December 22, McLeod had to sadly record: "All hopes given up of saving any of our horses. Every effort has proved ineffectual."

McLeod had his bundles of furs, 2400 pelts, plus other skins, carefully dried, then cached them in the ground from which he had his men clear the snow. With no animals left, he could not get the packs over the Siskiyous come spring. (It was all in vain; his failure was made complete when snowmelt water invaded the cache and ruined his furs before they could be recovered the next season.)

Using sledges and snowshoes, McLeod and his party on January 17, 1830, fought free of winter's grip on the McCloud River. They managed to reach the Shasta Valley. As if Fate had been mocking him, all along, he found it free of snow. It was full of deer and antelope. There was beaver sign, too, and the local Indians were not hostile. McKay, who had wintered there in 1827–1828 with Ogden, had correctly advised McLeod that they were friendlies. (Only later did the Shastas become feared raiders of the Siskiyou Trail.) Only then did McLeod realize the magnitude of his error.

From the Shasta Valley the Buenaventura Brigade negotiated the Siskiyou Mountains without any major difficulty. When McLeod led his men into camp on the Umpqua he was in familiar territory. So, he left his men there and pushed ahead to reach Fort Vancouver on February 13, 1830.

CHAPTER EIGHT

Banks of the Sacramento

FOLLOWING THE WINTER of 1829–1830, the mountains walling off California from Oregon were finally named the Siskiyous. According to one tradition, the word was a corruption of the name for the ford on the Klamath (perhaps the very "reef" pointed out today as the Company crossing near Hornbrook, California), *Six Cailloux,* or "Six Stones." However, since the words really mean "Six Pebbles," it is more likely that the name came from one of McLeod's saddle horses—a favorite—which died in the snowbound camp. This racer was a bobtail, a *siskiyou* in Chinook, the word apparently borrowed from the Cree. McLeod's Canucks named the mountain crossing the Pass of the Siskiyou in honor of the dead bobtailed horse.

McLeod's lack of leadership was verified not only by his illogical choice of a wintering-in site but also by his inability to handle the malcontents of his party. Most of his freemen objected to hunting in California during another season; Lucier was determined to quit. A rebellious clique of Dubreuil, Johnston, Aubichon, and Jeaudoins was led by Perrault, one of Ogden's deserters to Gardner, long before. McLeod lacked the force of character to control such unruly spirits. All that he could do was complain to McLoughlin: "The men were orderly and obedient except J. B. P. Perrault, who showed a bad example and, against orders and rules of the camp, bartered a gun with a Spaniard for a horse and, the preceding day, he objected accepting one from us. I called him to account and as he could not give any satisfactory reason for such conduct (and that the example might not be followed by others), told him unless he gave up the horse to the Company he would be made to forfeit 30 beaver. To which he replied that he would do neither the one nor the other; at all events, he would keep the horse. I have reason to suppose Perrault much addicted to create dissension and would not wish to have him, especially in that part of the country we have been in. Mr. McKay apprised me in the early part of the season that several of our men were inclined to go to the [Mexican] settlements. Their intentions became more evident after the loss of their horses. Perrault is the most conspicuous character and, I believe, dictator to the others."

McLeod reported that it would take him three months to go back to California, counting the time needed for hunting and resting the horses. He was not anxious to return and his freemen loath to do so. He wrote: "The country that we have hunted has been drained of beaver and to make another hunt we would have to select other hunting grounds." Anticipating the displeasure of McLoughlin and Simpson at his fiasco, he concluded his report thus: "I have nothing further to add except the deep regret I feel for the heavy loss the party sustained, the cause of which could not be forseen."

With McLeod's horses dead, his men rebellious, and his furs buried in some godforsaken corner of California, both Simpson and McLoughlin completely lost patience with the chief trader. Simpson blamed "the whole catalogue" of misfortunes on him, reminding him that two years of the Buenaventura Brigade had yielded only £180. The doctor accused him of following neither the letter or spirit of his instructions: "This injudicious deviation has been the cause of all the disaster which has befallen your expedition and the consequent loss the Concern must suffer."

McLeod tried to defend his actions in an angry exchange of letters. He had trapped the Buenaventura "as near the limits of the Spanish settlements as my instructions would warrant." He blamed his failure (partly) on his powder shortage. He had had only thirty-two pounds of gunpowder left when on the Mokelumne, an insufficient amount to push on southward. He argued that to have wintered in the Sacramento Valley would have exposed his brigade not only to hostile Indians, suspicious Mexican officials, and contact with the settlements by his men, but also Perrault's machinations.

For these reasons, explained McLeod, he had decided to winter in the Shasta Valley and to trap the Shasta and Klamath from his camp: "With this object in view, I directed our route toward that quarter, never anticipating being arrested in our progress, much less the loss the expedition sustained, which a most extraordinary season brought on, as suddenly as it was unexpected, a circumstance I most earnestly deplore. I consider myself particularly unfortunate, as three days' travel would have saved the party from loss, and me the reflections cast upon my conduct."

The doctor was tired of McLeod's excuses. He brushed aside the ammunition argument by reminding him that he should have taken more powder from the Fort Vancouver magazine and that he could have bought some from either Russ or "Spaniards" in California. He further reminded him that he could have camped all over the Sacramento Valley without coming remotely near any settlement. However, McLoughlin betrayed his long preconception of a coastal trail and his ignorance of the actual terrain by telling McLeod that, in similar circumstances, *he* would have marched up the coast from California!

Curiously, Simpson and McLoughlin reversed their usual roles when it came to McLeod. The doctor was more severe than the usually abrasive Governor. The latter was cognizant of failing health as a factor in the chief trader's debacle. Though he believed that McLeod would use all of his energies in the field in California, the Governor informed London: "This gentleman has been exposed to the almost incessant winter rains on this part of the coast since he has been attached to the Columbia Department which, I am much concerned to find, has injured his health and broken his constitution also, so that it will be necessary to relieve him, likewise, as early as possible."

Nevertheless, McLoughlin ordered McLeod to rejoin his men on the Umpqua, and he did so, in March 1830. He hunted between that stream and Fort Vancouver while he awaited a hearing by the Northern Council of the Company. This body of field partners met annually during the slack summer season to promulgate rules but was also virtually the sole consultive, legislative, and judicial body in northwesternmost America. On July 29, McLeod was back at Vancouver to report he had hunted as far south as the Shasta Valley, but had found few beaver. With no word on the hearing in his case, as yet, McLoughlin had him take McKay and eleven men on another hunt. This time, he searched the headwaters of the Willamette.

When the Council heard McLeod's case, he was censured not only for losing horses, traps, and furs, but for incompetence. The partners were aghast at his having left his almost-starving men on the Umpqua while he hurried to Fort Vancouver's comforts, mainly because he was homesick and eager to see the family upon which he doted. Because of McLeod's precarious health, the Company was lenient. He was not fired but merely re-exiled to the Mackenzie River Department. But never again would he be trusted with a Siskiyou Trail expedition.

The thumbnail biographies in Simpson's *Character Book* were often too critical. But the Governor evaluated McLeod far better than did wishful-thinking McLoughlin: "A stout, strong, active man, a good pedestrian, an excellent shot, a skilful canoe man and a tolerably good Indian trader, but illiterate, self-sufficient and arrogant; does not confine himself to plain matters of fact, annoys everyone near him with the details of his own exploits—'I did this, I did that,' and 'I did the other thing'—continually in his mouth. But it unfortunately happens that he rarely does anything well. Even his physical prowess has been greatly overrated and I have never been able to discover that he possesses beyond the most ordinary mental abilities; yet his own vanity and the partiality of friends have made him an aspirant to a place in the first class, to which—in my opinion—he has very modest pretensions as regards merit, and if he did succeed in gaining that stand he would be a most overbearing, tyrannical fellow; is capable of little mean tricks and, I suspect, is fond of a glass of grog in private. Would have made an excellent *guide* though he adds little respectability to the fur trade as a 'partner.' "

Alex McLeod's debacle almost put an end to the Siskiyou Trail before it was even well defined. On July 18, 1831, Simpson wrote: "From his report of the country and the difficulties to which a party could be exposed in hunting it, we do not think it advisable to maintain this expedition."

However, McLoughlin still feared that Americans would use the vacuum of montane northern California to penetrate Oregon in strength. He urged that the California brigades be continued, if only to displace American influence (and to give employment to Fort Vancouver men who would otherwise be idle and prone to mischief).

But McLoughlin was trying a new tack. As far back as November 24, 1830, he had written to Captain Aemilius Simpson, skipper of the Company's *Cadboro*. He asked if there were any settlers on the Buenaventura or Sacramento; if the Mexicans would allow a brigade to trap the river and San Francisco Bay area; and if they would allow cattle, horses, and mules to be shipped to the Columbia or driven there via the Siskiyou Trail. Passing on Abel Stearns's claim, he told Captain Simpson that a considerable quantity of beaver was being collected in Monterey. He ordered the captain to buy pelts at £0.17.6 in goods, or ten shillings in bills on England. For sea otter he was to pay twenty-five to thirty shillings in goods, eighteen to twenty in cash. The doctor cautioned the mariner that he was to get the information on trapping permission indirectly, from private parties; he was not to interview officials. In any case, indicated McLoughlin, he expected to continue sending trapping parties to the Sacramento, with or without permission.

On June 3, 1830, botanist David Douglas had returned to Fort Vancouver. His eyesight was failing badly after an attack of ophthalmia on the Columbia in 1826 had been followed by snowblindness. The fair Scot was now florid and going bald, too. But he was as zealous as ever. He determined the position of Fort Vancouver for McLoughlin, then visited Fort Nez Percés and the Blue Mountains, as well as botanizing around Fort Vancouver. The doctor detached William Johnston, the old man-o'-warsman, as his escort. In August, the naturalist rejoined his old friend McLeod and ascended the Willamette and Santiam Rivers with him. He collected specimens, took observations with his instruments (measuring Mount Jefferson, for example), and gave the name "Cascades" to the mountains which the Americans preferred to call the Presidential Range. He distributed presents of jewsharps, buttons, beads, and finger rings as he explored, so he had no Indian trouble. But, incredibly, he lost almost all of his zoological specimens on the Santiam near the spot where he had had a similar accident, earlier: "It is curious," he wrote, "on the 17th November 1826, I lost everything I had at the same place when returning from my southern journey. A *kelpie,* or elf, is the charm of that stream so unfortunate to me."

Returned to Fort Vancouver, Douglas was stricken with intermittent fever during ten days of a sweltering heat wave. He was, he said, between hope and fear. The malaria killed twenty-four Company men and brought trade, temporarily, to a standstill. Douglas wrote Sir Joseph Hooker: "Villages which afforded from one to two hundred warriors are totally gone; not a soul remains. The houses are empty and flocks of famished dogs are howling about, while the dead bodies lie strewn in every direction on the sands of the river."

Douglas packed his specimens for removal to Britain in October 1830. He had planned to march to California over the Siskiyou Trail but was put off by the hair-raising tales of Jed Smith's massacre. So, he took the Company brig *Dryad* to Monterey. He botanized and tried to ascend the nascent Siskiyou Trail from the California end

179

but got no further north than Sonoma Mission and Fort Ross. (At the latter point, his geography was so fuddled that he thought himself only sixty-five miles, not three hundred, from the Umpqua.) Douglas then sailed to Hawaii via the Columbia, meeting his tragic death in the "Doctor's Pit" on Mauna Kea in 1834.

McLoughlin's choice of a replacement for the discredited McLeod was not one of the doughty Scots, who were as tough (usually) as they were miserly. (They were said to keep the Sabbath—and everything else.) Instead, he picked John Work, born John Wark in Donegal in 1792; when he had enlisted in the Company in 1814, his name was misspelled, so he took the path of least resistance and changed it. Starting as a writer, he became steward, clerk, trader, and factor. He was not only loyal, experienced, and industrious, but sober as well.

Although he and Ogden were never close friends, Simpson's observation that Work was a man without chums was wide of the mark. He was well liked by Frank Ermatinger and Dr. John Tod, for instance. He married Josette Legace, half-French and half-Spokane or Nez Percé, and she bore him eleven children. This led Tod to comment in 1844: "Every letter I get announces the birth of another child." Between fur hunts and fathering children, Work pioneered agriculture at Fort Colvile on the upper Columbia. Perhaps because he had started out as a writer, he kept excellent field journals and McLoughlin learned much from them.

One trait of Work's gave McLoughlin pause. He was something of a complainer and hypochondriac. Like McLeod, he "enjoyed" poor health. He made it worse by anticipating its arrival and mourning its departure. And he invented it when the genuine article was absent. Tod predicted in 1831: "Poor Work. If he remains much longer in the country, neglected, I fear he'll die of spleen." A dozen years later, Tod wrote of his more disgruntled than sickly pal, who was venting philippics in regard to "the privations of the Service and 'this cursed country.'" Said Tod: "He is as far as ever from coming to any determination to quit it."

Nor was Work as tough as some of his peers. He was, in fact, a tender-hearted Irishman whose only tendency toward violence (they said) was his murder of the French tongue when addressing his Gallic colleagues. He was not foolhardy; he could not help worrying about his own scalp in such a dangerous trade. On September 6, 1831, he wrote John McLeod: "I escaped with my scalp last year"; and on August 5, 1832, he returned to the theme of his hair: "I enjoy good health, am yet in the possession of my scalp, which is rather more than I had reason to expect."

Simpson, of course, damned Work with the faintest of praise: "A very steady, painstaking man, regular, economical and attentive in business, and bears a fair private character. Has been a useful man for many years and must always be so from his persevering, steady and regular habits." However, the Governor felt compelled to add: "A queer-looking fellow, of clownish manners and address; indeed, there is a good deal of simplicity approaching to idiocy in his appearance. He is, nonetheless, a shrewd, sensible man and not deficient in firmness when necessary."

McLoughlin appointed Work Chief Trader of the Snake River Brigade but immediately ordered him in July, 1832, to California rather than Idaho. Work did not lick his "queer-looking" chops in anticipation. He wrote Edward Ermatinger (July 27): "I am going to start with my ragamuffin freemen to the southwards, towards the Spanish settlements, with what success I cannot say. I am tired of the cursed country, Ned, and becoming more dissatisfied every day with the measures in it; things don't go fair. I don't think I shall long remain." He told Ermatinger that he would have to leave Josette and his three little girls behind, because the Siskiyou passage would be difficult: "The misery is too great," he explained; "I shall be very lonely without them, but the cursed trip exposes them to too much hardship." Actually, the Irisher changed his mind. Though he did not once mention his beloved family in his official log of the expedition, Josette, Jane, Sarah, and Letitia joined his mess and made the arduous trans-Siskiyous march.

In April 1832, McLoughlin sent a party ahead under Laframboise. Michel took eighteen white men, seventeen Indian men, eighteen Indian women, and six children down the impossible coast "trail" to California. Freemen like Aubichon, Quesnel, and Alexander Carson were with him. He would not take John Turner because Jed Smith's comrade had contracted to work for Depaty for a year. Perhaps McLoughlin was not clinging stubbornly to the coast as an alternative route to Siskiyou Pass and the Sacramento. He issued orders for Laframboise to punish the Tillamooks for killing two Iroquois trappers. This would take Michel to the coast. But, said the doctor, "I shall not shackle you with copious instructions."

Left, thus, to his own devices, the ruthless Michel avenged the murders by killing six Tillamooks with no loss to his own force. He then moved southward, abandoning the precipitous coast as soon as he could, and crossed the Siskiyous to follow "McLeod's Track" (the first name for the Siskiyou Trail) into California.

By summer, Laframboise was camped on an oak-dotted, well-watered stretch of the San Joaquin plain near modern Stockton. He liked the site so well that it became a regular seasonal settlement of Company trappers. The first Mexican *diseños* or land-grant maps called the site Campo de los Franceses and the town of Castoria which ultimately grew there soon reverted to the name it bears today, French Camp. It is about four miles south of McLeod's Lake, now part of the port of Stockton, where Michel's one-time chief had earlier camped. Laframboise's orders were to trap both the Sacramento and San Joaquin valleys while he waited for Work, whose brigade he would join.

Understandably, Laframboise was a bit nervous, for he was flouting the laws of Mexico by hunting beaver without license or permission. James Weeks, a young English sailor who had jumped ship (the whaler *Fanny*) at San Francisco in 1831, met Michel in June of '32. He made clear Michel's uneasiness: "The Oregon party of trappers were at French Camp. That place is named for them. The commander was a Canadian, Mitchell Lafrumbois. I met him once at the Mission of San Jose. I went to the priest to interpret for him. The father provided him a room during his stay at the Mission. There was no furniture in it more than a hide-bottom bedstead. The room was about 12 feet high and, I suppose, about that much square. After consigning him to the care of His Reverence, I left for San Jose (Pueblo). I met him afterwards. He told me that he soon came away from San Jose. He was somewhat frightened and wanted to know what he had done, and could find no one to talk for him. He thought it was a prison they placed him into! The room had one big window with iron gratings; glass was not used in those days. So Mr. Lafrumbois skeedaddled, chuckling to himself at his happy deliverance from bondage, thrice glad to join his company and hear the beaver tails slapping the water again. His wild life appeared to him more secure than to be in sight of a church and well established mission."

Michel made French Camp his home until January 1833, when he moved his party to the junction of the Sacramento and Feather rivers. He was on his way to "les Buttes," which loomed out of the flat valley floor (near today's Marysville) because he learned that John Work was encamped there.

Work had finally got under way from Fort Vancouver on the warm, sultry morning of August 17, 1832. He joined his twenty-six

"Snake Trappers" at their upriver drunken *regale,* then embarked them in boats for the Dalles and Fort Walla Walla (or Nez Percés). His orders were to hunt either the Klamath Lake or Buenaventura country, "whichever might be deemed most advantageous." Work chose the Sacramento River over the Klamath basin, but not with great enthusiasm. If he found the season too far advanced, he planned to go to Ogden's River (the Humboldt, in Nevada) before it should freeze over. From there, he planned to move back to the "South Branch" of the Buenaventura—that is, the San Joaquin River. (He conveniently ignored the presence of the High Sierra between them.) "Either way," he wrote, "our prospects of making anything of a hunt are but very indifferent."

Work was taking the old, roundabout route to California of Ogden, rather than "McLeod's Track" which Ogden thought the best as well as shortest trail. Illness dogged his steps and Work was still at Fort Nez Percés on September 6 when he wrote that his second-in-command, François Payette, was too sick to accompany him. Reluctantly, he left him behind, noting: "This I much regret, as in the event of anything happening to me, he was the only person to take charge of the party." In his reports, McLoughlin worried over Work marching to California without a back-up man.

Though he was still dosing ten of his men and some women and children for the ague or "fever" (malaria), Work raised camp on September 9 and headed south-southwest to a Bitter Creek campsite. Trouble broke out when J. Rocquebin refused an order to go after five strayed horses, including three of his own. Hypochondriac or not, Work was no meek McLeod. He knocked the French-Canadian down and gave him a good drubbing.

From the John Day and Silvies rivers, and Harney and Malheur lakes, Work led his party to Goose Lake, which he called Pit Lake. He depended on Louis Kanota, probably either a Hawaiian or a Nipissing Indian to guide the party to brackish but potable water on the desert stretch east of the Cascades. Though Work ordered his men to treat all Indians kindly, Baptiste Guardapii (Gardipie) was attacked by Indians and his horse killed. The trapper was unhurt, although an arrow passed through his capote. Some of the improvident half-bloods were already killing their horses for food and four men were poisoned from eating what Work took to be toxic mushrooms. (They may have eaten the common poisonous cow parsnip, or hemlock, however.)

Work reached the willow-edged Pit River on October 28, 1832, and began to trap downstream to the Fall River. Near Hot Springs (and modern Alturas) Work found tracks of Indians, but they were "wild as beasts" and remained unseen. On Hat Creek he was surprised to find tracks of a party of mounted men with pack animals. He guessed that they had been lugging six "pieces" (fifty-pound packs) of furs. Ascending Hat Creek to the area of Doyle's Corners, he followed a trail over the mountains between Stony Butte (alias Tamarack Peak) north of Magee Peak and the height of Burney Mountain. This gap was already known to Kanota and Louis Pichette. Now, Work's hunters found themselves living off the fat of the land, their rifles bringing down bears, deer, and elk.

By dropping down McLeod's Canoe River (Cow Creek), Work reached the Sacramento on November 18. All the while, his men took beaver and shot game, including grizzlies. Work found the water so high opposite the later site of Anderson, California, that he gave up any attempt to ford the Sacramento. Instead, he had some of his men hollow out log canoes with their axes, à la McLeod. He had planned on doing this anyway, but further down the "Buenaventura." When he paid a friendly call on the natives, Work found them burning their dead. The latter had been killed in a "Chasty" (Shasta) attack on their village. The locals were simple and tame folk, who carried only rods or staffs as weapons, were naked as jaybirds except for deerskin cloaks, and were even more afraid of the dogs and horses than they were of the mountain men.

Work raised camp, divided his party into a land unit and river unit in canoes, and dropped ten miles down to the mouth of the "Sycamous" (Sycamore) River, now Battle Creek. He then went into camp on Deer Creek, which he called the Quesnel River after Amable. His next stop was Bear Creek, since renamed Pine Creek, where his men caught only a few beaver and an otter or so, though the stream looked eminently suitable for the furry rodents. Here, crowds of acorn-eating redmen were taking fish in a weir and hares or jackrabbits with nets. At this point, too, the Irishman found that he had passed an invisible political boundary. The natives spoke a markedly different language from the Indians upriver. He noticed that many carried immense loads on their heads, including wood for their winter homes, though many were so sick with malaria that they were staggering.

While camped on the Sacramento 10 miles north of Butte Creek on December 7, 1832, Work encountered two of Laframboise's men, C. Charpenteur and J. Boileau. They were on their way to Fort

Vancouver with dispatches. Work added them to his party since a delay mattered little to them. He learned that Michel had hunted from old Fort Umpqua until the coast mountains became impossible and impassable. He had then taken McLeod's Siskiyou Trail route, pushing all the way south to Mission Dolores on San Francisco Bay. He had found the latter abounding with beaver. According to the couriers, Michel was finding his best trapping in the very shadows of the mission settlements of San José, San Rafael, and Sonoma, which McLeod had earlier avoided.

Work was annoyed at Laframboise for leaving the coastal district to which he had been sent, in order to crowd the inland district. In fact, McLoughlin had written Work on August 21 that Michel was trapping the coast and would not possibly join him during that fall. Miffed, Work wrote: "They arr'd in August and have trapped it all from where we are here downward, as well as the Bay, so that after all our long journey here there are no beaver remaining for our party. . . . Thus, by their not attending to their instructions, the coast where they were directed to go remains unhunted and this quarter, which was left for our party, is hunted."

From Charpenteur and Boileau, Work learned that the mysterious strangers whose tracks he had seen were Yankee interlopers. The spoor was that of Ewing Young's trapping party. He also learned Michel had made his canoes opposite the very point where he was camped, and that Laframboise's catch was a disappointing 950 skins. This, he noted, was "far short of the number expected to be found. . . . The account given of this quarter was greatly exaggerated."

Working his way down the valley, Work ran into the Indians who had annoyed Laframboise. They stole traps and, without provocation, threw stones and shot arrows at *les canadiens*. At Butte Creek, which Work called Deception Creek, presumably because it ended in a swamp, the canoe men gave up their craft. On December 8, 1832, Work decided that there was no prospect of catching any more beaver in the Sacramento. He sent a note to Laframboise to arrange a meeting so that they could decide where to winter.

Work trapped Butte Sink and nearby streams; he dispatched hunters for *cabris* or kid (goat), by which they meant antelope. They also took elk or *biche*, bear, Columbia black-tailed deer, and the mule deer which his men dubbed *chivereau*. He sent ten men to search for J. Toupin, lost by his partner, a Walla Walla Indian. Though the Indians were peaceful and civil, he gave his men orders to punish the murderers should they find Toupin dead. However, on no other account were they to injure them, or even quarrel with them. He was amused to find that some Indians wore feather and rabbit-skin blankets about their shoulders, while others covered themselves from neck to knees with long grass or straw until they looked thatched.

When the rising Sacramento began to flood its plain, Work moved his men (December 15) to a "fountain" and a little creek fed by the spring on the high ground of the northeast slope of The Buttes. These snaggle-toothed remnants of a volcanic cone supplied the most prominent landmark of the Siskiyou Trail after Mount Shasta, a sort of Chimney Rock or El Morro for California-bound northerners. Perhaps Work camped on Little Snake River, barely a drainage ditch today. It may have been named by his veterans of the Idaho Snake River Brigade, but more likely was given its name because of the numerous rattlesnakes of the hot buttes. Much of the time, the camp was shrouded in *tule* fog, the low-hanging condensation fog which clung to ponds and *tules,* or bulrushes. The buttes were anything but hot in December; they were cold and damp, but the mildest and driest point in the otherwise featureless Sacramento plain. So dense was the fog that deer and elk were able to start and run—and disappear—before hunters could draw a bead on them. Still, Work was content to remain relatively high and dry as the great central valley flooded, especially since there was good pasturage for the horses.

When the messengers returned from Michel's camp, Work learned from them that Laframboise had changed his mind about trapping the San Joaquin and was coming to join him at the Buttes: "He is afraid of not being able to live, for want of animals this way," commented Work; "they have got themselves lately into some trouble with the Indians, who are stealing their horses notwithstanding they keep a regular guard." Work did not neglect to post pickets around his herd, either, since the local Indians were also inclined to be troublesome. But he sent men to Feather River to trap and when the fog burned off on December 21, he climbed the highest peak (South Butte) in brilliant sunshine to take a look at the surrounding countryside.

Late in the evening of December 23, Michel arrived in a rainstorm. Laframboise reported that Ewing Young had received some supplies from the Mexicans and even some beached sailors as reinforcements. The Americans had now crossed to the west side of the Sacramento Valley, in hopes of avoiding the flooding. Bad weather prevented Michel's return to his men, camped at French Camp, so he spent Christmas with Work. He planned to imitate Young by sending men to find the best route to higher ground on the Coast Range side of the valley.

For himself, Work hoped to drop down to a ford of the Feather River once the rain should stop. Then he would also cross to high ground, but to the east of the Feather and Sacramento. But he was getting an education in California climate. The rain did not stop. It continued for days as a steady downpour which turned the Buttes into an island in a vast lake. Although Laframboise managed his getaway to French Camp on December 27, Work was trapped in the Buttes until the twenty-ninth. He noticed the water dropping in the little creek and laid his plans: "By cutting across the [saddle of the] Butte, there is a passage by which, with some difficulty, we may get out. The Butte is almost completely surrounded with water and where there is a little spot of dry ground it is so soft that the horses bog in it."

On December 30, Work's men, women, and children cut across the Buttes to a precarious camp. Next day, they sloshed their way across the miry plain for twelve miles to Feather River. There, Work was overtaken by Louis Shanagoronte from Michel's party. The Iroquois had been attacked by Indians but had killed two of them and made his escape, losing his horse in crossing the flooding river to join Work.

At the Feather, Work ran into two hundred Indians loaded down with antelope meat after a successful "surround," though they were poorly armed with only a few bows and arrows and short, stone-pointed lances. And the antelope were fleeter than the freshest horse.

On New Year's Day 1833, the bourgeois detected the level of the Feather River falling four feet by night but rising five inches by day. This, of course, was due to nighttime freezing in the distant Sierra Nevada, where the river had its source. Work did not raise camp but joined the holiday celebration. He issued a dram of Demerara rum and some cakes to each man.

Now the water really began to fall as winter closed its icy fist on the sierra. The Feather dropped six feet in only a few days. He found the valley sheathed in frost but the Indians more numerous as he made southing. One short day's journey took Work past six different villages where all were living on acorns and salmon. He mused: "The country must be rich in [such] resources, when such numbers of people find subsistence." He figured that the population of each village amounted to some hundreds of souls.

At the traverse of the Feather just below modern Nicolaus, Work found the waters almost overflowing the river's banks. He did not dare let the women and children test the dangerous-looking ford: "Even could we," he observed, "it would be imprudent to risk with the camp when, with a night or two's heavy rain we might lose all our horses and perhaps ourselves." Work decided to follow the Feather back up toward the mountains in hopes that its waters would fall enough for a crossing back to the Big River, as he called the Sacramento. He hoped to reach it via the Little Camas River, the Cosumnes. In a Maidu village of twenty-eight lodges, he saw how the local Indians managed to survive the annual floods: They used as canoes two flat logs of pine or cedar, from the mountains, tied together. "Our people have borrowed all that the Indians have," he reported, "and, by tying two or three together, make good rafts and have everything ready to cross tomorrow."

On a raw, cold Sunday, January 5, 1833, Work ferried his party across the Feather on the rude craft. He lost only a single horse. He ascended the east bank to a fork, took the easterly branch (Bear River) for ten miles of northing, and camped on a dry plain close to the mountains. He was near modern Wheatland and historic Johnson's Ranch of Donner Party days. Curiously, John Turner—who did make the march, after all, but with Laframboise—became a member of one of the rescue parties which headed into the Sierra to rescue the snowed-in, cannibalized, Donners in 1847, from almost that very spot, on Johnson's Ranch.

Work sent word to Michel to join him if he was unable to cross the Sacramento as planned. They could cross together, up above. Hunting and trapping remained good, but the ground was soft and mucky as Work closed with the Sierra and made a good camp, probably on Auburn Ravine, and another on the South Fork of the American River. There, messengers brought word that Michel was coming from his starving campsite on the east bank of Camas River, the San Joaquin. Michel's camp was now virtually surrounded by water and Ewing Young's Americans had recrossed the Sacramento to the east side and were also floundering toward Work. All of Work's own seemingly aimless wandering in the Sacramento Valley was either to find high ground on which to camp or to find a ford of the river which would lead him to the higher foothills of the Coast Range, where he could hunt for beaver, once winter should end, as well as game. He could not understand why the foothills of the Sierra were empty of elk; Ogden had found many in 1830. On January 10, Work gave up his meandering in order to return to the Sutter (Marysville) Buttes. "We must also turn back [to] where we may find some elk to subsist on, about the Butte," he recorded, "which we left on the 30th ult."

Two of Ewing Young's Americans arrived, next day, virtually starving. They had had not a scrap to eat in three days of travel. But mid-January brought fine weather, at last. Work was able to cross to the north side of Bear River, where he was joined by Michel's party, less one man. Jed Smith's old pard, John Turner, had paid off his debt, delivered up his traps and horses. He was quitting Company employ to join his fellow Americans with Young. The merged Company parties, 163 persons in all, forded the Feather just north of later Marysville and returned to *les Buttes* via an eighteen-mile march along the line of modern Butte House Road.

At last, Work found the missing *biches*. The elk were all congregated in and around the Buttes, where the Indians were busily running them down, in relays, then dispatching them with spears or arrows. In just two days, Work's hunters killed fifty-two elk and a bear. The animals were very lean, but their meat was welcome. During a spell of fine weather, the women were kept busy dressing the skins of one bear, ten deer, and eighty-one elk.

Michel joined Work on another climb up South Butte on February 5 to view the flooded valley. Once again the Irishman wrote: "We are now nearly on an island as the Butte is surrounded with water." Then Laframboise and four men sloshed their way to the forks of the Feather, intending to continue to the Sacramento to locate Young's gringos. The hills were tinged gray with quickly melting snow on the fourteenth, but the Sacramento's banks were still overflowing and they could not even reach the river, much less find a ford.

The next night, Indians stole Michel's horses from near the bank of the Feather. This led to immediate action by Work, who wrote: "This is the first trick of the kind they have played upon us as yet. We must not allow them to pass with it." He sent Laframboise and thirty-seven men to recover the stock and to punish the rustlers, but without bloodshed if possible. "Quarrels with the natives are by all means to be avoided," observed the Gael, "but on occasions like the present, it cannot be well got off with." Laframboise retrieved the horses and the Indians cooperated by pointing out one of the two thieves. Michel gave him a good whipping, which Work thought would deter him from future larceny. These Indians seemed to have less excuse than most to rob strangers, being much better off. They had caches of acorns and of weirs to catch fish, and were netting wildfowl, using stuffed goose skins as decoys.

Work appreciated the high ground of the Buttes: "We have been a month here [on February 22, 1833] and could not have fallen on a better place to pass a part of the dead winter season, when nothing could be done in the way of trapping on account of the height of the waters. There was excellent feeding for the horses, and abundance of animals for the people to subsist on—395 elk, 148 deer, 17 bears and 8 antelopes have been killed in a month, which is certainly a great many more than was required, but when the most of the people have ammunition and see animals they must needs fire upon them, let them be wanted or not."

From the Buttes, Work and Michel led the company along the Feather for fifteen miles to the Oroville area, closer to the Sierra Nevada. It was the only route off their high "island." Two men trapped Butte Creek but got only one beaver, and Louis Pichette lost two traps to thieving Indians. The river was over its banks, anyway; trapping was hopeless. So the brigade marched up a well-beaten Indian trail on the east side of the Sacramento Valley, an aboriginal highway destined to form part of the Siskiyou Trail proper, as laid out on Pierson B. Reading's important 1849 manuscript map, now in the California State Library.

Work was startled to see the aborigines grazing on all fours in fields of clover, like animals. "The country is full of Indians," he observed. "They are spread all over the plain and gathering and eating different kinds of herbs, like beasts. A kind of small clover and a plant resembling parsley seem to be the two principal [ones]."

At last, on March 3, the rains stopped. Shortly, the skies cleared and traps were set again. In fine weather, the Canadians moved fifteen miles southwest to the Sacramento River, part of the way through a swamp. Next day, they reached an old campsite of theirs at a good river crossing near modern Jacinto. By evening, five skin canoes were finished. Humans, horses and baggage were shipped across the river as the Indians continued to pilfer traps, mainly to take out the beaver for food. The jerky put up at the Buttes was nearly exhausted and the men on short rations again. But it was a small loss, as Work explained: "The very lean meat, when dried, is scarcely eatable."

The brigadiers continued southwestward to a little river near the Coast Range, probably Willow Creek, then traversed a plain which was treeless except for tufts of willow in the little creeks. Antelope were numerous and the valley strewn with elk horns. Work noticed that the west-side *biches* were in better order than those of the Sacramento's left bank. By the eleventh, Work was on Cache Creek, about where it issued from a gap in the Coast Range, bearing the waters of Clear Lake. Most of the water in the stream was brackish and bad. Continuing south along the base of the mountains on a soft, swampy road, he found every little gully now a bog, difficult for the horses to cross. As the party followed the low range of hills jutting into the valley, Knight's Landing Ridge, hunters kept their eyes peeled for elk but had no luck.

Work's scouts reported that Young had managed to cross the Sacramento and, after camping in the Capay Valley, had entered the Coast Range by means of a small river. This was Putah Creek, called Young's River on the map of Duflot de Mofras. After eighteen miles, Work reached Putah Creek and set up camp around modern Winters. So many sloughs were filled by Sacramento River water on March 16, 1833, that Work reported a chain of lakes in the valley.

The bourgeois sent Michel up the creek into the gorge where, today, Monticello Dam blocks the waters of Lake Berryessa, to see if he could determine the route which the Yanks had taken. He found that they had crossed the Coast Range to the north fork of the Russian River, which emptied into the Pacific south of Fort Ross. The trappers argued among themselves as to how far ahead was Young. Some said ten days, others thirty.

When Work's advance party returned with thirty-four skins, he split his force in twain again. Half followed the Americans into the coastal mountains; the rest remained with him. Since he had sent Laframboise to Mission Dolores on San Francisco Bay for ammunition, he put the Coast Range party under the command of Alexander Carson. He was an old-timer, a veteran Astorian of Wilson Price Hunt's historic march of 1811. Carson took twenty trappers and eleven Indians, with their traps and two horses apiece.

Laframboise, as usual, had difficulty in following orders. He did not go to Mission Dolores but to Mission San Francisco de Solano at Sonoma. There was no ammunition to be had there, but the priest referred him to the Russ at their port of Bodega. He was able to get just ten pounds of powder and thirty pounds of lead from the Slavs, plus ten pounds of very welcome tobacco. And the Russians charged all that the traffic would bear—five pelts for the ammunition and two

191

plews for the *tabac*. But they treated him as civilly as had the "Spaniards" (Mexicans).

The Russian "Governor," apparently the manager of the colony, Peter (Don Pedro) Kostromitinoff, told Laframboise that he had been up the coast for thirty leagues. The route was bad, but passable. The rivers were small, the Indians hostile, and the beaver nonexistent. Work, like Jed Smith, McLeod, McLoughlin, Simpson, and probably Michel, had the idée fixe that there *had* to be beaver on such a timbered, well-watered coast. He wrote: "[He said] there was no sign of beaver, but it may be policy in him to not tell whether there were beaver or not."

Two Americans, two Englishmen, a Mexican, and three Indians who visited his camp told Work that the Indians were growing hostile. The gringos were probably George Yount and Moses Carson, Kit Carson's brother. The Englishmen were John Martin and Jerry Jones. Martin reported that Indians had raided his *rancho* at Botoque, the junction of San Antonio Creek and the Petaluma River. They had driven off all of his fifty cattle. Fearing that they would come back for his horses, he temporarily abandoned his ranch. He moved his family to Sonoma and rounded up his horse herd to sell to Work. Most of the thirty-two animals which changed hands were young, leading Work to say: "The most of these can be of little or no service to us, [but] it is true they did not cost us dear."

Work trapped the fens of the Cordelia area of Freshwater Bay (Suisun Bay), describing the area as bearing "the resemblance of a swamp overgrown with bulrushes and intersected in almost every direction with channels of different sizes." It looked like beaver country; the natives said it was. Work was delighted to find, at last, an area rich in *Castor*.

Meanwhile, Laframboise trailed Carson's party and brought it back. What a disappointment! "I am much dissatisfied with the men's conduct," reported Work, "particularly in turning back before they had come up with the Americans. They did not push on with the expedition as they might have done. Had they continued on for two or three days longer, even slow as they went, they would have been up with the party whose road still descended a river [the Russian] running to the southward and which falls into the sea between the Mission [Sonoma] and Russian settlements."

Work was especially unhappy over Alex Carson's failure as a leader: "The old man who was at their head and who appeared the fittest person among them, is too easy, tho' sufficiently experienced for the task, and listens too much to the babbling among the people."

When two Mexican officials visited him, probably Don Mariano G. Vallejo and Juan Miranda, the Steward of the Sonoma Mission, Work sent Laframboise with them to San Francisco Bay. He hoped to be able to buy powder and lead from a vessel which the Mexicans said was in the bay.

Few beaver were now being caught in the Suisun marshes, but the hunters were bringing down many deer, antelope, and bear. An American from Ewing Young's party, perhaps Moses Carson or Jonathan Trumbull (José Joaquín) Warner, came to Sonoma Mission. They told Work that they had followed a bad road with Young over the Coast Range—which had few beaver. Work, as ever, was suspicious of such negative reports: "Information from runaways like this can be little relied upon."

Michel brought back twenty-four pounds of powder and forty of lead, though he had missed the ship. He had had to pay the commandant of the Presidio at San Francisco, Luis Arguello, a pretty penny. Work scrawled in his journal: "What a set of mean scoundrels!" But Arguello also sent him a passport and a bottle of rum, without being asked for either.

The booshway was worried because two of his men were down with malarial ague again: "This disease again breaking out among us at this season is a serious evil, especially as we are without any proper medicines for it." For religious as well as health reasons, Work did not raise camp on April 7, 1833. It was Easter Sunday. He let his men have a rare treat. They attended Mass at the Sonoma Mission. On Easter Monday, Work was again visited by an official, probably General Vallejo, most powerful officer in northern California. He came from Sonoma and sold two horses to Work.

At this otherwise happy time, a tragedy intervened. One of the Iroquois hunters, Michel Oteotanin (or Oteotanie), was torn badly by a grizzly. The padre offered to keep him at the Mission. But the father had no medicines, and the Iroquois balked at staying with people whose tongue he could not fathom. So Work slowed his pace and let Oteotanin rest up at the mission before he continued his search for new trapping areas.

Since more of his people were falling ill with fever, the Irishman bought an ox at Sonoma, in exchange for a blanket and a yard of red strouds, and divided the meat among the sick. His men continued to trap the area, of course, dumbfounded by the lack of beaver in the Napa River, which looked just right for the animals.

Near Napa River a ludicrous accident occurred which, at least, broke the monotony of life for the mountain men. A sort of joint stampede took place, for which Work took the blame and apologized to the padre at Sonoma, José María de Jesús Gutiérrez. The latter tut-tutted that no apology was necessary. He had only been worried about some of Work's party, especially the young children, being hurt. (None were.)

Work later recalled the incident: "On approaching the Mission and at the end of a heavy shower, there was a very large flock of sheep a little to one side of the road and an Indian keeper with them. After a good part of the camp was past, the stupid animals broke from their keeper and rushed among our horses. The horses took fright and ran off and the sheep with them. All the efforts of the people could neither get them stopped or separated until, after a number of turns of several miles, when the sheep were completely knocked up, and the horses ran to the mountains. It was with difficulty they were stopped. What made it worse, a number of unbroken horses belonging to the Mission joined them. At length, they were all collected. A good deal of the people's baggage was also scattered about. There are some kettles and other articles not yet found. A great many of the sheep were killed or maimed. The stupid animals formed themselves into a mass 10 or 12 feet wide and the whole length of the flock, which was [of] no small extent, and kept winding after and among the horses, whereever they went."

Three miles west of the Mission, Work found Sonoma Creek. It was much smaller than the Napa River but, at least, it had beaver in it, so he camped. Father Gutiérrez sent Miranda to Work with his compliments, a going-away present of two bottles of wine—and a request that he, please, not trap quite so close to the Mission. Otherwise, he was free to hunt anywhere he chose.

Work did not like the looks of Oteotanin—he was not mending well at all. Besides grizzly-mauled hunters, stampedes, and malaria, the Irishman had to put up with something new—woman trouble. J. S. Larocque's wife ran off in the night without any apparent provocation from her husband. But Work guessed: "It is suspected that she has made an engagement with some of the Spaniards at the Mission. She is a very bad character."

While camped on small Novato Creek, about four miles west of Petaluma River, Oteotanin died. Work (and probably the Iroquois, himself) welcomed death. The Indian had suffered terribly from his torn and "mortified" (gangrenous) arm. It is not clear where Work buried him, but, since no interment of a Christian Iroquois is recorded in Sonoma Mission records, it is likely that the Irishman buried him near Novato Creek. Perhaps the grave was dug on one of the handsome, rounded, and live-oak-dotted hills flanking the stream. Work noted in his log that the burial took place on April 17, 1833, and that Oteotanin left a wife and two children.

Crossing the Coast Range from the Novato area to Russian River, Work engaged in a rather silly altercation with "Governor" Kostromitinoff. In his halting French, the latter objected to the Britisher's taking his men past the Russian settlements of Bodega and Fort Ross. Testily, Work noted: "We told him that we *must* pass, but that we meant to pass at some distance. He was told that our two nations were at peace and that we did not see any reasons for his objections, and we must pass. He then said that, as there was no other way, he would allow us to pass."

In an uncomfortable atmosphere of truce, the bourgeois dined as a guest of the Russians and heard out all their claims that it was useless for him to search the coast for beaver. Like all his predecessors, he could not believe that such a likely coast was without the animals, so he ignored their advice. Laframboise was ill with fever, and Work himself had a bad cold, but he doggedly led his men in an exploration of the foggy and rugged Redwood Coast.

Work crossed stream after stream, the Gualala and García rivers, Alder and Elk (later, Greenwood) creeks, then the Navarro and Albion rivers, without taking a single beaver. The Russians had not been talking through their hats. He cut the trail of Ewing Young's party on a line with the modern route of the so-called "Skunk" locomotive of the California Western Railroad from Willits to Fort Bragg.

A few horses were lost crossing the steep-sided streams and, although he successfully negotiated Big River, Work decided to raft across the gorge of the Noyo River. These craft were built with the help of local Pomo Indians, who wore skins—but of jackrabbits, not beaver. Their lack of furs, combined with the total lack of beaver sign, such as cut timber, finally convinced Work that the Russians were right: There *were* no beaver on the coast.

As the Brigade moved upcoast, the canyons ran deeper, the forest grew denser—and the Indians turned warlike. Luckily, some were armed only with sticks and stones. Others, however, had short stone knives and bows and arrows, the latter of great length. But they were afraid of Work's horses, if not always of his own "warriors," so he managed to extricate his party from the unfriendly region without serious loss.

Beyond Needle Rock, Work found the mountains beginning to dive directly into the sea, without shelf or beach at waterline. It was a formidable obstacle, the Coast Range of what is now northern Mendocino County. He had done his duty to McLoughlin, searched high and low for beaver and found none, only a little otter sign. His men had shot seals and sea otters in the surf but had not been able to retrieve them. All he had to show for his exploration of the rugged littoral was a pile of deer and elk hides and some venison.

Since Laframboise was mending, Work sent him ahead to try to clamber over or around the forbidding mountains ahead. At the same time, he sent a party under Louis Kanota in a reconnaissance to the east. Although Kanota was threatened by bow-and-arrow-brandishing Indians in the area, Larocque was so much in love with (or jealous of, or determined to thrash) his wife that he deserted Work and, alone, made his way to Sonoma. He shortly rejoined the Irishman, dragging his wife along behind him over the precipitous coastal mountains. Work admired the French-Canadian's gumption and remarked: "He has travelled well."

Michel reported that the seaside gullies ahead, perhaps the sea-cliffed King Range country, were far worse than those to the south. Some were downright perpendicular. Kanota, on the other hand, reported the terrain a short distance inland to be relatively clear of timber, though still rugged, ravined, and bushy. Naturally, Work was tempted to turn his back on the Pacific and swing inland. At Shelter Cove, tucked in the lee of Point Delgada, he finally gave up his attempt at finding a coastal Siskiyou Trail: "We might probably in time be able to pass with our camp, but it would take so long that we have decided to cut across the mountains and pass along behind them, where we expect the deep ravines will not be so frequent."

Work did his best to satisfy McLoughlin's curiosity about a sea-level trail from Oregon to California. He sent Michel and thirty men, traveling light, to hug the coast while he took the remainder inland. He split his party on May 13, 1833, just beyond the Mattole River, logging: "Not falling in with beaver along the coast as we expected, we have arranged to divide the party. . . . It was always our plan to separate the people at the first large river we found where there was any beaver and where we could do so by giving the people all an equal chance and not creating any jealousies among them. But the bad road we have passed, and not finding any beaver, discouraged the men so that a party of them desired to return and the opportunity was embraced of separating the parties. We are very short of ammunition, which is much against us. It requires a great deal to feed so many people and particularly when, as at present, there is only deer to be had."

Work expected that Laframboise would fall upon Jed Smith's old coastal trail beyond "a mountain" (the King Range?) and would soon make better time. Curiously, he was right. Once Laframboise turned the corner of Cape Mendocino, the mountains lowered, and he found easier going around Humboldt Bay and Trinidad. But beyond the latter point he had to return to cliff scrambling.

loose to try, once more, to find a
Work followed the warm valley of
about the Garberville area south-
d fogs of the Redwood Coast. He
's drainage and that of the Russian
found the tracks of Alex Carson's
ursuit of Ewing Young's band of
ght, Work observed one of those
ruth far stranger than fiction. Out
an Umpqua Indian from Lafram-
York. Why? He had had a quarrel
with one of Michel's men. With whom? No one else but Alexander
Carson.

Since Work had heard rumors of beaver in the lower Russian
River, he sent a group to trap there before hurrying the balance of
his party to the Sacramento. He took a direct route but the larder did
not suffer, for his hunters took both deer and bears as he skirted the
south shore of Clear Lake and entered Berryessa and Redwood valleys. In Redwood Valley, a large war party tried to surround the detachment he had sent to the Russian River. The trappers escaped the
ambush but had to abandon three horses, twenty-four precious traps,
and other baggage. They retreated and joined the main command,
picking its way across hills and valleys to some lagunas (lakelets)
and, finally, Putah Creek.

Safely back in the Sacramento Valley, Work sent men ahead to trap the Napa River which, earlier, had hardly yielded a beaver. By May 26, he was almost on the site of his March 28 campsite near the headwaters of Suisun Creek. After traveling a stony road, which made the horses' hooves sore, he was glad when Putah Creek again led him down to the Sacramento floodplain. There was yet a swamp to flounder across and a willow thicket to push through, but there were plenty of elk and antelope for the cookfires at the end of a fifteen-mile march from his Putah Creek crossing. Work camped near today's Woodland, where elk hid in the tall *tules* but were betrayed by their tracks in the mud. A halt was necessary, not for hunting but for the building of canoes. The river was high and impossible to ford. Although mosquitoes laid siege to the camp where eight canoes were taking shape in sultry weather unrelieved by even a breath of wind, the men were cheerful. Hunting was improving, after all, and the river falling. The latter phenomenon enhanced their chances of taking beaver. Traveling would be easier, too, as the plain was becoming so dry that, already, Indians were burning it to drive game.

Work contrasted his current easy marches with his recent coastal clambering: "Since we passed the Mission, we have passed a very rugged country and exceedingly bad roads and [have found] very little for our trouble." Around Verona, at the Feather River's mouth below the great bend of the Sacramento, where sandflies joined the mosquitoes as allies in assaults on the trappers, Work turned eastward. He crossed the Sacramento to its left bank below a large Indian camp. Work's progress was then blocked by a horseshoe-shaped lake, the one which McLeod had found dry in 1829. He moved along its east shore to some woods, then cut back to the Sacramento and its junction with the Little Camas, or Cosumnes, River. The latter was swollen to the size of the Feather. The Canadians had to ascend it for a while to find a ford. Yet the surrounding countryside was, to Work, "scorched ground, as hot as the floor of an oven."

While his men cruised for beaver in the canoes, Work marched the main party south to a rendezvous on Sand (Mokelumne) River. It was so overflowed that he could not camp near its banks, as planned. Only occasionally was the oppressive heat relieved by a light breeze sweeping up the Sacramento from distant San Francisco Bay. The Canadians were joined by some christianized Indians from Mission San José who wore "civilized"—Mexican—garb and made no trouble. Still, Work was wary of them, for some of his horses had been stolen just before they visited his camp. It was the second such local loss he had suffered—and one which he could ill afford.

The long beaver drought was broken when four canoes reached camp from the lower Sacramento. They brought twenty-nine beaver and nine otter. Two more craft arrived with ten beaver. The trappers reported beaver on the margins of San Francisco Bay but "shy," hard to take. There were also plenty of beaver in the Suisun marshes but the high state of the water, plus the rising and falling of the tides, precluded trapping at the moment.

Work sent the canoes out again and soon had thirteen more pelts of beaver and five of otter from three of them. When two more returned, they bore fourteen beaver and six otter, followed by another craft with eight beaver. Delighted, Work agreed to meet his little fleet in six days at a rendezvous "beyond this river, as near the Bay as we can go."

Although two horses were rustled by Indians, Work raised camp and marched his men to the Calaveras River, some nine miles. He crossed it on an Indian bridge, a toppled tree, and swam the horses to the muddy south bank. Then, by a roundabout route, he avoided the Sacramento's still flooded banks. When seven more horses were stolen, an exasperated Work rushed men in hot pursuit. His orders were to shoot the thieves on sight. But his men lost the trail on the hard, dry plain. Increasingly, the bourgeois was suspicious of the local natives: "Some Indians assisted in seeking for the horses but it is probable that they were seeking to lead astray instead of aiding." He set up nighthawks or guards over his *remuda,* giving the sentinels orders to shoot every Indian who approached the horse herd (or the camp) by night.

Well aware that Indians were shadowing him, Work marched nineteen miles southeast across the plain on June 26. Across a point of land, he found the oaks of the south fork of the Calaveras and then reached the site of McLeod's old camp on French Camp Creek. There, Larocque's wife redeserted him. This time, she took with her an Okanogan woman, the wife of Iroquois Pierre Satakaras. Work was puzzled: "No cause is known for their running off. There were no women in the camp better treated by their husbands."

Work found a campsite two miles from the flooding San Joaquin on a slightly elevated plain covered with fine clover. It was paradise for his horses. His hunters shot many elk and antelope too, though many took to the water and could not be followed. Less welcome was the abundance of other "wild game"—mosquitoes. At French Camp Work wrote: "As we are here nearly surrounded by water, we are like to be devoured by mosquitoes." However, he was cheered when three canoes brought in twenty-five beaver and an otter. This was very good work for such a short cruise, and five of the craft were still out hunting or, as the Mexicans had it, "fishing" for beaver. Work immediately pointed the prows of the three canoes towards the river, ordering an eight-day cruise.

On the twenty-ninth, Indians whom he had hired to chase the runaway wives returned. They had found the ladies' horses but had picked up no further sign of the women. The animals were found not far from French Camp. Although they had searched as far as the Cosumnes, the scouts had not been able to dislodge the women from their hiding place.

At sunset on another sultry day without even a puff of air to alleviate the suffering of the men in the suffocating, mosquito-breeding heat, horse thieves carried out their most daring raid. Apparently immune to skeeters and heat prostration alike, the Indians on July 1, 1833, stole five mounts right from under the very nose of the wrangler. He turned his back for a moment, the Indians slipped out of hiding in the tall grass, and the horses were gone. Trappers returning to camp through the oaks actually saw the stolen animals in the dusk but mistook them for elk. The loss was not noticed and the alarm not given until next morning, when the trail was cold.

An angered Work recorded his feelings: "We will be obliged to destroy a village or two of these scoundrels. So many of the men being absent in the canoes prevents me from going after and punishing them immediately. Besides, we are very scarce of ammunition."

When the long-absent canoes returned, Work was disappointed. They had only three dozen beaver and a dozen otter after two weeks. "In hopes of making more of it, they marched too much and spent their time to no purpose. There are plenty of beaver in the Bay, but they are shy and difficult to take. Besides, the hunters complain that the water is too high and that they cannot find ground to set their traps. The rising and falling of the tide is also against them."

In spite of the falling off of returns, Work sent five canoes out again on a nine-day cruise. When two more returned through the smoke and haze of the burning plain, just fired by Indians, he was so annoyed with their small catch (eight beaver and two otter) that he hardly let them beach the craft before sending them packing on another hunt of six days. When Larocque brought his canoe in, he had the same sad story to tell—and four pelts. Said Work: "Like the others, they say there are plenty of beaver but that they are shy and will not take the traps."

The Indians were becoming downright annoying. A Walla Walla hunter came in, his clothes torn to tatters. Alone, he had tried to take back four or five Company horses from six local Indians. He had failed; the odds were a little too much, even for a Walla Walla. He had lost his gun and cap in the scuffle, but, for some reason (probably the fear of reprisal by Work), the "gentiles" had returned toque and gun. They even let him keep his own horse. But they refused to give back the animals they had stolen from the herd.

While Work was camped on July 9 on a bay or slough, perhaps McLeod's Lake, near modern Stockton, a Spanish-speaking neophyte (Christian Indian) came in. He vehemently denied that his people had taken the horses. He blamed the "gentiles"—the pagans, the heathens, that is, the wild Indians of the locality. But Work had plenty of doubts: "It is most likely that they are all of a piece." Probably he was right. The Christianity of many *neófitos* was only skin-deep and they did not honor the final Commandment of the Decalogue. *And* he lost six more horses when the attention of the entire camp (including the horse guard and a boy he had posted as a lookout in a tree) was distracted by the noisy visit of six "civilized" Indians. The visitors' skillful kin, or whoever, led the animals quietly away through bulrushes and water in which Work thought it impossible for horses to avoid bogging down.

Finally, Work was able to throw a scare into the horse-hungry Indians. One of his own Indians shot a would-be thief right through the head. His frightened companions left blankets and other belongings as they fled pell-mell into a thicket. Sadly, Work commented: "Notwithstanding our wish to pass through the country peaceably, we will be obliged to go to war with these daring scoundrels."

Five canoes brought in thirty-seven beaver and twenty-eight otter. They were followed by the two deserted husbands prodding their bedraggled runaway wives along. The ladies had been stripped naked by the ungentlemanly "gentiles" but were unharmed.

That same day, July 13, 1833, John Work had his closest call: "A little before noon, eight Indians on horseback and nine or ten on foot arrived, headed by the Spanish-talking Christian who visited us on Tuesday last. They received food and some tobacco to smoke and were engaged in trading different little articles among the people for meat and other things. When their men were detected among the horses, attempting to steal them, they were brought to camp but attempted to escape. The others, at first, told them to submit but, afterwards, bent their bows and seemed determined to aid them in their object. The thieves were instantly fired upon and they all fled. Two of them got off on horseback. The others left their horses and rushed into the pond among the bulrushes. Two were killed and others wounded but they concealed themselves among the rushes and could not be found. One of them had bent his bow to fire an arrow at me behind my back, but one of the women attacked him with an axe and he fled with the others.

"It was, no doubt, a made-up plan," opined Work, "that those who came to the camp would amuse the people while the others would steal the horses. They took time to shoot a few arrows but, luckily, without effect, though some of them were very near. Towards evening, a party again approached the camp [but] on the opposite side of the pond. Some of the young men went to meet them and fired a couple of shots. They barely waited to shoot a few arrows across and then made off and hid themselves. We have strengthened the guard and made everything in readiness, should they be inclined to assemble and attack us in the night."

The same day as the skirmish, Laframboise turned up at Fort Vancouver. His exact route is unknown but he had given up the shore itself, to march along the ridge of the range paralleling the coast. He had hunted the headwaters of coastal streams without success. Turning inland, he received startling news (either in the Shasta or Siskiyou mountains)—word of the fatal attack on a party of seven Americans and an Englishman by Rogue River Indians.

The party had, indeed, been attacked but not wiped out as some rumors said. Five men escaped death to eventually reach the Willamette settlements, half-starving. Most prominent was Dr. William J. Bailey. He was disfigured by a horrible gash in his face delivered by a Rogue battleax. He was cared for by the folk at the Methodist Mission which had sprung up athwart the Siskiyou Trail near modern Salem, Oregon. Later, Dr. McLoughlin treated him at Fort Vancouver. Luckily, Laframboise's journey was as devoid of incident as Bailey's had been adventurous and disastrous.

On Bastille Day, as Laframboise relaxed in Fort Vancouver, Work was taking precautions against attack. He wrote: "The Indians approached the camp in the night and in the morning watch, a little before daylight, began their attack at my end of camp. The people immediately assembled to the spot to meet them and the horses were moved a little farther off to avoid being wounded with the arrows. The arrows were falling thick among us but it was so dark that the

Indians could not be seen where they were, concealed among the long grass and bulrushes and among some trees beyond a part of the wood. We, therefore, in order to not uselessly expend our ammunition, waited patiently for daylight so that we might see to fire with effect, but before daylight came they raised a war yell, fired their arrows a little thicker than before, and then ceased. And when it became light, none of them could be found. Probably they expected to find us asleep and when they found that not to be the case, they had not the courage to rush into the camp or wait until daylight, when they were sure they would not all escape." The only injury sustained by the Brigade was a horse wounded in the neck by an arrow.

From the ambush site, Work moved to the site of modern French Camp. When two canoes brought in only *one* pelt, he decided that it was time to move. "We determined not to return to the Bay, as they were working for nothing." He had his men jerk some venison, then moved to a camp at the forks of the San Joaquin and Jed Smith's river, the Stanislaus. Few elk, deer, or antelope showed themselves now—and fewer permitted themselves to become targets. Most fled precipitately into the impenetrable swamps and thickets. The few animals killed were unappetizingly lean.

Nine Indians were on the verge of attacking Pichette and Kanota but changed their minds when the trappers showed fight and raised their rifles. Five canoes brought only forty-five beaver and fourteen otter for twelve days of hunting, a sorry showing. Work was disappointed in the canoe hunt as a whole. Though the pelts taken were in better condition than anyone had dared to expect during the summer season, there were only 249 beaver (thirty-eight of them cubs) and eighty-five otter, of which sixteen were small pelts. Work decided that it was time to return to Fort Vancouver.

Another reason for moving on was the growing hostility of the trappers' "hosts." Work explained: "The Indians are becoming troublesome and we are very short of ammunition, scarcely enough to defend ourselves, let alone to enable the people to live [by hunting]." He sent out a party of scouts which walked right into trouble. They found a village of Indians drawn up for battle. The Canadians did not politely wait to become targets. They attacked and put eighty to ninety Indians to flight in a dry channel so guarded by low tree branches that trappers, who were mounted, could not charge o' horseback or even fire their rifles accurately. Still, they managed to kill some Indians and wound others. They seized eighteen horses but found them to be lean nags. The only casualty in the ranks was, again, one of Baptiste Guardapii's horses wounded in neck and thigh by arrows.

On July 26, Rocquebrin was wounded in one wrist by a shaft when Work sent a party to a village of sixty to eighty warriors on the Mokelumne River to look for stolen horses. Work reported: "As these Indians had offered no hostilities, the men were directed to do them no injury if they gave up the horses peaceably. But on approaching the village, the people were met by the Indians who immediately raised a war yell and discharged their arrows at them. But they were soon driven into the village and thence into a low swampy part of a lake overgrown with wood and bulrushes, where they could not be approached on horseback without much danger. The village, consisting of near forty huts, was burnt, some of the Indians killed and several wounded, and twenty-one horses taken. Among them are four of those which were stolen from us. . . . The chief of this village is the Indian whom the Indian from the Mission recommended to us as being a good Indian and converted to Christianity. . . . The visitation which this village has received may perhaps deter them from stealing again. On account of the scarcity of ammunition, we must defer punishing the other two villages for the present."

The rivers were falling with amazing speed. The Canadians on July 28 crossed the Cosumnes at their old June 10 station, where the Indians broke camp before their eyes. Word of their fight preceded them and the villagers fled in all directions. Next day, they were at the junction of the Sacramento and American rivers, where Captain John Sutter would build New Helvetia in a half-dozen years. Hunters, ranging as far as the lowest village on the Feather, found two of the missing horses and hazed them back to camp. They were pursued by Indians, who fired at them. One of them boasted that an arrow had pierced his trousers, but Work doubted the braggart's tale—"They are so given to vaunting that their story cannot be relied upon."

Bear River was reached on August 1 after fourteen miles of scorched, waterless, burned-over plain. Horses and dogs suffered greatly from the heat and from sore feet. The hot sand was torture. Work marched his brigade to the middle fork of the Feather, as he reckoned it. Here on the Yuba River, he let men and animals rest, for another hot day had been devilishly hard on them. Some of the men were feverish—not malaria but a touch of the sun. At the Nicolaus ford, Work crossed his men to the far side of the Feather and halted on the site of his December 15 Buttes camp.

To his amazement, he found the once heavily populated area

deserted. A sense of foreboding made his skin crawl. He knew that the depopulation was not due to fear of vengeance by him, nor of starvation. There were winter stocks of acorns about, untouched. There could be but one explanation—disease. He was right. The Sacramento Valley was being swept by a great epidemic, part of the pandemic afflicting much of the Far West. Villages along the faint line of the Siskiyou Trail had once swarmed with inhabitants. Now the settlements were desolate-looking and all but deserted. A few wretched natives remained, lying on the ground, scarcely able to move.

An uneasy Work gave orders to his men, strict orders. They were to give all villages or *rancherías* a wide berth, in case the mysterious malady should be infectious. Misjudged by some whites to be cholera, smallpox, typhus, or measles, it was actually a virulent malaria or intermittent fever. The Canadians called it ague and fever or tertian fever. Some, like Ogden, blamed it on "the miasmata pervading the atmosphere" of swamps. He was near the truth, of course, but it was no *tulare* miasmas but clouds of Anopheles mosquitoes which were the vectors of the dread disease. White men usually recovered; Indians almost always died of malaria.

Work learned that the "malaria of the marshes" had been unknown to the Indians until 1830. It apparently came in the bloodstreams of trappers following Jed Smith or Pete Ogden—men who were carriers but not suffering from the shakes. The Canadian did not know the long and roundabout route of the Siskiyou Trail's peculiar plague. Introduced to Fort Vancouver from Hawaii (where the disease was already prevalent) by the American *Owyhee* or the British *Dryad* around 1829–1830, it swept the Columbia and then the Sacramento Valley. The Siskiyous split the epidemic into two areas; it was not found in the high country.

Work, himself, was unconsciously a villain of the piece. He almost surely spread the disease among the California *rancherías*. His party had been slowed by malaria at the Dalles in August 1832. By September, he had a dozen cases of ague in the ranks. By December he noticed sickness among the Feather River Indians. This was the dawning of the pestilence he met on his retrograde march to Vancouver.

Work did not raise camp at the Buttes until his men had collected a large supply of provisions for the march back to Oregon. He noted, "This is the last place [in] which we can expect to find any." Along with several other men, Work was ill. But he gave orders to march through tormenting clouds of mosquitoes as the heat mounted. Several of the dogs gave up, from thirst, and had to be abandoned. More men fell ill, shaking with fever, between the ford of Deception (i.e., Butte) Creek and Chico Creek. They stumbled along under a hazy sky but one unswept by even a whisper of cooling wind. Aching bones and violent headaches became the commonest complaints. The marches were not only long and fatiguing, but thirsty: There was no water to be had except near the decimated villages pressed down by the hand of death. The men began to find bodies of Indians, dead of disease. Some were half-devoured by wolves and coyotes. The survivors were now too weak even to repair their fishing weirs when they tumbled down.

Still cursing the sun, "glaring through the hazy atmosphere like a ball of fire," Work reached the winter ford of the Sacramento on August 15. This was the traverse which came to be known as the French Ford and is so labeled on Pierson B. Reading's pioneer map of the Siskiyou Trail's California leg. It lay just above the bend near Red Bluff where Bear Flagger William B. Ide would locate his adobe, just below the west-side tributary of Red Bank Creek and the ocherous bluff itself.

Work tried to hurry his men north, from Bear River (today's Pine Creek) to the Quesnel River, now Deer Creek. When Guardapii fell from his horse and hurt himself, Work found that he was the fifty-first person with some kind of ailment. Most were malarial, suffering from alternating hot fits and icy, shaking chills. As the road grew more stony, more men fell behind. Still, even the weakest managed to stagger into camp by evening.

Briefly, Work felt heartened when he saw Indians across the Sacramento who were healthy-looking. Indeed, they were diving for freshwater shellfish. But when he reached the Sycamore River (Butte Creek), he had sixty-one men ill, most with trembling fits. One child was dead. There was no medicine to use in treating anyone. With dampened hopes, Work wrote: "Our condition is really deplorable. . . . I am afraid to stop lest we die like the Indians. . . . I endeavour to keep up their spirits as well as I can, but it is become now of little effect."

On August 21, Work was camped on Cow Creek with his disheartened party. He did not raise this "Canoe River Camp" next morning. The men were about at the end of their ropes. Dangerous or not, he simply had to stop and let them rest. With leisure available, he wrote more fully in his journal: "Many of the men are so discouraged that some of them proposed remaining here and let the strongest proceed on to the Fort. I pointed out the folly of such a step and the little chance those who remained would have of escaping, and that the distance to the Fort would not take more than a month, and that we were sure of getting medicines and every necessary, and that the mountains were now near, where we would experience a difference of climate which would, most likely, effect a change for the better."

Work was very worried, for seventy-four of his party were ill as of August 24, 1833. "The men are now beginning to fall. Our case is becoming more alarming every day. Indeed, we are in a most deplorable condition and all my efforts can scarcely keep up the men's spirits. Our only chance of escape is to push on to the Fort, and a long road it is. At the rate we can possibly march, at least a month's march, and some ill-disposed Indians before us at two places. But we must push on, as it is our only means of safety."

The next day, an old Cayuse *berdache* (homosexual) died. He was buried near modern Hat Creek Forest Service Station. (His grave was found in the 1930s by Ranger Reuben Box.) Work's men could now make only six to eight miles of progress per day. They were beginning to kill their horses for food. Guardapii managed to kill a bull elk. He generously distributed the meat and made broth for the sick.

The bourgeois confided to his journal: "I am endeavoring to inspire the people with confidence that a change of climate in the mountains will be of great advantage to them. I have been for some days unwell myself, with a violent headache and pains in all my bones." The Irishman's unscientific instincts were right again; there was safety from malaria in the Siskiyous, once he got above the altitude of the Anopheles's habitat.

The weather grew colder, heaping patches of snow on the higher peaks. Blankets and capotes were worn by everyone. After a sunrise start, the party crossed "the mountain" by noon. But not till sunset did the last stragglers drag their way to the campfires on the swampy plain of Hat Creek. He rested the sick, next day. He had now been ill himself for ten days, and it was damned difficult to keep up the spirits of the party through his own recurring attacks of the ague, which left him dispirited. He was further distressed to find a horse shot dead by Indian archers. Another four animals were wounded. Sourly, he commented on *les peaux rouges:* "This is the reward we meet for treating the barbarians kindly and endeavouring to conciliate them. Nothing but severe treatment is of any avail with such savages. Did they find opportunity, they would use the people as they did the horses. We have now to begin watch in the night, and I can muster just 12 men to attend to that duty."

The last day of August saw Work's enfeebled brigade creeping across the Pit River, to camp on the north bank in a thunderous rain-storm. It was a miserable night for Work; he shook with a severe trembling fit. Indians skulked about the herd, sizing up their chances until the night guard put them to flight with a gunshot.

When the company continued to Fall River, Indians fired arrows across its waters, wounding two horses. Some of the men responded with rifle fire. So many of Work's force had fallen ill by September 3 that it appeared to the booshway that his brigade might go the way of McLeod's snowbound outfit, only much worse: "We will, in a short time at this rate, all be down," he wrote. But the stubborn Irishman dragged his men over Dead Horse Pass, where McLeod's horses (and hopes) had perished, and reached the headwaters of the McLeod (now McCloud) River.

Sheep Rock, a major landmark east of the Siskiyou Trail and a perennial Company campsite, was reached on September 7. It lay at the crossroads of several ancient Indian hunting trails just north of Mount Shasta. The Indians dogging Work's steps like wolves began to move in closer, to pick off laggards. Seven horses were lost to them on the road to Sheep Rock and four more at the camp at the mono-lith's base.

After Groslui, ill, barely escaped being cut off by Indians, Work wrote, despairingly: "The greater part of the people are so ill that it is impossible for them to take care of their horses. Indeed, they can scarcely take care of themselves. Our whole party is now becoming exceedingly hopeless." Though an oasis of a small, grassy banked creek briefly cheered him, Work soon slipped back into his funk: "I tremble regularly every night, myself, and am becoming weaker daily." He knew that his feeble men could not march all the way to the Sasty or Shasta River (by which he really meant the Klamath proper) so he halted in a small swamp. The unseen, hounding Indians promptly stole a packhorse, and Groslui, overexerting himself in his sickly con-dition, began to bleed at the nose and mouth.

The next day, Friday the thirteenth of September, should have been the blackest of the journey. Instead, the "unlucky day" proved to be a red-letter day for Work. He led his men on an eight-mile march, good going for them at this stage; successfully negotiated the

Klamath River crossing; and came upon Laframboise's homeward trail of two months earlier. Only then did he learn that Michel had given up on the coast route.

Because Groslui was too weak to move, Work did not raise camp the following day. Perhaps he realized that the man was dying. On the fifteenth, he chose a campsite at the foot of the Siskiyous, to end the day's march. Next day, he led the party in a hike of eight miles over rugged slopes to reach the Coquin River, actually a branch of the Rogue. This was very good going for sick men in desperate straits.

Groslui gave up the ghost on the seventeenth, but his comrades made it to the main branch of the Rogue. There the Indians shot some horses and made off with three more. Raged Work: "There is no manner of dealing with such barbarians but to punish them whenever they can be caught." On the Rogue, Work overran the trail of Ewing Young (1832), as well as that of Laframboise.

The Rogue was well named for the rascally conduct of its people —"Rivière des Coquins." On September 22 Work stated: "The Indians here bear a very bad character. During the first watch last night, a party of them came to the other side of the river opposite to us, made a large fire, and raised the war cry. I was in a paroxysm of fever and could not stir out. . . . Owing to our helpless state, there being only 15 men in health in the camp, I felt uneasy for some time. All the people who were able were ordered to arms. The Indians in a short time went off and we saw or heard no more of them."

On the twenty-sixth, Work lost another companion when Bernie died after becoming so weak that his pards had to tie him to his horse. Work also gave up hope for one of the Indian women, bleeding at the nose and mouth as Groslui had done. Crossing the Rogue, Work slowly led his men up the track blazed by Joseph Gervais. Though the sick were no better off, the road was improving. And, by a miracle, the Indians left the sick travelers alone. By October 4, Work had reached the South Fork of the Umpqua, and its main branch near modern Roseburg by the eighth.

Slowly, the plummeted hopes of the men began to rise as they recognized familiar landmarks. But Work practically collapsed, because under the strain of leadership he had been traveling so long on raw nerve: "I am rendered so weak that I am with difficulty able to make the day's journey, short as they mostly are. For some days, I have had no shaking fits, but the hot fever visited me regularly." As he wrote, a sixteen-year-old boy was dying and the "friendlies" were stealing yet another of his surviving horses.

211

But the worst was over. Work was now on the homestretch. From Yoncalla Creek, he reached the road over Elk Mountain, somewhere west of today's Highway 5, and dropped into the Willamette Valley. Many men were still sick, including himself: "I am very feeble, myself, and still attacked every day with trembling fits and the hot fever."

Sunday, October 13, 1833, was a glorious Sabbath. Laframboise and some men, bound for the Umpqua, found Work's bedraggled camp on a swampy plain north of Elk Mountain. Michel told Work that he had arrived at the fort in July. The rumors of trouble on the Siskiyou Trail which he, and perhaps others, had brought to the post worried McLoughlin. He was anxious over Work's fate. To calm his fears, the Irishman hurriedly wrote a letter and sent it ahead to the doctor by one of Michel's Indians.

Next day, as Laframboise proceeded southward, Work shepherded his faltering men through cold rain showers to the Long Tom River. He was pleased to see the gait of a few of his men picking up again. They were responding to Laframboise's cheering visit, familiar terrain, and the nearness of Fort Vancouver. After he reached the Rivière des Souris ("Mouse River," now Mary's River), Work's messenger returned from Fort Vancouver. The courier handed him a letter from McLoughlin, then gave him foodstuffs sent by the doctor to restore his morale. They did the trick; he jotted in his notes that the tea, sugar, bread, and butter were "very acceptable to me in my present feeble state."

Making fifteen miles, Work reached the Yamhill River on October 19. He laid over on it because of heavy rains until the twenty-third, his men too weak to build rafts to cross it during highwater. So Work dropped down the Yamhill to its junction with the Willamette River, borrowed a canoe from a pioneering settler and ferried his people over to Sand Encampment or Champoeg. At this outpost settlement of Company folk, he borrowed another canoe to take himself and his baggage down the Willamette and across the Faladin (Tualatin) River, "the only stream now in our way."

His men were beginning to recover, so Work let them proceed by land while he embarked in Depaty's canoe with two Indian guides. Alas, they were incompetent and by the time he got to the Chutes, the Falls of the Willamette, his land party was already there. Work crossed the baggage and horses over the portage and had his men spend some time drying furs. On October 28, he set out in fine weather on the last leg of his Buenaventura expedition.

The Irish bourgeois beached his canoe below Fort Vancouver on October 29, 1833. He was received with a hearty welcome. On the last day of the month, his men arrived by boat. Some had to be placed in the doctor's care, but most of the hardy mountain men were already recovering.

As the last entry in his journal of the California expedition, Work again referred to his good fortune in reaching the Siskiyou Mountains in time: "Several times during our journey the people were so weak that I was apprehensive the greater part of them would die on the way before reaching the fort. I attribute their recovery in a great measure to the change of climate in the mountains, but as this had not an immediate effect, they did not begin to get better until some time after we crossed the mountains."

Then, in a single paragraph, John Work summarized his view of California as a field for Company activity. He was not optimistic: "We had a great deal of trouble and some skirmishes with the natives on account of their stealing and killing some of our horses and attempting to kill some of the men. . . . Our hunt only amounts to 1,023 beaver and otter skins. Indeed, the country is now so exhausted that little can be done in it."

McLoughlin listened carefully to the opinion of this veteran of the Siskiyou Trail. Once again, it appeared that the trail to California would be abandoned, closed, almost before it was named—and barely opened—by the Hudson's Bay Company breed of mountain men.

Yankee Interlopers

HARD ON THE moccasined heels of Jedediah Smith came other unwelcome Yankees to the southern end of the Siskiyou Trail. All were eager for a look-see at fabled California, and many wanted a gander at the beaver country of the Sacramento and San Joaquin valleys.

James Ohio Pattie was first in line. He arrived in California early in 1828 with his father and a trapping party. Unfortunately, Governor José María Echeandía took them for spies and clapped the Patties in the *calabozo*, where the elder died.

James was released by the suspicious governor in order that he vaccinate California's population against *viruela*—smallpox. He immunized his way all the way to Bodega and won his freedom and the thanks of the government. But he was never able to lead a trapping expedition up the Siskiyou Trail, as planned. He was only able to join a Portuguese in some sea otter hunting before sailing away from California in May 1830.

With the failure of the Patties, the chances of Americans giving the Honourable Company a run for its money in northern California fell on Ewing Young. There was no threat from native Californians. They were familiar with the beaver (Castor) and the land and sea otter (both called Nutria), and an engraving of a beaver decorated a cartouche on the classic map of the province in Miguel Venegas's book of 1757 about Alta and Baja California. And, legally, none but Mexican citizens could secure trapping licenses in the territory. But few *californios* were interested in such cold and hard work—not when

215

cattle and horses could be raised almost without effort. They preferred to barter with Indians for skins to trade to the occasional Boston ships putting into the bays of Monterey and San Francisco. Americans in Taos, New Mexico, like Joaquín Joon (Ewing Young) knew this— hence his determination to fill the trapping vacuum in California before the Hudson's Bay Company could attend to it.

The strapping mountain man from "Tenesí" had had his appetite for California fur hunting whetted by the tales of Richard Campbell and men of Jed Smith's expedition. Not only did he wish to trap California, he wished to check out the possibility of a horse and mule trade from there all the way to Missouri. Campbell had told him that Californian riding and packing horses were of outstanding quality.

In August 1829 Young left Taos for California. Among those tagging along with him was a ten-year-old grass-green mountain man, an excook named Christopher Carson. Earlier, Kit had run away from a saddler to whom he had been apprenticed. His master did not miss him too much; he had advertised a reward for Kit Carson of just one cent! Young feinted toward the north to fool the governor of New Mexico into thinking he was going to trap in U.S. territory, then slanted down to the Gila Trail and the Colorado River boundary of California.

Via the Mojave River, Ewing Young reached Mission San Gabriel, where Father Martínez received him with the same hospitality accorded Jed Smith three years earlier. But Young tarried only a day at the mission; he was eager to wet his traps. He climbed over the Tehachapi Mountains and dropped into the swampy San Joaquin Valley. He took a few beaver in the Lago de Chintache (de los Tulares), Tulare Lake, and the bulrushes were thick with game which kept men happy and company dogs pot-bellied from stuffing themselves with the plentiful meat. But he soon moved northward to the San Joaquin River and followed it down into what he thought was *tierra desconocida,* "unknown country." To his surprise and disappointment, he found unmistakable signs that another trapping party had recently preceded him there. It was a large company and its presence explained the paucity of beaver in the *tule* country. When he caught up with the mysterious strangers, he found them to be members of Peter Skene Ogden's Snake River Outfit. Young was amazed to find it a huge family affair—not only sixty men but a passel of women and children, too. Already, Ogden had taken a thousand pelts in the San Joaquin Valley. There was not much in the way of leavings for Young.

Ogden was friendly, so Young traveled with him for ten days. They worked their way north on the Sacramento portion of the Siskiyou Trail, then split up on Pit River. The Canadians took their leave of California, heading for Oregon on a northeasterly course. Young, finding traces of yet another trapping party (Alexander McLeod's brigade), gave up the chase. He decided to return to the lower Sacramento to loaf about until a fall hunt should be feasible.

Ewing Young arrived in the Central Valley at a critical time. A renegade Indian, Estanislao, was leading an uprising against the Mexicans. He was successful in encouraging Mission Indians to run away and join him in the interior. Sergeant Antonio Soto led a punitive expedition against him but Estanislao turned back the soldiery after wounding Soto fatally. When an Indian *alcalde* led the next force, a party of neophytes from Mission San José, the officer had the good sense to ask Young for help.

Ewing Young wanted the Mexicans to be in his debt. The Indian official's request for aid was a godsend to Young. It gave him carte blanche in the interior. According to a statement of July 15, 1830, by José Berryessa, eleven of Young's men had a three-hour fight with the "gentiles" before the latter fled. Having killed and wounded several warriors, the mountain men next put the Indian huts to the torch. Kit Carson, who led the raid, expanded on Berryessa's account: "We returned to the village and made an attack and fought for one entire day. The Indians were routed and lost a great number of men. We entered the village in triumph, set fire to it, burned it to the ground. The next day, we demanded the runaways and informed the Indians that if they were not immediately given up, we would not leave one of them alive. They complied with our demands and we turned our prisoners over to those from whom they had deserted and returned to our camp."

Carson recollected that he and Young took the Indian runaways to Mission San Rafael. Perhaps—but more likely it was to Mission San José. And Berryessa reported that Young's twenty-three-man party went to the latter mission to present their passports. Young brought along some peltries which he sold to a ship's captain, Juan Asero.

As he had predicted, Young was very much persona grata after trouncing Estánislao. Father Narciso Durán was very happy with Joaquín Joon. Carson recalled that, shortly, "We traded our furs with him [Asero] and with the money we obtained, purchased at the Mission all the horses we required, and returned to our camp." Young also bought mules. These were handsome brutes, much bigger even than the sturdy Missouri mules of American tradition. Young was sure that they would bring good money in the St. Louis market.

(If chronicler José Berryessa of 1830 was the aged José de los Reyes Berryessa of 1846, as seems likely, he was ironically reporting on the activities of his future murderer. During the Mexican War, Kit Carson captured José Berryessa and the De Haro twins near San Quentín. When his superior, John C. Frémont, told him that he was taking no prisoners, Carson had the peaceful and unarmed *californios* shot. It was the most despicable act of Kit Carson's career and has not yet been forgotten in Marin County, California.)

Young's horseflesh looked mighty fine to the hungry local Indians. A raiding party struck the camp one night and ran off sixty head. Next morning, while some of the men rounded up fourteen horses and *mulas* which had strayed from the rustlers, Carson led a pursuit. He and his dozen men chased the Horse Thief Indians all the way to the foothills of the Sierra Nevada—a hundred miles.

Long after, Carson recalled that ride and fight: "We surprised the Indians while they were feasting off some of our animals they had killed. We charged their camp, killed eight Indians, took three children prisoners, and recovered all of our animals with the exception of six that were eaten." Ewing Young's figures, in an October 10, 1830, letter to Captain Juan Bautista Rogers Cooper in Monterey, differed slightly from Kit's, but substantiated the plainsman's account: "Since I saw you in St. Joseph [San José], I have had my horses and mules stole by the Indians. I followed them and recovered all my caviard [*caballada*] but five of my best mules they killed to eat. We killed ten or twelve of the Indians."

Rustling was not Young's only headache. He was plagued by desertion. His French-Canadians, all of whom owed him money, threatened to mutiny and remain in California. But his Americans were loyal and put down the abortive emeute. Young was grateful to Carson and his three pards, whom he called "Americans that is men of confidence." Though the mutiny was put down, three of the Canadians merely bided their time and managed to bolt at the next opportunity. His was a sorry crew. J. J. Warner described Young's band: "It was composed of discordant material, being some Americans, some Canadians and Missouri Frenchmen, and a considerable number of New Mexicans of Spanish blood."

About September 1, 1830, Young struck camp and left the tag end of the Siskiyou Trail behind. He continued south in the San Joaquin Valley to cross the Tehachapis by way of the Cañada de las

Uvas, "Grapevine Canyon." From Mission San Fernando he marched his men to the tiny pueblo with the big name—Nuestra Señora de los Angeles de la Porciúncula. Shortened to Los Angeles (or "L.A.") today, it was then abbreviated more often to "the Pueblo" or, to distinguish it from the pueblo of San José, "the lower Pueblo."

In Los Angeles, the briefly popular Young soon wore out his welcome. It was because of the ragtag, bobtailed group of misfits under his command. His wild rovers indulged in *vino* and *aguardiente,* wine and brandy, and then in fistfights. The spree of fisticuffs turned violent and might have led to gunfire, but Corporal José Antonio Pico and his three common soldiers were no match for the twenty-odd mountain men, and knew it. They refused to tangle with them, even when they were sodden with brandy.

But when they could not pick a fight with the Mexican soldiery, Young's followers saw to it that a quarrel broke out among themselves. There was bad blood between two of Young's rough lot, probably the result of name-calling in the cantina La Rosa de Castilla. John Higgins, angered by some slighting remark or action of James (Big Jim) Lawrence, nursed his grievance until the party was on the road again. Then, according to Kit Carson, he calmly dismounted and, without warning, shot his erstwhile comrade to death. J. J. Warner commented on the murder: "These two men were both Irishmen, and Big Jim was a burly, overbearing man by nature, and when under the influence of liquor was intolerable, and Higgins in like condition was uncontrollable. The men were all suffering from the effects of days of debauchery and the major portion of them were intoxicated at the time and could not be controlled by Young."

The fur trader had hoped to trap the lower Colorado before returning for a December hunt on the Buenaventura portion of the Siskiyou Trail. But mutiny, desertion, brawling, Mexican annoyance, and now murder in his ranks discouraged him. He decided to go back to New Mexico with the beaver and stock he had on hand. Young did not even stop to bury Big Jim; he left his corpse on the road.

Young explained his change of plans to his friend, J. B. R. Cooper: "Having this difficulty with my men, I cannot have any confidence in them." He passed out of California via Cajón Pass and the Colorado River crossing. But in another letter to Cooper, dated August 24, 1831, in San Fernando de Taos, Young told his amigo that he would return to settle permanently in California. He planned to trade horses and mules, hunt sea otter, and trap beaver.

Dutch George Jundt, better known as George Yount, after talking to Jed Smith and Arthur Black, decided to head for California in 1831 with Ewing Young's partner, William Wolfskill. No wonder— Yount never forgot the tempting description of California by Black: "The valleys swarmed with Indians, peacefully disposed . . . the hills and mountains and streams with a profusion of game of every kind. . . . Beaver are abundant in all the creeks and rivers."

In February 1831, Wolfskill and Yount reached California, unaware that Young had gone back to Taos. The season was too far advanced for a successful hunt and the party fragmented. Wolfskill, in time, settled down as a successful rancher, with one of his properties being just off the Siskiyou Trail near Putah Creek. Yount, sometimes called Captain Buckskin, put his sharpshooter's eye to work hunting "nukies"—*nutrias*. He was a successful sea otter hunter and even devised a new craft for his Hawaiian boatmen. It was a sea-going skin canoe, a cross between a bullboat of the plains and the kayak and *bidarka* of the Aleut hunters sent along the California coast by the Russians. Yount used the thick, tough hides of sea elephants for the boat's skin. These critters were even bigger than the *lobos de mar* ("sea wolves") or sea lions off San Francisco.

Yount's new canoe and trusty Queens flintlock musket brought in many thirty-dollar skins. But, though beaver plews were worth only $4 and land otter a mere $2, the Dutchman's thoughts turned back to trapping. He built another boat, this one for river cruising parallel to the Siskiyou Trail.

Meanwhile, Ewing Young had written his friend Cooper about returning to California and made a cryptic reference to a trapping expedition or outpost-establishing expedition—"I think it is likely we can make some further arrangements about the establishments above San Francisco." On April 14, 1832, Young reached Los Angeles. He had only a dozen men, with defective traps. But, again, his men were more defective than his equipment. Cambridge (Turkey) Green was tired of being bullied by hulking Jim Anderson. He complained to Young, according to Job Dye, who jokingly, and foolishly, replied: "What makes you let him do it? If I could not prevent him any other way, I would shoot him." Going to a pine, Turkey steadied his rifle against it and shot Anderson. The latter took two or three short steps, muttered "You damned rascal!" and fell dead.

The ugly incident recalled the aftermath of the Rosa de Castilla bar fight and also the words of Jed Smith's clerk, Harrison Rogers, in regard to their Yankee trappers of 1827: "Friendship and peace prevail between us and the Spaniards, [but] our own men are contentious and quarrelsome among themselves, and have been since we started." Perhaps Green and Anderson were primed with Mexican *aguardiente* or tanked with William Workman's Taos lightnin', the ten-cents-a-gallon Missouri grain alcohol colored and flavored for Indian palates by soaking plugs of chawin' terbaccer in it.

In Los Angeles, Young turned Turkey Green over to the Mexican authorities. Some say he was lodged in the *calabozo* for a few months; Job Dye reported, "He was kept in prison over a year, when he made good his escape and joined the Apache Indians"; George Nidever claimed the Mexicans simply let him escape, to be rid of him.

After a go at sea ottering with some of his men and two *kanakas,* Ewing Young had his fill of seasickness and dumpings in the cold surf. He returned to beaver trapping in 1832, taking fourteen hunters over Tejon Pass and down Grapevine Canyon to check out marshy Tulare Lake before moving to the mouth of the Kings River, usually reckoned to be the end of the Siskiyou Trail, in October. Like Jed Smith and others before him, Young had to learn for himself that there were no beaver in the High Sierra. He moved across the ballroom-flat San Joaquin Valley and built a canoe for a three-man trapping expedition into the Delta. At the same time, he marched his men along the base of the Sierra to the Merced River, which he trapped down to its junction with the San Joaquin. He pitched his tent in a slough there to await the return of the canoe.

When no news arrived from the canoe party, an apprehensive Young sent out a search party. They saw no sign of the craft but left a note, with directions to camp, on a split stick stuck into the ground at the very point of land where the slough fed the San Joaquin. They found beaver to be very scarce in the "Sulphur River," probably the Fresno. No wonder: Young again found the tell-tale signs of a large trapping party (Laframboise's?) which had already worked the stream.

In order to outflank the opposition, Young collected his land party and hurried to the Sacramento, hoping to hunt its feeder streams. He did not yet realize how crowded was the Siskiyou Trail area that year. Laframboise was now poaching on his compatriot Work's territory; the combined British parties totalled 163 persons! Only forty of these were trappers, the rest women and children.

The Siskiyou Trail was already *too* crowded. Work's 1832 hunt was disappointing. Frank Ermatinger wrote his brother Edward about it on March 11, 1833: "Work was unsuccessful last year and [yet], this summer, went off with his party towards the Spanish settlements. There is some talk of its being the last year of the party."

McLoughlin would have liked to quash such loose, pessimistic, defeatist talk. Unfortunately, it came from the horse's mouth. John Work, himself, wrote Ned Ermatinger (February 24, 1834) to say: "My last expedition was the most unpleasant I have yet had. It was to the southward, to California. We had a good deal of trouble and some skirmishes with the hostile tribes of savages, who are very numerous. Some parts of the country are very rugged and difficult to pass, but what was worst of all, the fever broke out among my people (near 100 in number) and spread so rapidly that, in a short time, more than three-fourths of the party—myself, the three little ones, and their mother among the number—were attacked by it. 2 men, an Indian, and two children belonging to the party died on the way." Commented Frank Ermatinger to his brother Ned: "Poor fellow, he has suffered much, last trip, by the fever."

By settling the Willamette Valley with men loyal to the Honourable Company, McLoughlin hoped to hold the Oregon half of the Siskiyou Trail against American incursions. As early as 1828 he had encouraged old-timers like Gervais, La Bonté and Lucier to farm it, though he had never seen it himself. In 1832 he belatedly corrected this oversight with a tour of inspection. The doctor found the valley to be deserving of the praise heaped upon it: "It is the finest country I have seen, and certainly far finer than Red River for Indian traders to retire to. And, before long, [he warned John McLeod on March 1, 1833], you may depend [on it], it will be settled, as there is now a plan afoot to colonize it from Boston."

Others in the Company were worried by sharpening American rivalry. Archibald McDonald, chief trader at Fort Langley, agreed with McLoughlin. He also wrote John McLeod, to say: "If he does not look sharp, His Majesty will, ere long, be apt to lose his valuable domain."

With Jed Smith dead, Ewing Young would have to be the one to throw a scare into George IV. He gave the Sacramento Valley a careful going-over. It was a well-watered land of prosperous Indian villages of from 1000 to 1500 souls. J. J. Warner, with Young, was amazed that an uncultivated country could support such a large population. The explanation was the great quantity and diversity of food, readily available to people who were only mediocre hunters. There were great herds of elk, deer, and *chivereau* or mule deer, there were hares and rabbits, antelope, ducks and geese, sandhill cranes, herons, and, in the streams, not only salmon and perch but giant sturgeon. Warner and his comrades gave the Indians low marks as hunters but there was such a surplus of game that they had no trouble in filling their bellies.

When game grew temporarily scarce, the Indians fell back on edible roots and bulbs, grass seeds, acorns and pine (piñon) nuts. Even the handsome but noxious horse chestnuts or buckeyes were rendered into food. A farina was made by leaching, in a process similar to that which made acorn flour palatable. Warner did not think much of acorns and buckeyes as food, but understood their need: "So great was the number of inhabitants that no source from which subsistence could be derived, in this most abundant and productive valley, was neglected."

The indifferent hunters of the Sacramento Valley did not make great warriors like the Rogues of the Siskiyous proper. But they were practiced, even skilled, horse thieves. And, for all the wild game of the Sacramento plain, they had voracious appetites for horseflesh. Shortly after Young began his exploration, they started to make off with his animals. The American quickly seized two braves and put them in irons. He shackled the two men together by a trap chain connecting their right legs. The spectacle of the demobilized and humiliated warriors so shocked and demoralized their comrades that they began driving the stolen stock back to Young's camp. These horse herders reached the river bank across from Young but the water was too high for a night crossing. They settled down to wait for daylight. Unfortunately, the captives tried to make it over to their camp. They bolted, got into the river and began to swim, but the weight of the trap chain dragged them down to a death by drowning. That night, the sleep of the trappers was disturbed by the wails of the Indians grieving for their dead friends.

The chastened Indians gave Young no more trouble, but the weather made up for them. By January 1833, California's short but violent winter was in full sway. Torrential rains and wind storms lashed at the tents in cold fury. The rivers flooded, turning the Central Valley into a great inland sea. The Sutter Buttes became islands on which the Americans, like the Canadians, took refuge. Warner recalled that Young's party was trapped for twenty days on the east bank of the Sacramento ten miles south of the American River's mouth. Finally, the Yanks were routed when the river gushed over its natural dikes. They slogged through a vast quagmire to reach the American River's bank, still standing like a storm-washed berm or parapet. There, Young had his men build a rawhide boat in which to cross the torrent. The trappers then made their way north to the Feather's mouth at the ghost town of Verona, then swung westward in search of higher ground near Putah Creek and the Coast Range foot-hills. Young abandoned (temporarily) an amphibious life on the drowned Siskiyou Trail without regret.

On January 16, 1833, Young welcomed Jed Smith's old com-panion, "Honest John" Turner to his party. His knowledge of the lay of the land, picked up in Company service, was most welcome. But Young must have ignored his advice in one respect, since Turner knew that there were no more beaver on the California "outside" coast than in the Sierra. Young insisted on seeing for himself. While Padre Luis Martínez was complaining (in April 1833) to the governor about forty men in the Suisun area who called themselves hunters but were buying stolen cattle and, thereby, corrupting civilized Indians, Young departed for the coast. He ascended Putah Creek from the Winters area, entered Berryessa Valley and surmounted the Coast Range. His route lay along the southern and western shore to Clear Lake through a low jungle of resistant chaparral—scrub oak, buck brush, manza-nita, chamiso, and Ceanothus or mountain lilac. The going was very slow, but he made the shore about seventy miles north of Fort Ross, where he found the deep-cut Noyo River as beaverless as all the other Redwood Coast streams. With great vigor, Young pushed north-ward through very difficult country to reach McKay's old, abandoned Umpqua Fort. Marching smartly up the Umpqua River past the site of modern Roseburg Young rejoined the Siskiyou Trail. He negotiated the mountains, trapped a few beaver at Klamath Lake, then followed the Klamath River downstream. (On September 21, 1833, John Work crossed his trail as the Britisher headed for home.) Young dropped out of the Siskiyous to coast Mount Shasta's eastern base, pass Mc-Leod's old Dead Horse Camp, and trap the fast-moving Shasta River. From the piñon and juniper country, he then descended to the Sacra-mento Valley. Young reached the river in the area of Fort Redding, where the two major California forks of the Siskiyou Trail split to straddle Mount Shasta. Young's reconnaissance was a remarkable ac-complishment, of the caliber of Jed Smith's and Pete Ogden's explora-tions—but it yielded little profit in beaver.

Young was shocked by the change in the Sacramento Valley since his spring departure. The great river now flowed through a valley of death. After the floods, clouds of mosquitoes had come, in-cluding the deadly Anopheles. They infected the entire Indian com-munity with malaria. J. J. Warner could never bring himself to shut out the memory of the hapless Indian villagers: "We found the valleys depopulated. From the head of the Sacramento to the great bend and slough of the San Joaquin, we did not see more than six or eight live Indians, while large numbers of their skulls and dead bodies were to be seen under almost every shade tree near water, where the uninhabited and deserted villages had been converted into graveyards."

Conditions were no better across the Cosumnes River and into the San Joaquin Valley. "On the San Joaquin River, in the immediate neighborhood of the larger class of villages which, in the preceding year, were the abode of a large number of those Indians, we found not only many graves but the vestiges of a funeral pyre." At last, on the Kings River, the trappers found a *ranchería* not yet abandoned. But it was even more horrible than the dead encampments, for it was dying before their very eyes. Warner never forgot "the cries of the dying, mingled with the wails of the bereaved, [which] made the night hideous in that 'valley of death.' "

Suddenly, the horror of the pandemic was intensified for Young. His own men began to come down with intermittent fever near the confluence of the Merced and San Joaquin. Two Indian boys, one from New Mexico, the other from Oregon, died. Nearly every man-jack in the company fell ill, but all recovered. Warner was so badly afflicted with the shakes that he believed he was near death. Just south of the Kings River crossing he was completely prostrated by fever. Only the crisp air of evening saved him. He revived enough to haul himself aboard his patient and loyal mule, which had stuck by him. The beast carried him to camp and safety.

As a new winter approached, the disease waned. All thought of it, in fact, was driven from the mountain men's minds on the night of November 12–13, 1833, when stars fell on California—literally. In fact, they dropped on the entire country. It was the most remarkable storm of meteors in America's history, and it was reported in text and woodcuts to a curious public. A Boston observer estimated that 250,000 meteoric particles fell in five to six hours. He reported: "I never saw snowflakes thicker in a storm than were the meteors in the sky at some moments."

Young's trappers were amazed, frightened, and awestruck by the celestial show. A few were doubting Thomases. They pooh-poohed the idea of so many falling stars, and insisted that the display was not astronomical but only "swamp meteors"—that is, lightning bugs or fireflies. But, shortly, even the doubters were convinced because of the magnitude, direction, and brilliance of the display.

For his part, J. J. Warner remembered the meteor shower for as long as he drew breath. "During the early part of the night, our attention was called by the camp guard to the display of shooting stars. The whole company was aroused to look upon the unusual phenomenon. There were no clouds in the sky and the heavens presented an appearance as though all the celestial orbs had been cast adrift and were flying promiscuously through the celestial space in every direction."

Dutch George Yount and George Nidever, sixty to seventy-five miles north of Young, were fascinated by the astronomical fireworks but had their hands full calming their *kanaka* trappers, who thought some mighty *kapu* had been broken for the gods to carry on so. The Hawaiians were brave enough when faced with whitewater rivers, raging surf, or surging rapids. But heavenly pyrotechnics were beyond their ken and they trembled, frantic with fear, as they prayed to Pele and other deities.

Still another trapping party was enthralled by the barrage of meteors. Captain Joseph Reddeford Walker had marched a company of Bonneville's men over the Sierra Nevada, skirting Yosemite Valley's north rim. He had decsended the Merced to the "Two Laries [*tulares*] or Bush River," the San Joaquin, and reached tidewater in the Delta. Like the others, Walker's men were both frightened and entertained by the star shower. His clerk, Zenas Leonard, recalled: "Our men were again thrown into great consternation by the singular appearance of the heavens. Soon after dark, the air appeared to be completely thickened with meteors falling towards the earth, some of which would explode in the air and others would be dashed to pieces on the ground, frightening the horses so much that it required the most active vigilance of the whole company to keep them together. This was altogether a mystery to some of the men, who probably had never before seen or heard of anything of the kind. But after an explanation from Captain Walker, they were satisfied that no danger need be apprehended from the falling of the stars."

In the provincial capital, Monterey, Walker secured permission to hunt and trade with the Californians. But he was expressly forbidden to either trap beaver or trade with the Indians. Since Walker's word was his bond, he shut himself out from any exploration of the Siskiyou Trail, though some of his men sneaked off to trap the Sulphur (Fresno) River. Walker moved his camp there in mid-January 1834. Zenas Leonard probably spoke for his captain, too, when he enthusiastically described the lower Siskiyou Trail country: "The soil in the plain is very strong and deep, producing heavy crops of wild oats and grass—affording excellent pasture for horses at that season of the year."

Joe Walker joined a company of Mexicans chasing runaway neophytes from Mission San José. They had eloped with three hundred head of horses. Probably, Walker was promised some of the mounts as payment for his services. The allies closed in on the Indians in a thicket of timber on a mountain to the east of the gringos' camp. But the warriors slipped away, leaving only a few oldsters, plus women and children. To the horror of the mountain men (pictured, themselves, as bloody brutes by Washington Irving), the Mexicans not only proceeded to kill these noncombatants in cold blood, but cut off their ears! When the Americans protested the taking of these gruesome souvenirs, the *californios* explained that the grisly trophies were necessary in order for them to prove the success of the punitive expedition upon their return to the settlements.

The Americans found it difficult to understand their hosts. As long as the Indians minded their manners, the ambivalent Mexicans were paternalistic and protective of them, if not always kind. Zenas Leonard noted: "The Spaniards manifest a warm friendship for the Indians under their jurisdiction, as those who were friendly towards us were constantly reminding us of the danger of wronging the Indians." But, when the Mexicans turned on the Indians to punish them for transgressions, it was with a cruelty alien to the Anglo-Americans.

Captain Walker did not ascend the Siskiyou Trail but left Monterey on St. Valentine's Day 1834 and exited California by the gap in the Sierra Nevada which he discovered and which is, today, Walker Pass. Although he reported to Benjamin Bonneville that California's streams were already mostly trapped out, Clerk Leonard publicized California's many other attributes: "The country through which we passed still continued as charming as the heart of man could desire. . . . A great number of streams flung out, flowing out of the mountains and stretching afar towards the Pacific. The prairies were most beautifully decorated with flowers and vegetation, interspersed with splendid groves of timber along the banks of the rivers, giving almost romantic appearance to the whole face of nature."

The Mexican authorities might not have been so amiably disposed toward Captain Walker had they seen his clerk's notebook. The journal was later published as a book which, long before the coinage of the term Manifest Destiny, urged the annexation of California by the United States: "Most of this vast waste of territory belongs to the Republic of the United States. What a theme to contemplate its settlement. . . . The Spaniards are making inroads on the south, the Russians are encroaching with impunity along the seashore to the north, and further north and northeast the British are pushing their stations into the very heart of our territory. . . . [They] more resemble military forts to resist invasion than trading stations. Our government should be vigilant. She should assert her claim by taking possession of the whole territory as [soon as] possible."

George Nidever had secured his discharge from Captain Walker while in the San Joaquin Valley and joined George Yount in trapping expeditions. He told Yount that Walker was the best leader he had ever met, a good man at hunting, trapping, and "auguring" in sign language with the Indians. And absolutely uncanny in his ability to find water on desert marches.

Dutch George liked the looks of Nidever. The thirty-one-year-old Tennesseean was the very opposite of such braggarts as Jim (Gabe) Bridger or the Black mountaineer Jim Beckwourth. He was modest, unassuming, and honest. His reason for coming to California was simplicity itself: It was not to get rich in the beaver trade on the Siskiyou Trail—no, he had found the Rocky Mountain winter too cold for him and had headed for a milder clime.

In later years, Yount remembered his beaver expedition to the watery southern reaches of the Siskiyou Trail as one of "only indifferent success." But, from Nidever's point of view, it was a venture of "very fair success." They took a boat crew of Hawaiians to hunt San Pablo Bay and Petaluma River. After taking a few otter, they next worked the richer Suisun Bay (near modern Benicia), then hunted the lower San Joaquin River.

One afternoon Yount, Nidever, and the Owyhees were camping in the *tulares*. A quarter-mile away, they spied Indian huts in the reed beds alongside the San Joaquin. While Yount got supper, Nidever strolled over for a look. He peered into several shacks but found them all deserted. The whole village was empty. He continued his walk past the limits of the *rancheria* but saw no sign of the natives, so he retraced his steps to the campfire. As he repassed the huts, he thought that he heard a moan or a whimper. Again he looked into their interiors. This time, he recalled: "I saw nothing at first, but my eyes becoming accustomed to the darkness, I made out a small child seated in the farther end of the hut. I went in and the little thing tried to talk to me. But I could not, of course, understand nothing of its language."

Nidever left the naked child, a girl of about three years, on her *tule* mat. He reported his find to Yount, who was becoming worried by his absence. Dutch George would not hear of it when Nidever suggested that they go back and get the child. Yount told his partner that he was sure that the Indians would return, after dark, to collect the abandoned girl.

All night long, it seemed to Nidever, he could hear the piteous whimpering of the girl. Yount later stated flatly that he *did* hear the child crying through the night. At first light, the trappers returned to the hut. They found the little one now too weak to even sit up. Nidever brought her outside and found her to be mostly skin and bone, and crawling with vermin. He guessed that she had been without food for three or four days, though there was a beaver's head left near her, with a few shreds of flesh still clinging to the skull. Yount exterminated the bugs which were torturing the child and washed her— "purified" her in his own terms. Nidever then recalled: "We took her to camp and gave her a piece of boiled beaver, and it was pitiful to see the eagerness with which she caught it to her mouth and sucked it voraciously. We feared to allow her to eat too much at first, and so took the meat from her after she had sucked it a few minutes. But so tightly did she have it pressed to her mouth that main force was necessary to take it from her." Yount made some garments for her out of his own trail-worn clothes. Then he arranged a bed for the wretched child in the boat.

After a few days, Yount moved the camp upriver. He met a party of fourteen Indians. When he urged them to take the child off his hands and to nourish her, they all refused. To his horror, they offered to kill the girl for him, when he refused to throw her into the river as they suggested. Although the child could articulate a few words in some Indian tongue, none of the natives met by Yount and Nidever could understand her.

After carving their names on the stout trunk of a tree on the San Joaquin's bank, to mark the limit of their ascent, the two trappers turned back. Under the care of her two "uncles," the little girl soon recovered her health. They treated her very well. Yount took her home with him after having her baptized and christened at Mission San Francisco Solano. The girl grew up, in time, and rejected several white suitors because she preferred an Indian husband. Eventually, she married an Indian and bore him several children before he murdered her.

During their 1833 hunt, the partners observed the unwelcome Siskiyou Trail visitor seen by Young and Warner—the Fourth Horseman of the Apocalypse. The dark rider was malaria. Yount believed that nowhere on earth was the disease more fatal than among the unprepared Indians of California. Ironically, he and Nidever found the San Joaquin Valley a land of plenty for them, though a deadly vale for the Indians. Since malaria had wiped out virtually all Indian fishermen, the river was thick with salmon.

But, otherwise, the San Joaquin was (like the Sacramento Valley) a valley of death. Recalled Yount: "The poor, ignorant creatures knew no remedy. They resorted to their charms and flocked to their sweat houses and there, in groups of several hundreds, would dance frantic around a blazing fire and while thus dancing around, the malady would seize them and they would fall down in agonies of death, till the sweathouse could contain no more. First, they would bury the dead; then they resorted to the practice of burning the bodies in heaps of several hundreds and, at last, in despair they would flee from them to the mountains, where many sickened and died, while a remnant who survived wandered desolate and forlorn to bemoan their deceased companions. The bodies of untold thousands lay whitening the plains and fertile valleys, in some cases in scattered groups and in other cases might be seen in heaps of the dead, 'a very great army.' So impregnated was the atmosphere with the effluvia of decomposing and putrid bodies that it was almost impossible to navigate the rivers. Deserted and desolated villages stood tenantless all over the valleys. . . . Here and there wandered a scattered few, in sullen and mournful indifference to everything around them. They were unwilling to hold any intercourse with the white man, half suspecting him of some agency in the calamities which had befallen them."

The northern end of the Siskiyou Trail, like its Sacramento segment, was busy in 1833–1834. Nathaniel Wyeth, a follower of Oregon promoter Hall J. Kelley, in January 1833 fumed with annoyance at McLoughlin's reluctance to let him tag along with the brigades: "Today, a party sent to enquire after another reported to be cut off beyond the Umpquoi or near the Clammat River under a man by the name of Michelle [i.e., Laframboise] returned, having ascertained that one white and two Indians only of said party had been killed. This party (I am informed) was under a man by the name of Dupont [Depaty]. I requested to accompany them but the Governor would not consent, alleging that they would conceive that I came to avenge the death of Mr. Smith's party, who was cut off by the Umpquoi Indians. All which I interpreted into a jealousy of my motives. This party brought back 200 skins, which they traded. They did not go beyond the Umpquoi."

Wyeth's colony failed but he returned again to Oregon in 1834 for another try, but it too failed. Before its collapse, however, he had time to look at the Willamette portion of the Siskiyou Trail. Accompanied by the American naturalist Thomas Nuttal, Wyeth went only as far as Willamette Falls in September 1834.

Another American newcomer, however, made a permanent settlement athwart the Siskiyou Trail. Reverend Jason Lee had made the overland march with Wyeth. He built a Methodist Mission near French Prairie in the Willamette Valley. Compared to the missions of California, it was hardly successful. But it managed to hang on, tenuously, as a colony and accelerated the trend toward settlement of the Willamette, first, and its Americanization, second. Jason Lee, Daniel Lee, two teachers and a clerk planted the mission on the site of later Wheatland, near Salem. The Methodists soon became more secular than clerical and transformed themselves into loud advocates for U.S. annexation of Oregon. It was the presence of these Protestants that reminded McLoughlin of a major deficiency at Fort Vancouver, the lack of a Catholic priest. He asked for a padre in 1834. When none came, he instituted services himself, using a French Bible and a *Penser y Bien*.

On March 20, 1833, McLoughlin warned Governor Simpson of "Boneyville's" crowd of mountain men on the Snake: "Some say they are coming here to establish themselves as colonists in Willamette." At the same time, he was worrying about declining Company influence and the loss of a lieutenant. "I am sorry to say that there are reports that Laframboise and his party have been cut off. However, the Indians here are so apt to raise false reports of this kind that I hope this is also false." He need not have worried; the Indian was not born who could lift Laframboise's scalp.

Ewing Young returned to California in May 1834. He planned on making a fortune, though not with traps but a sawmill. Times were slow, and mill irons, tools and skilled labor almost nonexistent in California. So he gave up the project almost before he began. So discouraged was Young with California, trapping and all, that he was on the point of leaving for good. But Thomas Oliver Larkin, the quasi-U.S. Consul in Monterey, persuaded him to remain. Like Micawber, he was sure that something was bound to turn up.

While idling in Los Angeles, Young met the great Oregon booster Hall J. Kelley. He had hypnotized Wyeth and others with his grandiose colonizing plans. Kelley was doing his best to start an emigration which, by sheer weight of numbers, would wrest Oregon from Hudson's Bay Company control.

At first, Young declined Kelley's invitation to guide him up the Siskiyou Trail. But, after mulling it over, he joined the eccentric promoter in Monterey at the end of June and agreed to pilot him. He gruffly warned Kelley that if he were deceiving him on the promise which the Willamette offered enterprising settlers, he would have his hide. "Woe be unto him!" were his words.

By now, Kelley had worn out his welcome in Monterey. Already, Larkin was deriding the enthusiast as "The King of the Beggars" and describing him as "the greatest bore I ever knew." It was time for Kelley to leave.

Young drove forty mules and horses from the Salinas Valley to San Jose on August 8, 1834. Provisioning there, he moved his *caballada* to San Francisco Bay and picked up more animals. He was not only going to pilot Kelley; he would drive a herd to Oregon to start his own stock ranch. As he started up the Siskiyou Trail, Young had seventy-seven head. His men, and Kelley, had twenty-one more animals.

Ewing Young welcomed nine strangers to his company in order to build up its strength for any test with the hostiles of the Siskiyou Mountains. Now he had sixteen men. But Kelley did not like the newcomers' looks. He found it strange that two of Joe Walker's "deserters" and a few on-the-beach sailors should possess fifty-six horses. And there were far too many brands in the *remuda*. Young did not ask any questions. Later, he would only say, "Whether they bought them or stole them, I do not know." Kelley was a greenhorn who deferred completely to the veteran Young. Though he guessed that the *caballos* were stolen, he was scared by the looks of the toughs. Later, he tried to exculpate himself by saying, of their joining the party, that "Captain Young did not object."

In private, Kelley called the nine marauders and expirates. Unable to hide his disgust for them, he soon made enemies of them. They talked darkly of days with Joe Walker, "the black flag, the rifle, and the arsenic"—pure bunk designed to throw a scare into Kelley. They fired a rifle at him—or, more likely, in his general direction— as part of their hazing of the tenderfoot. This act convinced Kelley that they meant to kill him and that only Young's intervention saved his life.

Ewing Young's drive of so many horses up the Siskiyou Trail

in 1834 was a turning point for the route. Its abandonment, now, was unthinkable. He pounded out a real road over the mountains to Oregon. He proved the feasibility of profitable stock drives on the track. But, alas for Young, the immediate effects were harmful to him. The horse drive brought him "grief" and notoriety. The drifters' horses had, indeed, been stolen from California *ranchos* or missions. Governor José Figueroa rushed a letter to McLoughlin by the ship *Lama,* dated September 9, which implicated Young in the rustling of the *rancheros'* horses. It was guilt by association, but it stuck. Figueroa asked the doctor's aid in recovering the two hundred (!) missing animals. He attached a sheet of drawings to his letter. They reproduced the brands on the stolen stock.

Unaware of the letter being hurried ahead of him, Young slowly turned inland from San Francisco Bay to ascend the east bank of the Sacramento. Three of the ruffians deliberately lagged behind, slipped into an Indian village from which the men were absent on a hunt, and raped several young women before stealing all the articles which took their fancy. Young did not punish them. Next day, one of the herders cried out a warning—"Indians advancing towards us!"

Kelley—of all people!—boldly rode toward them. He halted about two rods away from them. He was so sickened by the brutality of his "comrades" that he felt that he must do something, since Young was so insensitive to their brutishness. A tall, good-looking chief greeted the greenhorn. He wore a red card pendant from a plumed cap as a symbol of authority. He had nerve, too, and seemed undaunted, unperturbed, by the mountaineers' long rifles, whose barrels were impolitely slanted in his direction. In his right hand he carried a bow, in his left a quiver of arrows. He spoke to Kelley in an Indian tongue.

The Bostonian tried to reply in a combination of English and sign language. If the king's English made no sense to the chief, Kelley's dactylology did. He urged the Indians to retreat, right away. He compared their bows and arrows with the whites' deadlier rifles, then gestured at the ground—where many warriors would fall, dead, if they did not leave.

The "marauders" were itching for a fight and even some of Young's men were "fierce" for one, Kelley noticed. But he persuaded them not to attack (probably with the backing of Young), and the redmen slowly turned back. The chief stood his ground for a time, unwilling to condone with impunity the behavior of the whites. But, finally, he also left.

Kelley's relief turned to anxiety when he saw two of the ruffians slip away after him. When he begged them to stay, they scorned him. Jokingly, they swore to God on high that they meant the chief no harm. In fifteen to twenty minutes, Kelley heard the sickening report of their rifles. On the return of the cowardly bullies, he asked if they had shot the Indian. The sarcastic reply was, "No, we fired a salute." They flaunted the bow and quiver of the man, and the red card which had taken the Bostonian's eye. And Kelley wept.

A few days later, just south of the American River, the men in the van spied a dozen Indians across the Sacramento. Young said that they looked warlike and Kelley thought that they were the wronged natives he had warned away. Although he was riding in stifling heat, his blood chilled. The Indians stayed on the west bank but when Young ordered his men into camp he found that seven of his horses were dead from arrow wounds.

Young assumed that the killing was done by the Indians across river. When seven peaceful villagers brought gifts of fresh-caught and dressed salmon to camp, with a bag of "pinions" (piñon nuts), Young was ready for them. Ignoring their peaceable gestures, the angered Young said just one word—"Yes!"—when one of the blackguards muttered, "These are the damned villains, and they ought to be shot!" A blaze of fire issued from the long rifles. Five of the visitors fell dead, some still clutching their gifts. The other two were pursued to the river and killed there.

Ewing Young, perhaps feeling a twinge of guilt or remorse, turned to Kelley: "What do you think of this?" The shamed but fearful Easterner could only give an evasive answer—"We must protect ourselves while on the wilderness among hostile Indians." It satisfied Young but, inwardly, Kelley knew that he was uttering a cowardly lie.

From the uppermost Sacramento, Young's cowboys—or, rather, wranglers—herded the horses over the Siskiyous to the Rogue River. Since several of the men were down with malaria, and the Rogues already had a reputation for being rough customers, Young did not bother the "Rascals." But when he laid over to rest his shaking companions, he took the precaution of camping on an island in the Rogue River which afforded some security from surprise attacks on either horse herd or men.

Kelley's heart sank when he observed two braves making their way, openly, toward camp. Some of the trappers were wary, if not hostile. Young was uneasy, largely because of the weakened condition of his malarial party. Talking with a couple of the brutalized hangers-on, Young allowed himself to be convinced that the pair were spies who would return to their band in the hills to lead a war party against the camp. Always impetuous, and now as ruthless as his despicable followers, Young gave the order that the pair were not to be allowed to return to their people. Kelley was so horrified that he could not describe what followed. His journal is silent on the subject. But another eyewitness, Webley Hauxhurst, refused to remain mute. He later wrote: "The two young hunters were killed, their remains covered with rocks and brush and then, as soon as they (the Americans) could get away, they pursued their way northward to the Umpqua."

Of course, the Indians found the corpses of their missing hunters. And Hauxhurst correctly asserted that much of the blame for the Rogue River Wars must be laid at Ewing Young's feet. Henceforth, said Hauxhurst, the Rogues "considered it their special and legitimate vengeance to slay the travelling white men, who they supposed were affiliated to those ruffians who so ruthlessly slew their brothers."

Hall Kelley was ill and faint with malaria when Young had to backtrack near the site of Roseburg to find some strayed animals. When the Bostonian fell unconscious and dropped off his horse on a mountain slope, Young left him in the dubious care of the "marauders." When he came to, Kelley shook in his blanket like an aspen leaf, wondering if the villains might finish him off, then and there. Then, through the malarial booming in his ears, he heard the strange voice of a visitor. In French accents came the question, "Where is Captain Kelley?" It was Michel Laframboise.

McLoughlin had sent the Canadian with the 1834 Buenaventura Brigade to hunt all the way to San Francisco Bay. On his return march, he had picked up Young's track and followed it. He was curious about the New Englander, of whom he had heard much around San Francisco Bay. So he had decided to pay a call on him.

Michel moved the sick man to his own camp. He dosed him with quinine to bank the heat of his fever, then fed him venison broth in order to win back some strength. By the third day of the French-Canadian's patient nursing, Kelley was on the mend. Laframboise then put him into a hired canoe to make forty to forty-five miles of progress down the Umpqua, rather than making the fatiguing journey overland on horseback.

The river voyage of a day and a half worked like a tonic on Kelley. Released from the threatening company of the rapist-murderers, he found himself passing through a charming countryside in relative comfort. The trip both excited and cheered his spirits. His Indian paddler was both skilful and loyal. He delivered him to one of Michel's men, Charles Rondeau, at the agreed-upon landing. A grateful Kelley overpaid his boatman (scandalously), pressing not only a saddle and bridle on him, but a horse, a salmon knife, and a scarlet sash of velvet. Rondeau started off for Laframboise's camp, only a few miles away, with Kelley in tow. The latter recalled: "I mounted, with a little help, and rode off, feeling like a new man."

Kelley reached Fort Vancouver with Old Man Raspberry or Big Mike (not that he was that big in stature), as Michel was called. (Laframboise means raspberry in French.) It was October 27, 1834. To his shocked surprise, no one came down the riverbank to meet him. Michel helped him out of the boat and slowly and feebly Kelley made his way up the slope to the fort. He met an icy reception. Though Kelley was weak as a kitten, McLoughlin segregated him from the other gentlemen at the post. He put him up in a little cabin outside the walls. Only when his health necessitated it did the doctor allow him to use the hospital. He would not allow him to eat in the officers' and gentlemen's mess.

Figueroa's letter had done its damage. Kelley's promised land turned into an ashpit for him. He was treated with cold contempt by the gentlemen because he was presumed guilty of complicity in the California horse rustling. Genteel snobs like George B. Roberts were delighted to find a reason for their sneering at the penniless visionary, whom they found "too rough," in any case, for companionship. The caste-conscious Briton even feared that American egalitarianism would harm the fort's discipline: "A general conmingling would not do," he sniffed.

Perhaps the costume of the wild Bostonian hurt him, too. His five-foot-nine-inch frame was topped off with a white Mexican sombrero or slouch hat, and he wore a blanket capote or, rather, a California *serape* in place of the coat worn by gentlemen. In place of wool trousers, he wore the leather pantaloons of a *vaquero* or cowboy, decorated with a red stripe down the outside seam. Yes, the romantic from Boston was "rather *outré*," even for Vancouver!

Young's progress had been slowed by his need to graze his horse herd to recruit the animals' strength after the Siskiyou crossing. He worked his way down the west side of the Willamette to avoid wasting their strength again in swimming the many left-bank tributaries. He found the grasslands skirting the mountains to be a heaven for horses. Leaving the animals with some of his men in the Chehalem Valley, he struck out for Fort Vancouver.

Young was as completely unprepared for the doctor's ostracizing as had been Kelley. When he reached French Prairie, he was astounded, then angered, to'find notices tacked to the trees which forbade the settlers to have anything to do with him since he was a horse thief. A furious Young tore down the sheets, showering them— and McLoughlin—with curses. He sternly warned the wide-eyed *gens du pays* against believing such damned lies.

As the bow of his canoe rasped against the beach at Fort Vancouver, Young leaped ashore. He stormed up to the fort to have it out with the doctor. He was not about to accept his tarring with the meekness of Kelley. An angry meeting ensued, but no blows were struck. Young freely admitted that horse thieves had joined his company, but he vehemently denied having had anything to do with horse stealing. The doctor was adamant: He refused to have any dealings with him or his men until Figueroa's charges should be cleared up. McLoughlin explained to London that Kelley was the only exception to his rule. The New Englander was still sick with malaria: "Out of humanity, I placed him in a house, attended to him, and had his victuals sent him at every meal."

Young stomped off, muttering and swearing. He told his followers that the doctor was hostile toward them simply because he opposed American interest in Oregon. Before he took his angry leave of the fort, Young paid a call on Kelley. His ranting accusations against the doctor were, to Kelley, "a full demonstration of a deadly hate."

Before a crushed Kelley left for Hawaii in March 1835, his dreams of Oregon colonies gone a-glimmering, he had a number of visitors, including Jason Lee and his own disciple, Nat Wyeth. Even the latter's mind was poisoned against Kelley by McLoughlin's hostile attitude. Astounded, at first, that his mentor was not "received" at the fort, he shortly explained the case to his diary: "He came in company with Mr. Young from Monte El Rey and, it is said, stole between them a bunch of horses."

Later, Kelley said that the only people who treated him with decency and respect while he was "in conventry" were the Indians and the common people of Fort Vancouver.

Cowboys from California

EWING YOUNG wasted precious little time and energy raving against McLoughlin. He preempted fifty square miles of the Chehalem Valley and settled down there. Though an exile, a pariah, in his splendid isolation he proved (better than Methodist missionaries or discharged Company servants) that ranching and farming were practicable where the Siskiyou Trail followed the lower Willamette. In only a few years, Young's example would lead to increased American immigration and the humbling of the mighty Hudson's Bay Company in Oregon. And McLoughlin would be forced to concede (in 1836): "Everyone knows, who is acquainted with the fur trade, that as the country becomes settled, the fur trade must diminish."

Young began to "civilize" the northern tip of the Siskiyou Trail with a vengeance. He started a sawmill in 1836 and planned a distillery. When Jason Lee and settlers of a temperance society petitioned him to give up the latter project he, surprisingly, acceded. Meanwhile, his horses grew fat and sleek on the grasses of Chehalem.

Cattle had been brought to Oregon by Hudson's Bay Company ships as early as 1825. But, a dozen years later, the herd was still so small that McLoughlin steadfastly refused all entreaties to butcher so much as a single animal. Beef just did not figure in the diet of Fort Vancouver's complement. Nor would the doctor outfit with stock the retired French *engagés* who were beginning to settle on the Siskiyou Trail—or at least that safe portion of it at Champoeg and French Prairie in the Willamette Valley. And, of course, he was not about to provide American squatters with any cattle.

239

At the same time, cattlemen—*rancheros*—in California suffered from an embarrassment of riches. They had thousands of head but no market for them. There were hardly any takers, only a few hide droghers sailing along the coast to supply New England shoe factories with leather. By 1837, the province had half a million longhorns wandering its valleys. No one bothered to count them. A few sufficed for the small hide, tallow, and meat business.

Ewing Young wanted cows as well as horses on his Chehalem Creek spread in Oregon. But how to get the critters? He still bore a grudge against McLoughlin, and he reckoned that the feeling was reciprocated. There was no hope that the doctor would break his cattle monopoly—break his own rule—for the likes of Ewing Young.

Help turned up from a completely unexpected source. U.S. Naval Lieutenant William A. Slacum sailed into the Columbia with the chartered brig *Loriot* in December 1836. McLoughlin treated Slacum well enough, as he did all travelers, though he must have guessed that he was a Yankee spy—the Navy's answer to the Army's Captain Bonneville in the West. And he could not have appreciated Slacum's ready assurances to lower Willamette settlers that they were well within the territorial limits of the United States.

Slacum really got off on the wrong foot in Oregon when he was ill-mannered enough to criticize his kindly host for allowing the men of the Fort to keep slaves. McLoughlin hotly denied this but, of course, he did not pretend to interfere with the tribal customs of his men's Indian wives. Their mores allowed them to keep servants who were virtually slaves. Still, the doctor thundered publicly: "We disapprove of anyone having slaves and consider everyone about the Establishment as free."

If Slacum did not hit it off well with McLoughlin, he found a friend in the doctor's enemy, Ewing Young. The Lieutenant visited French Prairie's farms and Lee's Methodist Mission in a canoe provided by McLoughlin. But he was most interested in Young, and the two men became fast friends. When the newcomer asked Young what his greatest need was, in order to make the Willamette solidly American, the ex-mountain man answered, without hesitation, "Cattle!" Slacum then suggested that Young take some men down to California on the *Loriot* to buy cattle to drive to Oregon.

Ewing Young thought that Slacum's plan was a fine idea. He had already driven more than 150 mules and horses over the trail, so he knew that it was feasible. The two men put their heads together and, by January 14, 1837, when Slacum addresesd a meeting at

Champoeg's Campement du Sable (Sand Encampment), the Willamette Cattle Company was formed. He not only offered his associates free passage to California but invested $500 of his own money in the project. The Lieutenant and Young estimated that $1600 would be needed to buy five hundred cattle.

The Methodist Mission chipped in $620. Two French-Canadians put up a modest sum and offered their services as drovers or cowboys for the balance of the investment. Herders were to be paid $1 a day for every day's work on the trail, but in cattle rather than in scarce cash. To the surprise of the Americans, the "monopolist" himself joined the enterprise. McLoughlin, with two Company associates, contributed $858 more. Young swallowed his ire; kept his head; held his tongue—and pocketed the money.

Not everyone, by a long shot, thought that the wild Siskiyou Trail would permit trail driving of a herd of cattle. Frank Ermatinger wrote his brother, Ned, at Flathead Post on June 1, 1837, to observe: "Several of the great folks have already sent to the Spanish settlements for cattle in order, I believe, to commence a hide and tallow speculation. I, my dear Edward, must change in opinion greatly if ever I can be brought to join them." Perhaps Ermatinger's coolness toward the plan was not due entirely to the dangers of the Siskiyou Trail and his own fatigue from working with Indians and risking his scalp. He was now critical of McLoughlin, because the latter was passing him over for James Douglas as second-in-command at Fort Vancouver. There, in 1834, he had written Edward to say of the doctor, "I never had more respect for anyone in my life." Now, less than a half-dozen years later, the disgruntled Ermatinger was denigrating the doctor as "a bickerer."

Perhaps because McLoughlin was leery of Young's trustworthiness after the Figueroa accusation, Philip Leget Edwards was sent along as a kind of supercargo, or purser. He was to keep his eye on the cattle company's funds and property. The ex-Kentuckian proved to be a poor sailor, seasick during much of the voyage, and not much of a cowboy. On the other hand, he turned out to be an excellent chronicler of the cattle recruitment venture.

The would-be cattlemen left Lee's mission on January 17 by canoe. They stopped at Pudding River and Etienne Lucier's cabin before camping at sunset of the nineteenth on the shore opposite the *Loriot*. The brig lay at anchor below Wappato Island. All of the tentless men—Young, Edwards, Dr. William J. Bailey, Webley J. Hauxhurst, the *canadiens* "Esquette" and "Despau" (Despain?

Depo?)—were soaked to the skin by the drenching rain. Edwards complained to his diary that he was so benumbed that he could hardly exert himself to get his baggage safely ashore from the canoe. The little party was joined on the beach by Slacum, Jason Lee, and Captain Bancroft of the *Loriot*.

On the twenty-second, after Reverend Lee prayed for Divine blessing on the enterprise, Bancroft weighed anchor. But the voyage did not go well. Perhaps God had not been attentive to Lee. In any case, the brig ran aground above Sand Island. Bancroft got her off, but gales then kept her penned inside the Columbia bar. Edwards, who had vomited away almost all desire for life itself, much less his earlier yearning to see the Pacific, sourly wrote: "Seasickness is an infallible remedy to poetic fancies." A storm parted both anchor cables and again drove the *Loriot* aground in the river. A small boat, trying to help, capsized. The detention at the river's mouth caused provisions to fail. Luckily, liquor was in greater supply than food, and the boat crews were happily drunk most of the time. When the sailors finally ran out of rum, they traded away their blankets to the Indians for liquor in a curious reversal of the customary practice.

Not until February 10 was the Columbia bar deemed by Captain Bancroft pacific enough for a crossing. After an uneventful run south, the *Loriot* fired a gun on the nineteenth. Its fire was returned by a salute from Fort Ross. A pilot came out in a skin boat, though a northwest wind prevented the brig's anchoring in the exposed doghole port of Fort Ross. Next day, however, Bancroft was able to put into the cove and drop the hooks. He was welcomed by Peter Kostromitinoff, who let most of the men debark to camp at Captain Juan B. Cooper's mill, where they would work until a herd coud be put together by the leaders.

Young and Edwards continued on to San Francisco Bay to transact their business, armed with almost $3000 in funds. After nearly being wrecked in Drake's Bay by a blow, the *Loriot* entered the Golden Gate and anchored in Whaler's Harbor or Richardson's Bay, off Sausalito, on March 1. Next day, Slacum and Young hurried to Monterey to dicker with the Governor for the purchase of cattle from General Vallejo at Sonoma. Although Young had saluted Vallejo with five guns, coming and going, when the California grandee visited the *Loriot*'s consort, the *Laura,* he had gotten nowhere. Edwards explained: "Gen. Vallejo declines having anything to do in giving us permission to drive out cattle. Says that is the prerogative of the Civil

Governor." The latter had removed from Monterey to Santa Barbara, so Young had to pursue him overland to that southern port.

Meanwhile, Edwards was treated with the utmost cordiality and hospitality by Padre José Lorenzo Quijas and others at Mission San Rafael and John Reed's *rancho* near modern Mill Valley. Two of the drovers joined Edwards in Marin County, Dr. William Bailey and George Gay. When Edwards returned to Monterery, he found Young, who told him that the Governor had given permission for them to purchase seven hundred head of mission cattle. (These, noted Edwards, "the authorities have unjustly seized from the friars.") There had been opposition to the project. In fact, two votes of the Governor's "deputation" had to be taken before his motion in favor of the sale was pasesd. Growled Edwards: "All this rumpus on account of an old colonial law yet unrepealed which forbids the exportation of male and female animals from the colonies." Luckily for the Oregonians, Vallejo and the *pardre presidente* of the missions joined Governor Juan B. Alvarado in his opposition to the narrow old policy. Alvarado appointed Vallejo agent for the government in the cattle sale.

More of the cowhands began to drift in, inclding John Turner and James O'Neil, while Young bought the seven hundred head at $3 cach. Of these, two hundred were to come from "Mission San Francisco," presumably Sonoma's Mission San Francisco de Solano rather than Mission Dolores (San Francisco de Asís, actually *in* today's city of San Francisco), though Edwards usually called the northern mission "San Solano." The other five hundred head would come from Mission San José. The *administrador* of Sonoma Mission tried to pull a fast one on Young. Instead of the agreed upon 170 cows and thirty bulls, he wished to reverse the ratio. Young, of course, protested and finally won the day. He collected the animals and moved them from corral to corral, after grudgingly paying the accustomed *mordida* ("bite") or bribe, in the shape of a thirty-dollar rifle, six $2.50 shirts, and $20 cash, to the Mission's civil administrator. The latter said that he planned to divide up this bonus with his Indian cowboys.

Ewing Young wanted to collect the full thousand head of cattle which Vallejo would allow him to have. But he could buy no more than eight hundred with the money he and his associates had scraped up with such difficulty. His efforts to secure more stock were counterproductive. On June 8 he became embroiled in what Edwards called a sharp altercation with the authorities. He had returned to the pueblo

243

of San José to haggle for more cattle. The exact details of the contre-temps are not known.

Meantime, Young's cowboys penned the first herd in an old thrown-down corral near Robert Livermore's ranch, tying up a yawning gap in the wall with elk and bullock hides. When the five hundred head arrived, they were a shocking sight. They were even worse than the original 200—wild, hungry, thirsty. Some were downright starved. The *californios* might not have selected all of the culls in the province, but they had certainly found a fair number of them. Edwards, almost as hungry as the "cows," was in the saddle all day and half the night, rounding up spooky stock which bolted at every opportunity from herd and corral. He reported that some of the San José herd had gone without water or grass for seven days, except when they had been escorted to pasture and pond, a few minutes at a time, during the short drive. Seven beeves were so enfeebled by starvation, and so crippled by the rough usage of the Indian *vaqueros,* that Young cut them out of the herd and abandoned them on the spot. He was sure that they would die on him before they were well up the Siskiyou Trail, costing him $21 at the outset. He gave his men orders to rope an equivalent number from any ranch herd on their way.

Young decided to go up the west bank of the Sacramento River rather than the better-watered and -grassed left bank, with which he was more familiar. He feared that he would lose too many head in swimming the numerous tributaries on that side. The herd made good time as far as the first major obstacle, Carquinez Straits, which he called the San Joaquin River though both that stream and the Sacramento pour their waters through the narrow passage to reach San Francisco Bay via San Pablo Bay. But, a week later, he was still trying to cross the herd to the north side.

On the twelfth, Young first drove the cattle into the water and tried to swim them across the strait. The deep water terrified the beasts. Instead of swimming ahead, the frightened animals began to mill. Since they would soon tire and drown in this stupid maneuver, Young had to let them return to the south bank. He next caught up a number of calves and, with a few horsemen, towed them across. Their mothers followed, and also a few heifers. But the bulk of the herd would not budge.

Despite his losses from drowning and straying, Young still had seven hundred cattle in his corral on the shore. This suggests that his *vaqueros* were doing a bit of mavericking, taking more than the seven additional animals which he felt California owed him. On the thirteenth, Young decided on a desperate effort. He mustered his whole force of drovers and tried to force the herd bodily into the narrows. He was unsuccessful. He then dismounted his men and had them try to move the herd while afoot. This also failed. Next, Young divided the corral by building a partition of logs and brush and tried to drive half the herd into the water. The recalcitrant beasts bore down on the partition. Some of them burst through. When the brush fence of the compound as a whole was threatened, he gave up.

Young removed the interior fence, strengthened the corral, and once more called all hands to action. By dint of great effort, they managed to crowd the animals into the water. A few got halfway across but soon began to mill. All returned but five which made it to the far shore by swimming, two which were towed there behind canoes, and sixteen which made it safely to neither side, drowning in midstream.

Edwards pictured his boss's plight: "In these sallies, when we huddled up the cattle on the bank and had formed a circle around them, then came the tug of war. Jump as we would, strike as we would, threaten as we would, our line was broken. A furious bull would anon rush by, horning and kicking. We were exposed to broiling sun and enveloped in clouds of dust. The latter article was seized upon by sweat, and soon we presented faces hideous enough to appal either man or beast."

The stubborn Young tried yet another technique. He had a rope stretched across the entire width of Carquinez Straits. His cowboys caught individual cattle with their lassos and towed them across by means of *tule balsas* (rush rafts), each pulled along the guiderope by hand. Two or three men crewed each crude boat, pulling and holding onto the two, three, or four cattle attached to it. Young also tried ferrying his animals with skin canoes, but they did not answer as well as the reed craft. Finally, he got all of the beasts across and safely corraled on the other side. Just when he was ready to celebrate his victory, Benjamin Wood chased the packhorse carrying his powder supply into a bulrushy pond where the creature bucked its entire cargo into the water, wetting everything and ruining the precious gunpowder. How Ewing Young cussed that Estrecho de Carquines!

Before Young returned to Yerba Buena (San Francisco) for more powder, Edwards made it clear that his chief did not wish to cross any more water for a spell: "Horrors! We chased cattle until after the moon rose, to get them across water no more than knee deep." All of the cowmen were worn down with too much exertion on too little food and rest, too little sleep—and far too many mosquitoes. The skeeters were so thick, except during the blaze of midday and in the coldest part of the night, that the men found it difficult to breathe because of the dense clouds of the insects.

Cattle were forever bolting, even when held in a herd just beyond the strait. In Edwards's words, they were "breaking like so many evil spirits and scattering to the four winds. Men, ill-natured and quarreling, growling and cursing." However, Young recovered most of the lost cattle and purchased (or simply rounded up) others to fill out his herd. On the twenty-seventh, he crossed the last stragglers to the north bank as Edwards joyfully wrote: "Adiós, San Joachin!" Then he added a note: "Another month like the last, God avert! Who can describe it!"

The trail herd reached the Sacramento proper on August 14. For some reason, Edwards termed it the Jesús María and the Bonaventura. Since leaving the strait, Young had lost a total of seventeen head. Ten had given out on the trail, five had drowned, and two had been sacrificed for food. But when he made a count he was pleased to find that he still had 792 head, some of which were finally becoming "trail broke."

Ten or a dozen Indians approached the drovers timidly on the eighteenth. They stopped three hundred yards away and only four could be enticed into camp. They had only (unstrung) bows and arrows as arms. Young ordered the one warrior who was actually ready for action to unstring his weapon before coming to the campfire. He complied. Wrote Edwards: "We understood them to say that they once had some difficulty with Mr. La Frombois and that he had killed some of their people."

At this halt, Young tried to prepare his stock for the mountainous portion of the Siskiyou Trail ahead. He decided to round up and dress the feet of his lame cattle. Edwards thought that this action was worse than a waste of time. The critters bolted, of course, as Young's cowboys tried to lasso them with rawhide *reatas*. As a result, the cattle reinjured their hooves at the same time that the cow ponies became tired and winded. But Young nursed his beasts and they responded. Rest and good pasturage on the Sacramento recruited not only cattle and horses but men, too, from August 18–20.

Young then started the animals out, to cross what Edwards confusingly referred to as "the long dreaded passage across the largest river on our route." Since the west side had *no* rivers of any consequence, only creeks which often failed to even reach the Sacramento, it is difficult to know his meaning. But probably Edwards was looking ahead to the Sacramento itself. When finally, way up-valley, Young forded his animals (somewhere north of present-day Redding), he did not lose a single beast. Edwards exclaimed: " 'Admirable!', every lip said and every heart responded."

Barely two hours after wading the Sacramento, Young picked up the Siskiyou Trail proper, in the form of Laframboise's well-marked track. McLoughlin, curiously, had ordered Michel to imitate Young and to buy some beeves to drive up the Siskiyou Trail, should the fur catch prove to be poor. But Michel had no yen to nursemaid cows across the Siskiyous, and, since the beaver were plentiful enough, he did not play *vaquero* for his employer.

On the twenty-sixth, the cattle column began to leave the Sacramento Valley behind. The men had increasing difficulty in following Laframboise's trail as the terrain roughened in the foothills of the Klamath, Shasta, and Siskiyou mountains. Edwards remarked that the Sacramento Valley had not only soil of excellent quality but a fine climate, if a bit hot at times. But Young was less enthusiastic, even though sea breezes fanned the evening air well up the Sacramento Valley. He reminded his associate that he had passed through it with a trapping party in 1831 without having a single man sick, only to repeat the march with Hall Kelley in 1834 with every man-jack of his company down with malarial fever, himself included. He described for Edwards the horrible sight of Indian villages strewn with the dead and dying, with birds feasting on the carcasses.

Although Edwards wrote that "on every hand we see revolting signs of its [malaria's] ravages"—probably bones and skulls—he found that the Indians had made a come-back. They were once again numerous. The scribe did not think highly of their funeral customs. They did not bury their dead, nor burn them, but simply lugged the corpses a few hundred yards from their huts and left them exposed as carrion to the vultures and crows. Even in a disease-free period, he found skulls and bones scattered all around the villages. Nor did the live Indians impress Edwards. They were naked, wore their hair all but cut off, and were of a mild deportment. He blamed the latter more on a want of energy than anything else. When two of the men complained of an attempted theft of a horse and a gun, both foiled, Edwards was reluctant to believe the natives capable of the attempt, and noted "Of neither instance have we proof."

Perhaps because the ford had been so easy, or the western trail was becoming so prominently marked, Young decided to chance it—

the direct north-south Sacramento River leg of the Siskiyou Trail—rather than the easier but roundabout route via the Pit River. Young was unaware of the westernmost of the three choices of Siskiyou Trail routes through the Sacramento headwaters country. This route, which became busy during stagecoach days, ran from the site of Shasta to the area of Fort Jones and Callahan before rejoining the main strand of the Siskiyou Trail in the Shasta Valley near modern Yreka. In tackling such deeps as Iron Canyon, Young was attempting the impossible with horses and men—much more so with cattle.

With each day of northing, the mountains grew more difficult. This led Edwards to write: "Hills peep over hills and Alps upon Alps." Four years later, members of the U.S. Exploring Expedition mapping the Siskiyou Trail traversed this upper Sacramento River portion of it, but moving in the opposite direction. They reported that men of the party familiar with the Rockies, and even the Andes, found the California terrain twice as hard to cross. (And they drove no herd of cattle.) As for the idea of a railroad along the line of the river, already a-glitter in some expansionists' eyes, the Wilkes expeditionaries stated flatly that "no sane or civilized being would ever recommend such a thing."

By now, the grass was burned off by the Indians. Consequently, the stock grew feeble at the very point where they needed their strength the most. Already, the horses were so exhausted from lack of grazing that they were almost more trouble than service. Thirst also slowed progress. Once, when the cattle were driven to the water to drink, they were so overheated and thirsty that they plunged into the rapidly rushing stream. Strangely, despite their fatigue and normal fear of the water, they foolishly continued right on across the river and, incredibly—and foolishly in their fatigued state—climbed to the summit of a mountain several thousand feet high! It was with great difficulty and exertion that the tired horsemen managed to recover the delirious cattle by a road, of sorts, found by Turner and Calvin Tibbetts.

Grazing grew even more scarce in the steep and rocky chaparral country, leading Edwards to predict (on August 26) "Unless grass is found tomorrow, we have every prospect of starvation to our animals." Young went ahead to climb a tremendous mountain which blocked the way. When he returned, he swore that there was still a higher mountain atop the one in view. "Now," he said to Edwards, "if you are a philosopher, show yourself."

All of the drovers were exhausted from trying to guard the cattle with too little to eat. Some of them, tired of eating dried meat, insisted that Young kill a beef. He would not consent to it. He did not wish to have to carry the meat over the mountains ahead. It was a nervous moment for Edwards and Young. The men nearly mutinied. Recalled Edwards: "A very rough and disagreeable quarrel ensued. Some had sworn they would kill one at all events. Mr. Y. defied them, and told them to 'Kill one at your peril!' " (Years later, a member of the cattle caravan confessed that a plot was hatched to kill both Young and Edwards at this critical point of the drive, but that the machinations fell through.)

On August 27, the herders assaulted the dreaded mountain which had long held their gaze, almost hypnotically. They hoped that beyond its fearsome height they would find a friendly valley. Instead, their worst fears were confirmed. Beyond lay still a higher peak.

With both horses and cattle "lazy" (exhausted), and the men heartsick with disappointment, Edwards reported that "every inch of ground we gained was contested." The cowboys shouted at their charges, barraged them with stones, pummeled them with clubs, all to achieve a few yards of progress. Of the dumb beasts, Edwards now wrote: "They would turn off from the road, wander down the sides of the mountain, take refuge in the dense brush, stop to fight each other and, in short, appeared willing to do anything but go quietly along the trail."

Three of the best horses and some of the once-strongest cattle were now completely tired out. They sank to the ground alongside the faint trail. The men were unable to force them to their feet. Edwards was so hot and tired from such activity that he drank three quarts of water in fifteen minutes when he reached a small rivulet. He recalled: "At the first hearty draught, it did not have the usual taste in my slimy mouth."

Even with the life-giving water, the low point of the drive was reached at this place on August 27–29, 1837. Morale was nearing zero. The clerk reported: "Few of our party, perhaps none, would have ventured upon this enterprise had they forseen all its difficulties. . . . Most of the party cursed the day on which they were engaged, and would hardly have exchanged a draught of cool water for their expected share of the profits."

All bad days come to an end, but those at the tag end of August 1837 seemed interminable. Even when the herders dropped down at last from the heights to the river valley again, and found wood and grass, morale was not restored. In fact, one of the men, Henry Wood,

249

engaged in a fearful quarrel with Captain Young. This was so even though the latter gave in and finally slaughtered one of the cattle for his hungry and rebellious cowboys. By now, the horses were too worn out to be of any use. For the first time, both the *remuda* and the cattle herd had to be guarded by men on foot.

August 29 saw the men floundering up another mountain in the Dunsmuir or Mount Shasta area. It was as high as any they had assaulted before. And the cattle were as stubborn as they were weak. But, just beyond the summit, the men in the van met three Indians. The natives encouraged them to push on, indicating "Go on, there are no more mountains ahead." Not one of the whites would normally have bet a copper on an Indian's veracity. But they were now clutching at the flimsiest of straws, so the good news produced hoarse shouts of joy from parched and dust-clogged throats. Men not before noted for their Christian devotion cried "Thank the Lord!"

The chance meeting with the Indians infused a little new life into the drovers. At length, they arrived at the most pleasant encampment they had seen anywhere in the mountains. Young immediately issued orders for a day's layover to rest animals and men. There, he recounted the herd and found that he had, amazingly, lost only forty-nine head since leaving the Sacramento crossing.

Nothing much of consequence occurred on the drive until September 6, except for the loss of seven more cattle and two horses. On that day, Edwards and Woods followed Despau in a climb up a towering stony peak, to see what lay ahead. The sound of the French-Canadian's gun encouraged them to hope that they were finally reaching an area of game animals. But they were so exhausted when they stopped for a rest that they fell asleep almost as soon as they got out of the wind. When they came to, they resumed their climb to the ridge. From it they found that the great granite peak seen from the valley was really four or five peaks. They could find no practicable way up the highest, so they settled for the second most lofty pinnacle. (Could they have been clambering over Castle Crags?) To their intense frustration, the view from the peak revealed only more mountain barriers on every side, except for one small break in the granitic horizon. Sadly, if poetically, Edwards wrote in his log: "On every hand 'Alps on Alps arise,' and mingle with the clouds." After rolling some stones into fearful depths, to see them tumble and smash their way down, the two men began their own slow descent.

Back in camp, Edwards wrote: *"Chagrin pour la terre!"* But he reported to Young the one possible exit from the mountainous maze.

Moving on, and losing only a mare which slipped off a brush-clogged trail and fell down a precipice into the river, the men made another arduous march before camping at a spring. Although grass was scant and the water so impregnated with iron that it acted as a purgative, the camp was a happy one. At least, the encampment was adjacent to a dozen vacant Indian huts and some of the men thought the country looked familiar. Someone told Edwards that the Chasty (Shasta) Valley now lay only three or four days ahead.

The camp of the seventh was even better, the best since Carquinez Straits. Young let men and animals rest up there over the eighth and ninth. Indians began to appear now, but never in large numbers. Edwards never saw a group larger than fifteen souls. They were friendly. Surprisingly, he was pleased by their language. It was a clear and distinct tongue, with none of the harsh gutturals of Indian speech to which he was accustomed. However, the natives were exceedingly long-winded. They delivered tedious harangues of which the whites understood hardly a word.

Edwards observed: "One old man, after seating himself in silence and smoking his pipe with much formality, raised his voice to its highest key, and began as follows: 'In yonder mountains I was born. There I sucked my mother's breast. There I have grown up . . .' and doubtless many other items of equal importance, could we have understood them. I never failed in getting a grave harangue when I addressed one of these mountain orators."

If Edwards was of mixed emotions over the Indians' loquacity, he was delighted by their friendliness. The company was tired and spread thinly along the road as it advanced, now, much exposed to any attack. Nor did the Indians seem to wish to raid the herd. Edwards, who had estimated a loss of forty-nine of the brutes, made a count and came up with 680 surviving beasts, most of which were recruiting well from their brief rest. Some, he thought, were even putting on fat as they cropped the welcome grass.

On September 12, after another long and difficult march, the men reached the Shasta Valley. They had been aching to reach it, for days. Without regret, they began to leave an old acquaintance— Snowy Peak (Mount Shasta)—behind them. But some of the men grew uneasy since they were nearing the Siskiyous proper and the border area of warlike Shastas, Pits, and Modocs. Thus, when Wood and a pal named Jim pursued two lost packhorses, their comrades began to worry after a couple of hours. But they finally turned up, having found the pack animal but not the escaped riding horse.

Alas, the day on which the cattle company crossed the Shasta River, September 14, 1837, was the day which saw the first real violence of the march. Five or six Takelma Indians followed the drovers into camp. One of them was a boy of only ten years. Edwards was already mildly worried because some of the herders were repeating threats to kill some Indians, once the Shasta River was in the party's rear. Some brute suggested that the child be killed. The diarist recalled: "It had generally passed as idle braggadocio, and I was hoping that present threats were of the same sort. I, nevertheless, intended telling Mr. Young. In the hurry, however, of unpacking, I could not do it unobserved."

Perhaps Dr. William Bailey was one of the men who muttered to Edwards that he intended to bag a few Indians before the march was over. The rough-hewn medic was one of the most colorful men to ever traverse the Siskiyou Trail. To escape the nagging of his mother and three sisters (over his drinking problem), he had sailed before the mast in a British ship. He quickly tired of the life of a foremast hand and took French leave in California. After jumping ship, he wandered about the province. In 1835 he had decided to go up the Siskiyou Trail on a "trapping excursion" with several other drifters who were momentarily at loose ends. But, as the author Miss A. J. Allen recalled: "Having selected no leader, and all aspiring to that honorable office, their journey was a continual scene of bickering and contention. At the first point of danger, when attacked by the Chaste Indians, they experienced all the evil effects arising from such an iniquitous course, proving the truth of the saying, 'a house divided against itself cannot stand,' for in the contest most of the number were killed four hundred miles from their destination. Bailey himself was badly wounded. The survivors, having been robbed of everything, wandered in the wilderness, suffering much from want of food till, at last, they were obliged to slay their only remaining horse. After devouring the emaciated carcass they subsisted on snails and insects for many days, just enough of them to sustain life."

Eventually, Bailey and his comrades made it to the bank of the Willamette opposite Lee's mission. They were too weak to cross or even to call loudly enough to attract attention. But luck was with them; they were found. Margaret Jewett Smith of the Methodists nursed Bailey back to health. (He later married her.) The bitingly sarcastic doctor, soured by alcohol, never forgot or forgave the Indians who had, almost literally, chopped his face in half. So he had signed up with Ewing Young as much for revenge as for profits.

Edwards had just loosed his horses and sat down to rest when he heard the explosion of a gun behind him. He turned to find that George Gay, without warning, had drawn a bead on an Indian sitting only ten feet from him and had fired. Incredibly, the mountain man missed at the murderous point-blank range! The Indian sprang to his feet and ran. After twenty paces he fell sprawling down the hillside as Doctor Bailey calmly put a rifle ball into him. A scoundrel took up a chant, "Shoot the boy! Shoot the boy!" But Edwards was pleased to see the young fellow dart into a point of rocks, then plunge into the thick chaparral and escape.

Ewing Young came up, demanding "What's that?" Though the knavish Bailey and Gay tried to excuse the murder as being necessary —to prevent word of their coming being transmitted to the tribe— Young joined Edwards in censuring the two men. The clerk had sprung to his feet, calling the shooting a base and dastardly act. He angrily pointed out to Young that such murderers were not to be trusted in times of real danger. He was confronted by Bailey. The dissolute doctor retorted: "Are *you* to be depended upon in danger?"

"Yes," replied Edwards.

"We'll see," said Bailey.

Meanwhile, Carmichael, who had joined Edwards in denouncing the senseless attack, had second thoughts. He suddenly reversed himself. Joining the others, he exclaimed: "We are not missionaries. We will avenge the death of Americans." Though a couple of the men were silent, only one of them really opposed the shooting. Young and Edwards quickly saw that there was no use in wrangling with the cowhands. Turner loudly joined Gay and Bailey in justifying the murder as an eye for an eye, revenge for the unwarranted attack on their party two years earlier.

The angry, vengeful men would not listen when Edwards tried to point out to them that the company was at least four days short of the 1835 ambush site and probably in a different tribal area. Edwards simply could not understand how the trio's thirst for revenge could possibly justify endangering their lives all over again, plus those of the rest of the company. Bitterly, he wrote: "We must now prepare ourselves for fighting our way through the hostile Indians." The diary keeper, cast in the role which Hall J. Kelley had had to play a few years earlier, quoted Ewing Young: "This fool act [may] cost us half our animals!"

Before the party moved on, two of the men ("Camp" and Pat) committed another barbarous act. They stripped the dead Indian of his skin clothing and left him naked and unburied. Edwards noticed sadly that, of the ten or fifteen arrows in his quiver, only two had stone points. The warrior had come in peace.

The sullen men continued the march before sunrise on the fifteenth. The cattle were now in three distinct bands. Some of the laggards could not get up a slope. They were shot by their herders. Perhaps because Young gave them only a half-hour's rest, or because he had halted on a brushy hill rather than in a grassy valley, some of the men grew mutinous again and refused to obey his orders. Again Edwards saw the success of the drive threatened by rebellious hotheads. Turner, Gay, Bailey, and Carmichael ganged up on Young, but only vocally. They were still in awe of the tough trapper. Recalled Edwards: "A most horrid quarrel ensued. Curses, guns and knives were bandied for 15 minutes." For all the waving of weapons, not one of the rebels dared to attack Young. But, on the other hand, only Edwards and Depo stood by their leader and tried to quash the ugly business. The rest of the men, as in so many fights, stood silent, almost indifferent; ready to jump one way or the other.

Edwards tried to explain to the men how foolish, how mad and dangerous, was the quarrel. "Here we were, in a most difficult pass, where a dozen Indians might have killed the half of us and numbers of our animals before we could gain a good road. And, no doubt, we would here have been attacked, if the Indians had had time to collect [together]. . . . And we were in equal danger from each other!" Perhaps Edwards's words had some effect. In any case, Young got the men quieted down and the drive continued. The faint trail led through a dense wood and down a brushy ridge to a prairie.

That night, Young put out five guards around camp instead of four. Edwards was on post just beyond a brook, protecting the camp and horse herd from potential Indian fire from the nearby brush. About an hour after he took up his position, the moon rose. By its wan light he saw five Indians stealing along through the trees on a hill to the east. He brought the butt of his double-barreled fowling piece to his shoulder and discharged one barrel. The blast of the shotgun brought the skulkers to a momentary halt, then a precipitate retreat. When Edwards tried to reload, he could get no powder out of his horn. Thinking it was empty, he retreated into camp, where he found that the rag wrapped around the stopple had come loose and plugged up the mouth of the powderhorn. By the time he had reloaded, all was still outside camp in contrast to the bustle within it. Young ordered every armed man to go on guard, leaving out only two men who carried no weapons. But there was no trouble that night.

All was quiet the following day, too, until about two in the afternoon. At that time, the cattlemen were passing between a patch of woods on the right and the dense shrub brush of a mountain slope on the left. Edwards was carrying a young calf before him as he rode so that its mother would not hang back with the slow-moving young animals and slow the pace of the entire herd. A shot, to the rear of the cattle, caused the clerk to spur his horse forward so that he could drop the calf beside its mother. He then hurried forward to tell Young of the shot.

When Edwards rode to the aid of the dust-eating drovers in the rearguard, he saw arrows fly from both sides of the road. Luckily, the horses were herded ahead of the cattle and unmolested. Although only one of the cattle was seriously injured, five or six were wounded. Since the men were in need of meat, the worst-off animal was killed and butchered. Not one of the concealed enemy could be seen until the cowboys reached an open plain. When they looked back, they saw their ambushers plainly enough: They showed themselves on a hill just beyond gunshot range.

Again Young posted a heavy guard around the camp that night. There was no attack. But at breakfast a few arrows were launched into camp from the thick woods. No man was hurt, but Williams's horse was wounded in the left hip.

Another day and night passed without an attack, but on the morning of the eighteenth the drovers saw Indians running along the mountainside to their right. Mused Edwards: "There could be no doubt that they were intending to attack us at some difficult pass. Our 'braves' occasionally fired on them where there was a mere possibility of doing any execution." At high noon, the Indians struck. The whites were again trapped in a brushy pass, this time with the river on the right and a wooded mountain to the left. Firing and yelling announced the raid, and this time from up front. Young, apprehensive of an attack, had just scouted ahead but had seen no hostiles. When he gave the brush and rocks a second look he found Indians posted on both sides of the narrow road, awaiting the herd and its drovers. He halted the cattle and some of his men fired four rounds at the Indians. Edwards started to join him but Young waved him back. No more men should leave the herd, which might stampede in a fight.

The gutsy Young headed straight for the ambushers with only two or three men to help him. He snapped off a quick shot at a warrior, who popped up only ten yards away. Another Indian shot an arrow into Gay's back. Young, having dismounted to save his wounded horse, slapped him on the head to drive him away. But the loyal animal stubbornly stayed by his master and was struck by two shafts meant for Young. Edwards now disobeyed orders and, joining four or five men scouting ahead, cleaned out a brushy area. They were not molested.

That night, Young set up camp on a gruesome spot—the very site of Turner's earlier defeat. Some of the men on day guard spotted three Indians in a small grove three hundred yards from camp. They surrounded the copse, fired into it, then made a sweep through it like a squad of infantry. But they found no Indians; the birds had flown.

That night the camp was jumpy, more nervous than ever because of the connotation of the once-bloody site. The horses, tied that night, were nearly famished. Nightfall brought neither moon nor starlight, only threatening clouds chased by rain squalls: "The guards could hardly have seen an Indian ten paces off, until the moon [finally] rose about ten o'clock." In this tight spot, Edwards—understandably—abandoned his diary entries. His last note was "I was on watch the first half of the night. . . ."

Diligent attention to security thereafter paid off for Young. The march continued to be tiring, nerve-wracking, but the skulking Indians did not dare to attack the trail herd and its men.

Early in October, Young reached the Willamette with his cattle column. Of the eight-hundred-odd animals with which he had started, he still had 630 head. His share was 135 cattle. The arrival of so much stock broke the Honourable Company's beef monopoly and brought milk to Oregon for the first time.

Young's success made him relatively well-to-do. He returned to his old calling, trapping, but also farmed 150 acres of bottomland in wheat. He also tended his cattle, expanded his lumbering of oak and Douglas fir on Chehalem Creek, built a grist mill and erected a larger cabin for his home. By the time California-bound Captain John Sutter visited him in 1838, Young was far and away the leading settler on the civilized north end of the Siskiyou Trail. (Sutter, briefly, thought of imitating him exactly, driving a herd north and settling near the ex-mountain man. But, when he saw the Sacramento Valley, he decided to squat there on the opposite end of the Siskiyou Trail.) Young imported *kanakas* from Hawaii to be his ranch hands. He entertained travelers like writer Thomas J. Farnham and Abbé François N. Blanchet, who brought Catholicism to the Trail by setting up a church at St. Paul on the Willamette. Young even sent huge bones of prehistoric animals to Boston for study. He took them from a local "dig."

But the sturdy six-footer never took to the Siskiyou Trail again. Suffering from "dyspepsia"—probably a stomach ulcer—Ewing Young died in February 1841. He was probably all of fifty years old, despite his long career on the Siskiyou and other trails of the West.

Young's Siskiyou Trail cattle drive, for all of its troubles, was masterful, as later imitators would learn. But his success was unknown in England, where J. H. Pelly could not have been more wrong, when he crowed to the Lords of the Committee of Privy Council for Trade (February 7, 1838) of Simpson's and McLoughlin's supremacy in the Columbia River and Willamette areas—"They directed their efforts so vigorously to that branch of the business that they compelled the American adventurers, one by one, to withdraw from the contest." Poor Pelly; unknowingly, he was talking through his hat.

Perhaps London did not realize the gravity of the situation in Oregon because Britain was active in exploring both ends of the Siskiyou Trail. Laframboise led the annual California brigade south, as usual, in 1837. Fort Vancouver was saddened, shortly after he left, by the death of his six-year-old daughter Josette on March 12, 1837. Curiously, no one was more touched than the chaplain of Fort Vancouver, Reverend Herbert Beaver. He had arrived at the post on the very day that Michel departed it. They did not meet. Beaver, an impossible bigot and prude (whose wife was even worse—"Haughty Jane," they called her), alienated McLoughlin and James Douglas by insulting the doctor's Indian wife and accusing his officers of keeping Indian slaves. Eventually, McLoughlin became so infuriated at the cleric's aspersions on his wife's character that he gave him a good drubbing before he left the post for England.

But because Laframboise was away and Josette's mother, a "chieftainess" of the Tsallel band of Umpquas, had died two years before, the Beavers virtually adopted the little girl. The detested chaplain showed a streak of humanity in regard to poor Josette. He wrote an obituary poem in her honor which began, "Last scion of a royal, yet savage, race,/An absent, widow'd sire's only solace . . ." The saddened minister, in writing a friend, betrayed the fact that he was a compassionate human being after all: "The hearty manner of her prayer for her father can never be forgotten. . . . Excuse my mentioning this, but we loved her. . . ." He asked his friend to engrave his poetic epitaph on a small marble slab and to send it, at his expense, to Fort Vancouver. Pathetically, the ostracized parson ended: "I know you will sympathize with our loss of almost the only thing we had begun to love at Vancouver."

Late in the year, Captain Edward Belcher of *H.M.S. Sulphur* explored the two ends of the Siskiyou Trail with his surgeon-naturalist Dr. Richard Brinsley Hinds. After investigating the Columbia and lower Willamette, Belcher sailed for San Francisco Bay to continue the surveying and charting begun in 1827 by Captain William Beechey of the *Blossom*. Beechey had gone no further than the Carquinez Straits.

Belcher took the *Sulphur's* consort, the large cutter *Starling*, up-river, along with a pinnace, two small cutters, and a gig. He started out gingerly on October 24, 1837, letting his pilot convince him that the *Starling* could go no further because of shoaly water. Too late, Belcher learned how wrong he was. He could have warped the cutter all the way up to the American River. But he left her in the "third basin" of San Francisco Bay, apparently Suisun Bay.

The Royal Navy officer hired as a guide an Indian converted to Christianity. Beechey was surprised to learn that he used to hunt for runaway Christian Indians for the Mexicans, usually along the San Joaquin River.

Belcher and Hinds carefully observed the oaks, cottonwoods, ash, plane trees, willows, chestnuts, and poplars of the valley. They were particularly interested in the wild grapevines which entwined around the boles of giant trees. The Captain several times used the fruit of the California walnut trees as dessert. He had several huge oaks felled by axmen. The most remarkable was twenty-seven feet in circumference and did not extend its branches from the trunk until they were at a height of sixty feet from the ground. "It was truly a noble sight," wrote Belcher. Hinds was disappointed at the late start. Autumn was already far advanced; the leaves of deciduous trees had sifted down on the river bank. Sadly, he remarked, "The season is past when botany should be pursued."

But Belcher was determined to make the most of his opportunity. He observed the geese and ducks which flocked to the Sacramento in great numbers. He counted herds of twenty and thirty elk and deer. But, to the disgruntlement of his men, he announced that there was not time for a hunt. He was anxious about delays; at several points along the river, he landed to make astronomical observations.

To Belcher's distress, the Sacramento became a rather narrow stream only twenty miles above the *Starling's* anchorage. He was confused and disappointed in not having met either the San Joaquin River or the Jesús María. The former's mouth was hidden by islands far below him, in the Delta. The latter was not a separate stream, as he imagined, but just Gabriel Moraga's 1808 name for the upper Sacramento, above the Feather. Belcher soon guessed that the large "fork" had to bend southward from the Delta, which he described as an "intermediate, extensive sheet of water forming a large archipelago." But he was hopelessly confused in his geography. He placed "Montes Diavolo" in the Elk Range, the bald mountains to the west, whereas Mount Diablo is the main peak of the Mexicans' Sierra de los Bolbones —now the Diablo Range—southeast of the Carquinez Straits. The guide was as much in the dark as Belcher. He was more familiar with the San Joaquin than the Sacramento River. Whenever he was asked a question, he fell back on his ignorance, stating: "I only know where to find the Indians."

Captain Belcher was pleased to find the Sacramento widening again as he progressed up it. He dismissed the San Joaquin as unnavigable and unworthy of the company of its majestic neighbor, the Sacramento. At his noon station of the second day, the latter was fully a third of a mile across. Moreover, the marshy terrain now gave way to firm ground, well wooded, grassy, and brushy. Again he noted the fox grapes: "Wild grapes in great abundance overhung the lower trees, clustering to the river, at times completely overpowering the trees on which they climbed, and producing beautiful varieties of fruit." He hurried along to reach the navigable limit of the river, allowing only nine, noon, and three o'clock stops to rest his men while he took his latitudes. Belcher allowed only his boat to make stops. It was the swiftest, and he soon caught up with the others when they passed him as he shot the sun.

The naval officer first observed Indians when he was about halfway up the Sacramento to the American River. His guide assured him that they were friendly. Shortly, he examined a *laissez passer* given them by General Mariano Vallejo which attested to this fact. The document allowed them to absent themselves from Mission San José to treat with the wild Indians and to trade for furs. When two of them volunteered to join his cruise, Belcher signed them on as impromptu guides.

The boats reached the American River on the last day of October 1837. He patriotically dubbed the fork area Point Victoria, then sent Lieutenant Henry Kellett, the *Starling*'s commander, to examine the American with his small craft. The Lieutenant returned, without having even passed from sight. He reported, "No water for our lightest boats." The two natives reinforced this view of the shoals by assuring Belcher that this was "the ford where the hunters cross"—that is, the American River ford of the beaver men near the 1839 site of Sutter's Fort.

When Belcher landed at his Point Victoria, the natives fled before him, leaving acorns and other provisions behind, their fires still burning. He tried various experiments to get the hidden natives—Wallocks his volunteer guides called them—to come to him. He had them call out to the locals, but it was in vain. He left a knife, some tobacco, and beads for the Indians to pick up during the night. Next morning, he saw some of the timid redmen crouching in the grass. One wore a metal headband into which some feathers were poked. They were naked, and Belcher thought them "wretched looking fellows." As his two hired Indians tried to persuade them to come up, he observed through his telescope that they waved their hands slowly in a gesture which plainly indicated that they did not care to join the strangers. He left more presents for the Wallocks and quit the forks after firmly warning his two Indian allies against "easing them of [the] bags of acorns" which the Wallocks had abandoned. Probably the Indians in hiding were Miwoks from just south of the river junction or Nisenans of the American River.

Captain Belcher inspected some of the river bank Indian *rancherías* or villages. They were all on artificially constructed mounds, rounded piles of earth no more than a hundred yards in diameter or fifteen feet above ground level. The pits or trenches from which the earth for the eminences was removed formed ditches to carry off river floodwater. Belcher's Indian-napping pilot told him that each village belonged to a separate tribe (really a band, at best)—then, confusingly, attributed several to the Onee-shan-a-tee or Nisenan tribe.

The Englishmen shook their heads at the cramped quarters in which the riverine Indians lived. Belcher observed: "Confined within such a compass, it is fearful to contemplate the ravages which disease must make in an inclement season, or the misery which the survivors must endure thus pent up with the dead or dying. Lately, fever and ague carried off whole tribes, and the spots they had thus so carefully reared were but their own tombs! On one of these I had fixed a station and on digging to insert the post, the parts of a skeleton, with hair perfect, mixed with ashes, were turned up. It is therefore probable that they burn their dead to destroy the animal matter and prevent contagion."

The officer noted that the Indians often made temporary sojourns under oaks and horse chestnut trees. Apparently, they could make buckeye meal palatable, like acorn meal, by leaching. They took ducks, geese, deer, and elk. There was a great profusion of antlers everywhere. The river abounded in fish and mussels. Belcher guessed that the Indians were not skillful enough fishermen to take many of the huge sturgeon he saw leaping in the river.

The pilot told Belcher that the Sacramento's banks had once been thickly clustered with populous *rancherías*. Now, many of the bands were almost extinct. Belcher realized that it was not the movement of wild tribes to the missions nor the pressure of fur trappers which had thinned out the natives. He wrote: "Let not theorists too eagerly advance the opinion that the introduction of foreigners depopulates whole tracts. A higher power operated here. It is probably that the hunters and Delawares which frequent these grounds, may have in some measure caused them to shift their ground. It is also known that they have most valorously contended against the rifle and suffered slaughter rather than retreat, generally severely and fatally wounding their adversaries." But he put his finger on the real cause of the depopulation of the villages—malaria. "The mortal sickness which scourged the Columbia and its tribes as far south as the Colorado in one year, and even penetrated to the Rocky Mountains."

Belcher realized that the day of the beaver hunter on the Siskiyou Trail was nearing an end, too. He recorded: "The Sacramento was once famous for its beaver and land otter." Then he added: "They are not scarce at present, but our Mission Indians were anxious to induce us to become purchasers of furs which would certainly be termed *refuse* to the northward."

Doctor Hinds' scientific collection was enriched by some fine specimens of ducks, owls, hawks, and other birds. But few four-footed animals were killed for study, other than land otters, weasels, raccoons, squirrels, and "jackalfoxes" or coyotes. Belcher fired at "small tigers or tiger cats"—probably wildcats (bobcats) rather than shy mountain lions—but the birdshot in his fowling piece did not penetrate the thick fur of the felines enough to bring them down.

A midshipman, Simpkinson, wrote a memoir of the Royal Navy expedition up the watery southern stretch of the Siskiyou Trail. He was dazzled at San Francisco by the deadly accuracy of marksmen Isaac Graham and Jacob Primer Leese. Mountain man Graham could hit a *real*, a silver Spanish coin the size of a shilling, with a rifle ball from as far as he could see it, perhaps one hundred yards or so. Leese dramatized his skill for the watching Britons by sticking a nail into

261

a post then driving it in with one shot and punching it all the way through the post with a second ball from his long rifle. Simpkinson said of Leese: "He had just come across the Rocky Mountains with nothing but his rifle and the clothes on his back, but was now in pretty affluent circumstances."

Although Simpkinson did not go upriver, he talked to some of his buddies who had manned the boats during the October 24–November 24 exploration. Not surprisingly, the *matelots* had not been as excited by the countryside as their officers. Wrote the Midshipman: "From all accounts, I am glad I was not selected to be one of the party, for a more uncomfortable, uninteresting expedition was never undertaken." Simpkinson blamed the monotony and boredom of the ordinary seamen on Belcher's caprices and bad temper. According to the Midshipman's informants, their commander reserved to himself alone even the privilege of shooting at ducks and geese, though the wildfowl were so plentiful that they quite literally darkened the sky when they rose off the river. But game was much scarcer than the boat crews had expected. Only one deer was shot—and that one by luck, for the stag chose to swim the river near the boats. A good number of deer and elk were seen at some distance, but they always fled at the sight of humans. And, of course, the stiff-necked Belcher would not let hunting parties go out for fear of delaying his exploration. Once or twice, the men ran short of provisions. How they growled when they went two days with nothing to eat but flour and water dumplings!

Still, the twisting Sacramento (taking 170 miles to make one hundred as the crow flew) was, to many of the sailors, a beautiful stream, fringed with trees, shrubs, and parasitic vines. The floodplain was handsome—"covered with the richest pasturage, and interspersed with park-like groups of trees." The sailors observed Indians who were perfectly naked and "in the wildest state of nature." No attacks were made on the boats, carefully moored so that they protected one another, though Simpkinson's confidant observed of the Indians: "They are, I believe, a very treacherous and savage race and in a more primitive state than any of the tribes we have seen to the northward. [But] no symptom was ever discovered of the Indians meditating an attack, and they probably thought the force too formidable."

Simpkinson and his friends were astounded at the size and weight of the racks of horns carried by California elk. None of the animals were taken during the cruise, because they fled at first sight of the Britishers. But in San Francisco the visitors examined a typical specimen. Its six branches measured six feet across and weighed (with part of the skull) forty-five pounds.

Back in San Francisco, Belcher made a final comment about the Sacramento Valley—and it had nothing to do with elk. He noted the deteriorating state of the Mexican province. The government was not even able to protect itself against American mountain men and "renegado deserters" from whaleships and merchantmen. As proof of the helplessness of Mexican California before American puissance, he cited one example of aggression by Yankee trappers: "A party of Delaware Indians or American hunters had a permit from the Governor to hunt for furs in the back country. Their time having expired, the chief returned [to the States] but the remainder, having appointed a new head, are now carrying on land piracy throughout the state. In open day, they rode to the Mission of St. Louis and took from the corral all the horses belonging to the mission (said to be a thousand!), desiring the administrator to keep clear of rifle range."

Captain Belcher was more aware of the real state of affairs on the Siskiyou Trail, and in California in general, than were Pelly and the Governor and Committee in London, of course. Far to the south of the Trail, as Belcher was on the point of exploring it, a mystery man was mauled by a grizzly. Probably he was a trapper or a "land-pirate" (horse thief), to use Belcher's term. When he died, his Anglo comrades buried him beneath an oak tree and carved an epitaph into the trunk: "Peter Le Beck, Killed by a Bear, October 17, 1837." To this day, no one knows exactly who Peter Le Beck was. Chances are good that he was one of the horse thieves of whom Belcher wrote, perhaps the "Pierre Lable" who rode with Pegleg Smith. Or was he Pierre Leveque or Levesque, a lone free trapper far from home?

In any case, Le Beck's very presence in the bleak Tehachapi Mountains, far to the south even of the faintest trace of the Siskiyou Trail at King's River, indicates how far-ranging were the freebooters who had taken a shine to California. These wanderers were scornful of national boundaries, and, in less than nine years, a party of roughnecks flying a Bear Flag would attempt to wrench the province from Mexico. Long before then, the filibustering of Sutter and Graham and others would swamp the fur trade and number the days of a viable Siskiyou Trail.

Captain
of the California Trail

JOHN WORK—"reduced to a perfect skeleton," in his own words—recuperated at Fort Vancouver during the winter of 1833–1834. He made a Siskiyou Trail expedition in the summer of '34, but only as far as old, decaying Fort Umpqua. Work could not handle the strenuous demands of the Southern Party any longer. So McLoughlin posted him to the coastal trade and replaced him with Laframboise.

Michel, born Jean Baptiste Eugène Laframboise on May 5, 1797, in Varennes, near Montreal, had more than earned the position. Experience the *canadien* had aplenty; it was his long suit. He had come with his father on the ill-fated *Tonquin* in March 1811. He had served in Astor's aborted American enterprise at the Columbia's mouth and trapped for the North-West Company before joining the Hudson's Bay Company in 1821. From 1824 on, he had been a skillful interpreter for expeditions to all corners of the fur country.

Laframboise was the idealization of the Oregon and California mountain man legend. He became more Indian than the Indians themselves. The lusty Canadian used to boast that he had a wife of high rank in every single tribe along the route of the Siskiyou Trail. Certainly, he moved from one Indian nation to another with a security which was the envy of other travelers. And he was the main thorn in the side of latecomer (1839) John A. Sutter, when the Swiss not only squatted on the trappers' ford of the American River, but tried to corral the entire Sacramento Valley fur trade for himself.

Sutter recalled Laframboise's visits in his *New Helvetia Diary:* "Every year the Hudson's Bay Company sent trappers to the region, who annually collected a vast quantity of furs. Their women squaws and half-breeds made moccasins, shirts and pantaloons of dressed deerskins, a commodity greatly in demand. I bought large quantities of this completed clothing, but they could not sell furs. They entered the valley in the fall, trapped during the winter, and left in the spring with their skins. Before I settled there and assumed judicial powers, the Mexican Government had been unable to prevent this annual incursion into the rich Mexican fur territory. When their tents were pitched, the scene had the permanent look of a large tent city. When I complained, the Government assessed a heavy duty against these furs, and soon my trappers were the sole fur seekers in the Valley."

If only Laframboise could be relied upon to follow orders! McLoughlin had acquired some of Governor Simpson's many misgivings about the man. He simply could not be depended upon with anything like the faith they accorded Work or Ogden. In 1825 he had earned a black mark by lying about the number of skins he delivered to the *William and Mary* for shipment. He had disobeyed Alex McLeod's orders in the 1826–1827 outfit and had gone off on an unauthorized hunting expedition when he should have been trading furs away from the Indians. Other minor failures, when totted up, convinced Simpson that his true worth was something well below the £60 at which he was salaried. In fact, the Governor rated him in his secret book as "a lying, worthless blackguard who begins to conceive himself a man of consequence and sets such a high value on his services that I am very much disposed to allow him to take them to another market."

As fur trade historian Doyce B. Nunis has pointed out, McLoughlin kept Laframboise on a close rein from 1828 until 1832, because of a growing distrust of him. But he appointed him postmaster at Fort Vancouver for 1830 and 1831; and, when Laframboise performed well enough in the recovery of Jed Smith's stolen goods, McLoughlin allowed him to lead the winter hunts on the Siskiyou Trail as far as Fort Umpqua and over to the coast at Coos Bay. But his pay was reduced to £50 a year during this period of McLoughlin's reduced confidence in him. In 1831, Laframboise demanded a raise to £80 per annum. His demand was ignored. Michel swallowed his pride and continued to work for the Company.

Since George Simpson had never had any faith in him, Laframboise could salvage nothing in that quarter. But by 1832 he had won back McLoughlin's trust. The doctor sent him in that year to punish the Tillamooks for their out-of-character murder of two Iroquois trappers. He killed six braves, added Indian auxiliaries to bring the strength of his force to sixty-three men, and promised to forward a good beaver catch to Fort Vancouver.

Alas, Laframboise once more broke orders. "Forgetting" his instructions, he strayed far from the coast, indeed all the way to interior California via "McLeod's Track," the Siskiyou Trail. After running into Ewing Young and then joining John Work, he split away near Fort Ross in May. Reaching Fort Vancouver on July 13, 1833, he mollified an annoyed McLoughlin by turning over to him a good catch—755 large beaver, eighty-four small beaver, and 152 other skins. Since Work had delivered 1023 beaver in October, this was a fine California bonus. McLoughlin gave Laframboise not only a handsome raise, to £75, but the sobriquet of "Captain of the California Trail."

Ordered back to California in 1834, Laframboise abandoned the Pit River route for good. With this expedition, the Siskiyou Trail settled down to its permanent track along the Sacramento, avoiding only such impassable stretches as Iron Canyon and staying west of Mount Shasta.

That summer, Laframboise had to move his base camp from the usual Trappers' Landing or French Camp on the San Joaquin River to a site near Sonoma. This was the result of increasing Mexican umbrage over his illegal trapping. General Mariano Vallejo gave him just twenty-four hours to either vamoose from the province or to camp near Sonoma, under his surveillance. Confined to this area, Laframboise could not make a good hunt. The irascible Simpson, in a report to London of June 19, 1835, put the blame for falling profits at Fort Vancouver squarely on Michel. But it was the restrictions of Vallejo and Governor Figueroa which forced Laframboise's return from California without making a hunt worthy of note. (It was on this march that he succored Hall J. Kelley.)

Governor Figueroa was trying to establish friendly intercourse with the Company, said Simpson, because of his hostility toward Ewing Young and other fur freebooters from the United States— "adventurers of various nations who have lately defrauded them of their beaver and robbed them of their horses." Thus, Simpson blamed the failure of the hunt on Laframboise's stupid neglect to provide himself with proper papers, passports. Had he brought such credentials, Simpson assured London, he would have been allowed free range to hunt beaver, under the protection of the "Spaniards." Only a small grain of truth hid in Simpson's argument. Vallejo, Figueroa, et al., were not pleased to see the Honourable Company stripping the central valley of its wealth in furs. But they did dislike—and fear—the Americans more than the Britons. And, doubtless, they were inclined to the belief that their enemies' enemy was their friend.

The Americans had received a severe setback in 1835 when the ubiquitous John Turner was attacked at Rock Creek on the south side of the Rogue River en route to Fort Vancouver. In this battle—for which Turner, Gay, and Bailey took revenge during the cattle drive of 1837—Turner's woman had been killed outright in the surprise attack, along with Dan Miller and Edward Barnes. A trapper named Sanders died later on the South Fork of the Umpqua from wounds received, as did an Irishman called Big Tom in the area of Winchester.

It was at this time that Dr. William J. Bailey had received a tomahawk blow which split his lower jaw from the point of his chin to his throat. He recovered, but his jaw mended poorly, giving him not only an ugly scar but a lopsided look to his face, which terribly distorted his appearance for life. Turner had led the bloody Bailey to the Willamette, mistaking it for the Columbia, and both made it to Lee's mission, though their companion, Woodworth, drowned almost at the very door while swimming the river to safety. George Gay, who had cut up his buckskin breeches in order to make moccasins for his barefoot pards, went alone along the foothills west of the Willamette. He crossed the Rickreall River at the site of Dallas, the Yamhill near its falls (at Lafayette), then reached the Tualatin Plains by way of Wappato Lake. He made it to safety in Nat Wyeth's colony on Sauvies (then Wappato) Island at the mouth of the Willamette. Since he was wearing only tattered remnants of an old shirt, the virtually naked Gay was almost eaten alive by Columbia River bottom mosquitoes by the time he reached the island.

Still unconvinced of Laframboise's worth, Simpson ordered McLoughlin to send a strong and well-appointed party to the Buenaventura in 1835, one which would not be cut up like the Turner-Bailey company. But he was *not* to give the command to Michel. The Governor wanted it to be headed by a commissioned gentleman like Chief Trader John McLeod—or at least by an experienced clerk. For the record, he explained that Laframboise, though very zealous, did not have sufficient weight of character for such a charge. But it was too late. McLoughlin informed him that Laframboise was already in the field with the brigade. Simpson had to make the best of what he saw as a bad bargain. McLoughlin, for his part, had been nervous about the eviction notices of the Mexicans, so he told Michel to hunt only between the Umpqua and the Klamath, and to erect a small fort in the area. On no account was he to go to the Sacramento Valley.

As ever, Laframboise disobeyed his orders. When he returned to Fort Vancouver on May 10, 1836, he blithely explained that he had had to proceed to the Buenaventura since the other area was completely hunted out. Moving along the shore to a point near Bodega, he had skirted the Russian colonies and turned inland to the Sacramento River, to camp in June on an island perhaps on Steamboat Slough or near the Sacramento's mouth in the Delta's "archipelago," as Belcher had termed the maze of low-lying islands. He chose a secure position in case Vallejo should come with a force to oust him.

Michel thus laid himself wide open to censure again. Luckily, Simpson relented enough to permit McLoughlin to give him another command *if* his 1836 outfit should prove profitable. It was a great success, grossing £805.5. McLoughlin was pleased to continue him in command of the brigade, and Simpson, on receipt of the fur returns, concurred on June 30, 1837.

As the decade of the 1830s neared its close, Michel was at the apex of his career. He was very much the "Captain of the California Trail," though he was not without critics. A priest (Blanchet?) in 1839 wrote that his Southern Expedition members had "revolting exteriors" and added: "The Brigade is a hideous assemblage of persons of both sexes, devoid of principles or morals." But to Dr. Elijah White, Michel and his ilk cut a very striking figure: "The style in which they travelled was rather novel, bringing with them beds, bedding, tea, coffee, sugar, bread, cakes, cheese; and not even the wine was left behind. They were attended by a numerous suite, never forgetting the cook." Miss A. J. Allen, in her *Ten Years in Oregon* (1848), paraphrased White in describing Michel and his entourage passing the Methodist Mission en route to Vancouver from California: "This company, just before entering the settlement, which was early in the morning, stopped to remove from their persons stains and traces of travel and [to] dress themselves carefully in their best attire. They then formed themselves in Indian file, led by Mr. La Fromboy, the chief of the party. Next [to] him rode his wife, a native woman, astride —as is common with the females—upon her pony, quite picturesquely clad. She wore a man's hat with long black feathers fastened in front and drooping behind her very gracefully. Her short dress was of rich broadcloth, leggins beautifully embroidered with gay beads and fringed with tiny bells, whose musical tinkling could be heard at several hundred yards distance. Next, the Clerk and his wife, much in the same manner, and so on to the officers of less importance and the men, and finally the boys driving the packhorses, with bales of furs, one hundred and eighty pounds to each animal. The trampling of the fast-walking horses, the silvery tinkling of the small bells, rich, handsome dresses and fine appearance of the riders, whose numbers amounted to sixty or seventy. The array was really patriarchal and had quite an imposing appearance."

Because Laframboise had seen sea otter on his earlier coastal marches, McLoughlin sent him on a special hunt in 1836. Transported to the Oregon coast by the Company schooner *Cadboro,* Michel brought back a very disappointing three months' catch of only twenty-two sea otter skins on August 5.

Hopeful of still salvaging something from the season, the doctor hurried him out again on September 6 with twenty-five trappers on a wintering hunt in the "Calamut" country. Whatever were the returns for the Klamath hunt (they have been lost), they were undoubtedly dwarfed by the success of Michel's next Buenaventura expedition. He took the Southern Party out in April 1837 and returned on July 6. The short, late four months of work, largely around San Francisco Bay, yielded 1185 large and 251 small beaver and 431 otter. His catch was worth a remarkable £2314. Naturally, the chief factor rushed Laframboise back to California on August 1 with twenty-seven hunters to trap the Feather River. But he also touted his protégé in his official reports, and raised his pay to £100.

In 1837 McLoughlin sought ways to outflank the Americans. He hoped to repeat Ogden's greatest exploit, asking Laframboise to take his company all the way to the Gulf of California and, instead of marching all the way back to the Columbia (a great waste of time), to meet the *Cadboro* in May 1838 at Trinidad Bay on California's Redwood Coast. The ship would collect his catch and reequip the brigade for another, immediate hunt. It was a grand design, a bold, amphibious version of the rendezvous system of the Americans. It was one way of outflanking the difficult terrain and hostile Indians of the Siskiyous, too. And it would separate the Company men from Yankee interlopers—in the words of McLoughlin's chief assistant, James Douglas, place them "beyond the influence of opposition."

Laframboise left the Columbia on August 1, 1838, and reached the Sacramento in November. As usual, he had no trouble with the Indians, his only problem being the perennial one, the weak condition of Company horses. Because of heavy snow that winter, he could not hunt very much on the Feather. So, once again, he adjusted his orders and trapped instead the Sacramento River and low, marshy and snow-free grounds of the interior basin which opened off San Francisco Bay by way of the Sacramento-San Joaquin Delta. He did not set up his headquarters at old French Camp but at the confluence of the Feather and Sacramento rivers, where the Hawaiian fishing village of Vernon grew after the Gold Rush. Begging Indians bothered the trappers, but they took 2700 skins, a fine catch.

On May 4, 1838, James Douglas, acting for McLoughlin, who was on leave, ordered Charles Ross to take charge of the Southern Trapping Party as Laframboise's superior. He was to sail with Captain James Scarborough in the *Cadboro* to Trinidad, the shallow, exposed little port visited by Captain Charles Vancouver in 1793. Douglas estimated that it lay 180 miles north of Port Bodega of the Russians. (It is actually near two hundred miles.) Small wonder the amphibious fur operation became a bit waterlogged.

Laframboise's geography was not much better than Douglas's. He broke camp on May Day and, after a fourteen-day march, much of it over the rugged Coast Range, reached the shore. But he did not realize that he was one hundred miles south of Trinidad Head. So he just sat there "in anxious suspense," perhaps near Bear Harbor.

Douglas gave Ross a copy of Laframboise's instructions, so that there could be no mixup, no failure to rendezvous. The trappers were to assemble at Trinidad no later than May 15 to transfer their plews to the ship's hold. Should Laframboise arrive before the *Cadboro,* he was to strip the bark off a prominent tree on a conspicuous point of land and inscribe a large "L" on it. He was also to leave a note at the tree, concerning his plans, should he have to absent himself. If Ross were to arrive first, he was to square off a tree by hewing it and was to engrave a huge "C" on it. Should the vessel be driven to sea by bad weather, he was to leave a letter of directions for Michel at the tree. Douglas assigned July 10 as the absolute limit of the schooner's stay and recommended that the loading of furs and unloading of supplies be rushed. The stevedoring should not take more than four or five days.

Since Ross was to leave the ship and take overall charge of the seasonal hunt, Douglas briefed him on the Company's intentions in the Siskiyou Mountains and Sacramento Valley: "In maintaining this party, we are desirous that the country should be kept closely hunted, a system hitherto but too successfully pursued in the intermediate district north of the Buenaventura Valley and south of the Columbia

271

River, no part of which can, at present, afford employment to a strong party."

Then Douglas either again betrayed his ignorance of distance in California or expressed misplaced faith in Ross's ability as a wideranging traveler. After the transshipment at Trinidad, his orders were: "If you cannot find profitable occupation in the Bay of St. Francisco, instead of returning in this direction you will push further south to Red Bay at the mouth of the California Gulf, a country little known or explored, but reported by trappers who have casually passed through it to be well stocked with beaver." The Colorado's mouth is a full eight hundred miles from Trinidad, even as the crow flies.

The remainder of Ross's orders had to do with subsequent hunts. He was to remain either at the mouth of the Colorado, or anywhere else in California where the hunt was good. Then, in the spring of 1839, he was to take the trappers back to Trinidad Bay for another rendezvous with a supply vessel on or about May 15. The ship would bring him new instructions from Fort Vancouver. Douglas wanted him to depend on his own good sense, so he gave him only three direct orders in regard to the *modus operandi* of his brigade: to post a strong guard over all of his camps, to be especially watchful of the security of his horse herd, and to keep his trappers always on the move.

Hope of the ship's arrival faded from Laframboise's mind. Probably he guessed that he and the schooner were waiting for each other, but far apart. In any case, he moved his camp to a point thirty miles inland, then set out for Fort Vancouver with a few men to get supplies and new orders. He told those remaining in camp to wait for him until August 1. If he should not be back by then, they were to trap their way up the Sacramento Valley, where he would rejoin them on the Siskiyou Trail.

On July 9, 1838, Douglas expressed his displeasure to P. C. Pambrun, commanding Fort Walla Walla: "Greatly to my surprise and disappointment, Mr. Laframboise, with seven men, arrived here yesterday from the confines of California, where he passed the winter with his party. He visited the sea coast early in May but, unfortunately, did not find the *Cadboro* and, despairing of her arrival, he returned to the interior, quitted his people in the mountains, and has made his way through many dangers to this place."

Once more, Fort Vancouver's distress at Laframboise's failure to follow directions was soothed by the magnitude of his California catch—1361 large and 225 small beaver, and 884 otter. Profits were almost £981, some £120 more than the returns from that year's Snake Country Outfit.

Michel also brought news of heavy traffic—and tragedy—on the Siskiyou Trail. An American cattle party, composed of Willamette Valley men emulating in 1838 the great drive of the prior year, were reportedly cut down to a man. It was true that Nat Wyeth's gunsmith, Thomas Jefferson Hubbard, led a party down the Trail. He had probably been a cowboy with Young; Miss A. J. Allen wrote that "Hubbard started a second time for California for herds." And, barely three weeks after he set out, the Shastas struck his company. Gloom smothered the Willamette settlement when Michel brought in rumors that all the cattlemen had been killed. Some gave them up; others hoped against hope that it was a false report.

The settlers' anxiety was relieved, one day, by the reports of signal guns across the river from the Mission. When they hurried toward the sounds, they were delighted to find nearly all of the party safe. Recalled Miss Allen: "They had been defeated by the savages, driven out of the way, and wandered about in the mountains, some of them suffering pretty severely from their wounds." James Douglas, in keeping London posted on Siskiyou Trail activities, briefed his superiors (October 18, 1838) on the debacle: "Eighteen or twenty Americans and Indians left the Willamette last June with the intention of penetrating to California and returning from thence with cattle. They were attacked on the route by the Saste tribe, who repulsed them with loss after a sharp engagement, and they arrived here, empty-handed, and have since quietly remained on their farms."

Laframboise had passed the attack site only a day or two after the battle. He had had no trouble; in fact, he had not seen an Indian. But Douglas worried about the effect of the defeat on Siskiyou Trail travel. He told Pambrun: "I am now very anxious about the way and means of sending Laframboise back, as the Indian population are excited and much elated with their success." He had planned to have Pambrun supply the twenty-man Southern Party with horses for the overland trek to California by way of the Siskiyou Trail. But with the Trail effectively closed by the Shasta Indians, he ordered Scarborough in July to take Laframboise by ship to the Northern California coast, where he could point out a landing near his trappers' campsite.

Wisely, Douglas did not entirely believe Michel when he bragged that he was quite familiar with Cape Mendocino and described a small cove just south of the point, protected (he said) by a projecting angle of the Cape. Fearful of more missed connections, Douglas warned his skipper: "Laframboise cannot furnish the accurate information so desirable in such cases. He is, in fact, ignorant of the exact geographical position, as it is laid down in our best charts. But he supposed that the place is 100 miles north of Bodega, probably in the vicinity of Cape Mendocino. [The Cape is actually 160 miles north of Bodega Head.] If the trappers be not found there, you may run to the southward, keeping as close in with the coast as may be consistent with security, until you meet the party, who are in some point between Cape Mendocino and Point Delgado, beyond which your researches need not be continued." (The distance between Cape Mendocino and Point Delgado is 30 miles.) Scarborough's chore would have been that of the legendary needle in the hayrick, even had Douglas not mistakenly believed that Cape Mendocino formed the south end of Trinidad Bay, whereas it lies forty-five miles south of Trinidad.

On July 17, 1838, Douglas gave Laframboise his rather complicated orders. He played it safe by giving them in both French and English. Michel was to hunt the Sacramento Valley during the winter, but was not to go to the Feather River. He was then to march to the coast by May 15, 1838, and to wait till July 15, if necessary. Should no ship arrive, he was to return to the Sacramento to provision his party by hunting game, since an accident would have befallen the ship to delay her. He was to return to the sea again by October 25 and to wait there until November 10. Should no ship arrive during that time, he would know that none was coming until the following (1840) May 15. Arriving off Cape Mendocino on that date, the vessel would wait for him until June 10 before sailing back to Fort Vancouver. Douglas would again send a ship south to rendezvous with the trappers on October 25. If the captain should find no one on the coast, he would proceed to San Francisco.

Douglas replaced Ross with John McLeod as the *Cadboro*'s supercargo and Laframboise's overseer. The chief trader was to equip the trappers and to return as quickly as possible. And the Scot was to be sure of his (Laframboise's) men—"You will make every man sign a new agreement for two years, as we cannot retain irresponsible persons in our service."

From Cape Mendocino south, the *Cadboro* hugged the coast but the lookouts sighted no white men. All the trappers had departed the littoral for the Sacramento Valley. Because Scarborough could not find a safe anchorage anywhere on the rugged coast, in which to put ashore Laframboise and his men and supplies, McLeod decided to chance the resentment of the Russians. He ordered Scarborough to conn the *Cadboro* into the tiny, exposed, harbor at Fort Ross. His fears were groundless. The Russian Commandant was friendly and provided a pilot to get the schooner past the reefs and into the doghole or cove. Then he welcomed his visitors with graciousness and, even better, fresh provisions.

Peter (Don Pedro) Kostromitinoff, Manager and Commandant of Fort Ross, whom Chief Trader McLeod mistook for the Governor of all Russian America, including Alaska, was much interested to learn that Laframboise was one of his visitors. Since Laframboise was, already, something of a legend in California, Kostromitinoff (in McLeod's words) "expressed a great curiosity to see the person so celebrated in California." He added, "Captain Michel, no ways deficient in tact, during a subsequent interview took the liberty of entreating His Excellency's aid in enabling him to rejoin his people, & with much address obtained the loan of twelve horses."

McLeod realized that a dozen horses would not suffice to refit Laframboise's hunting party in the interior. Recalling how wrong had been his misgivings about the Slavs, he took another gamble and sent a courier to Mariano Vallejo in Sonoma. (The General had virtually run Laframboise out of California.) To McLeod's delight, Vallejo had, indeed, enjoyed a change of heart. He sent a small herd of horses and a note containing not only the price but an offer of further help, if needed.

Faxon Dean Atherton, an Anglo pioneer of Mexican-California, ran into McLeod at Sonoma during the end of August 1838. The Scot had just come from the *Cadboro* to buy thirty horses from Vallejo. He sent them with ten men to Michel, inland, then set out for the schooner with Atherton, who was keen on seeing the Russian settlements.

Atherton rode west with McLeod and his Canadian trapper, servant, and guide, Luis. They laid over at Vallejo's great Petaluma adobe before making a curiously difficult crossing of the Santa Rosa plain. So hot was the summer of 1838 that the muddy ground had split open like a desert riverbed, leaving some cracks six inches wide. This led Atherton to misjudge the rich valley of Sonoma County. He wrote, "Was it not for them, it would be beautiful land for cattle." At Rancho Laguna de San Antonio, on the modern Marin-Sonoma County line, McLeod and his companions were attacked by a grizzly as they dismounted, tightening their saddle girths. All escaped without injury, however. After a nice lunch (ragoût!) at Edward M.

McIntosh's Rancho Estero Americano, the trio rode into Bodega at dark.

McLeod hailed the *Cadboro* but could not be heard over the boom of the crashing surf. So Atherton halloed to the Russian house across the inlet. Luckily, Kostromitinoff had come the few miles from the fort to Bodega Bay. He sent a canoe for them from Bodega Head. After they signaled three or four times with pistol shots, the watch on the *Cadboro* noticed them. Acknowledgment came in the form of the firing of a ship's gun. A small boat soon picked up the travelers and took them to the schooner. There the lanky Atherton had to sleep in a bunk only five feet long, curling himself up like a snake.

On the last day of August, Atherton accompanied McLeod and Luis to Fort Ross. There he met with Kostromitinoff and the man who would shortly become his successor, (Don) Alexander Rotscheff.

Meanwhile, Laframboise made a fast trip to the Feather River, collected his trappers and their furs, and hustled them back to the *Cadboro,* rocking at anchor in Bodega Bay. Once his party was reprovisioned, he led it out again for the Feather River hunting grounds, promising to assemble it at Trinidad in May 1839.

While the Britons were basking in Russian hospitality, James Douglas was writing optimistic letters to London. On September 1, 1838 he reported that the "Buonaventura" trappers were uncommonly fortunate, having killed in their winter's hunt 2300 beaver and otter. He had equipped and reinforced the party to enable it to maintain its position in the Sacramento Valley and, if necessary, to extend its hunt into the more populated country "situate on the southeast [?] of California." Whatever Douglas's bewilderment over the number and location of Mexican settlements, he was correct when he reported good hunting in California to the chief factors and chief traders of the Northern Department in a November 9 communiqué.

The Governor and Committee in London, which approved the supply ship plan, were pleased as punch with the good news. But they were uneasy about Mexican reaction to expanded trapping. Wisely, they told Douglas to warn the leader of the "Bonaventura" Brigade against visiting ranches or settlements. Laframboise was to have no unavoidable contact with any parties of whites, especially Americans. This was very difficult. For example, General Mariano G. Vallejo contacted him (September 1838) about a mixup over horses. Some of Michel's men had bought horses at Russian River after John McLeod had authorized rancher Edward McIntosh to claim five horses (supposedly) bought from Vallejo by the Company. Michel replied that he had urged his men to take their horses to Sonoma to get the proper brands and receipts, but that they had "declined." He admitted that he believed that these particular animals had neither been bought or sold honestly. But he sent what papers he had, on his legally acquired horses, to Vallejo. And he asked the General to write him if he wished to see the horses in the flesh. But to write in English or French—Spanish he did not understand. This was obvious from the very salutation of his letter—"Comendent Byaco"—when he sent Vallejo a note (October 19, 1838) via two scouts he had out searching for deserters.

Laframboise asked for the return of the horse receipts he had sent to the General. He then approached him again on the purchase of more animals: "I have been very unfortunate and my people also. We have lost a good many of our horses by a sickness that got among them. At the same time, to ask you if you could assist me of about twenty horses. I have goods here to pay for. The goods I have on hand are blue cloth jackets, white trowsers, white cotton stockings, black silk handkerchiefs, different kinds of calico, and white cotton in pieces. If you wish to sell that number of horses, I wish you would send them by your people. . . . I have no horses here that is able to make the trip. The horses I ask for is not of the best, but good packing horses, not too old."

Alas, Michel went too far in trying to curry the favor of both Vallejo and his rival, Governor Juan B. Alvarado. His hope was to get permission from one or both to trap widely in California. Instead, he got himself roped into an agreement to aid the Mexican militia in a campaign against marauding Horse Thief Indians. Luckily, Laframboise never had to take the field. But London in 1840 expressed its shock to McLoughlin that he had entrusted the "Buena Ventura expedition" to a man of such bad judgment as Michel. His rash action, combined with his earlier want of firmness in management (which had caused considerable inconvenience and loss), surely rendered him ineligible for such an important command.

Largely ignorant of the chronically unsettled, near chaotic, sociopolitical conditions in California, London chided Laframboise for his impolitic and injudicious actions. By this, they meant his going about so near the coast, with its pueblos, missions, and ranchos—and doing so in direct opposition to instructions given to each successive commander of the Buenaventura Brigades since the expeditions first set out down the Siskiyou Trail. So the Governor and Committee flatly recommended that the southern trapping be placed in better hands than those of Laframboise, since "his having entered into an offensive and defensive treaty with General Vallejo was, to say the least of it, a most indiscreet proceeding."

The grand ship-rendezvous plan was abandoned when word trickled into Fort Vancouver in the spring of 1839 that the situation in California was deteriorating further. Laframboise was experiencing serious difficulty with the *californios*. In fact, he was already en route home with his entire brigade at the time the rumors reached the Columbia.

Since Alvarado and Vallejo were deadly rivals, Laframboise was placing himself in an untenable position in trying to befriend both of them. He might have done better in choosing sides (or he might have hastened even more the collapse of the fur trade, and the Siskiyou Trail, in California). When he finally veered toward Alvarado and tried to bind himself to the Governor's destiny, Vallejo—in control of the northern frontier of California, where the beaver were—ordered him out of California. He reiterated the order and backed it with the threat of arrest. Vallejo was not just exercising bombast; he meant what he said. And Laframboise got going.

Douglas stood up for Michel. He wrote London that Laframboise had been placed in an impossible situation. His party was in a constant state of alarm because of the General's enmity. Then, too, the party had been beset by petty traders who sought to "swindle" the men of their furs. Despite these difficulties, stressed Douglas, Laframboise had not retired to Oregon but, instead, had held out long enough in California to pull off a brilliant winter hunt. The proof was in the pudding—1404 large and 204 small beaver, and 695 otter.

James Douglas brushed aside Vallejo's threats and cruelly (for Michel had just married a French-Okanogan girl, Emilie Picard) hurried Laframboise back down the Siskiyou Trail. He set out on July 20, 1839, with thirty-three *engagés,* some Indians, and the doctor's son, Joseph McLoughlin. The latter, described as a young man of determined character, fell ill on the march. He returned to Fort Vancouver not, presumably, because of the fall which gave the name to Jump-off Joe Creek, but because of a pulmonary attack. He may have had "mountain fever"—pneumonia.

Laframboise continued south without his lieutenant for a brief stay on the "Dumais" River to collect winter provisions, thence to the banks of Smith's River, the American River, to hunt there all season. For once, Michel obeyed orders to the letter. He had no intercourse with settlements or Indians. He did not have to use the note from Douglas to Alvarado, reserved for emergencies. In short, he did everything right and proved London wrong. When he reached Fort Vancouver on June 22, 1840, he was hailed as a conquering hero of the fur trade, for he brought as "booty" some 1380 large and 210 small beaver plews, worth a neat profit of £1408.14.11.

But the times were changing. Laframboise now objected to further Siskiyou Trail hunts. Not only were Vallejo and Alvarado both hostile by 1839, they were joined that year by Captain John Sutter, the Swiss-born Mexican citizen who ordered the Hudson's Bay Company out of the Sacramento Valley so that he might have a monopoly of its fur trade. But, worse, Laframboise was becoming afraid of his own men! They were so wild and lawless that he actually feared for his own life at the hands of members of the Buenaventura Brigade.

McLoughlin hoped to replace him in 1840 but could not spare any other officer. So, although Laframboise's heart was not in the task, to say the least, McLoughlin sent him forth with twenty-four men to hunt the Siskiyou Trail south of the Umpqua. He was to return by June 1841. It was a good year for Michel to begin phasing himself out of the Siskiyou Trail hunt, for 1841 was the year in which the United States Government decided to survey and map the route between a territory it claimed (Oregon) and a Mexican province for which it lusted—California.

CHAPTER THIRTEEN

Exploring Expedition

THE UNITED STATES came of age, scientifically, in 1838–1842 when Lieutenant Charles Wilkes's U.S. Exploring Expedition vessels cruised among South Seas atolls, nudged Antarctic floes, and coasted Oregon headlands. For the first time, naval officers were aided by civilian scientific researchers. Uncle Sam's belated response to Captains Cook and Vancouver was not entirely scientific; there was an element of "showing the flag" on the California and Oregon coasts.

Some officers, like Lieutenant George F. Emmons and Passed Midshipman Henry Eld, became genuinely interested in research and formed friendships with the professionals. Emmons was Wilkes's choice to lead his Overland Expedition, charting the Siskiyou Trail to California, with Eld his second-in-command. Emmons literally put the Siskiyou Trail on the map.

Others of rank found the researchers to be a ruddy nuisance. Lieutenant William M. Walker typified them when he disdainfully gave the final order at Sandalwood Bay in the South Pacific: "Bring off the yams, hogs, and scientifics."

Lieutenant Wilkes was, of course, hospitably received at Fort Vancouver in May 1841, and McLoughlin loaned him a canoe in which to explore, personally, the lower Willamette portion of the Siskiyou Trail. Wilkes met Joe Gale and his "Young Americans, building a boat to sail to San Francisco where he hoped to buy cattle and drive them up the Siskiyou Trail." He met William Cannon, the Revolutionary War veteran whom he mistook for a veteran of the Lewis and Clark Expedition. And he patched up a quarrel between

281

Gale and McLoughlin by persuading Gale to fire troublemaker Henry
Wood. The latter, trying to secure rigging under false pretenses, flew
off the handle when the doctor turned him down. "Well, Doctor, you
may keep your pretty rigging! But, remember, Sir, I have an uncle
in the States who I expect here shortly, rich enough to buy you out
and send you all packing!" McLoughlin, who stammered when he
was excited, blurted: "I am gl-glad to hear that so ri-rich a man as
your uncle is co-com-coming to this country. Who is it, Mr. Wood?
What's his name, Mr. Wood? I should like to know him, Mr.
Wood. . . ." The arrogant Wood retorted hotly: "His name is Uncle
Sam, and I hope you *will* know him!"

The officer found his fellow Americans lazy, dirty, and full of
fleas. He was disgusted because the Canadian settlers in the Willamette
were as cheerful and industrious as the Yanks were discontented and
slothful. Laframboise served as Wilkes's guide and impressed him as
being exceedingly civil and better acquainted with the country than
anyone: "He had traveled in all parts, among all tribes, and says he
has a wife in every tribe."

The Methodist Mission was rundown; the hospital was a dwelling; the only threshing machine in Oregon lay rusting alongside "the
public road" (the Siskiyou Trail). Wilkes did not complain about the
fare when he dined there but did not cater to his hosts. Coatless, with
dirty, unwashed arms, they sat higgledy-piggledy on rude benches.
"We dined *à la* Methodist," recalled Wilkes, "on salmon, pork, potted
cheese and strawberries, tea and hotcakes. . . . The meal was eaten
by us in brotherly love, but hunger assisted me or I should never have
been able to swallow mine."

Worse than the Mission's general air of decay was its neglect of
its Indian wards. Of two thousand natives in the area, only twenty-
five were under missionary instruction—"if such it may be termed,"
added Wilkes scornfully. Only farmer James O'Neil was half diligent.
He worked only one month of the twelve each year in a benevolent
climate with a rich soil, yet he had one hundred cattle and forty acres
of wheat. Unlike his mates, he spoke in the kindest terms of McLoughlin who, of course, had helped all the Americans.

Though Wilkes was "doomed" to breakfast again with the
Methodists, he enjoyed a fine view of the Willamette from the Yam-
hills. The scene reminded him of the Connecticut River Valley from
Mount Hope, New Hampshire, or Mount Holyoke, Massachusetts.
The oaks spread over the prairie in clusters, like Eastern orchards.

George Gay also served Wilkes as a guide, besides Michel. The violent veteran of Ewing Young's cattle drive intrigued the officer: "George is fully as much an Indian in habits as a white can be, and bears them [Indians] no love, and is a terror to them, having not infrequently taken the law into his own [hands] and applied it after the Lynch fashion. . . . In the words of one of the settlers, George is not a man to be trifled or fooled with." Gay drifted about with his Indian wife and two children, breaking, earmarking, branding, and gelding stock, and taming wild cows for milking. He was the handiest man in Oregon with a lasso and, as Wilkes observed, "few things with him are deemed impossibilities."

Gay said his parents were English, but he was, by now, more than half Indian. Wilkes agreed, adding: "And I will add, fully equal to them in all artifices." For all his roughness toward Indians, he could be kindly, too. Recalled Wilkes: "I have seen him, while with me, dash off for half a mile for a poor Indian's horse [which] he was unable to catch, and then return. This was done in a manner that showed it was his practice."

Wilkes visited Doctor Bailey but, strangely, made no mention of the horrible cicatrice which ruined the medic's features. John K. Townsend had hardly been able to look on the terrible mask of scarification without flinching: "This is, by far, the most horrible wound I ever saw. He simply bound it up as well as he could with his handkerchief, and his extreme anguish caused him to forget the necessity of accuracy in this respect. The consequence is that the lower part of his face is dreadfully contorted, one side being considerably lower than the other."

Returning to Fort Vancouver, Wilkes found the missionaries as baneful an influence as before ("low, vulgar and unclean"). "If they were Christian men, and readers of their Bible, they ought to practice cleanly habits. Mr. Waller was as filthy as any Indian I have met with in appearance and, taking our nation into consideration, more so."

At the fort, Wilkes observed, close-up, a fur brigade like Laframboise's Siskiyou Trail outfits. The newcomers were Ogden's men from New Caledonia: "They are to be seen lounging about in groups, decked off with feathers, ribbons, &c&c, with the conceit and flaunting air of a finely dressed country girl, evidently looking down upon all those employees who, with their somber and business-like air, are moving around the fort as if they were total strangers to the pleasure of life, while these jovial fellows seemed to have naught to do but attend to the decorating of their persons, and [to] pleasures." The Lieutenant was entranced by the ritual of the fourteen *voyageurs* as they dug their paddle blades deep to thrust their canoe forward. They wore ribbons in their oilskin-covered hats and sang a rousing Canadian boat song as they worked, much as deepwatermen employed a chantey to ease their labors.

Wilkes issued orders for Lieutenant George Emmons to head the Siskiyou Trail expedition to California on September 1, 1841. Its original object, according to Passed Midshipman George Colvocoresses, was to explore only as far as the Siskiyous or the Shasta Mountains, then return by a different route. If so, orders were changed almost immediately and the party's destination became the anchorage of the flagship *Vincennes* in San Francisco Bay.

Emmons felt pressed to get under way by the threat of winter snow closing the Siskiyou and Shasta passes. Horticulturist William D. Brackenridge arrived in Fort Vancouver from a strenuous Columbia exploration only to receive his marching orders for California. He wrote: "We had already had a pretty hard campaign, but as it was a new field, we were anxious to get into it." He barely had time for a tour of the fort's grounds, led by gardener William Bruce. The latter showed his colleague the muskmelons, watermelons, gooseberries, strawberries, various vegetable crops, the peaches, nectarines, and apple trees (four to five hundred of them), all raised from seed, which made the post such an oasis in a wilderness.

Colvocoresses noticed more the humming activity of the fort than its quiet gardens. He watched 30 to forty Sandwich Islanders felling trees and dragging them to the day and night shifts working the mill. Two gangs of saws ripped out three thousand board feet of lumber a day for foreign ports. The Midshipman was watching the beginning of the metamorphosis in Oregon's economy, from furs to timber.

On September 2, Eld led a party by canoe to join Emmons, already at Champoeg. Brackenridge scribbled in his log as they turned into the Willamette: "As this river has been denominated the paradise of Oregon, I kept my eyes about, in order to catch some of its beauty."

Above the Willamette Falls portage, progress was slow as the current strengthened. The boat had to cross and recross the river to take advantage of every eddy. Colvocoresses learned from the Indian crew that the stretch of river was considered to be so dangerous at high water that the natives left propitiatory offerings of food for the gods, to beseech safe passages. But the waters were docile in September and the night clear and serene for travel, so the Indians continued to paddle until the Champoeg canoe landing was reached. There, the gentlemen bedded down in a barnyard.

Next morning, Eld and Colvocoresses breakfasted with Tom McKay, already familiar to them from many a trapper's tale of adventure. At forty, he was tall, straight as a spruce, and with a face expressing firmness and nerve—"daring character"—to Colvocoresses, no less than shrewdness.

McKay furnished horses to reach Emmons's bivouac, fifteen miles south. All but Brackenridge rode. The Scot botanized his way on foot. The thriving Canadian farms and American mission colony reminded Colvocoresses of home, with good roads, enclosed fields, schoolhouse and smithy. Unlike Wilkes, he was impressed by the large and seemingly prosperous Methodist settlement. He shortly found appearances to be deceiving. True, the climate was so benign that stock did not have to be taken inside during the winter; barns were used only for storing grain. But the colony was rotting away. Colvocoresses found that only Reverend David Leslie had a good reputation among the settlers. He was, they said, the only sky pilot who gave a damn for his brood. Added the passed midshipman: "This statement, if we may judge the tree by its fruit, is not very erroneous." He found the Methodists more wrapped up in farming than missionizing. He estimated that only twenty Indian children were receiving any instruction and that the clergy, save Leslie, ignored the adult Indians entirely.

Eld found that Emmons was having a hard time finding a guide. He had wanted Laframboise or McKay, since the bare mention of their names would be a kind of passport through hostile Indian country. But neither was available. He thought that mountain men Montero, Boileau, or Aubichon might pilot him, though Sanders and Conner flatly refused. They were willing to guide him east over the Rockies, but wanted no part of the Siskiyou Trail. It was easy for Emmons to learn why: "Almost daily, reports reach camp of the bad character of the Indians. Some said that they had fortified themselves at the different passes, and all generally agreed in pronouncing them determined to put to death all whites who attempted to pass through the country."

Emmons, eager to increase his strength in the face of Indian threats, was not choosey about whom he took along. Thus he added Joe Gale's troublemaker, Henry Wood, as well as Joel Walker and other California immigrants. His next recruit was the watchdog of missionary-farmer Josiah Whitcomb. The latter's ostensible business was teaching agriculture to the Indians, but he freely admitted that he kept his bulldog chained in front of his house to keep the red race at a distance. He agreed to let Emmons hire the dog for $15 but, shortly, became ashamed of his un-Christianlike avarice. He let the animal join the Navy for nothing. Whitcomb's only proviso was that Calvin Tibbetts, put in the dog's charge because he was returning to Oregon, must not leave the beast behind if it developed sore feet on the Siskiyou Trail.

The transfer of the "bull" was a happy arrangement. He had kept the neighborhood in an uproar with his lamentations. The bulldog did not cease its barking, but entered upon his duties with zest, keeping an eye on all strangers about camp. It kept all Indians at a respectable distance and did not hesitate to bite them if they encroached on the camp. Although he called off the dog when it attacked them, Emmons was nervous over the Calapooyas. He was sure that they had no other object than to spy on his camp movements.

While Emmons delayed his departure in hopes of finding a guide, Brackenridge collected seeds. The flowering season was largely past, but he took specimens of the evening primrose, California poppy, monkey flower, and lily of the valley. Emmons had been a close friend of another naturalist, Titian R. Peale. But after a quarrel, they barely spoke. Without naming him, Emmons referred in his diary to the unexpected, hidden character traits of the scientist who had been his messmate for three years. He convinced himself of Peale's dissimulation and added that it only confirmed the predictions of some brother officers. He swore that he would be more cautious, in future, in choosing friends and bestowing confidences. As for Peale, Emmons wrote: "Hereafter, I shall not recognize him as an acquaintance."

Naturally, Peale took offense at being clapped in coventry without a trial. His natural hostility fostered further resentment between Emmons and himself. Thus Emmons later wrote: "An allusion to personal matters, however brief, is unpleasant and would not have found its way into this journal had not the subsequent conduct of this gentlemean, while on the route to California, evinced vindictiveness highly unbecoming an officer and gentleman." Emmons later placed the quarrel before Wilkes, so that his superior would be on guard should Peale's complaints reach the Navy Department because of the artist-naturalist's "presumptions."

Probably, well over half the blame for the ill feeling was Peale's. The forty-two-year-old Philadelphian was high-strung and spoiled. He was "difficult" all of his life. Though a talented draftsman and natural historian, Peale was not brilliant like geologist Dana. He resembled more the botanist, William Rich, and horticulturist, Brackenridge. Though classed as a scientist or naturalist, and paid $2500 a year rather than the $2000 of an artist, Peale was prickly and self-conscious about his limited schooling. Long after the Siskiyou Trail expedition—in May 1845, in fact—Wilkes commented to Senator Benjamin Tappan: "Peale is very proud, as you well know, and is difficult to manage."

The Peale-Emmons quarrel was most unfortunate. It was detrimental to Peale's work on the Siskiyou Trail. And he was no "closet naturalist" or denizen of libraries and laboratories, but a veteran of field work with Stephen Long's Great American Desert expedition (1819–1820) as well as having ranged Spanish Florida in 1818. Moreover, he was the best marksman of the whole Wilkes Expedition, well deserving of the title given him by the Samoans—"Good Shot."

When no pilot arrived by September 7, Emmons decided to march without one. He sent men to search for missing horses, had the tents struck, and the riding and pack horses saddled. He then made a short shakedown cruise of six miles on a southwest compass course. Camp was made near John Turner's place, on a stream at the base of the Yamhills where Joel Walker and other "Californy"-bound Oregonians awaited Emmons.

The forty-year-old Turner, who had complete charge of five hundred Methodist cattle on a five-mile square ranch, was called "the Mission butcher." He supported himself and his Calapooya wife by supplying the settlement with semi-weekly deliveries of beef. Eld was astonished to find that the Turner "farm" consisted of a rude log cabin. It had no bed, no chair, no other furniture—only a few kitchen utensils. Nor were there any cultivated fields. Wrote Eld: "This man lives on the open prairie, upon the meat of the cattle he kills. . . . Has been for 13 years living in the precarious way I have stated. He appears to be a good-hearted, simple fellow and, apparently, lives as happily as he would do in a palace, having not a spark of pride or ambition beyond his present situation."

The kindly Turner had already killed a steer for his visitors. Though a poor man, he supplied them with beef for nothing while the stingy missionaries would not let the Lieutenant have meat for less than six cents a pound. To Colvocoresses, Turner seemed completely content with his life. Tall and robust, he was (to Emmons), "so careless in his dress and tanned by constant exposure in the sun that, at a distance, he might be taken for one of the Kalapuyah tribe, to which he is already allied by marriage." Turner told Emmons a moving account of his early life, full of incidents and narrow escapes. He recounted Jed Smith's Umpqua massacre and his own, later, ambush by the "Rascally" Indians (i.e., Rogues or Rogue Rivers) on the Siskiyou Trail. He had held off a night attack though armed only with a flaming faggot snatched from the campfire. Miss A. J. Allen later wrote: "This young Hercules, like Samson of jawbone memory, seized a large pine knot and [began] making such havoc among the copper-colors that he, at last, succeeding in driving them off."

That night, Baptiste Guardapii (Gardipie) came in, to join up as guide. Emmons now had thirty-nine souls, about twenty-eight capable of bearing arms. The remainder numbered both women and small children. Under him were Eld, Colvocoresses, Assistant Surgeon J. S. Whittle, Peale, Brackenridge, James D. Dana, Rich, and artist Alex Agate. Noncoms were Sergeant Stearns and Corporal Hughes. There were two Marine privates, March and Smith, and two seamen, Doughty and Sutton. Waltham and Mercer were servants. Mountain men besides Guardapii included Baptiste Molair (Molière) and Ignace, an Iroquois hunter known to the Anglos as "Junass." Oregon emigrants included Henry Black, the troublesome Henry Wood, James Warfield, and Calvin Tibbetts. The latter was suffering from a sore throat which had nothing to do with a cold. He had been one of a party spending Sunday at Leslie's place. While the Reverend was droning his sermon, Cal was drowsing on a bench near one wall. Nodding, he had unconsciously thrown back his head. His skull knocked loose the prop supporting a raised window. Down slammed the sash like a guillotine, awakening Tibbetts but almost decapitating him, too.

Joel Walker, whom Emmons confused with his more famous brother, Joe, had his wife, her sister, and his three boys and two girls with him. He had already had an adventurous career. Born in Virginia in 1797, he had been wounded while fighting with Andy Jackson's command at the Battle of Horseshoe Bend, had helped capture British agents Arbuthnot and Armbruster in Florida, and served in the seizure of Pensacola. Burrows had a small family, a wife, an adopted child, and her Indian womanservant. Curiously, a Dutchman with the non-Netherlandish name of Nichols took care of Warfield's wife and child. He may have just come across the plains with the Bidwell-Bartleson party. Walker was the most impressive of these auxiliaries. Wilkes said of him: "He is a good specimen of a border man, and appears to think nothing of a change of domicile although he is much past the middle age."

Emmons had seventy-six animals, forty-four of them the private property of individuals who had to guard them against loss. Unfortunately, the strength of his horses was overrated. Their loads had to be lightened at the very start. Then too, many of the pack saddles were found to be either too small or too large.

The company laid over on September 8 while men searched for missing horses and mules. Emmons used the delay to have some men smoke beef for iron rations. Though he had just hired extra horses, he barely had enough stock to carry everyone and everything. Determined to run a tight ship, Emmons organized a four-man horse guard for both night and day duty.

The inventory count of animals, government and private, gave Colvocoresses time to visit a Calapooya village. He found five families, each with its own fire and tent. All of the Indians were poorly dressed and their homes a-crawl with vermin. A few Calapooyas, snooping about camp, were bitten by the bulldog before it could be collared. Emmons mused: "I am sometimes surprised to see how soon these animals discriminate between the Indians and settlers, when there is frequently not a shade of difference in their color."

When the horse hunters returned empty-handed, the charitable Turner furnished Emmons with two of his own animals, volunteering to run the risk of finding the missing beasts in order to replace his own horses. Just before starting out, Emmons had his men drive the band of horses into a corral for a last count. To his great annoyance, he found that two more animals were missing—one of them his own horse.

Emmons recalled that his saddle horse had been much coveted by a foreigner with the "go-by" of Williams, who had loitered about camp, wishing to join the party. He was sure that the wretch had stolen his animal during the night, perhaps to get even. Emmons was ready to welcome almost any reinforcement, but he did not like the looks of Williams and turned him down. Angered, the fellow had told Black that if he could raise force enough, he would go ahead and cut the party off. And, reported Eld, "after applying some very tender epithets to some of us, regretted that he had not us in his power."

Turner took a description of the missing horses from Emmons, and let the officer select another animal from his *remuda,* or remount herd. Emmons gave him permission to seize the three missing animals, should they turn up, commenting: "Mr. Williams may find himself duped, at last."

For his many kindnesses, Emmons gave the trusty Turner several little presents and promised to return him the best of the horses. He would send them back with Tibbetts. Unwittingly, Emmons then betrayed his uncertainty as to the success of his exploration. He wrote that he would return the animals "should I ever reach California." He began to suspect that other settlers were in cahoots with Williams. He singled out as a likely accomplice none other than Wilkes's old pal George Gay. But, at least, he could write that one man was above suspicion, John Turner.

Bad luck dogged the expedition as it moved out. Emmons's riding horse became spooked. When lassoed for its own good, it was accidentally thrown to the hard ground and lamed. Since the beast was unfit to carry any burden, Emmons had to claim one of the few remaining "private" animals. But at least the false starts were over. The Overland Expedition really got under way with a good day's march on September 9, 1841.

The route lay across three-hundred-foot hills, dotted with white oak groves, and alternating grassy rolling prairies. Several Willamette tributaries were crossed. Emmons saw many "wolves" (doubtless, prairie wolves or coyotes), and he killed one. The air was full of smoke from Indian-set grassfires which shut out any view of the countryside and prevented Emmons from getting an altitude at noon with his instruments. He had to follow a compass course, south-south-west. A few packs got "adrift," but there was no damage to their contents. Yellowjackets stung some of the children, too, but the chief inconvenience was the burnt-over plain. All vegetation, save trees, was destroyed by the fires of the Indians intent on making root digging easier. Yet, somehow, Emmons managed to find patches of grass for the horses and mules.

The travelers camped, after fifteen miles, on Ignace Creek, named for Emmons's chief hunter. The expedition was already shaking down into a pretty shipshape endeavor. But Emmons worried about the horse herd. He had to let the animals loose in order for them to find sufficient grazing. This made it easy for straying—and rustling.

Coyotes, yowling all night, disturbed the lieutenant. But he was pleased, next morning, to find not one animal strayed. His night guard had done its work well. The full count was all the more remarkable when it was found that some horses had eaten their trail ropes off, presumably when the animals were lying down. The men found only short lengths on several of the animals' necks. Yet none had been attacked.

Carefully, Emmons examined the hooves of his horses and had them trimmed for shoes. Like most Oregon horses, his were not shod. He took the precaution because of the hard ground ahead, from summer heat and Indian fires. Already, two animals were so disabled that they could carry nothing. Luckily, he managed to swap one of the cripples (plus a blanket) to an Indian for a fresh horse.

With some officers and men sick, Emmons moved on, past an old Indian burial ground. He saw mounds of earth and heaps of stones on nearby hills, too, and learned that it was the Indian custom for girls arriving at puberty to build these strange monuments.

The company was joined by Boileau, his Chinook wife, and five horses. He had cached some traps in California and McLoughlin was now sending him ahead of Laframboise's Buenaventura Brigade to trap there during the winter. The naval expedition was now at peak strength, forty-one persons and eighty-six animals.

Just as the men started out on September 11, they heard a shot. They looked to their weapons but an Indian came running out of the woods, shouting, *"Markook manich!* Buy a deer!" Eld and the sergeant followed him. They found another Indian literally skinning a deer alive. The animal was still kicking as the butcher went about his flaying. Emmons bought the meat for six loads of powder and ball. His own nimrods were having poor luck, and the party had only two or three days of half-jerked beef, which would not keep.

The Indian hunter showed Eld the tree from behind which he had shot the buck, twenty to twenty-five yards away. This reinforced the opinion of Eld's which led him to write: "I think it is a mistaken idea about Indians being generally good shots. This is seldom the case with those I have come across and I have seen them try their skill often. In shooting game, it is generally by stratagem and slyly sneaking upon their prey. They use often a decoy which is the real head of a deer with the horns standing. This they either attach to their own head in some way or slip it over the head and crawl on their hands and knees, going through sundry antics, bobbing the decoy up and down in such a way as the deer would be supposed to do. In this manner, the unsuspecting animal becomes an easy prey. If they have not a decoy, they steal up on him behind the trees until he is in a few yards and easily killed."

When Joel Walker's wife joined four men on the sick list, Emmons mused about her usefulness in an Indian attack. But the Indian women of his party were making shot pouches, and he knew that, in time of danger, they would use the guns they carried to protect themselves and their children from attack.

At deep but muddy Mouse Creek one of the men told Emmons that he had helped bring a flock of sheep up the Siskiyou Trail from California for the Hudson's Bay Company. In crossing the little steep-sided stream, he and his fellow-sheepherders had lost several hundred woolies. The stupid sheep in the rear had run across the backs of the animals spanning the stream. The lead animals had thus been beaten down by the others and drowned.

Near Mouse Creek, Emmons had a minor accident of his own. He fired at a coyote which was trailing his rearguard. His saddle horse was unaccustomed to rifles going off in its ear. The beast reared and spun around until the officer was dizzy; but he stayed topside, avoiding a nasty fall. The coyote got away.

Smoke limited vision to two miles on Long Prairie and Marsh's Creek. The men skirted Lake La Mali or Guardapii Lake, a bizarre *laguna* only four feet deep and eighty across but three-quarters of a mile long. In the afternoon, the La Mali or Lumtumbuff (Long Tom) River itself was encountered, a roily but deep branch of the Willamette, fordable only at a few points. In places, it looked like a necklace of lakelets. Several pack animals bolted and rushed down its banks to drink. The regular crossing was impossible but, by trial and error, Emmons found one and got across, though some packs were wetted and he was, himself, thoroughly baptized. Brackenridge was grumpy that evening, after botanizing, but not because of his own immersion. He complained: "The Rascally Indians, by setting fire to the prairie, have deprived us of many fine plants."

Emmons always tried to put the barrier of a stream between his animals and home. They always drifted north, while grazing, so it was easier to round them up if he camped on a southside bank. Settled down on the Lumtumbuff, he figured he had made twenty miles that day. Eld put it at seventeen. Smoke and fog made celestial sightings impossible.

Just after dark, the hunters shot at three deer, but only one animal was brought in, by crackshot Peale. And even Peale had to wait for daylight to find the carcass. A dense fog so blinded the nighthawks that twenty-one horses were missing at dawn. Emmons sent out men in all directions and personally joined the search. All were found, but the chase was difficult since the animals were not yet fatigued enough to be easily captured. On the other hand, some were already developing sore backs, and the sandy, shingled soil was proving hard on their feet.

Again, next morning, many animals were missing, but they were located back up the trail at a marsh where they had watered. Only a little progress could be made after a late start. When Emmons reached the old campground on the Lumtumbuff's headwaters, near an Indian dam or weir, he called it a day. He had made no more than two miles but the Calapooya Hills provided fine grass, for a change. And the sky, for once, was clear enough for observations with the instruments.

Some Calapooyas drifted into camp after being verified as friendlies by Guardapii. Colvocoresses observed that some wore deerskins, and others affected cast-off white man's clothing. All preferred fox fur caps. As arms, they carried bows and arrows, the latter bone-tipped and stowed in sealskin quivers.

Again on the fourteenth, there was a late start because of scattered horses. Emmons had to relieve one animal of its pack because it could barely carry its own carcass. After ten miles of hills, he camped in a grassy prairie where Colvocoresses tried his hand at collecting specimens. That night, a different specimen blundered into camp—a grizzly. *Ursus horribilis* escaped after throwing a scare into the men.

New Indians who came to visit were friends of Mrs. Warfield, and one had worked for the Honourable Company. Emmons broke his cardinal rule and let them stay overnight. They were dirty and poorly clad in buckskins and remnants of Company dress. Some were hardly clothed at all. Most carried bows and arrows, but a few had fine rifles. The women toted baskets of seeds and *camas* roots. Ever the jolly tar, Emmons could not resist noting (even in an official journal) that he had "observed among them a very pretty squaw."

Alexander Agate sketched one old man who agreed to pose for him, motionless as a stump. Some Indians would pose—others would flee the artist's pencil as if Agate were a witch doctor who could seize their souls on paper. Eld was pleased and surprised by the Calapooyas' generosity and good manners: They vied with one another in sharing provisions and entertaining each other. He thought them to be poor, miserable, and degraded but simple-hearted and honest folk.

Sultry, smoky weather followed the company southward. As the day wore on, the air fanning past the men came to resemble the draft of an oven. Still, Emmons was pleased. The combination of hobbling and good grass had kept the herd together all night, insuring an early start and a good day's run. Alas, he congratulated himself too soon. His horse became mired in a slough. In extricating itself, the beast tossed its rider. Luckily, the bank was soft and Emmons unhurt. But again there was delay as pack animals became stuck in the mire and had to be towed out by horsemen wielding lariats.

Shortly, Emmons used the first—and only—improvements engineered on the Siskiyou Trail. He crossed two streams on rough bridges built by Hudson's Bay Company men to facilitate the trailing of sheep. One was Rivière du Pont (Bridge River), the other a fork of the Lumtumbuff. From the crude spans, Emmons headed for Elk Mountain, the divide between the Willamette and Umpqua drainages. Beyond a mixed forest of pines, oaks, and spruce at the foot of the mountain, he could see ridges covered with shrubbery. Only the high peaks were rocky and bare of the chinquapin, or dwarf chestnut, and the Ceanothus. He called the latter "redroot," but the shrub with the white or lavender-lilac blooms is the wild lilac or mountain lilac to most travelers.

Colvocoresses guessed that some of the pines were two hundred feet tall. These were lofty ponderosas, sugar pines, or possibly Douglas firs. Emmons measured boles four feet in diameter.

By using the tops of mountainous spurs, Emmons put together a circuitous route which paid off with only gradual rises and declines. However, deadfalls and trees overhanging the trail brushed men from their saddles. None was seriously hurt, though some were knocked silly, for the moment.

Encamped at the very foot of Elk Mountain, Emmons estimated its height at 1600 feet. Feed was poor but a natural corral bounded the herd nicely, with the aid of Tibbetts Creek. There would be no straying of horses that night. Hunters shot a deer but could not get it to camp in the haze and darkness. They marked its location with a white rag tied to a bush. The flopping cloth served not only as a marker for retrieval but as a "scarecrow" of sorts to keep predators from the carcass.

Two Indians who paid a call were on their way to Fort Umpqua with beaver. Emmons again relaxed his guard enough to feed them and let them stay the night. But ignorance of each other's tongues prevented their passing any real trail information on to him. For the first time, there was a hard frost that night. Water froze in containers. The whites bundled up in extra clothing but the natives paid no mind to the chill.

On September 16, the expeditionaries reached Elk River, an

affluent of the Umpqua about half the size of the Willamette. Wapiti or elk congregated along its banks. Hardly were the tent pegs driven home before hunters were bringing elk and deer meat into camp for the messes. They reported the countryside thick with beaver and bear, too. Eld found the elk meat to be good eating. He was impressed, too, with the size of the beasts. Hunters brought in an animal (minus head and horns) which he judged to be bigger than a horse.

A twelve-mile trail to Fort Umpqua diverged at Elk River from the Siskiyou Trail. Emmons wanted to visit the outpost as part of his exploration and mapping, but also to try to trade horses. He packed his four weakest animals with dried peas, spare packs, and equipment of little use. If he could not swap the little packstring for fresh stock, he was afraid he would have to cover the lower Siskiyou Trail via shank's mare. Leaving Eld in command of the camp, he took Agate, Stearns, and Doughty, with Boileau as guide.

Brackenridge and Rich took advantage of the halt to botanize. They discovered a new oak, among other species. Some men jerked meat over a slow fire. Eld had others run rifle balls in their bullet molds, to make up cartridges. He was able to serve out fifty rounds per man. Eld could see little of his surroundings for the smoke, but managed to shoot the sun at meridian to get the latitude. When the sun could be seen at all, it was of a dense blood-red color and the size of a doubloon. Eld recorded: "Terrestrial objects are literally shrouded in darkness [by day]; the horses cannot be seen and stray away in spite of every precaution."

Calapooyas who drifted into camp frightened some of the Oregonians attached to Emmons' party. They spread the word that the Indians beyond the Umpqua were planning to kill them. The ambushers were angry at the whites for spreading smallpox among them. Emmons's order prohibiting the firing of weapons around camp was enforced by Eld and incurred the enmity of Guardapii. Others were surly and grumbling; it was not a happy camp. Eld was sure that the reason for the discontent was not Navy discipline but fear: "The truth is they are afraid to encounter the Indians and are making every endeavor to retard the party until Michell [Laframboise], the person who headed the Company's party, shall overtake us."

After 21 miles of the most craggy, up-and-down mountain travel of his life, Emmons reached the Umpqua. He had crossed Elk River several times en route. He did not dare swim the Umpqua in the dark. There were no canoes, and Fort Umpqua lay hidden in fog pressing down to the opposite shore. But Emmons could see lights, dimly, and hear the baying of dogs, though the sound was muffled and made eerie by the thick mist. He hobbled the horses to graze, then fired a signal shot. It was answered by a "shriek" from the opposite shore. His second gunshot only seemed to add to the excitement at the fort. Frequent hails received no answer until Boileau's voice was recognized. Then the fort's manager, Jean Baptiste Gagnier, sent two canoes to ferry his visitors over. Each man carried his saddle, bridle, blanket, and firearms, hoping that lurking Indians would leave the horses alone.

The Lieutenant found Fort Umpqua to be a picketed miniature Fort Vancouver, measuring 200 by 150 feet. It squatted solidly in an opening 150 yards back from the river. On his way to it, Emmons noted Indians dodging furtively into the brush. He found Gagnier nervous as a cat, almost trembling with fear that the Indians would attack. He had mustered his tiny force of five men, two women, and nine dogs, determined to sell his life dearly. He had no cannon and no arms other than hunting rifles. Gagnier had thought that the dreaded hour was at hand when he heard the commotion across the Umpqua.

The factor told Emmons that there was an unusually large number of Indians about—also that some had threatened to storm the outpost. The Umpquas were angered by the spread of malaria and smallpox by Laframboise's brigades and by the Company's unwillingness to sell them powder and ball, which (said Emmons) "they [Company officials] had every reason to expect would soon be used against them."

The terrified, sleepless, Gagnier had not dared show himself outside the stockade gate, for days. He was keeping a vigilant watch, night and day, and on the point of sending a messenger to Fort Vancouver for help.

As an Indian woman prepared tea (the factor's wife was unwell), the alarmed—almost panicky—Gagnier filled Emmons in on the true character of the Umpquas. Several times he repeated *"Terribles mauvais sauvages!"* as the Lieutenant took a cup of bad tea sweetened with dirty sugar. But the hungry sailor appreciated the coarse, wholesome bread offered him, though the butter on it was dirtier than the sugar.

Gagnier had heard of Emmons's coming from the Indians. The news was that the Umpquas, Rogues, and Shastas were collecting together to oppose the passage of the naval party. The Siskiyou Trail was closed. They had sworn vengeance against all white travelers. Gagnier pointed out that, as an earnest of their intentions, the savages had killed two halfbreed boys living peacefully among them. They had murdered the pair because of their mixed blood and their friendship with whites while working for the Company—most of all, however, because the youths had been raised by terrible Tom McKay.

Gagnier tried to dissuade Emmons from proceeding any further south. He insisted that the party was too small to face the Indians in combat. They were "a brave race." He feared that Emmons and all of his party would be killed. He offered to bet that already the Umpquas were gathered in ambush at the Umpqua River crossing of the Siskiyou Trail. When Emmons refused to turn back, Gagnier persuaded him to shift to an alternate ford ten miles above the usual Trail crossing. The factor urged him to never permit an Indian to enter his camp, for any reason. There were many spies about. Under their seemingly friendly intentions, they sought only the destruction of the whites.

Because of bad weather, Emmons could not take observations in order to fix the location of Fort Umpqua, but Gagnier told him it lay thirty miles from the river's mouth. The Umpqua was navigable by small craft all the way to its junction with Elk River, three miles from the fort. Emmons estimated the outpost lay in 43° 23′.

Emmons feared that the Indians could wipe out the little bastion, should they dare to rush it. But he doubted that they would ever make the assault. They were in habitual dread of the Company, represented by the White Headed Eagle, Dr. McLoughlin. Also, they were completely dependent on Fort Vancouver for arms and ammunition, as well as clothing and tobacco.

Emmons found little in the storehouse but beaver, otter, bear, and deerskins. The plews were testimonials to the Company's scorched earth policy. Many pelts were small, from cubs which normally would have been allowed to grow to adulthood. He remarked to himself that the Company was not very scrupulous in contested Oregon, which he patriotically called "our portion of the country."

Though Emmons presented a letter from the doctor, Gagnier had only two horses he could spare. Emmons leaped at his offer, chosing a big, black horse which was a favorite of the factor's. The latter gave it to him without asking any further remuneration than for the other animal. He gave him bearskins for sleeping robes and deerskins to replace buckskin shirts and trousers already wearing out because of the hard going of the Siskiyou Trail.

That night, Gagnier made beds of blankets for Emmons and his companions on the storeroom floor. Then the trader locked them in!

He took the key with him and locked himself in the adjacent building, where his living quarters were located. There was no doubt in Emmons's mind that Monsieur Gagnier was in fear of his life.

Next morning, the trader let his guests out at daylight. Emmons found a thick fog smothering the fort. But he was happy to be able to put some distance between himself and the fierce fleas of Gagnier's storehouse. After breakfast, Agate sketched some of the Indians who did not vanish into the underbrush.

Emmons escorted Gagnier's wife and her Indian womanservant back to his camp. Madame Gagnier wished to consult Dr. Whittle on some ailment or other. The Lieutenant found his men unsettled by all the scary rumors of war. He took great pains to dispel the apprehensions of the "breeds" and Canadians. He was only partially successful. Boileau was so worked up that he decided to leave his wife in the security (!) of Fort Umpqua. She would accompany Madame Gagnier back and stay put until Laframboise should arrive. Michel knew the trail and the Indians well, had better riding horses, was less burdened with pack animals, and had fifty to sixty mountain men. Laframboise expected to make much faster time than Emmons and the latter recalled: "Michel had, several times, told me that he would overtake me before I reached the Umpqua Mountains."

Emmons was distressed by the relaxed vigilance of his main camp in his absence, despite the Indian scare. This, plus continuing illness and thick atmosphere, resulted in his band of horses scattered all over creation. His planned getaway was delayed from dawn to 10 A.M. by the old story of missing stock. Progress was through fog- and smoke-shrouded country ridged with pine and spruce and flanked with oaks, hazel, Ceanothus (with sky-blue flowers), and arbutus or madrone, its warm-colored bark peeling as if sunburnt. The steeper country then gave way to flats occupied by clumps of dogwood and ash. It was cool enough for peajackets in the evening, but the travelers, at midday, would have been comfortable marching in the raw.

At noon, Emmons was slowed down by a message from the rear. Marine Corporal Hughes was so sick with malaria that he could not sit his horse. Surgeon Whittle halted with him. Emmons could not camp immediately because there was no water and the Indians had fired the grass along the trace that very morning. He was now sure that they were kindling these fires to harass him. It became difficult to urge the horses forward now, because raging brushfires, feeding billowing clouds of smoke, lay dead ahead. The fire was not moving fast, just creeping along ahead of a light wind. Once or twice, the trail led smack through a smouldering or even flaming swath. But, luckily, the grass was sparse and no animals were burned or otherwise injured. Deciding to push on to find an adequate campground, Emmons detached Colvocoresses and some men to protect doctor and patient.

Just before reaching a pretty camping spot, four deer trotted across the trail. They were greeted by a barrage of fire but all escaped, as Emmons shook his head at his hunters' "skill." The tents were raised under shady oak trees on Billy Creek, named for a Company trapper bitten to death there by a "white bear," or grizzly. Eld thought it the best campsite yet selected. It afforded excellent pasturage and water, and a kind of natural corral for the stock. Colvocoresses brought up the sick detachment and Emmons set a strict guard over horses, mules, and camp.

At this point, Guardapii told Emmons that he wished to return to the Willamette. His main reason was solicitude for his little boy, due to come down the Siskiyou Trail with Michel. The guide had been dejected all day by tales of Indian treachery. Emmons needed him badly and feared that, if Guardapii left, the other *canadiens* would follow. So he took great pains to dissuade him. He was greatly relieved when he finally won him over.

Eld sensed a change in the camp's atmosphere once the pilot decided to stick with Emmons. The discontent among the woodsmen subsided. Emmons knew that Guardapii was not faking his deep affection for his child to cover fear. He had heard him say with the utmost sincerity and fervor of feeling that he prayed that God would protect his child. This emotion was common among "the French," and Emmons respected it. Still, prudishly, he had to note his surprise at such strong parental affection and sniff (like the good New Englander he was) that the children, in most cases, were "the pledges of an unlawful union."

Winds swept clean the atmosphere on the nineteenth. An alert night watch guaranteed an early start but new trouble arose when Burrows and his woman took fright and hung back, half resolved to return to Fort Vancouver. Eventually, like Guardapii, Burrows succumbed to Emmons's powers of persuasion and caught up with the party again.

Emmons branched off from the traveled trail to intercept the Umpqua's north fork, following Gagnier's advice and determined to avoid any collision with Indians. His party was not strong and, anyway, he had his orders: "You will use your best endeavors, wherever you may go, to leave behind you a favorable impression of your country and countrymen." Should his disaffected Canadians pull out, the Government's transit of the Siskiyou Trail would have to be aborted. Once he could put the Umpqua behind him, he would feel better: "Having once passed this barrier and entered the domains of the hostile Indians, they would not, for their own safety, dare [to] separate from the party."

The north fork was low, barely two feet deep but rushing fast over a slippery, cobbly bed. Brackenridge estimated it as ninety yards wide. Finding the boulders so slick, Emmons had the trail ropes of his animals "cast adrift." He had his men take the packhorses in tow. They crossed diagonally, headed upstream, so that the current should not sweep them too far, and they carefully skirted the potholes in the river bed. A few beasts slipped, lost their footing, and were carried downstream. But Emmons's precautions prevailed. Skillfully, they were roped by horsemen stationed at the ford. Aside from "sundry duckings," the floundering animals made it across without accident. Only a few packs were even wet through. And with relief Brackenridge noted: "We anticipated opposition from the Umpqua Indians in crossing, but none of them showed their faces till we all got safe over and encamped."

Because of wet packs and fatigued horses and men, and the illness of some—including himself—Emmons decided to camp right on the south bank. He chose a shady grove, and, after his horses had enjoyed a good graze, he had them staked out for greater security.

Shortly, an Indian signaled his desire to cross the river to camp. Since his language was unintelligible, Emmons doubted that he could learn anything from him. Anyway, it was imprudent to allow Indians into camp, spies or not. So, by shouts and signs, he indicated his refusal of admittance.

Colvocoresses was not as suspicious of the natives as his superior. He sized them up as friendly, trying to warn the whites of dangers ahead. Certainly, the tribesmen did not look dangerous. One large party was composed entirely of root-digging women. All were old— passé to Colvocoresses—and extremely ugly. One hag reminded him of Juvenal and he unkindly quoted in his journal:

> "Such wrinkles see
>   As in an Indian forest's solitude
>   Some old ape scrubs amidst her numerous brood."

Since this was now enemy territory, Emmons wrote out regulations for the security of the party. The one major rule was that no Indians be allowed into camp. But he did not forbid communication with them. While Agate took his turn with the malarial shaking and freezing, Emmons sent out hunters. He had other men arrange tents and baggage into defensive positions. To make sure that everything was shipshape, Emmons took the first watch that night. He informed his officers that such would be his custom in subsequent camps.

The weather cleared and the sun came out for the first time in days. Midday heat became oppressive to those suffering from ague and fever. But the well and the half-well enjoyed a spirited hunt on that day's march. A large grizzly was mistaken, at a distance, for a pack-horse because it "trotted" along toward the party without deviating either to left or right. The men only discovered the bruin's true identity—and temper!—when it reared up on its hind legs to accost them. Peale put a rifle ball in the monster's lungs. The "white bear" bounded away, with Emmons and two other horsemen in pursuit. Though several more slugs struck home, the animal did not fall—in fact, the horses faded. When they were reduced to a tired walk, Emmons gave orders to give up the chase. He did so just as a couple of trappers were shaking out lassos in hopes of roping the beast, California-fashion.

Like Meriwether Lewis thirty-six years before, Emmons marveled at the tenacity with which *Ursus ferox* clung to life. The grizzlies were, indeed, "strong in death," as he put it. The mountain men confirmed that "grisly" bears, when closely pursued, usually turned and became the attackers. Hunters put balls into grizzlies every day but brought down few of them. This led Emmons to write: "Among all the animals I have ever seen I do not think that I have ever witnessed so formidable an enemy." He regretted that he did not have time to take and cure a bearskin for the National Museum, which he was sure would soon be built in Washington. (James Smithson had already left his money to the United States for a national museum —today's Smithsonian Institution—but it had not yet been received by the government when Wilkes sailed in 1838, with Emmons et al.) The Siskiyou Trail grizzlies far exceeded in size any specimens which Emmons had seen in museums.

The south fork of the Umpqua was neither broad nor deep, but rapid flowing. It was easily fordable on a rocky bottom between ten-to-fifteen-foot-high cliffbanks. Emmons followed it through rolling country and excellent bottomland, with scattered pines and oaks.

The only harsh note was the blackened aspect of the earth, fired by Indians.

Emmons had to make Hobson's choice. He let his animals graze freely (in order not to starve), knowing they could easily be run off by Indian rustlers. But, should he pen, hobble, or stake them for safety, they would grow thin and feeble from lack of grass. They would then let him down just when he needed them most, to cross over the Siskiyou and Shasta mountains into the Sacramento Valley.

Friendly Indians again warned of hostile parties gathering ahead. But some said they were planning to attack Laframboise, not Emmons. The latter would not allow himself to be lulled into a false security by such poppycock, of course. One informant was an old dame whom Gagnier had described as friendly. She begged for powder charges. Emmons would not give her any but tried to maintain the peace by bestowing brass rings on her.

In spite of the continued warnings, Emmons was astonished to find discipline sagging. He had to send two men to look for a missing packhorse. Eld, in charge of the night watch, next reported neglect of duty by one of the men.

That night, while his men tried to sleep through the din of bawling coyotes, Emmons spent part of his watch writing: "Here is one of the prettiest rivers we have seen in the country. From a nearby perpendicular height of a couple of hundred feet, you look down upon the limpid Umpqua winding its way gracefully among the mountains in death-like silence. Not a living thing to animate the beautiful scene; not even a canoe is skimming on its waters. The inhabitants, the few remaining, are scattered in the dells and glens lying in wait and meditating deep and dark vengeance against the white men who, by disease, have depopulated the country and who they wish to make accountable for the crimes."

How these worries must have pressed on Eld's mind the next day. Alone, he became lost while sketching. As he tried to quell the panic in his chest, which sent him hurrying forward in hopes of finding either comrades or trail, he stumbled into a party of Indians. By signs and gutturals, they demanded to know what he wanted. He tried to explain in gestures that he was only passing through their country. Eld's sign language was intelligible to them, and the Indians motioned him in a direction which they suggested his friends had taken. But they gestured toward the *north*—the one direction in which they could not have gone. So, boldly, Eld rode right through them on a rough southwest course. After eight miles, he struck the Siskiyou Trail again and almost went limp with relief. Shortly, he felt so much easier that he took a shot at a coyote—and his heart sank, for his rifle, the weapon on which his life had depended only a short time before, misfired! The percussion cap snapped, but the weapon did not discharge. Quickly, he reloaded his piece before rejoining his comrades.

After the company passed an Indian graveyard surrounded by poles hung with mats, blankets and bows and arrows of the entombed, a halt was made for the eighteenth encampment. The southerly main fork was now only fifteen feet wide; they were nearing its headwaters in the Umpqua Mountains. Once more, Emmons damned the natives for burning off the summer-parched grass (perfect hay for his failing animals); but now he decided that he would, henceforth, camp between established sites, hoping to find more feed. On this occasion, however, he had to squat in the ashes, as it were. For the trail crossed the Umpqua Mountains abruptly and did not reach water (and a possible camp) until it entered the valley on the far side of the range.

Parties of Indians who passed Emmons all vehemently declared themselves to be friends. But he politely refused all requests for powder and ball. He and four others were ill with malaria and the odds too great, already, to risk handing out ammunition to possible enemies.

Peale was distracted from the danger by a herd of wapiti neighing nearby. The "whistling" of bull elk could be heard a good quarter-mile away. From 140 yards, he brought down two does and a buck. Even though the male was lung-shot and wounded in the heart, it refused to die. Instead, the bull lumbered into a charge. The bloodied beast circled the tree behind which the hunter hid and plunged its antlers at him. Before he could be forked into the air, Peale dashed for better cover. The elk chased him down a hill but collapsed and crashed to the ground, finally dead, before it could overtake the artist. Peale measured the neck of the elk and found it to be five feet around. Each horn was four feet, four inches long. Its body size was that of a full-grown horse.

After his strenuous chase, in which the roles of hunter and hunted had been so startlingly—frighteningly—reversed, Peale was disappointed to find the elk meat too rank to eat. He contented himself with the tongue and marrow bones. Luckily, the trusty Iroquois Ignace shot a white-tailed deer and supplied the camp with tasty venison.

The picture of his downhill dash remained long in Peale's mind. He later recalled the bellicose elk: "A deliberately aimed rifle ball I thought would be sufficient to settle matters, but it seemed as though it had produced no effect other than to make him rush on so quick as to get between me and the trees."

That evening, the camp crackled with the electricity of suspense and apprehension. Colvocoresses recalled: "We expected an attack during the night from the hostile tribes, and had prepared to give them a warm reception, but none came."

As he broke camp early next morning, Emmons noted an Indian man and woman watching the company's movements. While his men and animals fell into a single file almost a mile long, to ascend the mountain, he rode with Guardapii to the hill where the pair stood. The guide's fluent Chinook patois was lost on them, nor could he pick up what they tried to say. Shortly, Emmons met four or five young Indian men, carrying bows and arrows. Curiously, they were led by an old woman. Somehow, they were able to communicate better with the whites. They said they were friendly with the men of pale visage but that other Indians hated whites. These hostiles had recently killed some of their own tribe, they said. Then, to Emmons's amazement, the supposedly stoical warriors began to sob in grief. He half suspected that they were dissimulating but could not be sure. Probably, their dolorous wailing was meant to win sympathy—and powder and ball. Sure enough, they stifled their lamentations shortly and begged for ammunition. Emmons refused them, albeit politely. Nor would he let them in his camp. When they asked pointed questions about Laframboise's whereabouts, he felt uneasy about Michel. He predicted trouble for the booshway: "If he is not strong in numbers, I shall not be surprised to learn that he has been attacked by the Umpquas, particularly if he takes the lower crossing."

The climb into the mountains proved difficult. Several pack animals rolled over and over for a hundred feet down a steep slope. After watching one dramatic fall, Eld wrote in amazement: "I at first thought we should be obliged to kill him and leave his load behind. But, on loosening his packs, found that he was not very much hurt and, after a while, he mustered strength enough to clamber up the hill again and we put his packs on."

Emmons rested his animals before assaulting the upper "Umpqua ridge of mountains," which looked more formidable to him than reports he had had. He found that the rugged, abrupt inclines made it necessary to halt the animals for a blow every few minutes. Some beasts fell and a few turned complete backward somersaults; packs were torn off some animals. To make matters worse, the Indians had fired the mountain—"doubtless to obstruct us," griped Emmons—and great trees had crashed across the path. Many times, men and animals could not go around, and axes had to be used to cut through the blackened, fire-hardened trunks as Navy cutlasses did machete duty in lopping off limbs. Emmons observed how "artfully tied together" were the tangled boughs which trapped his men or swept riders from their seats. Hacking through crosstimbers and brush, the men gained the summit, a forest of spruce and sugar pines towering over a thick undergrowth of madrone.

The travelers cut their way down a steep descent, transferring some packs to stronger animals. He also asked all of his men (except the ill) to dismount, to spare the horses. To the Lieutenant's disgust, the air was not even clear on the mountaintops. He could see nothing at a distance and grumbled: "As long as it continues in its present state, I feel that I am groping my way along, half-blindfolded, and consequently learning but little about the country beyond my reach."

That day, there were several close calls. Emmons, while in advance of the others, was caught in an Indian snare and swept off his horse. Luckily, he was unhurt. Nor was the man injured who, foolishly, tugged at his gun, caught in the brush, until the piece discharged. But it was a near miss. Next, a man returned to Peale one of his boots, found back along the trail. Only then did the artist-naturalist learn that his carpet bag had been torn from its moorings on a packhorse. It contained not only his bedding and wardrobe, but his journal, drawing instruments, paint box, sketchbook, and *camera lucida* (a device of lenses which threw an image of a mountain, an Indian, whatever, on a sheet of paper; then the picture could be drawn— really, traced—with great accuracy).

A lovely valley at the foot of the mountains was pocked with the tracks of wild cattle. A corral, or cowpen, was there, thrown up by Indians to trap the critters. Emmons guessed that they were escapees from Siskiyou Trail herds and their progeny. To his regret, his hunters had absolutely no luck in bagging beef; the wild cattle were wily beasts.

As soon as the tents were pitched, Emmons sent the animals to feed under a strong guard at the mountain's base. At sunset, he had them brought back. All unruly animals were hobbled for the night. He was about to send packing an Indian seen hanging around camp when Warfield recognized him as one of Laframboise's old trappers. He departed at sunset, promising to return next day with his horse, to accompany Emmons. But he did not show up, and the Lieutenant, his mind still full of Gagnier's warnings, immediately put him down as a spy.

Several horses were limping now with sore feet, so Emmons had them shod. His hunters were successful in shooting elk but the meat was stringy and unpalatable. Emmons could not bring himself to add more weight to the packs of the staggering beasts, so he did not tote the skins and antlers of the elk. Afterwards, he regretted that so noble an animal had been destroyed by his men. As predicted by several of the hunters, the Umpqua Mountains marked the southern limit of the white-tailed deer's range. From here on, they were replaced with black-tail and *chivereau* or mule deer.

Emmons lessened the loads of the pack animals by breaking up his casks of tallow or lard. He put the "grease" in light *parfleches* or skin bags. To insure an early start, because the animals tired so early in the day, he had his men cook breakfast the night before. But he was still delayed by Indian arson and the resultant scarcity of feed. His horses wandered all over. When he took special precautions, they sometimes backfired. Thus, when he hobbled his own horse one night, it cut itself badly with its new shoes. He had to set it loose in the herd of limping, sore-backed animals.

His men were as black as Africans from the incessant ashes and smoke of the trail and all of them were tired out. Emmons could not help feeling sorry for himself. He wrote: "Distance today 15 miles, but 50 on the plains would be shorter."

That night, the Lieutenant was awakened by a loud "Ho-ho!" He peered out from the tent flap and found that a horse had become entangled in the stretchers or tent ropes of the adjoining shelter. In its attempts to break loose, the brute had pulled the whole canvas tent down upon its occupants. The Marines inside were too sick or tired to even try to get out.

Corporal Hughes was so weak, in fact, that he fell off his horse several times. Emmons found that the Marine's senses were impaired by his continuing bout with malaria. With Hughes out of his head and Peale beside himself because of the lost equipment, Emmons threw up his hands and acceded to the request of his estranged friend for a layover. He gave Peale permission to retrace his steps in search of his lost articles. But he took the precaution of sending two armed guards with him.

Peale, with Wood and Black, found his "camera" but nothing else, other than Indians lurking in the woods and apparently trailing the company! He took them to be Rascals—that is, Rogue Rivers—

and alarmed some of them by searching the baskets and quivers of those who did not flee. But he did not find his goods concealed there.

It was with difficulty that Emmons prevented his racist dog from biting the Indians who passed him on the Siskiyou Trail. Although the redmen were well armed with bows and flint-tipped arrows, they appeared more frightened than warlike when they came upon the camp of the whites. Emmons let them pass. When he tried to question them, they pointed to their ears and shook their heads to signify that the English, French, Spanish, and Chinook meant absolutely nothing to them.

The Rogues looked little different from Umpquas or Calapooyas, though they were lightly tattooed on their arms and bodies. Always assuming the worst, Emmons sized them up as spies and couriers on their way south to warn the tribes of the coming of the whitefaces. He gave them all a hard, long look and confided to his journal: "I shall recognize them if I see them again."

Lieutenant Emmons got his latitude by both sun and stars that day, the readings agreeing. His pleasure at this result was dampened somewhat when Peale reported Wood for some neglect of duty. Since the latter was a worthless lout, and he had taken him along mainly in order to have the use of his pack animals, Emmons gave him his discharge on the spot. But he allowed him to continue to accompany the party. To have actually separated him, forcibly, in such hostile country would have been tantamount to signing his death warrant.

Colvocoresses, Rich, and others were on the sick list. But Agate and Emmons himself were improving in health, so matters balanced out. The march was resumed over a rolling prairie with rounded hills dressed with sugar pines, spruce, longleaf pines, cedar, and madrone. When another Navy packhorse broke down, it was replaced with one of Nichols's horses.

Fresh tracks were common, but the only redmen seen were skulking in the thick, concealing underbrush. Only three women were caught out in the open. All the men felt unseen eyes on them; it made their skin crawl. Colvocoresses was sure-for-certain that warriors were not only spying on him but also waiting for the opportunity to fall on him and his associates. Brackenridge, too, noted: "Observed several Indians lurking behind trees. Was ready to pay these rogues in round numbers, had they made themselves troublesome." Eld also encountered hidden Indians.

After working up a bad slope, the men in the van heard a rustling in the brush ahead. They approached a clump of undergrowth gingerly, rifles at the ready. They found nothing. But when Brackenridge fired at a "coyote" it turned out to be a half-starved Indian dog. In so doing, he accidently flushed a group of Indians, who left behind four agitated women and some dogs. Emmons let the "fair dames" and their verminous pets go their way in peace. Though Peale and others heard Indians calling from height to height in what seemed like preparations for an attack, Emmons wrote: "Notwithstanding all these symptoms, I did not yet feel authorized to commence offensive operations."

Peale refused to let his nervousness inhibit his scientific researches. He found that the Rogues eschewed established villages. They roamed from temporary camps of grass shacks, thatched on four-foot-high hoops which allowed perhaps five persons to huddle inside, whether prostrate or in a sitting position.

Further along, more Indians on hilltops hailed the whites. More than ever, Emmons was convinced that they meant to get into a row with him. It was imprudent to separate his sick into a second, slower-moving party any longer. So he halted his entire force, to enable the chills of Rich and March to wear off. Once the men were no longer incapacitated for riding, he closed ranks and moved his party off in a tighter formation.

A new anxiety was added to the load of worries which Emmons bore. He noticed that when he halted for nooning, the transport animals were so tired that they had to lie down, packs and all. And it was with difficulty that they could be coaxed back on their feet again.

On the other hand, most of the men were in good shape, barring those who had malaria. Peale took advantage of the break to do some birdwatching. He sighted a number of Lewis's partridges (grouse?), larks, goldenwing woodpeckers, ravens and crows, Steller and other jays, and huge California "vultures." He probably meant California condors, since he later listed turkey vultures and California's "buzzards" separately. Emmons was not as cool as Peale. When an Indian man and boy appeared with a few items to sell, he jumped again to the conclusion that their real intent was espionage. Before they could count his numbers or armaments (should they have wished to do so), he ordered his bewildered visitors away.

That evening, when he set up camp at (Ewing) Young's Creek, Emmons made ready for the Indian attack which he felt, in his bones, was sure to come. But Peale ignored the danger and examined mussel and snail shells in an old Indian camp, tasted the manna of sugar pines, and measured "large hares" or jackrabbits.

Indians scuttled about during the evening, "telegraphing" each other with signal lights which suddenly flared, then winked out. An Indian (a spy?) left behind a bag of cooked roots dangerously close to the perimeter of the camp. There was no attack, but even Peale finally began to appreciate the magnitude of the danger. He blamed it on his ex-friend, Emmons, and his lack of security measures: "Being imprudently encamped on the banks of the creek, the Indians last night approached within a few yards of our tents under cover of the bushes."

Ascending and descending burnt hills and dales interspersed with sugar-pine forests, Emmons saw fresh Indian signs everywhere. He also encountered another ambush site in the undulating country. But all of his men were on the qui vive as they dropped past "Joe's River" (Jump-off Joe Creek?) to reach the trough in the mountains carrying the clear, beautiful "Tootootunas" or Rogue River. Emmons estimated its size to equal the Willamette's at Jason Lee's mission. He forded the ninety yards of water and gravel without accident, the water coming only within two feet of the animals' backbones in midstream.

On the far side, Emmons set up camp, again "placing something of a barrier between us and our red friends in the rear." He now kept his hunters out in front as skirmishers, so he felt fairly secure. They wounded black-tail deer and antelope, but reported no Indians about. Once camped, Colvocoresses scrounged some of the crystallized sap of the Lambert pine which the trappers used in lieu of sugar on the Siskiyou Trail. It was slightly bitter. It was also cathartic. He noticed that the Indians collected it in a manner similar to that by which Vermonters took maple syrup. They wounded the trees by burning holes in their trunks. From these hurts oozed great quantities of the pitchy sweet. Peale labeled the resin-sugar "manna," but he, too, found it to be a purgative. He measured the sugar-pine cones and found them to be more than fifteen inches long. He noted that large, ground-dwelling gray squirrels fed on them. Eld was also curious about the Lambert pines. The sugary sap gave him both diarrhea and a three-hour stomachache. But he did not stay sick all day, and he, too, collected sugar-pine "buds" (cones) fifteen and sixteen inches long.

Just as tents were being pitched on the Rogue River's bank, probably at the later site of Evans' Ferry or, perhaps, Vannoy's (Fort Vannoy) Crossing, three miles west of modern Grant's Pass, two Indians got into camp. Emmons was annoyed by the breach of security but relieved to find them friends of Laframboise. One wore an arrow-proof coat of mail, which looked like a straightjacket to Eld. It was made of sticks the size of a man's thumb, woven closely together. They protected only his trunk. His arms were free of the garment, which was fastened with shoulder straps at the top and a strap at the bottom. The man was not bad-looking and the boy quite prepossessing. Emmons, nevertheless, let them stay only a few minutes, not enough time for artist Agate to draw them.

The Lieutenant ordered Ignace and Sergeant Stearns out on another hunt. The Iroquois bagged a deer but was surprised by twenty Indians as he skinned out his game. He remounted his horse, abandoning the venison, and rode for camp. The Indians shot arrows at him and he had to fire his rifle at them when they attempted to cut off his retreat. Since all were afoot, he easily outdistanced them.

Emmons, of course, became fearful for the Sergeant's safety. As the sun set, he caught some horses in order to personally lead out a rescue party. At that moment, the noncommissioned officer came in. He sheepishly admitted having chased a wounded buck so far that he had become bewildered and lost. Emmons noted that the Sergeant came into camp from the direction opposite to that in which he had been prepared to dash to his rescue.

That night, the Lieutenant kept an even stricter watch than usual. He heard many Indians prowling about in the fringe of pines edging the campsite. But the night passed without alarm.

Much later, while at sea aboard the *Vincennes,* Lieutenant Wilkes requested (May 30, 1842) a detailed report on the Ignace incident. Assistant Surgeon Whittle informed him that the Iroquois had wounded an Indian (Wilkes had been told nothing about it, earlier). Since he had given the most unmistakable orders not to molest the Indians, he demanded a report from Emmons. He explained: "The general subject of the character of the Indians of that part of the country and the conduct of the hunters towards them may hereafter be made a matter of inquiry."

Emmons responded, reminding his superior that he had been anticipating trouble with the Indians dogging his steps. He told Wilkes that Stearns had gone off with Peale, separating (against orders) from Ignace. He managed to get in a "dig" at his ex-friend by explaining that he no longer pretended to control the actions of the "scientific gentlemen." Unknown to him (Emmons), Ignace had sallied forth on horseback, alone. The Iroquois had returned within an hour, "with considerable animation." Since he spoke little English, Emmons had Guardapii translate. The hunter had been warned of danger by his horse. (Emmons explained, "This is not unusual, as all may know who travel through this country.")

Ignace had looked around to find natives stealing up on him. Leaving the deer, he had jumped into his saddle to beat a retreat. He had fired but one shot, in answer to their arrows. This was to slow his attackers' pursuit. He had not looked back to see if his ball had flown straight from powder to target. Emmons concluded: "I believed him then and, upon more mature reflection, have no reason to alter my belief. Ignas was a quiet, unassuming man of acute perception and but very few words—and this is another reason why I confided in him. The circumstances, however, hardly warrant the belief that an Indian was hit, much less killed."

No two accounts of Ignace's ambush agreed. Brackenridge wrote that the Iroquois cleared out only after he had killed an attacker. Eld wrote: "Ignas then gave them a rifle shot which wounded one of their number, as he supposed, as one of the Indians gave a jump and shrieked out when he fired." Peale wrote: "He was attacked by about 20 Indians with arrows, which he described as striking all around him. He remounted his horse, firing a shot from his rifle amongst them first, and then retreated at full speed to camp."

Emmons even drew a sketchy map for Wilkes. It showed his defensive position on the south bank of the Rogue and the arc of pines semicircling the grassy flat occupied by his tents. On the perimeter he had placed four sentries, evenly spaced, to watch the piny woods. They were to protect the camp as well as the horses. All these precautions against the Indians were necessary, he informed Wilkes, in order to "guard against their killing or crippling my animals, a game that they have practiced against the H. B. Company's parties with considerable success."

Whatever the exact facts of the fight, neither Emmons or Wilkes ever blamed the Iroquois for the encounter. The set-to at least served to waken every man-jack of Emmons's command to the danger he faced in the Siskiyous. But the troublesome Wood had to be shamed out of the idea of shooting his horse, which would not stand still for saddling. The long heavy rifle which the ruffian shook in the air was the one with which he had killed an Indian at a distance of a half-mile (he bragged) while herding with Young in '37.

Indians were seen hiding behind trees. Peale guessed that there were fifty. They came forward timidly when hailed, expressing their friendship for Laframboise. They asked after him and even volunteered to join Emmons. He waved them away but, before he left, the

311

chief of the band told the Lieutenant that he was at war with the natives controlling the area where the naval party would camp in the evening. But he doubted that they would attack.

Emmons halted the caravan to let Rich summon enough strength to ride, after a recurrence of his ague attacks. After slow-paced progress, camp was made to allow Rich to recuperate and to spare those animals in a bad way. In camp, Colvocoresses saw Emmons send away more Indians, these in rude, square-ended dugout canoes.

By a grim coincidence, Emmons found that he had selected a grisly and dangerous spot for a campsite. Peale thought that it was the site of Ewing Young's ambush, but it was actually almost the very site of John Turner's battle with Indian attackers. Two of Turner's men had been killed there and two mortally wounded. Since the whites and half-bloods had held their position long enough to bury the dead, the bones which Emmons and Peale saw bleaching under the clutter of tall pines must have been those of slain ambushers.

Peale reconstructed the action there: "The white people on that occasion suffered the Indians to come into camp in great numbers (more than 100), who professed friendship but who waited for an unguarded moment to attack the few whites, and would have succeeded in killing all of them to obtain their property had not a gigantic, iron-framed fellow [Turner] laid about him with a tremendous firebrand, keeping back the naked assailants until his red wife brought out his rifle, when the Indians retreated with considerable loss." Colvocoresses added: "We had one man in the party who had twice been assaulted at [nearly] the same place." He referred to Cal Tibbetts.

For a long time after the tents were erected, an Indian harangued the whites from across the river. Emmons did not have the foggiest notion of what he was shouting about. But, shortly, an Indian dog began to bark an accompaniment to the oratory. The irascible Wood, against orders, drew a bead on the ululating mongrel. Emmons heard it yelping ("ki-i-ing") in pain after the shot. He called Wood down, but the frontiersman ("a worthless vagabond" to Peale) saw no harm in his action: "It was an Indian dog, and his master would shoot any of us if he had the chance." Emmons could not necessarily deny the truth of that. But he still had to reproach Wood and try to convince him of his error, since it simply invited trouble with the Indians. The Lieutenant soon realized that his lecture was falling on deaf ears. Wood had been so long in the Far West, out from under any moral restraint, that he no longer made fine distinctions between right and wrong. Of his kind, Emmons wrote: "[They] are doubtless either the principals or accessories of crimes that would, under proper law, cost them their heads."

The Lieutenant found it difficult to say just how far the Indians were justified in their hostility and treachery toward whites, because of Wood and his ilk. He knew that the savages did not particularize their revenge; thus, innocent whites had to be prepared to pay for the acts of their guilty fellows. And he was sure that vengeance and mutual retaliation would continue until civilization should take over the Siskiyou Trail—if the red race were not extinguished first.

The Indians did not need an excuse for a war dance that night, though Emmons assumed that the wounded dog provided it. They built fires on the far bank of the Rogue and kept shouting until midnight. Even in his predicament, Emmons could not help sympathizing with the Indians: "They doubtless swore eternal vengeance against our party and very probably pledged to each other the final extermination of our race. Poor fellows! I have none of this feeling towards them and if it would avail me anything, I could shed tears for their (as appears to me) cruel destiny."

Though Dr. Whittle found his thermometer broken by the fall of a horse, another survived to show that it was just above freezing at sunrise of September 27, 1841. The party was on the move as soon as possible, with winter coming on, though horses were giving out and sailors and gentlemen both suffering from malaria. Travel, from time to time, became temporarily impossible.

Indians whooped and ran along the opposite bank as the men headed up the Rogue on a northeast course toward a narrow riverside pass. There, Guardapii informed Emmons, the redskins had twice before fortified themselves to ambush Laframboise. Accordingly, Emmons dismounted, checked his arms, and took a few skirmishers forward as a patrol. He kept well in advance of the main party in order to clear the way completely and he posted a special guard over the women, children, and baggage.

Emmons anticipated real trouble where the trail almost pinched out between the narrow bank of the Rogue and a chaparral-covered mountain slope. It was a perfect ambush site, with plenty of cover for snipers or bowmen. Peale recounted: "Indians on the opposite side of the river, running, apparently with the object of cutting off our passage across a rocky promontory covered with brush. The place was favorable to an ambuscade and, as there was no way to avoid it, we prepared for hostilities." Eld added: "All but a guard for the baggage, women and children, dismounted to use our rifles with the most effect. But on approaching, a few savages only were seen, re-treating up a mountain on the opposite side of the river, and we passed without molestation."

Emmons laid his success in clearing the trap strictly to his many precautions. These, he said, "the Indians do not like, for they much prefer taking us unawares." Seeing his preparations for a fight, the Indians lay concealed until the whites were out of gunshot. Then they showed themselves and taunted the travelers. Joel Walker's wife and her sister were alarmed at having to run a kind of gauntlet. But the Indian women with Emmons remained unperturbed. Like their men-folk, they were pretty much ready for anything.

Brackenridge commented on the mountain men: "They did not find a single Indian in ambush during the whole range, and 'twas well for them, as there were some deadly shots among the party, who wanted nothing better than to get a sight on one of the rascals." Eld saw no more than five Indians at any one time, and all of them safely across the river from the trail. They aimed their bows and arrows at the travelers, but all in bluff. He did not believe that they launched a single missile. He was close enough to see that one wore a Hudson's Bay Company shirt and another a conical hat like a schoolboy's fools-cap.

A few miles on, the Rogue turned abruptly away from the Siski-you Trail. All the whites were glad to see the last of the stream named for its rascally denizens. Exiting through another mountain pass, Emmons reached a large prairie. In it he found deer, bear, *camas* roots, rabbits, antelope, and coyotes. A few root-digging Indian women fled before him, and he noted the first hoofprints of a horse not of his own company. He guessed that it had been stolen from whites and that it now bore a messenger from the Rogues to the Shastas.

But the next day Peale spotted three mounted Indians. They rode off. Eld's horse gave out entirely and was left on the trail. Em-mons, already quite a husbandman for a sailor, could not bear to abandon the animal. He sent a man to fetch it to water. Now very fond of his loyal animals, he hoped to prolong its days: "I could do no more, nor could we well do less for an animal that had served us so faithfully." Though Eld had had to lead, whip, and drag the beast before he had finally "abandoned ship," Ignace managed to get the fagged-out nag to camp, and to water.

The tents were next pitched on Beaver Creek. Peale, curiously, failed to mention *Castor*. Perhaps this was because he was so busy spitefully chiding Emmons for his bad choice of campsite, one with "poor provender for our horses." But he explored the area with zest, finding jackrabbits and brush corrals thrown up by the Indians to trap both the big hares and deer, by means of drives. In the openings were snares made of a hemplike twisted fiber, perhaps iris fiber.

The air, which Peale described as "atmosphere loaded with smoke," cleared enough to provide Emmons with eight to ten miles of visibility on September 28. He saw high mountains to both left and right of the trail. These were the Siskiyous proper. No spare horses remained, so some of the men had to alternate between walking and riding. The sick were able to move and Rich was improved, but Colvocoresses's worsening condition caused several halts. Then Mercer became stubborn and lagged behind. Emmons was afraid to leave him where the Indians could pick him off, so he waited patiently until he came up.

Doubtless, Emmons thought himself as patient as Job, braking the progress of the company because of the sick with winter staring him in the face. He was eager to get out of such hostile country, too. But Brackenridge, under the strain, was becoming almost as critical of him as was Peale: "Several of the gentlemen who had already suffered from the tertian fever were again attacked today. But the leader of the party, instead of holding on for them, pushed ahead. But five of the party, who had a little more sympathy for their fellow-beings, remained behind to protect the sick individuals from the assaults of the savages, so that they did not reach the camp till after dark."

Notwithstanding the accusations of Brackenridge, Emmons several times halted the caravan to enable Rich and Colvocoresses to get up enough strength to climb back into their saddles. Whittle, Peale, and others watched over the passed midshipman when he was delirious and unable to ride. He finally became so frenzied that they thought it best to take away his weapons. No sooner was he calmed down than Walker and one of his children came down with malaria.

Progress was made in small stages but, finally, the tents were staked down at the foot of Emmons's "Boundary Range," the Siskiyou Mountains proper. The sugar pines were gone, the heights now clothed in brush wood. Because Mount Shasta peered through a gap in the sierra, Brackenridge dubbed the range the Shasta Mountains (which really lay far ahead of them). Peale guessed that the peaks climbed to three thousand feet, and Emmons thought that Mount Shasta lay about on the California line of 42°. (It is actually forty miles south.) When a cloud of smoke seemed to rise from the peak's very summit,

Emmons made the absurd guess that it was a signal from the Rogues to the Shastas to get ready for him. He was already very leery of the Shastas: "This latter tribe took the trouble to send word to the Umpqua Fort that they were prepared to kill any of the whites that should attempt to pass through their country."

Most of the more localized smoke was readily explicable. Peale saw only one Indian all day, a woman collecting roots and seeds into a funnel-shaped basket. She wore a deerskin mantle and a cup-shaped cap made of *tules,* and she carried a firebrand. She was so intent on setting fire to prairie and mountain ravines that she paid him no mind.

Though Dr. Whittle urged him to remain in camp for two days to let the sick recoup their strength, Emmons used the strict letter of Wilkes's instructions to keep moving. The site was so poor in grass and water that he could hardly keep the horses alive. He explained to his officers the many dangers consequent to a delay there, with Bloody Pass just ahead. He stressed the importance to the invalids of getting out of the dangerous border country while their provisions lasted and their horses could still walk. *And* while he had enough well men to tend the sick and protect them and the herd. Colvocoresses said that he could ride—though, he recalled, "Every moment we expected to be attacked by hostile Indians." Emmons tested his endurance by sending him back a short distance to camp, to retrieve a journal left there by Eld. But he sent Warfield with him.

On the penultimate day of September, Emmons began the transit of the critical point of the Siskiyou Trail, the summit of the Siskiyou Mountain range at dreaded Bloody Pass. This was the site of the ambush of nine Americans and eight halfbreeds in which Tibbetts had been wounded and, according to Peale, dangerously wounded. One man had been killed and several others wounded before the Oregonians had been driven to retreat, giving up their plan of driving cattle up the trail from California.

The climb was slow. As soon as the sun gained power, Colvocoresses grew worse. Emmons had to order a series of short halts. When he found fresh Indian spoor near the ambush site, he went ahead with a skirmishing party of flankers. Tibbetts expected that, at long last, he would be given the opportunity for revenge. But his wish was not granted. Emmons found the pass empty, though it was ideally adapted for ambuscades and easily defendable against great odds. He was, of course, as pleased as Tibbetts was disappointed. Eld described Bloody Pass as being bounded by hills on one side and beset with bunches of scraggy rocks and a small creek on the other—all highly suitable to shelter ambushers. There was every sign of recent occupancy, from fresh moccasin tracks to a large pine felled expertly across the Siskiyou Trail to halt the expeditionaries in the trap. But the trap was sprung.

Emmons, pleased to be again "disappointed" in his expectations of meeting an enemy, surmounted the next ridge. He was rewarded with a fine view of Mount Shasta from the Rogue-Klamath watershed. In spite of the boundary ridge being on fire and sending up great clouds of smoke, he could see Shasta easily forty miles away and the extensive Klamath River plain extending southward.

The company camped at Otter Creek, well within California, as winds formed small vapor clouds over snowcapped Mount Shasta. The animals delighted in the *tules,* or bulrushes, chomping them like some exotic dessert. Their starved masters made do with bread and tea for supper. Beaver sign was about but nowhere, reassuringly, any fresh Indian tracks. Curiously, no animals—not even birds—were to be seen near the Otter Creek-Klamath River junction. But, at least, plants provided a welcome touch of green to the landscape, and Peale collected the seeds of many strange botanical specimens about the little oasis in the rather barren land of cedars or junipers and brush.

Although the men were tired, some were still itching for a fight with Indians. They were bored with endless marches over an arid and often stony soil, through thorny brush and snaggy trees. Brackenridge cited the chagrin of Tibbetts and others at coming through Bloody Pass without a scrap: "One or two of the hired men of our party, who had formed part of another that was totally routed and beaten back at this place, were now anxious to meet their old opponents, but the Indians were too wily to show themselves against such a strong party."

The last day of September was warm and sultry. Emmons decided to belatedly accept his surgeon's advice. He let his men and animals remain stationary in camp all day. Even Brackenridge admitted that the lieutenant "condescended" to permit those who were well to leave camp. The great range of California temperature in autumn, from freezing at midnight to 100° at noon (in the shade), seemed to aggravate the ague. While Brackenridge made a collecting trip, three men were having malarial seizures.

Though the Rogue was behind him, Emmons continued his precautions. After all, the Shasta and Pit River Indians lay ahead. He sent the horse herd out to better grazing but warned the guard to bring them back to camp for their nocturnal feeding. Since the temperature bothered his sick, Emmons had the men throw up brush *ramadas* to shade the hot tents. Some of the party mended and washed clothes; others got out their bullet molds and cast rifle balls. Peale put up his seeds and other specimens.

Chills and fever kept the Overland Expedition's leader ill all that day. He blamed his attacks on the great heat and thought that Rich and Colvocoresses were suffering for the same reason. Peale took Agate on a hike up the Klamath River for a few miles. They saw fish in the rapid current, but no deer or other animals on its banks. It was an arid and treeless country through which the Klamath hurried, as if eager to find greener fields.

When the hunters returned without having even seen any game, Emmons crawled out of his sickbed to give orders to conserve rations. He reduced the amount of flour and lard issued to all hands. There was still a large supply of dried peas, but the dehydrated stuff was almost inedible and the men would use it only as a last resort. There was much grumbling that night, as always in a hungry camp. But Emmons was grateful for one thing. The horses were now so fagged out that they had no inclination to stray at night while grazing. Thus, early departures would be possible on the California portion of the Siskiyou Trail.

Buenaventura Reconnaissance

OCTOBER 1, 1841, dawned so smoky that even mighty Mount Shasta was invisible. Brackenridge did not look forward with pleasure to crossing the remainder of the "California Range of Mountains." From Guardapii, he knew that the haze and smoke hid a rugged sierra which might take seven days to cover with such weakened horses. As his eyes strained to pick out details of the barrier ahead, he commented: "The whole is one continuous series of valleys, hills and ridges, standing in all positions toward each other."

But Lieutenant Emmons was optimistic. His men were rested, fresh when they pulled out. They easily forded the barren-banked Klamath on a pebbly bottom between rapids. The water rose only to the horses' bellies. The ford was probably the one designated today as the Hudson's Bay Crossing (by the Siskiyou County Historical Society) at Klamathon Bridge near Hornbrook. The river looked as wide as the Umpqua or Rogue.

The men grew fatigued and sickly under a blazing sun as the journey took them across a parched, bleak, undulating volcanic plain rendered even more black and desolate by recent grass fires. They found no water until they reached the Shasta River, only a "generous rivulet" (Dana). Occasionally, buttes reared up through clouds of dust, some of them flat-topped mesas—Dana's "table summits." To Peale, all were "naked, barren-looking mountains," but to Dana they were interesting because of their pebbles of milky quartz, sandstone outcroppings, volcanic rock splotched with crystals of glossy feldspar, and salines or *playas* where only Salsola grew. The traveling was par-

319

ticularly hard on the unshod horses, for the valley floor was paved with small, loose stones. Yet, if Eld's figures were correct, it was the best day's march yet—twenty miles in only six and a half hours.

The solitary Indian that Emmons spied fled like an antelope to the timber on the hills. Camp was made at the only plot of grass seen all day. The patch of green lay in the midst of cairnlike conic piles of porphyritic rocks, fifty to a hundred feet high, and saline-incrusted ravines. But alongside camp chuckled the clear, handsome, and rapid "Southern Fork of the Klamath," the Shasta River. Though barely thirty feet across, it was full of fish. Antelope were nearby, but too shy to be approached. No one could even get a long shot at one. Quail were abundant but birdshot was too precious to waste on such small fowl. The only other birds seen were cranes and a few mallards.

Spying some Indians watching him, Emmons rode boldly out to a hilltop lookout and cut off their retreat. They waited for him, warily. He found them to be better-looking people than those of Oregon. He thought, at first, that they were armed only with fish spears. They wore no more covering than Pacific Islanders he had seen, though one had an elkskin robe. Using sign language, the Lieutenant was able to barter some salmon from them for buttons. He found the fish to be out-of-season and poor eating, and their tails were worn from beating their way so far upstream.

Once convinced of the white's friendship, the natives showed off their well-made bows and arrows, which they had hidden in the grass at Emmons's approach. He sketched one of their *balsas* or reed canoes on a page of his journal. But when they signified their desire to come to camp, Emmons would not allow it.

Emmons continued over a gently rolling plain so hazed with smoke that his view was obscured. Although the prairie was fertile in spots, most was so dry and waterless that the ground sounded hollow under the horses' hooves. Emmons was worried, as the animals grew crazed with thirst, but Brackenridge was pleased with the new flora —heliotropes, silvery-leaved bushes, patches of dogwood, and spiraea —he found between the salt-crusted soda flats.

When the horses reached waterholes, some could not be restrained. They plunged right into the "tanks" with their packs on until they submerged and had to be hauled out with lassos. Worse, the heat heightened the fever among Emmons's patients. The thermometer registered 90°, but it felt hotter. Peale found new plants but no birds other than a few curlews. There seemed to be no animals about, except the very shy antelope in the distance and the ubiquitous, slouching camp followers, the coyotes.

Several men were ill that day and Emmons so weak, himself, that he had to dismount and rest several times before camping again on the Shasta River. The stream, near its headwaters, was so narrow that Eld jumped across it. Brackenridge did not approve of Emmons's route west of "Snowy Mountain." He wrote: "Tis my belief that had we kept to the eastward of it [Mount Shasta], our route would have been shorter and easier."

Agate sketched friendly Indians as Emmons relaxed his guard enough to admit a half-dozen to camp. Earlier, Eld had written that most Indians loved to be sketched: "I do not know how it is that all mankind have [sic] such an insatiable propensity to see their own image on paper, but I have noticed that the most savage tribes will stand as mute as lambs to have themselves drawn and, after it is finished, contemplate the imitation with pleasure." Such was anything but the case with the Shastas. Now (October 2), Eld wrote: "Mr. Agate got a sketch of them after some difficulty in getting them to stand, for they seemed a little afraid that the evil spirit was about to act upon them. In order to draw the attention and fix the eye upon something, Mr. Agate took out a miniature of his father and mother, on either side of a locket. This, so far from having the desired effect, alarmed them considerably. Not one of them could be prevailed upon to look at this medicine worked in human shape."

The whites traded trifles for bows and arrows as souvenirs. Brackenridge found the sealskin or wildcat skin quivers and "yew" bows to be well made. Likewise the arrows of what he called tassle wood, barbed with points of volcanic glass or obsidian. The Indians used their weapons with great skill, especially in shooting fish. He encouraged them to target-shoot. One of them hit a button at twenty yards three out of four tries. The archers were rewarded for their marksmanship with a few buttons and some tobacco. Brackenridge spoke the words of all his comrades: "For my part, I would as soon —at one hundred yards—have a musket discharged at me as an arrow from one of these Indian bows."

The hunters saw not only deer and antelope but also mountain sheep. For the first time, Emmons found himself too ill to take his watch. Eld, who had somehow escaped the ravages of malaria, stood guard in his place that night. Poor Emmons was too sick to even enjoy the spectacular sunset which Peale noted: "The summits of Mt. Tchasty presented a beautiful view from our camp when its snow was illuminated by the pink rays of the setting sun, while the base remained invisible to us."

Shasta was visible from first light until half an hour after sunrise, then veiled again by smoky weather. But travel on October 3 shifted from a dusty open prairie to a pine and spruce-shaded forest. On this spur of the Shasta Range, Emmons saw fresh Indian tracks and traces of recent fires. Some pines were still ablaze, though the natives lay concealed. Perhaps the shudder which shook his frame was more from anxiety than malaria.

Dana described the last obstacle to the Buenaventura: "Before us were a mass of lofty ridges ranging from east to west and situated to the west of the Shasty Peak. They form a natural boundary across the country, dividing the Clammat region from the district of the Sacramento and, where passed by us, they occupied a breadth from north to south of about forty miles, though twice this distance by the zigzag course we followed." Dana particularly admired Shasta's little neighbor, Black Butte, a perfect cone of ejected cinders. To him, "It retained all the freshness and regularity of a recent formation."

Emmons now turned to botanizing, too. He measured sugar pines fifteen feet in circumference which bore heavy cones up to sixteen inches long. He was pleased to find specimens larger than those collected by David Douglas. The tree's sap or gum was pleasant to chew and the "sugar," which he likened to crystalline burnt alum, was sweet, soluble, and a good substitute for the real article. But it was rare, appearing only where the woods had been fired.

Emmons's twenty-eighth camp was on the headwaters of the long-sought Sacramento. He called it Destruction River, favoring the Pit as the true upper Sacramento. But Peale realized that he was on the "Buenaventura" and rejoiced that he had crossed "what might be called a natural boundary of California." Since it took its rise on Mount Shasta, it was only a creek about two feet deep and three yards wide. But Emmons determined to cling to it as a passage through a hundred miles of rugged mountains.

Emmons had a fine view of the peak. Someone—Emmons, Dana, or Agate—sketched it for inclusion in Wilkes's published report. Emmons estimated that its summit rose ten thousand feet above the plain on which Ignace was finally finding such good hunting. He was close; the top of the massif reached 14,162 feet above sea level, whereas Black Butte summit on the Siskiyou Trail lay at only 3920 feet.

Steep hills and punishing small stones slowed progress. Though the forest was more open, with the underbrush burned away by the Indians, the animals were now tender-hooved. Dana noted that the thermometer read $32\frac{1}{2}°$ at 2 A.M., and early-risers were greeted by frost-whitened ground. But the terrain soon regained its blackened aspect as the morning wore on. In places, the turf was aflame or oozing smoke. Brackenridge found a few large tree trunks still on fire. Still, it was not unpleasant traveling; the men found abundant wild grapes near the stream and Peale shot two deer for the larder.

Travel under the towering, sky-piercing sugar pines would have been pleasant save for a few nagging problems. The stock was deteriorating badly. Emmons had to exchange a horse with Molair in order to get an animal fit for riding for one of the sick men. When another animal proved useless, he abandoned its load, a sack of peas, to the unseen Indians. The party still saw no redmen but overran campfires, still alight, and even the hastily dropped bags and baskets of Indian women.

Brackenridge mused: "It appears strange that the Indians should so avoid us. . . ." But Guardapii explained how wild the local natives were, living on seeds and small fruits, building no village or even lodges but sheltering themselves under trees and overhanging rocks. Added Brackenridge: "For my own part, I have not seen an Indian hut since leaving the Columbia. The Indians, ever since we entered the mountains, have always avoided us, although they are very numerous, from the trails we saw."

Emmons's other anxiety, besides crippled horses and evasive Indians, was his sick list. Rich and Colvocoresses were both incapacitated by chills again and under Eld's care. A horse was lost, too, but Emmons reached Soda Springs safely. This Siskiyou Trail landmark, whose waters hovered at $50°$, looked "suspicious" to the men because its waters left a coating of rust on rocks. But the horses drank eagerly of it and even gnawed at the earth and stones. This was not because of salinity, though the animals were starved for salt. Dana found the spring to be acidulous and chalybeate—neither saline or alkaline, just "irony."

Peale tried a tentative draft of the water and found it delicious. Carbonic acid-charged, it was refreshing. All soon drank heartily of it. They experienced no ill effects. Brackenridge so appreciated the treat that he wrote that the spring's waters were "as agreeable as any manufactured in our large cities. . . . To be in possession of such a fountain in the U. States would be the having of a fortune."

Because the campground was a blackened ruin, Emmons pushed

on three miles to make a day's advance of fifteen miles. He settled down on the west bank of his Destruction River. Having been joined by a branch, it was now a respectable stream.

Two miles west, a much more dramatic landmark was visible. The jagged ridge of Castle Crags reared up against the horizon. To Peale the fold-faulted, glaciated massif of domes and turrets resembled Staten Island (the one off Cape Horn, not Manhattan). Dana was intrigued by the granite cliffs, colored almost as light as chalk. "A valley on the west opened to us a magnificent spectacle of needle peaks and lofty pinnacles of granite. This bold, crested ridge was about three thousand feet above the plain at its foot, and one massy peak overhung the valley. A few evergreen spires stood in the clefts of the ridge; otherwise it presented a bare surface of grayish white rock. A whitish debris covered the slope at its base and the valley was strewed with boulders of granite."

Emmons estimated that the "remarkable castellated peaks" were only three to four hundred feet in elevation. Even Dana was off; the spires soar a sheer six thousand feet in contrast to the valley's two-thousand-foot elevation. Emmons was properly impressed by the great granite wall erupting above the forest: "The noble scenery 'round is exceedingly wild and boldly romantic." He saw that the gray slopes were streaked not with snowbanks, as he had first thought, but with great strata of a very light-colored rock.

Blowing winds subsided on October 5, when Emmons took the morning watch because all three of his officers were sick. He turned out the cooks a half-hour before daylight in order to get everyone on the trail early. Travel was best in the cool morning hours when everyone was fresh and rested. As he moved along, he found a quantity of fox grapes. Though he was fond of the fruit, he did not dare indulge his appetite. He had learned that wild grapes and ague did not agree.

Leaving Eld with a party to protect Agate, busily sketching Castle Crags, Emmons piloted the main force on at a slower pace. This was to enable the rear detachment to catch up, but also because the animals were failing again. Frequent stops were necessary to rest them. Six times the track crossed the swelling Sacramento to avoid the worst mountain slopes, though it generally followed the west bank. The river was very rapid and clear, its bed filled with "pudding stones" —compacted conglomerates of flintlike stones. Dana thought that these would make good millstones.

Whichever side they chose, the travelers had to scramble a tortuous course in and out of tributary creeks and deep, dry *arroyos* which, in winter, would have been channels brimming with thundering torrents. They passed along deep ravines lined with large boulders, then a succession of mountain ridges and outcroppings whose small basaltic stones cruelly hurt the horses' hooves.

Emmons found Wood, who had gone ahead, hunting, at the bottom of a small natural corral with the carcass of a deer. He told the Lieutenant that the "wolves" (coyotes) had dogged his heels constantly and during the night, while he slept, had devoured part of the deer though he was lying beside it. They had done it quietly, without awakening him.

At camp that night in a rocky dell hard by the Sacramento, dashing along in its stony bed, Emmons had more of the animals shod. He was glad that most of his men were pretty fair farriers. The wonder of it was that more animals were not lost or crippled in the maze of mountain ridges, ravines, canyons, granite rocks, and pine and oak woods which led Peale to write: "The road today was the worst yet passed." Nevertheless, it proved to be a good day for him. He saw birds new to him and also two new species of marmots. And at the many fine springs along the route of march he observed "a botanic harvest," though Brackenridge grumpily lamented having to leave Soda Springs—"I regretted very much that we were not permitted to remain at this station for at least one day, as the mountains on our left presented a very alluring aspect for the botanist."

The atmosphere continued to be curtained with smoke which confined Emmons's view to a small area but, as far as he could see, there extended a succession of mountaintops—the "alps upon alps" of Philip Leget Edwards (1837). Some were wooded, others covered only with undergrowth. The madrone (*madroño* of the Mexicans) which the travelers called arbutus or "strawberry tree" now became abundant. These handsome shrubs and trees with skin-smooth underbark and a peeling coarse outer "skin" provided Indians and bears alike with tasty red berries.

The course of the party continued to be a serpentine one, determined by the writhings of the Sacramento River. Men, women, and children waded five creeks and as many more rivulets tributary to the river that day. The Sacramento, thirty yards wide, was one long staircase of rapids, fenced with the remains of old Indian fishing weirs. Tracks, recent campsites, and fresh graves, decorated with offerings (bundles of salmon and other provisions), proved that Indians were about, though unseen. Their absence began to suit Emmons nicely. He relaxed a bit and wrote: "Having passed several bad places where

325

the Indians might with apparent security have annoyed us exceedingly, had they felt disposed, [I] began to think that we shall escape their vengeance."

On the other hand, Peale ran into six Indians while he was hunting alone. They secreted themselves the moment they saw him. As it was near dark, and he did not like their looks, he hurried to camp without trying to hold any intercourse with them. According to Brackenridge, they meant to cut his colleague off: "Mr. Peale, while out hunting, saw six of them hid in the bush, about (as he thought) to entrap him—and a fine booty they would have had!"

Camp was again set on the Sacramento, still clogged with rapids and disintegrated remains of weirs. The water, only three feet deep, was transparent, but the only fish Peale could see, so late in the season, were the dead salmon cast by the current on rocks. Sitting on the river bank near a sandy bar, Peale was first surprised and then delighted with the antics of a rare bird: A Cinclus, better-known as the dipper or water ouzel, performed for him. Almost black and bearing itself in the oddest posture, it jutted or fretted its tail upward while teetering like a drunkard on stream rocks, keeping its body horizontal with this balancing act. Even more amazing were its underwater bug hunts. Fascinated, Peale watched the ouzel as it "clearly and distinctly walked on the bottom, *under water*." The rocks, six to eight inches below the surface, were clothed with moss and interspersed with aquatic plants—all of which the diving dipper carefully investigated. Confessed Peale: "I was so anxious to see the disputed habits of this bird that I lost the opportunity of securing the specimen."

Emmons began to travel even more slowly and to camp early, to favor the sick; Brackenridge described Agate and Colvocoresses as having "a good shake of the ague." Even short jaunts were exhausting in these rugged mountains. The terrain lacked feed, so the horses grew weaker with each step. Riders had to dismount, out of pity, and foot it over major portions of the march. Veterans of Rocky Mountain travel in the ranks told Emmons that California's "Shasty" Mountains, the tail-end of the Siskiyous and Cascades, were much rougher going than the Rockies, and they supported little game. So it was that the Lieutenant, on Dr. Whittle's suggestion, did not "start" (break) camp at all on the seventh. He decided to rest men and animals for the last mountainous stretch before the Sacramento Valley.

Emmons joined his hunters, but his presence worked no magic. All returned empty-handed. He blamed such ill luck on the presence of hidden Indians, who scared away all game. Men gathered seeds and fox grapes to fill shrunken bellies and others tried to fish. The latter had no success. Brackenridge commented: "The headwaters of the Sacramento is said to abound in a very large trout of a delicate flavor, but the day was too clear for us to catch any."

Against Dr. Whittle's remonstrances, Emmons broke camp on the eighth. But he consulted his sick charges before moving out. He hoped to avoid two high mountains looming ahead. Since Guardapii was unfamiliar with this sector, he had to depend on Warfield, who had been over the route. But the trail split and Warfield chose the fork which grew so faint that he lost it several times. Each time, luckily, he was set straight by his sharp-eyed wife. Three times, in dodging the two mountains—the worst-looking obstacles of the entire march—Warfield took the men across the river, now eighty to one hundred feet wide. The peaks appeared to be about three thousand feet high, rocky and uneven. The path which the men took lay over angular and sharp rocks on dry land and rounded and slippery boulders in the rapid flow of the Sacramento and five small eastside affluents which they waded. Perhaps only Brackenridge could enjoy that day's trek through good-for-nothing country. He was all wrapped up in *Quercus* collecting: "Oaks!" he wrote; "I do not know what to think of them, they are so varied in character. There must either be a vast number of species or a great many varieties of one kind."

Emmons was worn out when he camped, after thirteen very difficult miles, on the east bank of the Sacramento again. The sick bay dragged behind the main force; two pack animals with his vital powder supply strayed and had to be found. The last straw was when Peale, a better shot even than Ignace, joined the hungry hunters fanning out of camp. He sent one deer to camp with the horse guard when he ran into them. But he reported the other animal to Eld, suggesting he send men to bring it in. Dog-tired and sick with responsibility, Emmons blew up. He forbade his second-in-command to allow men to go and get the much-needed meat. Peale's journal told the story: "But Mr. Emmons considered the report *informal* in not being made to *him,* and refused permission to the men to bring in the meat. I therefore gave directions to the camp followers [Wood and Mrs. Warfield], who consequently were better supplied than we were." A presumably neutral Brackenridge observed the silly set-to and reported: "Mr. Emmons would not permit anyone to go and bring the venison to camp, saying that he [Peale] had fooled him often enough, already."

Difficult fords across a widening Sacramento succeeded the teacup tempest. Bare rock banks and slithery bottom were negotiated safely until a six- or seven-year-old Indian girl (Eliza, according to Emmons; Elsie, said Peale) belonging to Burrows was knocked from her horse and swept down the river. Dr. Whittle plunged in and managed to rescue her. But the current was so fast and the footing so bad that others, including Doughty, had to re-rescue both rescuer and rescued all over again. Both medic and girl were well dunked but otherwise uninjured. Emmons halted the advance to enable the soaked, shivering individuals to change clothing. More time was forfeited when the doctor had to search for his gun, lost in the rescue. He finally retrieved it from the bed of the river.

Passing east of the blockading mountains, Emmons reached the junction of Pit River with the Sacramento. It was a good place to rest after eighteen hard-traveling miles. The animals bearing the sick were staggering since their riders were too enfeebled to get off in order to walk them or rest them. Some horses had to be left behind. Brackenridge, as usual, rose above discomfort and fatigue because of his scientific zeal. He found the madrones covered with fine ripe fruit, the sweetish sub-acid berries which were such a treat to the Indians. He found local acorns so sweet and free of tannin that many of the tree branches were broken down by bears which had gorged themselves on the nuts.

Emmons scorned the Sacramento and Pit rivers as mere creeks in terms of the rivers back East. But he was impressed by the fact that the junction marked a boundary between the Shastas and the friendlier Kinclas or Kinklas. (The name is not now used. He may have been referring to Maidus or Wintuns.) Since they had a good reputation among whites, he began to feel confident that he would escape entirely the battles direly predicted for him by Oregonians.

On October 10, 1841, Emmons exited via a terraced slope from both mountains and stony barren foothills. It was now smooth sailing across the dry sea of grassland which was the Sacramento Valley. Vigilance against Indian attacks relaxed. It had been an exhausting strain on sick men.

Pines, firs, and madrones now gave way to cottonwoods, sycamores, and stately oaks, including the evergreen liveoak. Emmons collected specimens of acorns (which the Indians used for food) and oak leaves, while Peale botanized among plant species quite new to him, including a wild tobacco of offensive odor.

Naked Kinclas became numerous and friendly. It was with difficulty, however, that Agate persuaded some to pose for their portraits.

Though they were "full of jest and merriment" (Dana), they took Agate to be a medicine man, like later photographers of the West. They were fearful that he was practicing an enchantment on them and would seize their spirits with his sketching pencil.

Colvocoresses described the Kinclas as large-bodied, good-looking, sociable Indians. Brackenridge liked them very much: "These people appeared to be a very good-natured sociable set of beings, and behaved themselves very orderly." He gathered that they never lived in huts, any more than the Shastas, but, at best, erected barricades or flimsy *chevau de frise,* made of branches and stems of trees, to protect their camps. Most of them wore their hair long and bushy. Black as jet, it hung to their shoulders in natural ringlets.

Colvocoresses observed the Indian bowmen's sealskin and otter-skin quivers. Their bows were of yewlike wood, very elastic, and their arrows of the same or spiraea, barbed with obsidian. When they shot at a button at thirty yards, they hit the tiny pearl-shell target three times out of five attempts. They even shot birds on the wing. The archer stood firm, his left leg well planted and right leg thrown forward. Holding the bow horizontally rather than vertically, and, bracing it with the left thumb, he drew the nock of the three-foot arrow holding the bowstring back to his sucked-in chest. When he let fly it was with deadly power and precision. Many bowmen did not bother with quivers but carried a bundle of arrows in the left hand.

If they were great marksmen, the Kinclas were inexpert cartographers. When Emmons tried to learn something of the country ahead by scratching a map in the sand for them, they could not grasp what he was doing.

Because they were friendly, largely unarmed, and familiar with Laframboise, Emmons broke his own rule. He invited the Kinclas into camp. Only the men came. They were curious about everything. Emmons traded them knives and beads for dried salmon, pine nuts ("excellent eating," noted Peale), and some bows and arrows. The weapons were highly prized by them. Some would not part with their arms for any price, even the large Hudson's Bay point blankets which Emmons offered. He knew that all Indians set the highest value on these Company "robes"; yet they would not sell him one quiver.

These Indians looked like South Sea Islanders. They were relatively light-skinned and were tattooed. They carried fish spears as well as bows and arrows and wore little clothing (usually only a deerskin across one shoulder) even in cold weather. Their dances reminded the Navy of the South Pacific, too. To Emmons, these redmen were far superior in appearance to those he had seen to the north. Colvocoresses noted the strong, regular features of the men, many with oval faces and even roman noses. Some did not let their hair cascade down their backs but parted it and gathered it up at the back of their heads with a deerskin string. They marked the upper part of each cheek with a blue-black triangle of paint, one angle meeting the corner of the mouth. They painted their foreheads black, and some wore spots or zigzag lines of ocher on their faces.

Emmons had to agree that the Kincla women were far from being South Seas *huahines,* however. It was not so much that they were tattooed on the face, below the line of the mouth, but rather that they were careworn, wrinkled, and prematurely old from hard work.

While the whites accepted the Indian, the watchdog could not be reconciled to their presence. Emmons had to apologize to one fellow who approached too closely to the baggage and was bitten.

When some of the Lieutenant's men killed two grizzlies, the natives told him that the beasts sometimes invaded their *rancherías* or villages and carried off children. When Emmons visited the local *pueblo* or *ranchería* of rude "apartments" joining one another, he found them to be a cross between genuine huts and the simple shade shelters of many Indians, *ramadas* or brush arbors. They were made of poles, brushwood and coarse mats, partially roofed with the same material, and surrounded by the protective pole and brush fence. Rather harshly, Emmons compared the poor little stockaded camp to a pigpen at home, "in size, comforts, and cleanliness."

The Indians took salmon with weirs and long forked fish spears bearing detachable deerhorn points attached to lanyards or lines like whaling harpoons. Venison, acorn bread, *camas* roots, berries, seeds, and wild grapes were their staples. They were tolerably well organized and Emmons was surprised to find that they maintained a night watch and even called out passwords, like "civilized" sentries. For his part, Eld was astounded when the Kinclas brought wild grapes to camp in small baskets, without expecting anything in return. Generosity, as European-Americans understood it, was not a strong point with California redmen. Eld noted: "I have also noticed among these people that they have never begged among us, a quality I have never seen savages free of."

Accepting Guardapii's advice, Emmons had planned to shift from horses to canoes once he reached the Sacramento. The river, 150 yards wide, was navigable enough. But there was no timber for the construction of the craft. So he gave up the idea and continued slogging south on foot and horseback.

The gravelly plain was broken only by scattered oaks and some stunted pines which looked to Emmons like the casuarinas of the South Seas. These were scraggly digger pines. Eld, because of the shape of their big, round cones, called them "pineapple pines."

A good breeze from the north finally cleared the air of smoke and haze, but also carried the scent of the party before it. All game fled its path. But, surprisingly, that day's march over miserable, gravelly terrain was the longest so far—twenty-five miles. Most vegetation had been burned up by the sun; all small streams and rills were bone-dry.

The Sacramento slowed its racehorse pace, spread out to two hundred yards, and swept placidly, majestically along. Rest was sweet at sundown on the river bank, with the song of the coyotes a lullaby during the mild night. Next morning, the men were in good shape but the horses reluctant to move out after breakfast. Some lay down with their packs on to make their feelings perfectly clear. Once under way, crossing gravel beds and gullies, they startled a herd of antelope. But the horses were in such sorry condition that a pursuit was impossible. Deer and even bears could now easily outrun them.

But Ignace and Peale did not let their comrades down. Emmons found the former awaiting him on the river bank opposite an island. He had bagged and skinned out a large grizzly. Earlier he had bragged to Eld, *"Mica klatwa kokchit hyas silex siam*—I am going to kill a mad bear." Emmons packed the meat but left the heavy skin when the testy Peale told him that he did not want to preserve it.

Emmons now gave up the idea of canoe travel. He crossed to the east bank via the island. The water came only to the horses' girths. Yet the current was so strong that the horses could barely stem it at an angle. Broadside, they would have been carried downriver. After a uninteresting march of ten miles from the crossing, probably French Ford of the Hudson's Bay men at Red Bluff, Emmons had his force camp. Game abounded—antelope, elk, and black bear. Both deer and grizzlies were killed for the cooking pots.

The Lieutenant hoped to secure boats from Captain John Sutter to navigate all the way to San Francisco should he fail to fall in with Navy smallboats. He was afraid that he was too late for a rendezvous with the latter.

Guardapii, perhaps jealous of Ignace's success, came to Eld and told him that he, too, was going to kill a grizzly. Since Eld had been a scoffer of the "bear stories" of the mountain men, he wanted him to tag along. But Eld was busy making observations. Soon, he heard a crashing report from a rifle. Then he heard someone call out. Marine March told him that it was Baptiste, calling for a knife. Eld sent him one and found that he had, indeed, bagged his bear.

Five deer were shot and Eld and Ignace brought down a "vulture," either a California condor or a large turkey buzzard. The hunters then took on three bears. After the two men had repeatedly shot the largest *Ursus horribilis,* Eld impatiently started to rush from his hiding place behind a tree. He wanted to administer the coup de grâce. But Ignace pulled him back and said: *"Silex siam hyas kokchit mica!* —The mad bear will kill you!" When Eld still tried to get him to join in a search of the thicket in which the bear was hiding, the Iroquois refused. He answered: *"Tomalen siam kokchit klatawa esecum.—* Tomorrow he will be dead."

On their way back to camp, the hunters ran into Walker and Wood, who had killed four grizzlies. In one day, twenty-four bears were seen and six killed. Now they understood why the Hudson's Bay trappers had dubbed the site Bear Camp or Grizzly Bear Camp.

Peale was silent on the palatability of bear steaks, though not loath to give his opinion on elk ("not fit to eat"). Dana was noncommittal, though he observed: "Bear stewed, bear roasted, and dough fried in bear grease composed our evening meal." But Emmons and Eld both liked bear meat, though it was not as tender as beef. And Brackenridge wrote: "I must say that bear meat, when well cooked, is very palatable."

Besides "grisly" bears and deer, there were elk and wild cattle and vast flocks of antelope, leading Eld to exclaim: "Surely, a greater game country cannot exist in any part of the world than in this country." Brackenridge echoed his feelings: "Of antelope, deer, elk and bear, I never [saw] such number in my life." Peale added that the valley was a great aviary. He counted mallards, sandhill cranes, rusty grackles, cormorants, herons, and egrets as well as the ubiquitous ravens which had loafed about all their camps, cadging meals of offal.

The brazen coyotes grew bolder and sneaked, by night, right into camp to carry off a fresh bear skin hung from a limb six feet off the ground, near the fire and only six feet from a tent. But there was so much food that, next morning, the explorers threw even choice cuts to the ravenous ravens, turkey vultures, and "California vultures" or condors assembled to enjoy a feast.

The valley soil was fertile and apparently flooded each spring.

The prairie grew lush wild oats and Canary grass, escaped from the Spanish settlements. Brackenridge watched natives collect fat, meaty acorns from stately oaks, twenty to the acre. They waved their hands at him as if to say "Keep off!"

When the march was resumed, one of the packhorses fell into the river and ruined everything soluble in its pack—sugar, gunpowder, tea. Emmons tried to keep an eye on the Sacramento as the trail veered away. He feared that he might bypass a reach holding the squadron's boats, stopped by shoals, perhaps, and waiting for him. His anxiety led him off the marked route, several times, to interview Indians. But, when they did not avoid him altogether, they were incommunicative.

The hunters were coming into their own. Venison vied with bear stew for dinner. Emmons wrote his agreement with Eld—"This is one of the greatest game countries that I have ever been in." He probably agreed with Eld (unlike Brackenridge) that the Sacramento Valley, dry as it was—between floods—might be cultivated to advantage.

When two men broke their gunstocks, they showed themselves to be pretty fair armorer-artificers. They applied wet rawhide thongs which dried and shrank so tightly on the wood that the firearms were soon as strong as when new. That night, the repaired arms were grabbed up as a grizzly ambled through camp, capsizing things and creating a great hubbub before it blundered off into the night unhurt.

Because Guardapii was unfamiliar with the Sacramento Valley, the men meandered in close company with the river when straight-line shortcuts would have served. The hired hands now separated their privately owned stock from the government herd. They felt safe from Indians now and did not want to bother guarding them so tightly any longer. A closely herded or hobbled horse could not feed well enough to put any fat on its back. Nor did the frontiersmen see any point in standing watch anymore. Emmons acidly noted that they took full advantage of Peale's "negligence" in not sending out a guard relief during the night. Emmons had to bear the brunt of the anger of the unrelieved guard detail.

Dana compared the Sacramento Valley favorably with the Willamette, remarking on the alluvial black soil which, though cracked by drying, was fertile and caused oaks to groan under loads of spindle-shaped acorns whose rich meal was just right for the Indian "black loaf" bread.

October 14 saw an easy, overcast, and cool day of traveling across a dusty plain, once covered with ponds. But Emmons shook with chills. He dosed himself heavily with quinine but could not ward off a violent attack of the shakes: "I was a miserable man, all day," he scrawled in his diary. Though ill, he was blamed by Peale for lost time and effort, because of retraced steps: "By refusing the information of the guides, much time and distance was lost, as we were obliged to return nearly to where we started from, after several hours of travel."

As the animals lagged, Emmons changed course to intercept the river. He watered and rested his stock, and, when he found that two kegs of powder were spoiled by the wet, he let his men celebrate at the same time that they lightened the baggage. They amused themselves by making squibs, or firecrackers, which they set off. The kegs were a big failure. They had been painted on the outside and were so tightly fitted as to be considered waterproof. He observed, philosophically: "But constant exposure to the sun upon these prairies has unfitted them for submarine navigation."

The fourteenth started out like a bad day. A broken-down horse was abandoned and a mule was crowded off the riverbank trail and into the Sacramento. But the brute was undismayed by its fall and wetting. Emmons watched with alarm, then growing admiration, as the long-eared swimmer headed upstream—"like a young steamboat" —despite its heavy pack. The mule successfully breasted the current, scrambled up a steep bank three hundred yards above its mates, and quietly regained its old position in the caravan.

By keeping too close to the Sacramento, Emmons again lost time. A muddy tributary, too deep to ford, had to be rounded. With all its twisting turns, it took four hours, and Brackenridge bickered: "We did not go more than 7 miles in a direct line today."

Next day, however, eight hours of steady riding clipped off a record advance of twenty-eight miles over a flat destitute even of oaks, except on the banks of the river. Deer and antelope were shot and the commander took the horns of the latter as scientific specimens. Peale had noted on the fourteenth that the soil kicked up by the horses' hooves was full of bulbous roots. Now the ground was covered with goose dung and dead Planorbis shells, testifying to the valley's overflown condition in winter. Agate was seized with a chill but regained the party safely at a beaver dam on a small but deep tributary to the Sacramento. This was the Rivière des Buttes. Though Butte Creek was only twenty feet wide and muddy, it was sometimes called Beaver Creek because Company trappers had taken more than a hundred pelts from it in a season.

Emmons examined the Sacramento Buttes or Three Buttes, now

called the Sutter Buttes or Marysville Buttes. The mountains plunked smack-dab in the middle of the billiard-table-flat Sacramento Valley constituted a Siskiyou Trail landmark second only to Mount Shasta. No geologist, he decided that the volcanic ruin was a sedimentary sandstone formation! Because of the low valley at their base, the jagged, two-thousand-foot buttes, far from any other heights of land, could be seen all the way from hell-and-gone.

Peale did not attempt to determine the geological origin of the unusual, almost awkward "range of insular mountains." Colvocoresses was correctly convinced of their igneous origin. He described them properly as crater-shaped hills or low mountains, adding: "It is generally believed that each of these has been a volcano."

Brackenridge dismissed the buttes as simply "a number of barren peaks and, toward the summit, rocky and rugged, with a few scattered bushes and trees vegetating in the cliffs." But mineralogist-geologist Dana was fascinated, naturally, with the "isolated collection of summits." Putting the buttes into the singular—for he recognized them as the rotten remnants of a giant volcanic cone or *caldera* (crater), eroded away—he wrote: "It stands like an island in a vast prairie of mill pond smoothness."

Emmons sent the main party ahead under Sergeant Stearns while he worked on altitudes and Eld and the doctor nursed Agate and Colvocoresses along the trail. Since water was scarce along the proper route, Emmons diverged from its ruts to find a campsite and crossed a floodplain which Peale found offensively dusty. After floundering in a jungly swamp of willows and *tules,* and wading in viscous mud, he finally reached a *laguna.* The lakelet had served as a Company campground, but the water was now so stagnant that Emmons feared it would sicken his party. He turned his back on it.

Emmons made his way into the heart of the complex of buttes, entering via a southside pass, traveling seven miles and almost exiting by an eastern gap. His party straggled along in his wake. Guardapii had assured the officers that they would find a "Bay" camp, with water.

October 16 offered the expeditionaries a good sampling of California's climate, scorching sun by day and a cold north wind by night. The tents were pitched in a corral which Emmons found in a little valley amid the peaks. (Curiously, he used the South African spelling, "kraal.") The filthy corral had been occupied not only by Laframboise's men but by sheep and by cattle. Two of Emmons's followers found there traps they had cached in 1840. There was plenty of game in the opening, but the summer sun had sucked the waterhole dry. Two deep holes remained wet in an arroyo about a third of a mile away. The *aqua* was anything but *pura,* being aswarm with animalculae. In fact, it looked as bad as that of the pond at which Emmons had earlier turned up his nose. But both men and animals drank of the noisome liquid—Emmons even had to station men at the wells with buckets to water the horses and mules, to keep the beasts from tumbling in because of their roaring thirsts.

Emmons shot the sun to find the latitude of the Buttes. He was surprised to find that trappers and Mexican-Californians alike treated the Prairie Buttes as the de facto border between Alta California and Oregon. (Like a good Yankee, he called the latter, contested territory "our country.") The line of 42° was well within "greater" Oregon, like the Siskiyous themselves.

So gusty was the sharp-edged north wind that night, blowing in williwaws, that Emmons ordered all campfires extinguished to avoid setting the grassy slopes of the Buttes afire. Because of the difficulty of cooking breakfast in what Brackenridge called "a complete hurricane," a slow start was made the next day. Worse, one of the Indian women accidentally started a grassfire. All hands, not excluding Emmons, had to pitch in to fight the fire before getting the caravan under way.

Smoky weather and a dusty road could not hide the beauty of the great valley oaks, some six feet in diameter. The spread of branches of many was fifty feet, the equal of their height. Emmons, ever the practical seaman, examined the oak wood carefully as a possibility for naval stores. Though it was brittle, he guessed that some of the smaller species might provide good ship's timber for California markets, in time, "as the world grows older."

Less than twenty miles below the Buttes, Emmons led his men to the Feather River, named by the Spaniards for the many wild-goose feathers floating on its waters. It was more rapid than the Sacramento but of less volume. The hundred-yard-wide stream was lined with willows, and Brackenridge remarked, "Near this river I saw some of the finest oak timber observed during the whole trip from the Columbia."

The expeditionaries were a few miles below the Siskiyou Trail ford at today's Nicolaus, where they expected to find canoes. But they were gone, so Emmons searched downstream for a ford which could be waded. His animals were in no shape to swim. He found a splendid site where the water came up only to the horses' ribs. While he was congratulating himself as a pathfinder, Guardapii and his horse began to disappear. *Quicksand!* Hurriedly, Emmons pulled everyone back to the solid beach. (In his journal, he lapsed into shipboard jargon in his excitement, reporting that he had "hauled off.")

Night overtook the travelers as they continued downriver, looking for a crossing. Camp was made two miles from the Feather's mouth. Hardly was everyone settled down when a herd of antelope invaded the camp. A great ragged volley greeted them but the swift animals bore charmed lives: Not one was hit. Next, several male elk bulled their way into camp. Again, the men blazed away. And again their prey escaped, although some were wounded several times over. The almost grizzlylike stamina of the elk impresesd Emmons: "There is no doubt that many balls entered them, but one might as well shoot at a whale, unless he hits exactly in the right place."

Ignace had better luck, dropping a cow with a well placed shot into a herd of wild cattle—runaways from either Captain Sutter's ranch or Siskiyou Trail herds. Emmons was delighted with the quality of the meat, finding it "fatter than any I have ever seen in our markets in the U. S." Peale compared the beef with fresh-killed antelope and observed: "No game will compare with *beef,* excepting buffalo meat."

Emmons planned an early start on the eighteenth, to reach Sutter's Fort. But nine animals had strayed. The delay was extended when Rich fired his gun, for some reason. Since a gunshot was the agreed-upon signal for the horse hunters to come in, they did just that— and had to be sent out, all over again. Impatient, Emmons headed for New Helvetia and Sutter, leaving Eld in charge of the horse herd. Wood did not even wait for Emmons. He hurried ahead on a bee-line for Sutter's Fort.

Just above the mouth of the Feather, Emmons crossed the stream, diagonally, using a sandbar in midstream. The ford was only two or three feet deep but, again, quicksandy. All hands and their packs were wet through, but they floundered ashore safely on the site of the later Hawaiian fishing village of Verona. Emmons thought that the Feather and Sacramento, combined at their junction, spread out to the breadth of the Columbia at Fort Vancouver between high banks of sandy clay. Seeing "civilized" tracks on the beach, Emmons deduced that Navy boats had come this far in search of him.

Peale was poking about in the ruins of an Indian civilization. Between the two rivers he found the remains of a town, completely deserted. He later learned that it had once held several hundred souls. He explained its desolation: *"All* of whom perished in one season by a tertian fever. . . ." Brackenridge was horrified: "Their bones lay strewed about on the hills in all directions, there being not enough of the tribe spared—as we were told—to bury the dead." Peale added: "In one of the skulls a bird has built its nest." Eld also puttered about the Indian golgotha. He was told that five hundred natives had died there of the fever and ague during a single malarial season. Wrote Eld: "Their remedies for this disease, like the Indians of Oregon, was to jump into the river just as the fever was coming, which was often followed by instant death on the banks."

Travel on the nineteenth was unpleasantly warm and sultry, but Emmons had to hurry his animals to reach water before they should collapse. At one point, a large herd of curious elk milled in a great antlered circle about him. They held their massive heads high, every eye on him. His hunters tried to kill some of the beasts but the horses were quite unequal to the chase when the elk bolted. Sighed Emmons: "With fresh horses, well equipt, such a chase with such advantages would be grand sport. But with our poor, worn-out animals, it is cruel to see them attempt to run."

The only horse with any spunk left was Frying Pan. This eccentric brute in the charge of sailor Doughty had a vicious temper. The seamen had so named her because the kitchen equipment was entrusted to her—frypan, pots, and kettles. As the band moseyed quietly along in its fatigue on October 19, Frying Pan took it into her head to kick and menace the other animals. She also made a lot of noise, what with the clangor of dislocated cookware on her back. The sound further alarmed the other animals. Not wishing a stampede, even of jaded horses and mules, some of the men tried to catch Frying Pan with their *reatas* or lassos. But the mare was familiar with such cowboy tricks and, dodging, easily escaped the loops which they cast. She finally rejoined the pack train, but only when she was good and ready —and not for long. Next, Frying Pan created further mischief by (quite literally) busting her bellyband. Away the she-devil dashed, pots and pans flying to all compass points. Emmons confessed that he found the mare entertaining, if mighty troublesome.

Emmons found the American River ford just up from its junction with the Sacramento. The American, in October, hardly deserved the term "river." But the Lieutenant did not fail to note its wide bed and deep-cut banks, carved by in-season flooding. Eld, unlike Emmons and Brackenridge, called the American River (named for Jed Smith's trappers) the Jesús María. This was the name which the Spaniards had given the Sacramento in 1808. But it had not stuck.

Colvocoresses looked back up the Sacramento Valley and voiced his disappointment. He had heard much of its fruitfulness and had expected a vast greensward. He had been unprepared for its straw color during the summer. "We saw but little good land," he recalled, "and as for the landscape, it was extremely uninteresting, being utterly devoid of either beauty or variety."

Captain John Sutter rode out to meet Emmons on the south bank of the American River. He was ruddy-complexioned, fair of hair, and a bit stout, though well proportioned at five feet, eight inches. He was accompanied by some of his attendants and by Wood. The Swiss wore an undress uniform with sidearms buckled around his waist. Brackenridge described his costume as that of a French lieutenant of infantry. Small wonder: The vain Sutter liked to fib about his army service, actually limited to militia duty in Switzerland. He greeted his visitors with the utmost cordiality. Brackenridge later described his welcome as being in "the ceremonious manner peculiar to his country."

Sutter insisted that Emmons camp alongside his house in the New Helvetia walled compound. But, because of a water shortage there, the Lieutenant politely declined and ordered his men to the Sacramento's shore. Perhaps he was more concerned with brandy than water. Sutter's distillery made *aguardiente* or *pisco* out of wild grapes. All that Emmons needed, after his exhausting efforts on the Siskiyou Trail, was a company of drunken sailors, marines, and mountain men in Mexican territory!

However, Emmons accepted a luncheon invitation extended to him by Sutter (whom he called a Swede, in error). Before the *merienda,* he examined New Switzerland, from his host's "doby" (adobe) home—which Brackenridge thought was in "the Swiss style" —to the thick mud walls of the fort, pierced with loopholes for riflemen and buttressed by heavy supports. The compound was the heart of a thirty-league (ninety-mile) square agricultural and pastoral empire. Sutter told Brackenridge that he had a thousand sheep and 1200 horses but seven thousand cattle.

Sutter was planning to dig a moat around his fort and to lead American River water into it via a natural *laguna.* He was taking this precaution in case the Mexicans should dispute his landgrant. He told Brackenridge: "I shall fight them for it [if necessary]." The botanist added in his notes: "I understand he has secured the good graces of the Indians in his vicinity, who will, no doubt, assist him in case of any serious misunderstanding with the Mexican government."

To Emmons, New Helvetia was "an independent monarchy on

a small scale," and Sutter as powerful a figure on the southern end of the Siskiyou Trail as was Dr. McLoughlin at the northern end. The Swiss told him: "My assumption of power is quite necessary for my own well-being and self-defense." He described the California government as both weak and corrupt. Though he held a Mexican government commission as *alcalde* (judge) and commander of the northern frontier, he was the target of much jealousy from "some Californians of high position," by whom he meant Generals Mariano Vallejo and José Castro and Governor Juan B. Alvarado. Emmons correctly judged the situation: "Instead of looking to the Government for support, he is now actively engaged in fortifying himself against any attack." He noted that Sutter had purchased a park of artillery from the Russians at Fort Ross. There were already in position four twelve-pounders and four six-pound carronades, to add to the small arms and a few swivels which the Swiss had earlier relied upon for defense.

Captain Sutter was deeply involved in the beaver trade, using Indian trappers, whom he paid liberally. Emmons noted how kind and indulgent—paternalistic—he was with them, as with all his servants and employees. Brackenridge put in: "Captain Sutter keeps a number of individuals a'hunting beaver and otter and has prohibited the Hudson's Bay Company from trapping on his property. He is also by subtle-by-fair means securing the friendship of the Indian tribes about him and giving every inducement to foreigners of all denominations to settle about his vicinity in the capacity of farmers."

Brackenridge took the time, also, to size up his kindly host: "Being a Swiss by birth, his appearance and manner bespoke in him a man of volatile and unsettled disposition. . . ." Noting that Sutter was starting vineyards, using Bodega cuttings for wines in lieu of the local fox grapes, the horticulturalist opined, "I doubt not that he will succeed." But he felt it necessary to add: "Captain Sutter don't appear to be a very temperate man." Nevertheless, he liked him. "Like his countrymen, he certainly talks a little largely. But, granting him a little license in this respect, with the stock he has begun on, and the intelligence and perseverance which he possesses, in a few years there will be nothing in California to compete with him in point of strength, wealth, and influence."

Emmons feared that the Swiss adventurer had plunged too many irons in the fire and was bound to be burned. Sutter, himself, was aware that he was gambling with fate, but he was sanguine of success: "I will be a good Mexican so long as they guarantee to me my natural rights as a free citizen. But when they curtail them, I am prepared to help myself." With much enthusiasm and sincerity, he wished aloud for the day (not too far distant, he hoped) when the Stars and Stripes would fly over California.

Sutter placed a boat at Emmons's disposal. He also promised him the loan of a second vessel, expected daily from downriver. The Swiss, who took tea in Emmons's camp, detailed one of his men (probably a Black American from Boston) to kill a bullock for the naval officer whenever he needed beef for his men. Good steaks and roasts helped morale in camp, even among the "scientifics" who griped about not being able to stay in more comfortable New Helvetia. The Lieutenant dismissed them as men who consulted only their own convenience in such matters. Doubtless, Peale and Brackenridge were the miffed *científicos*.

Segregating provisions, Emmons formed up two parties. He would take the ill by boat. Eld would take the other detachment, by boat if possible, otherwise by land. From Sutter, Emmons learned that the *Vincennes* was at anchor at San Francisco but that Wilkes had not yet arrived with the rest of the squadron. He also found that Lieutenant Cadwalader Ringgold had surveyed the Sacramento by boat for some distance above the American River before returning to San Francisco Bay.

As he took his leave, the Lieutenant thanked Sutter for his information on California as well as his general kindness. He had a genuine liking for his multilingual host with the frank and prepossessing manner: "From a short acquaintance, I should take him to be an intelligent, generous and high-minded man with a good share of that enthusiasm which, I believe, is common with his countrymen."

Colvocoresses also admired the energetic colonizer: "We were most hospitably and kindly received by him; there was no ostentatious display, no pomp nor ceremony, but an easy and polite demeanor on the part of our host that made us feel perfectly at home."

Sutter had hired Walker to superintend his farm and herds. He also took on Burrows, Warfield, Wood, and Nichols and their families. Guardapii and Boileau wished to work for the Swiss, too, so Emmons gave them their discharges.

Since Sutter's launch did not nose up the river as hoped, Eld departed on October 20 with Peale, Rich, Brackenridge, Ignace, Warfield, Black, Molair, and Tibbetts. Guardapii was supposed to go but stayed at the fort, though Boileau made the march, perhaps out of curiosity about San Francisco. The servant, Thomas Mercer, and a Mexican guide, Romero, supplied by Sutter, rounded out the land party. Brackenridge described Romero as "an intelligent young Spanish peasant." Eld requested Acting Second Master Sergeant Stearns because he had been so valuable on the Siskiyou Trail as hunter and guard, so Emmons let him have the Marine at the last moment.

Eld's orders were to lose no time in meeting Emmons in Yerba Buena, as San Francisco was still called. He was to move there via the missions of San José, Santa Clara, and San Francisco de Asís, or Mission Dolores. Still fuzzy about California geography, Emmons threw in Santa Cruz Mission (too far south, had Eld gone there). The scientific gentlemen were instructed to continue their researches while on this last leg of the Siskiyou Trail.

With Emmons in the launch went Colvocoresses, Dr. Whittle, Marines March and Smith, Corporal Hughes, servant Waltham, the taxidermist, Sutton, and mineralogist Dana. The latter, somewhere along the Sacramento River, predicted the California Gold Rush. He told Joel Walker, "This is a golden country." Reported Walker, later: "He said he saw every indication of gold, but showed me none."

Eld led his men over the level prairie to the Cosumnes River, the dividing line between Sacramento and San Joaquin Valleys. Brackenridge was pleased by the terrain: "I felt a pleasant sensation, in passing along, to view the numerous flocks of cattle and horses which were in all directions seen grazing on the rich prairies, which brought forcibly to my recollection scenes of former days."

Eld, however, was unimpressed by the Cosumnes and denigrated the thirty-foot-wide stream as a mere creek. Romero told him that it had been perfectly dry twenty-five days before. Distant rain in the Sierra had given it a seasonal rebirth. On the march, the men saw many *berendos* (antelope) and "collotes" (coyotes), though the grass was sparse and Eld thought the soil was too poor and sandy for anything but grazing. Peale appreciated the fact that the Indians were not burning the prairie out from under them.

Probably because Sutter had warned him against the Horse Thief Indians of the interior valleys, who made a living—and a very good one—by raiding ranches and missions of their stock, Eld posted a mounted guard over his herd. Peale applauded the idea as "a decided improvement over our practice heretofore—men on foot can do little to prevent (cunning) Indians from stealing horses and riding off in the night."

Peale found the Río de los Mogueles (the Mokelumne) to be a rapid stream. On its sandy beach he saw the tracks of a grizzly bigger than any he had met. When the aching men tumbled into their blankets, they had covered thirty-two miles. The campsite was on the small San Juan River, now French Camp Creek, Laframboise's old base of operations. The stream was filthy with feathers and goose dung but it had to be drunk by men and horses; there was no other alternative. Eld had hoped to reach the San Joaquin River, but the horses had failed him on the long and dry stretch. Mercer's animal was abandoned, for the beast "had not strength enough to carry his own miserable carcass along."

Through the "toolie fields" (*tulares*) passed the party to the San Joaquin on October 23. The river was not fordable usually where Eld struck it, but the summer had been such a hot one that the river occupied only 150 feet of its wide bed. The men crossed it easily, hardly wetting the packs. Romero wished to halt at a lagoon filled with geese and ducks and surrounded by cranes and antelope. He warned that there was no more grass or water for a long day's journey. But an impatient Eld insisted on pushing forward since it was not yet noon and there was no feed for the horses. Brackenridge blamed Eld for overruling the pilot: "Mr. Eld, wishing to bring into play the very little power with which he was invested, rejected the advice of the guide and ordered the party to proceed."

Romero and Eld led the company across a plain barren of grass except for sunburnt stubble. The ground was so soft that the horses sank into it at every step. Many elk and antelope were sighted on the sun-blasted plain, leading Eld to ruminate: "What these animals find to eat is difficult to conceive." Next, he encountered naked hills one to three hundred feet high. They abounded in fossil oysters, and Peale learned that Californians had found fossilized fish, too. From the area of Altamont Pass or Corral Hollow they dropped toward Livermore Valley. Before they were out of the barren Puertezuelo Mountains, they ran into Dr. John Marsh, a Sutter-like pioneer of the *contra costa*—the inside coast (that is, the eastern shore of San Francisco Bay). He offered them some of his half-wild horses—if they could catch them. Eld found this impossible, so he pressed on.

Night caught the detachment on Robert Livermore's "miserable rancho" (Brackenridge), without a blade of grass or drop of water. They groped their way westward until eight and, at last, found water. But it was a quagmire. The *ciénega* or swamp was full of geese, ducks, and sandhill cranes. In this mudhole, trampled by herds of cattle and plastered with their droppings, the men had to make camp. Eld, in disgust, described the campsite as "little better than a cow yard." Brackenridge termed the filthy oasis "a morass." It was so dark that most of the men could not even find water—a "nauseous beverage," at best—though they were virtually on top of it. After riding forty-five miles with nothing to eat and hardly anything to drink, they had to turn in without tasting a morsel of food. The grass was rank and good but the stock so spent that they lay down in the wet *tules* and flags without eating.

Peale did not complain. In fact, he had a good word for the site—"the bed, however, was better than usual, being rushes." The racket made by the waterfowl should have kept everyone awake but it was a lullaby to men worn out by almost fifty miles in the saddle that day, without grub. And when they were finally able to kill a few geese and a steer, the detachment made a meal which, in Peale's words, "would astonish people who eat more than once in 24 hours."

Eld, like Emmons, was concerned over the sufferings of the horses. Some had galled or ulcerated backs. One such "ulcer" was an inch deep and eight inches long. Another beast had two broken ribs. A third had a place laid bare by a sore where every respiration was distinctly seen in the wound, which was the size of a man's hand. "And yet," sighed Eld, "I am obliged to drive these poor animals at the rate I did this evening that they may not literally starve to death."

Since he considered himself to be lost in a swamp, Eld was astonished when Romero asked permission to go to his *rancho* for a change of clothing in which to make his entrance into the settlements! The subaltern could not believe that the pilot could find his way about in a pitch-black night showing only a few stars. But the Mexican needed only the North Star. He was back, as ordered, by daylight. And he was metamorphosed, "having come out a perfect Spanish don, with broad-brimmed black hat, a big Spanish cloth cloak lined with red, his pantaloons on the sides studded with bell buttons, and a pair of spurs with rowels more than two inches in diameter which, having a little wire tongue attached to them, made as much noise, every time he stepped, as a string of hawks bells."

Breakfast was prepared with dirty, saline water, but Eld had Romero kill one of Livermore's steers. He had paid for it in advance at Sutter's with an old red Hudson's Bay blanket used all the weary way down the Siskiyou Trail as an *apishamon* or saddle blanket. Behind the cook-fire loomed the bulk of Mount Diablo, called Pul Pomie by the Indians. He noted that it was covered with the "remains" of verdure almost to its summit, then amended his entry—"To say verdure would be almost preposterous at the present time, for during our whole day's route we have scarcely seen a blade of grass."

Leaving the third-rate oasis, Eld and Romero led the men over and through the heat-blasted hills, Brackenridge's "base and bleak range of mountains," probably via Niles Canyon. The terrain flattened in the afternoon and Eld found himself in the Santa Clara Valley.

Mission San José was miserable and dilapidated. Its "dauby" (adobe) wall still enclosed a five-to-six-hundred-foot compound but the gates were missing. Of the many buildings, including schoolrooms and Indian dormitory, only the church looked to be in passable condition.

The midshipman presented a letter of introduction from Sutter to the administrator of the secularized mission, Don José Antonio Estrada. The *administrador* was annoyed by Eld's blunder—the latter took Estrada at first, because he was in shirtsleeves, to be a servant. Don José received his visitors without kindness and let them cool their heels in a decaying anteroom. There, several "mean looking" fellows asked Eld impertinent questions. No one offered to help him in any way. Finally, he asked if there was feed in the vicinity, to refresh the horses. "*Nada* [nothing]," was the answer. He then asked, "Where is there any?" He received a noncommittal "*¿Quién sabe?* [Who knows?]" When he asked if he could turn his animals into the enclosure, the reply was yes—but there was nothing for them to eat.

Eld's temper was rising. He recalled, shortly thereafter: "At this last reply, I got completely outrageous [*sic*], as I could plainly see that altho' what he said was very nearly true, but that he wanted the politeness to even do what was in his power. I determined to leave him forthwith, which I did, without being asked to partake even of a cup of chocolate or a morsel of food. This, then, was my first impression of the hospitality of California. . . . After having been more than forty-five days traveling over mountains and thro' arid plains for nearly 800 miles, fatigued, tired and fagged out, scarcely any of us but was more or less affected with fever. . . ."

Eld had believed what Captain Frederick W. Beechey, R.N., and other travelers had written of Californian benevolence. Hence his surprise at being treated like a *lépero*.

Peale had little to say about the inhospitable reception. He was more interested in the clean, well-dressed aborigines leaving the mission after Mass. He learned that, once a year (at the very time of his visit), they were allowed to return to their native mountains and valleys to harvest the acorn crop. Many of them rode horses, he noticed, loaded with beef. This meat was their weekly mission ration.

Brackenridge, like Eld, was miffed at Estrada. "Our own external appearance was certainly anything but prepossessing, but he might certainly have detected beneath the buckskin dress, and from the conversation that issued, some faint traits of gentlemen."

A grumpy Eld was mounted, ready to ride off, when a "gentlemanly looking" man stepped up. He addressed the officer in English and asked if he might be of service. The man was Hudson's Bay Company agent Alexander Forbes. He invited the travelers to accompany him to his home, distant about two leagues. "We were overjoyed to find ourselves in such good hands," Eld recounted, "as we knew by experience we should be, with anybody connected with the Company, and we of course readily assented."

But, first, Eld looked over the mission with Peale. He sent his men ahead, to camp at Forbes's place, six miles up the road, and he promised Forbes to join him and his lady at some point on the road to San Francisco Bay. Brackenridge, with little scientific curiosity about the mission, was eager to leave the "miserable, fallen place and its inhospitality."

Eld and Peale waited for the padre to finish his siesta but an old retainer and his wife offered chairs and a snack of grapes and water. Shortly, the man brought a key and showed off the church to the visitors. The whitewashed interior was unexceptional but one religious picture caught Eld's eye as being tolerably well executed, if not done by a Raphael or Michelangelo. Peale liked the "distemper" (tempera?) paintings on the chapel walls, done by a wandering Italian.

The mission's tailor, Ephraim Travel of Philadelphia, guided the two men through the four-acre garden of grapevines, fruit trees, and other plants, including tobacco. Despite the total drought, the mission had made forty barrels of wine that year. But the Indian population had dropped to one thousand from three thousand in 1831 and five thousand at its peak.

Eld and Peale rode hard to catch up with Forbes. They found his comfortable two-story adobe ranch house on a treeless, uncultivated plain at the foot of the hills called Monte de las Calaveras— "Skull Mountain." Peale noticed one nearby rancho with its fences composed of walls of longhorn cattle skulls. The plain was covered with carcasses in varying stages of decomposition, since only the hides and tallow were worth taking for commerce. He recalled: "As we traveled in the dark last night, the continued rattling and breaking of bones under our horses' feet had a most singular and unpoetic effect. Any but California horses would have been frightened by it."

At Forbes's place, Peale slept in a bed for the first time since leaving Fort Vancouver. His host escorted him and his comrades up the Royal Road (El Camino Real) until they could see Mission Santa Clara in the distance. He strongly urged them to bypass the pueblo of San José. There, they would surely lose their horses. Romero agreed. He called the town a nest of *putas y ladrones*—whores and thieves.

Crossing Penitencia and Coyote creeks and the Guadalupe River, Eld sent Romero and the men ahead to camp at San Francisquito Ranch. Meanwhile, he took Peale and Rich to investigate Mission Santa Clara. They were received hospitably by the priest, Padre Jesús María Vásquez del Mercado, a man with intelligent black eyes and a jolly countenance. He gave them a thorough tour of his church, then turned them over to the civil *administrador* of the property.

The old administrator treated the Americans with even greater rudeness than had Estrada at San José—in fact, with contempt. But, after his wife whispered something in his ear, his attitude altered somewhat for the better. Peale, who had mistaken him for the mission gardener, thought that the civil servant had sized up his visitors as roughnecks because of their travel-stained clothing. Rich refused to accept the man's inhospitality. He reproved him for his bad manners in tolerably good Spanish, and the man became a different person. He showed off the grapes and peach, pear, apple, fig, almond, and olive trees, and also the prickly pear cacti raised for their *tuna* fruit. He sat his guests down in his house and fed them fruits, *dulces* (sweets), and pear brandy.

Later, Eld realized the reason for the administrator's initial inhospitable conduct. It was because of the priest's keeping "certain females about the church for his express commerce." The old man had taken Eld and his friends for customers for the favors of the soiled doves under the friar's wing. He had been determined to drive them away forthwith.

San Francisquito was reached before dark on October 25. Eld decided to make a "long camp" there since the grass was good, although it was already occupied by two "fierce looking" fellows, Mexican soldiers on leave who raised horses and cattle. Eld believed that they were quite ready to steal his animals, at any time. Boileau traded a gun to them for a horse and the pair made no trouble, despite Eld's fears.

A botanizing Peale was particularly taken with the very fragrant species of Laurus, the California bay tree or laurel (pepperwood) which had entranced David Douglas, and which Oregonians called Oregon myrtle. Peale packed some of its olivelike nuts in a goose skin filled with dry clay, hoping to be able to introduce it into "the States" when he got back home. He had first seen it in the Umpqua Valley and recalled: "The foliage is so fragrant as to perfume the air to a considerable distance, when heated by the sun."

At dark, it began to rain. At last, the long summer drought was broken. Winter was on its wet way. Though it rained copiously all night, Eld tried for an early start for San Francisco. But, suddenly, the horses began to give out, one after the other. They were blown up like puffballs. He guessed that it was from drinking great quantities of brackish water. Against his will, he had to camp only four leagues from San Francisco.

En route to his camp, Eld fell in with a launch and some woodsmen on Pulgas Creek, cutting redwood. He was much amused when an obvious American persisted in speaking badly broken Spanish to him, although he answered in "broad English." When Eld finally said that he really wished that he would speak English, the fellow looked at the officer's grimy buckskins and fifty-day-old beard. He exclaimed: "My God, sir, where did you come from?" When Eld told him the Columbia River, the lumberjack's jaw sagged further in disbelief. He looked astonished. He said that he never would have believed it, were it not for the wretched condition of the horses.

The first question put to Eld by most Californians, who saw the emaciated walking carcasses which passed for horses, was, *"¿De donde viene?* [Where do you come from?]" When he answered, "The Columbia," they would repeat after him, in amazement, "Columbia! . . . *¡Es un país muy lejos!* [It is a far-off country!] *Su caballo es muy cansado y malo.* [Your horse is very tired and sick.]"

Eld's last camp before San Francisco was a hungry one. He wrote of his hunt. "I, as usual, got nothing." But, once more, Peale displayed his fine marksmanship by bringing down a high-flying goose —and with a ball, not birdshot.

The horses were somewhat improved by their rest so Eld rounded Mount San Bruno and headed for Mission Dolores (Mission of the Sorrows), as Mission San Francisco de Asís was familiarly called. Peale thought it aptly named: "It is a mission truly of sorrow, and is nearly all in ruins. But fifty Indians are left in it, who are the 'picture of poverty.'" Eld was frankly disgusted. He was shown about the decrepit buildings by the *alcalde,* or, as he understood it, "Don Juan," rather than the Mission's civilian administrator, Tiburcio Vásquez.

To Eld, "Don Juan" was a "dumpling-looking man, dressed in a trooper's light-blue cassimere, leathern lined pantaloons, and a bottle green jacket adorned with black braid and frogs; and mounted upon a great rawboned horse, he looked as fierce and military as such a lump of good nature well could."

Eld, remembering the descriptions of Vancouver and Beechey, was appalled at the state of the mission and its dissolute priest, an ex-muleteer named José Lorenzo Quijas, a disgrace to the Franciscan Order if there ever lived one: "This profligate, hoary headed, sycophantic wretch, disguised with a shaved head, hood and caul, keeps a harem of Indian girls, gets drunk habitually, and glories in his wickedness like a demon; chuckles and laughs at his depravity. When asked why he can do these things under the garb of religion, [he] answers with the utmost concern that he does not preach to them to do as he docs but as he says, and if they derive no benefit from his doctrine, it is not his fault."

Peale was pleasantly surprised by the town of San Francisco, still being called by its original name, Yerba Buena ("Good Herb"). It presented a contrast to the slovenly Mission Dolores. Several neatly built English and American frame houses flanked the bay. But, at first, Eld did not even realize that he had arrived in the port. The town was only a hamlet. He looked into the windows of a structure and found it to be a billiard parlor. When he asked some players, sailors from Wilkes's little fleet, where Yerba Buena was located, he was told that he was standing in it.

Eld met Emmons, who had a boat ready to take him to the ship. But, first, he wanted the passed midshipman to settle with the trappers and to dispose of the wornout horses. A notice was posted to inform the "public"—presumably the half-dozen loungers in the *plaza* or square. At two in the afternoon, a ridiculous, pitiful, and painful scene took place. The poor old Siskiyou Trail horses, veterans which had borne men and supplies faithfully for 840 miles from Fort Vancouver to San Francisco, were held up to contempt and ridicule in English, Spanish, and French.

The animals were knocked off in lots, for bids ranging from twelve *reales* to five or six *yanqui* dollars apiece, to the accompaniment of jeers from buyers and onlookers alike, who laughed and joked cruelly about the horses' and mules' sore backs and bare ribs. The strutting little *alcalde* took one of the hardiest horses for a paltry sum. Eld was so mad that, as he later recalled, "I could, with good will, have knocked down the little *Alcalde!*"

Before nightfall, a boat took the overlanders across San Francisco Bay to Whalers' Cove or Richardson's Bay, where the flagship lay off Sausalito. The thump of Eld's travel-worn moccasins on the holystoned deck of the U.S.S. *Vincennes* marked the last of thousands and thousands of steps of the government's historic official exploration and mapping of almost 850 miles of Siskiyou Trail between Fort Vancouver and San Francisco.

The Navy's exploration and cartography would be improved and refined in 1855 by one of Secretary of War Jefferson Davis's railroad surveys. But the completion of the investigation of Emmons and Eld on October 28, 1841, really put the Siskiyou Trail "on the map."

Epilogue

BERNARD DE VOTO described 1846 as the Year of Decision for the Far West. But 1841 was a decisive year, too, at least for California and Oregon. Not only did the U.S. Exploring Expedition map the Siskiyou Trail and reaffirm America's intentions toward the two territories, but the year also saw representatives of two other interested countries jockeying for political position in California.

Britain's agent was Dr. McLoughlin's right-hand man, the efficient James Douglas. On board the *Columbia* in Monterey Bay, he recapitulated for Governor Alvarado on January 11, 1841, the results of their discussions about expanded commerce. He understood that the Governor was agreeable to the establishment of a Company store on San Francisco Bay and to Company vessels trading on the California coast, as long as they flew the Mexican flag. But he spelled out again his third query: "Will the Governor also concede to the Honble. Hudson's Bay Company the privilege of bringing to the country a party, not exceeding 30 beaver hunters, in order to extend their hunting operations into every part of the country, provided the persons in question submit to the legal formalities and become subjects of Mexico?"

Alvarado's reply was that the hunters would be licensed to trap beaver "in all our frontiers" once they were naturalized as Mexican citizens and given passports. He also demanded that the trappers be *"hombres de providad y buena conducta"* (men of probity and good

351

conduct), a pretty hard bill to fill—as Laframboise was finding out with his unruly Buenaventura Brigade. And, finally, Alvarado wished the size of the party cut in half and some of it composed of young Mexican boys, who would become familiar with the beaver "fishing" (*pesca de castor*) profession.

France was not yet ready to cede hegemony over the Pacific Coast to Great Britain. The French were represented by Eugène Duflot de Mofras, apparently a secret agent of the stripe of America's Bonneville and Slacum. Duflot de Mofras investigated California, including New Helvetia. (Rumors had him attempting to recruit French-Canadian trappers in John Sutter's employ for a potential army of occupation in a French-seized California.) He then journeyed to Fort Vancouver—but by ship rather than overland via the Siskiyou Trail. Simpson greeted him with cool suspicion, though he carried a letter of introduction from William Glen Rae. The latter, McLoughlin's son-in-law, had just (September 1841) opened the store in Yerba Buena granted Douglas by Alvarado. Sir George could not bring himself to believe that the French gentleman was interested solely in commerce. Nor did he appreciate the splendid, almost patriotic recognition paid the distinguished visitor by his fellow Gauls of Champoeg and French Prairie.

Thus, when Duflot de Mofras returned to California on the Company ship *Cowlitz* in December 1841, he was not the only passenger. Also aboard were McLoughlin and his daughter, Mrs. Rae, and Governor Simpson himself. The latter was intent on personally mending trade fences in California, although he appreciated the efforts of the trusted Douglas. It was not easy, for Simpson despised Governor Alvarado. Privately, he rated him as "an ignorant, dissipated man, quite devoid of responsibility and character."

According to a resident *yanqui,* Captain William D. Phelps, Sir George was determined to wrench California commerce (if not the territory, itself) away from the clutches of the naïvely imperialistic Americans. Rae, the Company factor in San Francisco, was socially inclined and prone to indulge in the "barley brae." When he was in his cups, Company secrets were anything but confidential. Once, when drunk, he had bragged to Phelps and other topers that it had cost the company £75,000 to drive the Boston firm of Bryant and Sturgis from the Pacific Northwest Coast trade. Then he had added: "And they will drive you Yankees from California, if it costs a million!"

Rae was not fooling. Simpson was aware that the sun was setting on California's beaver era, but he had great faith in the province's soil and its agricultural prospects. He had his eye fixed on the great Central Valley, threaded only by the rough road of the Siskiyou Trail. He considered the interior plain to be the finest region of all California, teeming with fish and game, flanked by forest-clad mountains, and capable of supporting "millions of inhabitants."

Simpson had his information on the hinterland from the new chief of the Southern Party, Francis Ermatinger, as well as from Douglas. (The latter wrote: "California is decidedly one of the finest countries in the world, surpassing all that poets dream of beauty and fertility. . . . The government is arbitrary and feebly administered; otherwise, I would make it my home in preference to any other country I know.") Ermatinger had replaced Laframboise at the latter's request. He was tired of trapping, especially since his Siskiyou Trail subordinates were becoming more lawless each year.

Moreover, Laframboise nursed a canker of grievance against the Company for his lack of promotion. Wrote Lieutenant Charles Wilkes of him: "To me he complained that he had not received what he considered his due, and that he was no better than twenty years before, saying 'I am still Michel Laframboise, only older.' " The naval officer liked Laframboise and concurred that "All parties refer [to him] as possessing the most accurate knowledge of the country." But to Wilkes's mind, Laframboise was his own worst enemy: "I regret to say that, like too many others, he ought to look to himself as the cause of his misfortunes. Had it not been for his proneness to dissipation, I am informed that he would have risen in the Company's service."

Whilst Laframboise was settling his brood into a farm on the west side of French Prairie, on the wheat land over which Nat Wyeth had enthused ("I have never seen country of equal beauty, except the Kanzas country"), Frank Ermatinger was writing his brother Edward, October 20, 1841, that he was taking the trappers to California. He wintered there and liked the area quite as much as Douglas. Much later (March 4, 1843), he recalled to Nat: "I took a long gallop after him [Sir George Simpson] in California and had an interview in Monterey, when he promised me a furlough in 1844. . . . Sometimes I am half-inclined to give up all thoughts of the [Hudson's Bay Company] service and Canada, in favour of California. It is a country I like. I passed a jovial winter of it last year, let the trappers take care of themselves while I was galloping about the country, to the American shipping, to Rae's, &c."

William Glen Rae's drinking crony, William D. Phelps, was more impressed with "Captain" Ermatinger than with the lordly Simpson himself. Although the latter did not affect a retinue including a Scots piper and a Russian American Company liaison officer as he sometimes did in Canada, Simpson did dash about California, chatting, flattering, dancing, and cigar smoking with the *señoritas, señoras* and *señores* in the hope (vain) of offsetting American influence in the Mexican province.

Phelps was so impressed with Ermatinger that he mistakenly took him to be in command of all Company trappers west of the Rockies. His word picture of Ermatinger serves to describe all of the half-wild breed who dominated the Siskiyou Trail: "He was a fair specimen of many who have risen to positions of responsibility by long and arduous service. Beginning at the lowest round of the ladder with low pay, compelled to perform duty in any capacity and in any place of which they may be ordered, at the desk or chopping wood, pulling an oar or cultivating the ground; and the Company servants are promoted, from time to time, according to their capacity and merit. Ermatinger was a good representative of his class—hardy, vigorous and active, extravagant in word, thought and deed, heedless of hardship, daring of danger, prodigal of the present and thoughtless of the future.

"Twenty-five years' life as a trapper and chief of trappers had accustomed him to perilous encounters with bears and Indians. His simple and frank manner in relating them contrasted singularly with the wild and startling nature of his themes. I was amused at a remark of his which showed the contempt in which these sons of the wilderness hold the comforts of civilized life. 'Captain,' said he, 'This is the first time I have slept in a house for two years, and last night I did a thing I have not done for twenty-four years—I slept in sheets. But I was drunk, and Rae put me into them; therefore, the sin must be at his door.'"

Another time, Ermatinger's skin-deep "civilization" was clearly demonstrated. Mission San Rafael's priest called on Rae one evening. The good father was not only quite "sprung" from assaults on an *aguardiente* bottle but also quite overly familiar, by Anglo-Saxon standards. Although the company was entirely male, he tried to embrace and kiss everyone present, Latin style. When the padre attempted to give Ermatinger a bearhug of an *abrazo,* he was knocked sprawling across the room by a backhand blow. "Stranger," said Frank. "When I was in the Rocky Mountains I swore that I would never allow myself to be hugged by a Blackfoot Indian or a grizzly bear. But I would suffer the embraces of either in preference to those of a drunken priest."

At Sonoma, Simpson learned of Ermatinger's presence on the Sacramento River. He sent him a letter asking that he meet him at Monterey. Ermatinger hurried to San Francisco but just missed the sailing of the *Cowlitz*. Now almost as good a horseman as the *vaqueros* whom he emulated, Ermatinger rode overland to the California capital. Simpson's first view of him has suggested to some historians that Ermatinger was a spy, like Duflot de Mofras. Actually, his appearance was but testimony to his social acclimatization. Wrote Simpson: "While returning to our boat, we were saluted by a horseman in Spanish costume whom we, at length, recognized, through his disguise, to be Mr. Francis Ermatinger."

Simpson sat Ermatinger down and pumped him of his experiences on the trapping cruise down the Siskiyou Trail. The booshway reported that he had traced the Willamette to its source, crossed the "height of land" (the Siskiyous) to the valley of the "Calamet," then made it over the snowy chain of Shasta or Klamath mountains extending to Cape Mendocino. He called his route Pit Mountain because it was near the river of the Indian hunters' pitfalls. Sir George paraphrased Ermatinger's words as he wrote in his journal: "The latter portion of this route ran through a country which has been the scene of the cowardly atrocities of some Americans but, though the Indians did for a time make the Company's innocent servants pay the penalty of the guilt of others, yet, through the influence of kindness and firmness combined, they have within the last two years permitted our people to pass unmolested."

On "Pit Mountain" Ermatinger had had to march for three days through snow sometimes two feet deep. Recalling Alex McLeod's fiasco, Sir George added: "This mountain was notorious as the worst part of the journey for, about ten years before, our trappers, being overtaken by a violent storm, had lost on this very ground the whole of their furs and nearly three hundred horses."

Ermatinger described the Sacramento Valley as eighty leagues long and the richest, most verdant district anywhere west of the Rocky Mountains. But, alas, he warned, it was subject to astounding inundations. On December 12, 1841, for example, torrents of rain caused the petty Sacramento River tributary upon which he was camped to rise nine feet overnight. Next morning, he led his men out of the flooding camp and across a plain turned into a bog. So bad was the sucking mire, which pulled at the horses' fetlocks, that it was eleven o'clock at night before all arrived at a bit of higher ground only a half-dozen miles away.

While his men pulled off their soggy, cold, and shapeless moccasins, to rub warmth back into their feet, Ermatinger counted heads. An Indian woman and some horses were missing. Daylight revealed to Ermatinger that his party was "marooned" on a green knoll in a vast lake. Nearby, the woman and the bogged horses were found, dead. Ermatinger described the macabre scene: "The missing animals were standing, stiff and ghastly, upon their legs, with their loads on their backs."

From the swamped area, Ermatinger had proceeded to Cache Creek to send hunters out in different directions. His orders were that they meet him at a site two days from Sonoma on April 25—"The latest date at which the swarms of mosquitoes would allow them to carry on their trapping in the haunts of the beaver and otter." Ermatinger then moved to the rendezvous with two or three men and the women and children, to set up a headquarters camp and announce his presence to General Vallejo. His camp was on William Wolfskill's Suisun Valley *rancho,* near Freshwater Bay or Suisun Bay. California pioneer Joseph B. Chiles visited him there in January 1842 with some fellow ex-Missourians heading home via Sutter's Fort. "Urmatingle" made them welcome, not only by inviting them to camp with him but allowing them to sleep under the protection of his tent because of a rare Sacramento Valley snowfall.

Unfortunately for British attempts to rival the United States as a power in California, Simpson and McLoughlin had a falling out in 1842. They had long been at odds because of their widely differing attitudes toward their American rivals. McLoughlin not only liked the Yankees, he argued friendship and cooperation as a useful policy. When he had welcomed Nathaniel Wyeth to the Columbia in 1834, he had reminded London that all the Bostonian intruder had to do to make real trouble and expense for the Company was to open a bale of goods and tap a puncheon of rum. Moreover, McLoughlin probably—like Sutter and even Vallejo—saw the handwriting on the wall. That not only Oregon, but California, too, was bound to fall to the aggressive Americans. Simpson detested Yankees. Nor could the two men even agree on how to handle trapping and trade in California. Ermatinger noticed this and wrote: "They had a few words upon business in California—and rough ones they were."

The split between McLoughlin and Simpson became final in 1842 and, shortly, drove the doctor from Company service and from Canada to the United States. The doctor's son John was killed by some of his own men at his Stikine post. Simpson did not sympathize with the doctor since he had never been impressed with the son. He rendered a verdict of self-defense in the case and let the killer go free after an investigation by Donald Manson, "the ramping [rambling] Highlander."

Ermatinger was almost as outraged as McLoughlin with Simpson's handling of the bloody affray. He told his brother that Sir George planned to throw all blame for the murder on the victim. Frank was all for hanging the perpetrators of the crime. He wrote: "They fired two shots at him, some weeks before, and the depositions taken by Mr. Manson makes me doubt whether John did booze, wench, and cudgel the men as Sir George wrote the father; and, altogether, I think it was premeditated and as cool and heartless a murder as could be. . . . It is one of those cases in which Lynch Law is tolerable."

A grief-stricken McLoughlin was also shocked by what he saw as betrayal by his superior. He blasted the reputation of the recently knighted Simpson by exposing his hidden amours, then turned his back on the Company. He began to survey and improve his Willamette Falls property, already threatened by American pettifoggers. McLoughlin built his sawmill, began his grist mill, and named the little Siskiyou Trail settlement Oregon City. Later (1844), he would prevail on Ermatinger to give up trapping and to supervise the completion of his mills, canal, and road. Frank needed little persuading. California's fur trade was busted and Oregon was American. Worst of all, there was a shift in fashion in European markets from beaver hats to silk toppers. Frank wrote Ned: "The price of beaver is falling, owing to the use of silk."

The northernmost portion of the Siskiyou Trail was no longer a mere trail but a busy thoroughfare connecting scattered settlements. (In '44, old trappers Depaty and Tom McKay marked and improved the trace into a bona fide road to Oregon City.) But James Douglas, as early as 1841, was writing off the Willamette—the whole Siskiyou Trail—to the Americans. The day of their benign neglect, which he called "masterly inactivity," was over. For 1841 saw the beginning of the Westward Movement and Manifest Destiny which would reach flood stage during the California Gold Rush. The die was cast when the Bidwell-Bartleson Party reached Sutter's Fort in November 1841.

James Douglas continued to urge exservants to settle north of the Columbia. As long before as October 18, 1838, he had complained to London that "the Willamette settlement is annually growing in importance and threatens to exercise, in course of time, a greater influence than desirable over our affairs." But McLoughlin knew Douglas's efforts to be in a lost cause, remarking: "No man who can take a farm in the Willamette will remain at the Cowelitz or Nisqually." In time, Douglas—and the Company—had to fall all the way back to Victoria, on Vancouver Island.

The first real outbreak of "Oregon Fever" occurred in 1842 with the immigration of some 150 souls. Most were led by Dr. Elijah White and Lansford Hastings. Next year came the "Great Migration" of 875 people. Newcomers dissatisfied with the Willamette took the now well-established Siskiyou Trail down to Sutter's Fort. Hastings led off with fifty-three malcontents. His pilot was Stephen Hall Meek, mountain man and trapper, brother of Oregon's more famous mountaineer, Joe Meek. Steve was a braggart who claimed to have come to California with Joel and Joe Walker in '33 and to have trapped the Scott and Trinity rivers from Fort Vancouver in 1836 with Tom McKay. Maybe so. In any case, he told John Bidwell that he had said to his comrades in 1843, "Boys, when I get to California among the Greasers, I am going to palm myself off as a doctor." And he did just that, becoming Dr. Meek to the *californios*—a medic who could neither read nor write.

On their way south, Hastings and Meek ran into Joel Walker and his partner, McClelland, where the "Hudson's Bay Trail" (i.e., the Siskiyou Trail) cut through the Rogue River Valley. They were driving a herd of 1200 longhorns, two hundred horses, and six hundred sheep to Oregon. Walker had set out from Sutter's Fort in May 1843. Indians at the head of the Sacramento Valley pretended to be friendly —then killed a number of the horses. So, Walker told Meek, "The next day, we returned the favor by killing a good many Indians. We then resumed our journey and saw no Indians until next day, when they came within a hundred yards of our camp and killed a mule. We killed more Indians. They followed and annoyed us greatly from that time till we crossed the Umpqua River in Oregon. They would neither fight us or leave us." Joel later recalled: "We reached Oregon with our stock in good condition about the time the emigrants began to arrive, which circumstances enabled me to make money out of my cattle."

Before meeting Walker, Hastings and Meek had put guards on both sides of the Rogue as they crossed, with orders to fire in the air should any Indians appear. Hastings was sure that the Rogues would not be content just to loot the baggage. He said that they wished "to effect our indiscriminate extermination."

Hastings became nervous again when Meek and some men defected to Walker, to return to Oregon. He was left with just sixteen men. Thus, when he came on two Indians chasing a strayed cow from the Walker cattle column, he asked no questions. Instead, he fired at them without warning and probably hit one of them with his charge of buckshot.

Retaliation for offenses was never slow in coming on the Siskiyou Trail. At midnight, on Shasta River, a party of Shastas attacked the camp, wounded a man named Bellamy in the back with an arrow and injured two horses before being driven off. On the Sacramento, several hundred Indians massed to meet the party. The whites did not want war and they tried to discourage one by firing only in the air. But arrows began to zing around them so they lowered their sights enough to send fourteen braves sprawling in the dust. By the time the war party pulled back, twenty warriors lay dead. A strong guard was maintained by Hastings, and the company reached New Helvetia without mishap.

Increasingly, the Oregon portion of the Siskiyou Trail civilized itself in the forties. Preceding Laframboise as a Willamette settler was Joe Meek, with his pals and their Nez Percé wives who took up farm land on the Tualatin Plains. Dr. Elijah White in 1842 became the first U.S. Government official in Oregon when he was appointed Indian sub-agent. Self-government was already a reality; when Ewing Young died (1841), his estate had to be probated so a mass meeting set up a kind of town hall governance. The need for a wolf bounty was also taken care of, and, by 1843, there was a genuine provisional government in Champoeg with a sheriff (Joe Meek), constables, a probate judge, and a court clerk.

Travel increased on the Siskiyou Trail in the 1840s. Tom McKay tired of farming and milling, so he went to California in late 1840 and drove 3670 sheep and 661 cattle up the trace for James Douglas. In 1843 Jacob Primer Leese trail-herded cattle up the route and Thomas L. (Pegleg) Smith, California's greatest horse rustler, drove a stolen herd of horses up the Siskiyou Trail. Joe Gale herded 350 cattle north, losing many to the Indians of the Siskiyous, in '44, and William H. Winter led a party of thirty-seven emigrants down the trace in June 1844. He was lucky, having no real trouble with Indians. Winter contrasted California's soil unfavorably with that of the Midwest but admitted, "On account of the delightful mildness and uniformity of the climate of California, it will forever be the most healthy and happy country."

The most interesting overland party of all was that of Chief

Piopiomoxmox (Yellow Serpent) who led his Walla Wallas, and some Cayuses and Spokanes, south in the fall of 1844. He had a herd of horses to trade, along with beaver pelts and deerskins and elkskins, for "neat stock" (cattle). Unfortunately, one of his young men was killed at New Helvetia in a quarrel with a white roustabout, and Captain Sutter took the side of the latter. The Walla Wallas had to flee back up the Siskiyou Trail.

The Siskiyou Trail continued to be a busy thoroughfare between Oregon and California. Mountain man James Clyman, for example, made journeys over it in 1844 and 1845 with parties. But its days as a beaver road were numbered. Profit and loss figures for the early 1840s are confusing, at best, and often contradictory. The returns of the Southern Party for 1841 were either £475.18.1 *or* £848.5.7, depending on the source. Some of the discrepancies can be explained by the matter of gross versus net profit. Also, some figures included the value of furs traded from the Indians at Fort Umpqua as well as those trapped. Some totals even lump the Southern Outfit totals with those of the Columbia or the Snake outfits. Thus, where McLoughlin said that the *gain* of the 1841 hunt was £22,974 (for the whole Columbia Department), Simpson put the *profit* at only £1474. Likewise, in 1842 McLoughlin's figure was £16,982 in gain; Simpson's adjusted figure showed a loss of £4003. Manuscript records in Hudson's Bay Company archives in Beaver House, London, show still another set of figures—a gross of £31,186 and a net loss of £2813.8.11.

Finally, when the doctor indicated a gain of £1153.17.5 in '43 for the "California Establishment," in contrast with Simpson's estimate of a loss of £3136, the latter accused McLoughlin of "overvaluating" furs by at least 25 percent. Whatever the grosses, the nets were losses as the 1840s wore on. Fur sales decreased sharply after 1844 because of the silk hat vogue in Europe. (By 1859, beaver pelts were no longer being sold by the pound.) The Company decided to call a halt to beaver trapping along the Siskiyou Trail, since it had become a losing proposition. James Douglas reported to Chief Factor Tolmie (1866) that: "So far as I know, the Southern Party was not equipped after Outfit 1842, so that the record closes there."

Frank Ermatinger's catch had been a poor one, only 643 large and 120 small beaver, plus 387 land otter. This was only half the size of Laframboise's prior catch, so Michel was persuaded to make one last two-year hunt. Douglas had secured Governor Alvarado's sanction of Company trapping in the Sacramento Valley (over Sutter's violent objections), but not even Laframboise could work magic. The country was simply running out of beaver. He got only 462 large and 66 small animals in '42, plus 20 mink and 173 land otter. Nor was 1843 much better—only 586 large and 166 small beaver and 121 otter. Even though the skins were sent to William Glen Rae's Hudson's Bay Company store in San Francisco, rather than being packed all the way by horse to Fort Vancouver via the Siskiyou Trail, the hunt was hardly worth the effort.

Laframboise left the nearly worn-out California trapping grounds for the last time in May 1843 and slowly made his way up the Siskiyou Trail. Worse than the dearth of beaver was the anarchy in California. His own men were infected by it. They were insubordinate, virtually mutinous. The chaotic political conditions would bring the Bear Flag Revolt and Mexican War in just three years. McLoughlin reported to London Laframboise's last words about the Siskiyou Trail: "I am, through the mercy of God, come back safe, because I gave way to my men. If I had assumed the tone of master, I would have been murdered by them. I will not venture again."

Michel Laframboise's retirement effectively ended Hudson's Bay Company trapping in California and signaled the end of the Siskiyou Trail as a route of the beaver men. Michel was lured out of retirement, once, but went no further south than the Umpqua. Captain John Sutter continued to trap the Sacramento and San Joaquin valleys, but with only modest success. Grass was growing in the moccasin-pounded ruts of the trace by 1845. Travel was at its lowest ebb since the trail's founding.

Suddenly, in 1848, the Siskiyou Trail came alive again. On January 24, Sutter's millwright, James W. Marshall, who had migrated to California via the Siskiyou Trail in '45 with Jim Clyman, discovered gold at Coloma. Oregonian argonauts quickly reopened the road and rushed to the diggins of El Dorado.

By 1849, the Gold Rush was at its height. Peter Ogden complained to Donald Ross (March 6) that once the news of gold was confirmed in Oregon, settlers, Company men, and Cayuse War soldiers alike deserted to the placers of the Mother Lode: "In less than a week, two thousand of our population started abandoning large fields of wheat, ready for the sickle, and others began leaving them in stacks for the benefit of their cattle. Rely on it; gold has a charm about it that is irresistible. . . . Madness alone can be compared to it, and we already have men becoming insane from its effects."

Ogden was right about the virulence of gold fever in Oregon. Frank Ermatinger wrote Ned on July 11, 1849, that "The affairs in the Columbia [Department] are in a confused state—the men were all running off to California, and the clerks had all given in notices to quit the [Hudson's Bay Company] service."

In time, pack trains replaced the footslogging argonauts and were, in turn, succeeded by wagons and stages. In the 1870s and 1880s, the iron horse finally tied Oregon and California together along the route of the old Siskiyou Trail.

McLoughlin lapsed into a funk after he moved to Oregon City and became an American. In 1843 he rallied to the defense of Laframboise, however, when the "Captain of the California Trail" was defamed in Congress. The House's Committee on Military Affairs admitted quotations from the 1841 journal of Captain Josiah Spaulding of the *Lausanne* into the record. Michel was branded as a man "notorious for murdering the Indians." McLoughlin wrote a letter to London on November 15, 1843, to set the record straight: "From being Interpreter, [he] has been conspicuous in every difficulty that has occurred with the Indians, but when he did fight it was because he was obliged to do so in self-defense, and in punishing the wrongs others had suffered."

Laframboise lived on in retirement until January 25, 1861. McLoughlin, responsible more than anyone, perhaps, for the Siskiyou Trail, led an embittered existence during the 1850s. British demagogues called him a turncoat. Yankee ingrates stupidly asserted that he had caused the massacre of Americans by Indians, and "by the hundreds." ("I, who saved all I could!" he cried in despair.) In 1851 the doctor told Lafayette F. Grover, later governor of Oregon: "I might better have been shot forty years ago than to have lived here and tried to build up a family and an estate in this government. I became a citizen of the United States on good faith. I planted all I had here—and the Government confiscated my property."

When Dr. Henri De Chesne called on the dying McLoughlin on September 3, 1857, he saluted him with the customary *"Comment allez-vous?"* The old White-Headed Eagle of Fort Vancouver and the Siskiyou Trail responded with the last words he ever uttered on earth —*"A Dieu."*

Selective Bibliography ════════════════

IT HAS BEEN easy to be selective in compiling this brief bibliography: Since the volume in hand is the first book devoted to the history of the Siskiyou Trail, there are no similar works to list. I have used a number of secondary works on the fur trade, the history of Oregon and California, and so on; but I see no point in totting up titles used in backgrounding my study. There were no newspapers in the Far West during the Siskiyou Trail's heyday; few government documents throw much light on the subject; none of the handful of M.A. theses and Ph.D. dissertations on the Hudson's Bay Company in California, etc., are extraordinary.

But, on the other hand, the very words of the men who pioneered the historic trail—Ogden, McLoughlin, Smith, Douglas—are available, and not only in preserved original manuscripts. Most of these have been published and have been edited and annotated by historians of the caliber of Dale Morgan, John Hussey, Alice B. Maloney, and Doyce Nunis. *These* are the rich sources which I have used to tell the tale, and they are listed below.

Unpublished manuscripts:

Boronda, José Canuto. *Notas Históricas sobre California.* 1878. Bancroft Library. *Ms.* C-D 47.

Brackenridge, William D. *Remarks and Opinions of W. D. Brackenridge.* Maryland Historical Society.

Eld, Henry. *Diary of Passed Midshipman Henry Eld, September 7–October 29, 1841.* Beinecke Library, Yale University.

Emmons, George. *Journal, Overland Expedition, September–October, 1841.* Beinecke Library, Yale University.

Ermatinger, Francis. *Correspondence, 1823–1846.* Huntington Library. *Ms.* HM 16761.

Johns, James. *Diary*. Bancroft Library. *Ms.* (Film) C-F, 188.
Warner, J. J. (Jonathan Trumbull). *California Historical Society. J. J. Warner's Paper on Jedediah Smith and Early California Trappers (Read before California Historical Society, April 17th 1888)*. Huntington Library.

Published works:

Allen, A. J. *Ten Years in Oregon*. Ithaca, New York: Mack, Andrew and Co., 1848
Anderson, William M. *The Rocky Mountain Journals of William Marshall Anderson*. Edited by Dale Morgan and Eleanor Harris. Huntington Library, 1967.
Ball, John. *John Ball, Member of the Wyeth Expedition* . . . Edited by Kate Ball Powers, Flora Ball Hopkins, and Lucy Ball. Glendale, Calif.: Arthur H. Clark, 1925.
Bancroft, Hubert H. *History of California*. 7 vols., San Francisco: The History Company, 1886.
————. *The History of Oregon*. 2 vols. San Francisco: The History Company, 1886.
Barker, Burt Brown. *The McLoughlin Empire*. Glendale, Calif.: Arthur H. Clark, 1959.
Barrows, William. *Oregon: The Struggle for Possession*. Boston: Houghton Mifflin, 1885.
Beaver, Herbert. *Reports and Letters of Herbert Beaver, 1836–1838* . . . Edited by Thomas E. Jessett, Portland, Ore.: Champoeg Press, 1959.
Belcher, Sir Edward. *Narrative of a Voyage Round the World* . . . London: Colburn, 1843.
Belden, Arthur L. *The Fur Trade of America* . . . New York: Peltries, 1917.
Berry, Don. *A Majority of Scoundrels*. New York: Harper & Row, 1961.
Bidwell, John. *Echoes of the Past*. Chicago: Lakeside Press, 1928.
————. *A Journey to California*. Berkeley, Calif.: Bancroft Library, 1964.
Binns, Archie. *Peter Skene Ogden, Fur Trader*. Portland, Ore.: Binfords & Mort, 1967.
Bonner, T. D. *The Life and Adventures of James P. Beckwourth*. Edited by Delmont R. Oswald. Lincoln, Neb.: University of Nebraska, 1972.
A Brief History of the Hudson's Bay Company. Winnipeg: Hudson's Bay Co., n.d.
Bryce, George. *The Remarkable History of the Hudson's Bay Company* . . . New York: Charles Scribner's Sons, 1910.
Camp, Charles L. *George C. Yount and His Chronicles of the West*. Denver: Old West Publishing Co., 1966.
Carson, Christopher. *Kit Carson's Autobiography*. Edited by Milo M. Quaife. Chicago: Lakeside Press, 1935.
Carter, Harvey L. *Dear Old Kit: The Historical Christopher Carson*. Norman, Okla.: University of Oklahoma, 1968.
Chittenden, Hiram M. *The American Fur Trade of the Far West*. 2 vols. New York: Press of the Pioneers, 1935.
Cleland, Robert Glass. *This Reckless Breed of Men*. New York: Alfred Knopf, 1950.
Cline, Gloria Griffen. *Exploring the Great Basin*. Norman, Okla.: University of Oklahoma, 1963.

Clyman, James. *James Clyman. American Frontiersman, 1792–1881*. Edited by Charles L. Camp. Portland, Ore.: Champoeg Press, 1960.

Colvocoresses, George M. *Four Years in the Government Exploring Expedition Commanded by Captain Charles Wilkes . . .* New York: J. M. Fairchild, 1855.

Cook, Shelburne F. *The Epidemic of 1830–1833 in California and Oregon*. University of California Publications in American Archaeology and Ethnology, Vol. 43, No. 3. University of California Press, 1955.

Corning, Howard M. *Willamette Landings*. Portland, Ore.: Binfords & Mort, 1947.

———. *Dictionary of Oregon History*. Portland, Ore.: Binfords & Mort, 1956.

Cox, Ross. *Adventures on the Columbia River*. Norman, Okla.: University of Oklahoma, 1957.

Coyner, David. *The Lost Trappers*. Glorieta, N.M.: Rio Grande Press, 1969.

Creighton, Donald. *The Story of Canada*. Boston: Houghton Mifflin, 1960.

Dakin, Susanna B. *The Lives of William Hartnell*. Stanford, Calif.: Stanford University, 1948.

Dale, Harrison C., ed. *The Ashley-Smith Explorations*. Glendale, Calif.: Arthur H. Clark, 1941.

Davidson, Gordon C. *North-West Company*. University of California Press, 1918.

Dickens, Samuel N. *Oregon Geography*. Eugene, Ore.: University of Oregon Cooperative Bookstore, 1965.

Dobbs, Caroline C. *Men of Champoeg*. Portland, Ore.: Metropolitan Press, 1932.

Douglas, David. *Journal Kept by David Douglas During His Travels in North America, 1823–1827* . . . New York: Antiquarian Press, 1959.

Duflot de Mofras, Eugène, *Duflot de Mofras' Travels on the Pacific Coast*. Translated and edited by Marguerite Eyer Wilbur. Santa Ana, Calif.: Fine Arts Press, 1937.

Dye, Eva. *Hudson's Bay Company Regime in the Oregon Country*. Bulletin of the University of Oregon Historical Series, Vol. 1, No. 2, 1898.

Dye, Job F. *Recollections of a Pioneer*. Los Angeles: Glen Dawson, 1951.

Edwards, Philip Leget. *California in 1837*. Sacramento: A. J. Johnston, 1890.

Ellison, William Henry. *The Life and Adventures of George Nidever*. University of California, 1937.

Farnham, Thomas J. *The Early Days in California*. Philadelphia: John E. Potter, 1860.

———. *Travels in the Great Western Prairies*. 2 vols. London: Richard Bentley, 1843.

Fleming, R. Harvey, ed. *Minutes of Council, Northern Department of Ruperts Land, 1821–31*. Toronto: The Champlain Society, 1940.

Fletcher, Fred Nathaniel. *Early Nevada. The Period of Exploration, 1776–1848*. Reno, Nev.: Published by the author, 1929.

Forbes, Alexander. *California: A History of Upper and Lower California*. San Francisco: Thomas C. Russell, 1919.

Franchere, Gabriel. *Adventure at Astoria, 1810–1814*. Norman, Okla.: University of Oklahoma, 1967.

———. *Journal of a Voyage on the North West Coast of North America* . . . Toronto: The Champlain Society, 1969.

Frémont, John Charles. *Geographical Memoir upon Upper California* . . . San Francisco: Book Club of California, 1964.

Galbraith, John S. *The Hudson's Bay Company as an Imperial Factor.* University of California Press, 1957.

Geiger, Rev. Maynard, O.F.M., *Franciscan Missionaries in Hispanic California, 1769–1848.* Huntington Library, 1969.

Giffen, Helen S. *Trail-Blazing Pioneer: Col. Joseph Ballinger Chiles.* San Francisco: John Howell, 1969.

Green, Jonathan. *Journal of a Tour of the North West Coast of America* . . . *1829.* New York: Charles F. Heartman, 1915.

Gudde, Erwin G. *California Place Names.* University of California Press, 1960.

Hafen, Leroy R., ed. *The Mountain Men and the Fur Trade of the Far West.* Glendale, Calif.: Arthur H. Clark, 1965–1971.

Hammond, George P., ed. The Larkin Papers. 11 vols. University of California Press, 1951–1968.

Harvey, Athelstan. *Douglas of the Fir.* Cambridge, Mass.: Harvard University Press, 1947.

Hill, Joseph J. *The History of Warner's Ranch and Its Environs.* Los Angeles: 1927.

Holman, Frederick V. *Dr. John McLoughlin, the Father of Oregon.* Cleveland: Arthur H. Clark, 1907.

Holmes, Kenneth. *Ewing Young, Master Trapper.* Portland, Ore.: Binfords & Mort, 1967.

Horner, John B. *Days and Deeds in the Oregon Country.* Portland, Ore.: J. K. Gill Co., 1928.

Hussey, John. *Champoeg: Place of Transition.* Portland, Ore.: Oregon Historical Society, 1967.

———. *The History of Fort Vancouver* . . . Tacoma, Wash.: Washington State Historical Society, 1957.

Innis, Harold. *The Fur Trade in Canada.* New Haven, Conn.: Yale University Press, 1962.

Irving, Washington. *The Adventures of Captain Bonneville.* New York: Putnam, 1868.

———. *Astoria, or Anecdotes of an Enterprise beyond the Rocky Mountains.* Edited by Edgeley W. Todd. Norman, Okla.: University of Oklahoma, 1964.

Jenkins, John S. *United States Exploring Expeditions* . . . Auburn, N.Y.: James A. Alden, 1850.

Johnson, Overton, and William H. Winter. *Route Across the Rocky Mountains.* Princeton, N.J.: Princeton University Press, 1932.

Kane, Paul. *Paul Kane's Frontier.* Austin: University of Texas, 1971.

Lee, Daniel, and J. H. Frost. *Ten Years in Oregon.* New York: Published by the authors, 1844.

Leonard, Zenas. *Narrative of the Adventures of Zenas Leonard* . . . Chicago: Lakeside Press, 1934.

McArthur, Lewis A. *Oregon Geographic Names.* Portland, Ore.: Binfords & Mort, 1944.

Mackay, Douglas. *The Honourable Company.* London: Cassell, 1937.

McKelvey, Susan Delano. *Botanical Exploration of the Trans-Mississippi West.* Cambridge, Mass.: Arnold Arboretum, Harvard University Press, 1955.

SELECTIVE BIBLIOGRAPHY

SELECTIVE BIBLIOGRAPHY

Mackenzie, Cecil. *Donald Mackenzie, "King of the Northwest."* Los Angeles: Ivan Beach, 1937.

McLoughlin, John. *Letters of John McLoughlin from Fort Vancouver to the Governor and Committee, First Series, 1825–38.* Edited by E. E. Rich. London: Hudson's Bay Record Society, 1941.

———. *Letters of Dr. John McLoughlin Written at Fort Vancouver, 1829–1832.* Edited by Dr. Burt Brown Barker. Portland, Ore.: Binfords & Mort, 1948.

McNamee, Sister Mary Dominica. *Willamette Interlude.* Palo Alto, Calif.: Pacific Books, 1959.

Maloney, Alice B. *Fur Brigade to the Bonaventura. John Work's California Expedition, 1832–1833.* San Francisco: California Historical Society, 1945.

Merk, Frederick. *Fur Trade and Empire. George Simpson's Journal.* Cambridge, Mass.: Harvard University Press, 1931.

Minter, Harold A. *Umpqua Valley, Oregon, and Its Pioneers.* Portland, Ore.: Binfords & Mort, 1967.

Montgomery, Richard G. *The White-Headed Eagle, John McLoughlin.* New York: Macmillan, 1934.

Moraga, Gabriel. *The Diary of Ensign Gabriel Moraga's Expedition of Discovery in the Sacramento Valley, 1808.* Edited and translated by Donald Cutter. Los Angeles: Glen Dawson, 1957.

Morgan, Dale. *Jedediah Smith and the Opening of the West.* Indianapolis: Bobbs, Merrill, 1953.

———, ed. *The West of William H. Ashley . . .* Denver: Old West Publishing Co., 1964.

———, and Carl I. Wheat. *Jedediah Smith and His Maps of the American West.* San Francisco: California Historical Society, 1954.

Neihardt, John G. *The Splendid Wayfaring.* New York: Macmillan, 1927.

Newell, Robert. *Robert Newell's Memoranda.* Portland, Ore.: Champoeg Press, 1959.

Nonsuch, Hudson's Bay Company Ship Replica. London: Hudson's Bay Company, 1969.

Nunis, Doyce B., Jr., ed. *The California Diary of Faxon Dean Atherton, 1836–1839.* San Francisco: California Historical Society, 1964.

———. *The Hudson's Bay Company's First Fur Brigade to the Sacramento Valley.* Sacramento: Sacramento Book Collectors Club, 1957.

———. *The Trials of Isaac Graham.* Los Angeles: Dawsons Book Shop, 1967.

Ogden, Adele. *The California Sea Otter Trade, 1784–1848.* University of California Press, 1941.

Ogden, Peter Skene. *Peter Skene Ogden's Snake Country Journals, 1824–25 and 1825–26.* Ed. by E. E. Rich. London: Hudson's Bay Record Society, 1950.

———. *Snake Country Journal, 1826–27.* Ed. by K. G. Davies. London: Hudson's Bay Record Society, 1961.

———. *Peter Skene Ogden's Snake Country Journals, 1827–28 and 1828–29.* Ed. by Glyndwr Williams. London: Hudson's Bay Record Society, 1971.

———. *Traits of American Indian Life & Character, by a Fur Trader.* San Francisco: Grabhorn Press, 1933.

Palmer, Joel. *Journals of Travels over the Rocky Mountains.* Cincinnati: J. A. & U. P. James, 1847.

Pattie, James Ohio. *The Personal Narrative of James O. Pattie.* New York: Lippincott, 1962.

Peale, Titian R. *Peale in California* . . . Ed. by Clifford M. Drury. Los Angeles: Dawsons Book Shop, 1957.

Phillips, Paul C. *The Fur Trade.* Norman, Okla.: University of Oklahoma, 1961.

Physical and Economic Geography of Oregon. Salem, Ore.: Oregon State Board of Higher Education, 1940.

Pinkerton, Robert E. *Hudson's Bay Company.* New York: Holt, 1931.

Poesch, Jessie. *Titian Ramsay Peale, 1799–1885, and His Journals of the Wilkes Expedition.* Philadelphia: American Philosophical Society, 1961.

Rich, E. E., ed. *The Letters of John McLoughlin* . . . 3 vols. Toronto: Champlain Society, 1941–1944.

———. *Hudson's Bay Company, 1670–1870.* London: Hudson's Bay Record Society, 1958–1959.

Robinson, Henry Martin. *The Great Fur Land.* New York: Putnam, 1879.

Ross, Alexander. *The Fur Hunters of the Far West.* Ed. by Kenneth A. Spaulding. Norman, Okla.: University of Oklahoma, 1956.

Russell, Carl P. *Firearms, Traps & Tools of the Mountain Men.* New York: Knopf, 1967.

———. *Guns on the Early Frontiers.* University of California Press, 1957.

Russell, Osborne. *Journal of a Trapper.* Lincoln, Neb.: University of Nebraska, 1955.

Sandoz, Mari. *The Beaver Men.* New York: Hastings House, 1964.

Simpkinson, Francis G. *H.M.S. Sulphur at California, 1837 and 1839.* Ed. by Richard A. Pierce and John H. Winslow. San Francisco: Book Club of California, 1969.

Simpson, Sir George. *Narrative of a Voyage to California Ports in 1841–42.* San Francisco: Thomas C. Russell, 1930.

———. *An Overland Journey round the World during the Years 1841 and 1842.* Philadelphia: Lea, 1847.

Slacum, William A. *Memorial (December 1837).* Senate Document 24, 25th Congress, 2nd session.

Smith, Alson J. *Men against the Mountains.* New York: John Day, 1965.

Stewart, George R. *Take Your Bible in One Hand* . . . San Francisco: The Colt Press, 1939.

Sullivan, Maurice S. *Jedediah Smith, Trader and Trail Breaker.* New York: Press of the Pioneers, 1936.

———. *The Travels of Jedediah Smith* . . . Santa Ana, Calif.: The Fine Arts Press, 1934.

Tappe, Donald T. "The Status of Beavers in California." State of California, Department of Natural Resources, Division of Fish and Game. *Game Bulletin No. 3.* Sacramento: State Printing Office, 1942.

Templeton, Sardis W. *The Lame Captain.* Los Angeles: Westernlore, 1965.

Tobie, Harvey. *No Man Like Joe: The Life and Times of Joseph L. Meek.* Portland, Ore.: Binfords & Mort, 1949.

Vestal, Stanley. *Joe Meek, the Merry Mountain Man.* Caldwell, Caxton Printers, 1952.

Victor, Frances Fuller. *The River of the West.* Hartford, Conn.: Columbia Book Co., 1870.

Vincent, W. D. *The North West Company.* Pullman, Wash.: State College of Washington, 1927.

Warner, J. J. (Jonathan Trumbull). *Reminiscences of Early California, 1831–46.* Historical Society of Southern California Annual Publications, Vol. 7. Los Angeles: Historical Society of Southern California, 1908.

Weber, David J. *The Taos Trappers.* Norman, Okla.: University of Oklahoma, 1971.

Wilkes, Charles. *Narrative of the United States Exploring Expedition* . . . London: Ingram, Cooke and Co., 1852.

Wilson, Iris Higbie. *William Wolfskill, 1798–1866.* Glendale, Calif.: Arthur H. Clark, 1965.

Work, John. *The Journal of John Work, a Chief Trader of the Hudson's Bay Company* . . . Ed. by William S. Lewis and Paul C. Phillips. Cleveland: Arthur H. Clark, 1923.

Work, John. *The Journal of John Work, January to October, 1835.* Victoria, B.C.: Banfield, 1945.

———. *The Snake Country Expedition of 1830–31; John Work's Field Journal.* Ed. by Francis Haines, Jr. Norman, Okla.: University of Oklahoma, 1971.

Wyeth, Nathaniel J. *The Correspondence and Journals of Captain Nathaniel J. Wyeth, 1831–6.* Ed. by F. G. Young. Eugene, Ore.: University of Oregon, 1899.

Youngson, William W. *Swinging Portals.* Portland: Published by the author, 1948.

Index

INDEX

INDEX

INDEX